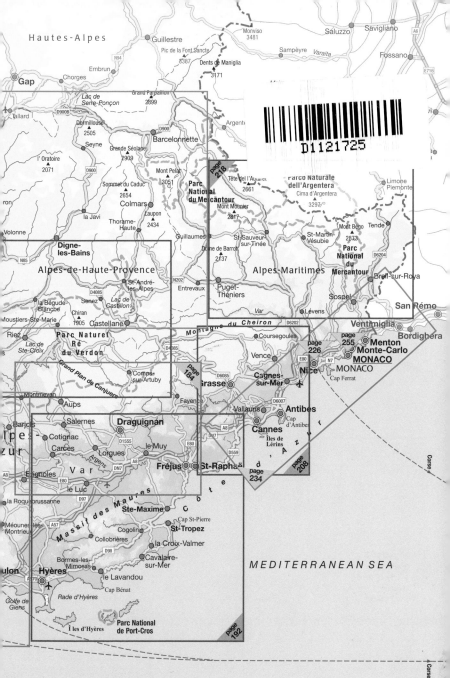

	Autoroute with Junction
	Autoroute (under construction)
	Dual Carriageway
	Main Road
	Secondary Road
	Minor Road
	Track
	International Boundary
	Province/State Boundary
	National Park/Reserve
	Ferry Route
	Airport
	Church (ruins)
	Monastery
	Chateau/Castle (ruins)
	Archaeological Site
	Cave
	Place of Interest
	Mansion/Stately Home
	Viewpoint
	Beach
	Border Crossing
	Autoroute
	Dual Carriageway
	Main Roads
	Minor Roads
	Footpath
	Railway
	Pedestrian Area
	Important Building
	Park
	Numbered Sight
	Bus Station
	Tourist Information
	Post Office
	Cathedral/Church
	Mosque
	Synagogue
	Statue/Monument
	Tower
	Lighthouse

INSIGHT GUIDES

PROVENCE

APA PUBLICATIONS L

Part of the Langenscheidt Publishing Group

✳ INSIGHT GUIDE
PROVENCE

Project Editor
Catherine Dreghorn
Picture Manager
Steven Lawrence
Series Editor
Rachel Lawrence
Publishing Manager
Rachel Fox

Distribution

UK & Ireland
GeoCenter International Ltd
Meridian House, Churchill Way West
Basingstoke, Hampshire RG21 6YR
sales@geocenter.co.uk

United States
Ingram Publisher Services
One Ingram Blvd, PO Box 3006
La Vergne, TN 37086-1986
customer.service@ingrampublisher
services.com

Australia
Universal Publishers
PO Box 307
St Leonards, NSW 1590
sales@universalpublishers.com.au

New Zealand
Hema Maps New Zealand Ltd (HNZ)
Unit 2, 10 Cryers Road
East Tamaki, Auckland 2013
sales.hema@clear.net.nz

Worldwide
**Apa Publications GmbH & Co.
Verlag KG (Singapore branch)**
7030 Ang Mo Kio Ave 5
08-65 Northstar @ AMK
Singapore 569880
apasin@signet.com.sg

Printing

CTPS-China

©2011 Apa Publications GmbH & Co.
Verlag KG (Singapore branch)
All Rights Reserved

First Edition 1989
Fourth Edition 2007
Fifth Edition 2011

ABOUT THIS BOOK

The first Insight Guide pioneered the use of creative full-colour photography in travel guides in 1970. Since then, we have expanded our range to cater for our readers' need not only for reliable information about their chosen destination but also for a real understanding of the culture and workings of that destination. Now, when the internet can supply inexhaustible (although not always reliable) facts, our books marry text and pictures to provide those much more elusive qualities: knowledge and discernment. To achieve this, they rely heavily on the authority of locally based writers and photographers.

How to use this book

The book is carefully structured both to convey an understanding of the region and its culture and to guide readers through its myriad sights and activities:

◆ To understand Provence today, you need to know something of its past. The first section covers the region's rich history and culture in lively, authoritative essays written by specialists.

◆ The Places section provides a run-down of all the attractions worth seeing, with the best restaurants featured at the end of each chapter. The main places of interest are co-ordinated by number with full-colour maps.

◆ The Travel Tips section provides information on transport, hotels, shopping, festivals and outdoor activities; the index is printed on the back cover flap, which also serves as a bookmark.

look at fast-changing cities like Marseille and Toulon, providing coverage on lesser-known inland areas and beauty spots, all accompanied by her reliable selection of local restaurants. She penned many new features on a wide variety of topics, from the new breed of chefs, wine and truffles to tropical gardens, perfumes, and the latest on the Avignon festival. She also planned and wrote the routes on the touring map that accompanies this guide.

Additional features on *Wild Provence* and *Architecture* were provided by London-based writer and editor, **Roger Williams**, who is knowledgeable on all things Provençal. He also co-wrote the *Provence Today* chapter and expanded the history section to bring it up to date.

Other contributors to previous editions include **Peter Capella**, **Peter Robinson**, **Ingrida Rogal** and **Caroline Wheal**.

This new edition was project managed and edited by Insight assistant editor **Catherine Dreghorn** and production work was carried out by **Rebeka Ellam**. The majority of pictures were taken by regular Insight photographer **Gregory Wrona**, with new images by **Sylvaine Poitau** and **Wadey James**. They have captured the timeless beauty of the Provençal landscape and its historic towns.

The book was proofread by **Leonie Wilding** and indexed by **Helen Peters**.

◆ Photographs are chosen not only to illustrate geography and sights but also to convey the moods of the region and the life of its people.

The contributors

This latest edition of *Insight Guide: Provence* was completely revised and reshaped by Paris-based journalist and editor **Natasha Edwards**. She writes on travel, contemporary art and design for the *Daily Telegraph* and *Condé Nast Traveller* among other publications, and is the Paris expert for the travel website www.simonseeks.com. Building on the foundations laid down by contributors to previous editions, **Rosemary Bailey** (author of the chapter on Provençal Artists) and **Anne Sanders Roston**, Natasha compiled a wealth of new information, taking a fresh

CONTACTING THE EDITORS

We would appreciate it if readers would alert us to errors or outdated information by writing to:

Insight Guides, P.O. Box 7910, London SE1 1WE, England. email: insight@apaguide.co.uk

NO part of this book may be reproduced, stored in a retrieval system or transmitted in any form or means electronic, mechanical, photocopying, recording or otherwise, without prior written permission of *Apa Publications*. Brief text quotations with use of photographs are exempted for book review purposes only.
Information has been obtained from sources believed to be reliable, but its accuracy and completeness, and the opinions based thereon, are not guaranteed.

www.insightguides.com

LEFT: the harbour at Menton.

THE BEST OF PROVENCE: TOP SIGHTS

Unmissable attractions in Provence range from a marvel of engineering to marvels of nature. Add a balmy climate, plenty of art and fine cuisine, and Provence cannot fail to enchant

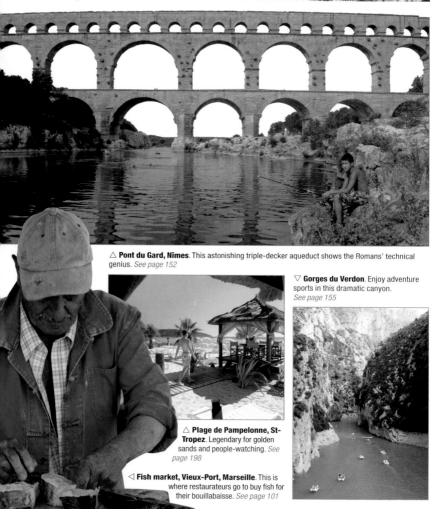

△ **Pont du Gard, Nîmes**. This astonishing triple-decker aqueduct shows the Romans' technical genius. *See page 152*

▽ **Gorges du Verdon**. Enjoy adventure sports in this dramatic canyon. *See page 155*

△ **Plage de Pampelonne, St-Tropez**. Legendary for golden sands and people-watching. *See page 198*

◁ **Fish market, Vieux-Port, Marseille**. This is where restaurateurs go to buy fish for their bouillabaisse. *See page 101*

◁ **Chapelle du Rosaire, Vence**. Matisse's spiritual masterpiece. *See page 208*

▽ **Promenade des Anglais, Nice**. Skate, jog, bike or just stroll and stare along one of the world's great promenades. *See page 228*

△ **The Calanques**. 20km of dramatic limestone cliffs and coves stretching between Marseille and Cassis. *See page 108*

▽ **The Luberon**. Oak woods, vines and the quintessential hill villages of Bonnieux, Gordes and Ménerbes. *See page 83*

△ **Palais des Papes, Avignon**. Palatial 14th-century home of the popes... and the elephant sculpture outside it. *See page 60*

▽ **Monte-Carlo Casino**. The casino that made Monte-Carlo's glamorous reputation, with opera house attached. *See page 256*

THE BEST OF PROVENCE: EDITOR'S CHOICE

Setting priorities, saving money, unique attractions... here, at a glance, are our recommendations, plus some tips and tricks even Provençals won't always know

MUSEUMS AND GALLERIES

- **La Vieille-Charité, Marseille**. View the exhibitions in a beautiful 17th-century hospice. *See page 102*
- **Musée International de la Parfumerie, Grasse**. Scents and smells in the perfume museum. *See page 213*
- **Musée Chagall, Nice**. Chagall's colourful Biblical paintings in a beautiful modern museum.

See page 230
- **Musée de la Préhistoire, Quinson**. Ultramodern museum of prehistory. *See page 159*
- **Musée Picasso, Antibes**. Works by Picasso in the castle where the artist had a studio. *See page 239*
- **Collection Lambert, Avignon**. Adventurous contemporary art shows in a classical mansion. *See page 65*

HISTORIC MONUMENTS

- **Les Alyscamps, Arles**. Vast Roman necropolis painted by Van Gogh and Gauguin. *See page 137*
- **Basilique, St-Maximin-la-Ste-Baume**. Provence's finest Gothic church. *See page 179*
- **Théâtre Antique, Orange**. World's best-preserved Roman theatre. *See page 70*
- **Synagogue, Carpentras**. France's oldest synagogue with a

pretty Baroque decor. *See page 74*
- **Cathédrale Orthodoxe Russe, Nice**. Ornate onion domes and icons. *See page 229*
- **Villa Noailles, Hyères**. Modernist Cubist masterpiece now used for exhibitions. *See page 192*
- **Abbaye du Thoronet**. A glorious Cistercian Romanesque monastery. *See page 183*

NATURE, WILD AND TAMED

- **The Camargue**. Mysterious wetlands of flamingos, cowboys and wild horses. *See page 139*
- **Prieuré de Salagon, Mane**. Medieval plants and medicines in an ethno-botanical garden. *See page 168*
- **Colorado de Rustrel, Luberon**. Colourful rock formations created by man and nature. *See page 94*

- **Domaine du Rayol**. Stunning tropical gardens overlooking the sea. *See page 195*
- **Ile de Porquerolles**. Silver sand and pine woods: Robert Louis Stevenson's Treasure Island. *See page 193*
- **Parc National du Mercantour**. Wild mountain landscape with prehistoric scratchings. *See page 217*

Top: Cathédrale Orthodoxe Russe, Nice. **Above Left:** a classic exhibit in Musée International de la Parfumerie, Grasse. **Above Middle:** flamingos in the Camargue wetlands. **Above:** Abbaye du Thoronet.

FESTIVALS AND EVENTS

- **Féria de Nîmes**. Bull-fights and costumes are the showstoppers of these events. *See page 149*
- **Festival d'Avignon**. Controversial, but still cutting-edge for theatre and dance, plus its gigantic Off. *See page 64*
- **Festival International d'Art Lyrique, Aix-en-Provence**. Top international opera in splendid outdoor setting. *See page 116*
- **Rencontres de la Photographie, Arles**. Photography's Oscars in the town with a commitment to the art. *See page 138*
- **Jazz à Juan**. The oldest, best and coolest of the Côte's many jazz festivals. *See page 240*
- **Carnaval, Nice**. Mardi Gras is the winter highlight of the Côte d'Azur. *See page 229*
- **Monaco Grand Prix**. Formula 1 racing in the Principality. *See page 256*
- **Fête du Citron, Menton**. Three fragrant weeks of oranges, lemons and parades. *See page 249*

ABOVE: eye-catching floats and costumes at Nice's Carnaval.
BELOW LEFT: tackling white water in the Gorges du Verdon.
BELOW: the St-Tropez quayside is perfect for people-watching.

OUTDOOR ACTIVITIES

- **Gorges du Verdon**. This is the place to experience white-water rafting thrills.

See page 155
- **The Camargue**. Riding through the magical wetlands allows you to get much closer to the wildlife. *See page 139*
- **Mont Ventoux, the Luberon and Mercantour**. Ideal for hiking. *See pages 78, 83 and 216*

PEOPLE-WATCHING

- **Cours Mirabeau, Aix-en-Provence**. The focus of Aix's chic café society.
- **Vieux-Port, St-Tropez**. For celebrity-spotting and yacht-gawping.
- **La Croisette**. Cannes' essential promenade with designer shopping.

MONEY-SAVING TIPS

If you're planning extensive sightseeing and museum visiting several cities have money-saving passes, such as Passion in Avignon, Pass Monuments in Arles, the Marseille City Pass and the ticket Nîmes Romaine. Some passes also offer discounts on public transport and guided tours.

All the municipal museums in Nice, including the Musée Matisse and Palais Lascaris, are free, and national museums, such as the Musée Chagall in Nice, Musée Léger in Biot and Musée Granet in Aix, are free for EU nationals under 26 (bring passport ID).

The sea is free: even at the Riviera's most fashionable beaches, such as the Plage de Pampelonne in St-Tropez, there are free public bathing areas amid the private beach concessions.

A helicopter shuttle between Nice and Monaco airport is speedier and doesn't necessarily cost much more than a taxi.

You are not obliged to buy mineral water in restaurants. Tap water is perfectly fine to drink: ask for a *carafe d'eau*. It is also worth noting that many restaurants have good value menus at lunchtime.

A service charge is included in French restaurant bills – any extra tips are purely optional.

PROVENCE TODAY

**"It was a pleasure to feel one's self in Provence again, the
land where the silver-grey earth is impregnated with the
light of the sky." – Henry James, _A Little Tour in France_**

Provence and the Côte d'Azur are the
ultimate pleasure zone. No other region
of Europe conjures up such familiar,
enticing images, and few places live up to such
continual hype. The region's unique combination of romance and glamour mixes a Mediterranean climate and a timeless Latin lifestyle
with youthful dynamism and French chic. From
beach resort to hill village, big city to nature
park, it manages to embrace all these things.

France's sunny south is also a magical,
mythical land where the ancient soil never
seems far from the Romans who gave Provence
its name. Long a poor, predominantly rural
economy, it was not until it was "discovered"
in the 19th century, first by foreign aristocracy and then by artists, that other Europeans,
Russians and Americans began to turn their
envious gaze towards this corner of the Mediterranean that was so benign in winter and
so frolicsome in summer. They brought their
millions with them and made it the world's
most expensive coast.

A hard life

For the people of Provence, however, life is not
one long holiday. Inland, in the hills and the
sparsely populated mountain areas of Mont
Ventoux and the Alpine foothills of the Alpes-
Maritimes, the soil is thin and the living hard.
Here, the people are conservative and cling to
traditions. This rural landscape is imbued with

a romantic quality, as immortalised in _Jean de
Florette_ and _Manon des Sources_, the books of
Marcel Pagnol turned into haunting films.

Keeping traditions

The deep conservatism of the countryside,
and the refusal to allow traditions to die, can
nowhere better be seen than at Arles, where
the cowboys of the Camargue don their
bright Provençal print shirts, and tenaciously
traditional women pull on their shawls and
full skirts at every festival.

Conservatism extends to food, too, and people coming here year after year will wonder why
the menus so seldom change. Many will be glad

PRECEDING PAGES: lavender field in Viens; boats in Sanary-
sur-Mer's harbour. **LEFT:** pavement cafés and beaches:
the social hubs of Provence. **RIGHT:** on the beach at Nice.

they don't. Even the new generation of talented young chefs remain faithful to authentic Provençal ingredients and seasonal produce.

Some parts of Provence seem to live in a nostalgia for lost glory, trying to keep a pre-industrial spirit alive, and for many visitors, this is how they want Provence to be. Many like to come on courses, to cook in the traditional Provençal way, to paint as the artists before them have done. But they should not forget to look out for the active cultural scene, which includes prestigious festivals and a dynamic creativity that can spring from anywhere. There are adventurous dance and theatre companies in Marseille and Aix, theatre and opera in Nice,

a million, is Nice, the silicon valley of France, where opinion polls consistently reveal that French people would like to live here more than anywhere else in their country.

Many other people not born in France would like to live here, too. Marseille, Nice, Toulon, Nîmes and Avignon are big multicultural cities with large immigrant populations, especially North and West Africans from former French colonies, as is evident in the local markets and street culture. Lying at a trade crossroads, Provence has long been multicultural, but this did not stop trouble flaring in towns and cities throughout the region during the civil unrest in 2005 that provoked long debates about

and a lively, often controversial annual festival in Avignon.

This creativity is propelled by a high student population. There are around 20,000 students in Marseille, and many of the foreigners who come to study in Provence inject a demand as well as a supply of new diversions.

Population

The population of Provence-Alpes-Côte d'Azur (PACA) is 4,600,000. Marseille, the administrative capital and a great Mediterranean port, is the largest city, with around 1.5 million inhabitants; Toulon, the naval port, has just over half a million. In between, with around

immigration and integration.

Italians are also a large immigrant group, though they only come from next door and feel quite at home, owning many of the properties and restaurants around Nice and Menton, a municipality that has cross-frontier administrative agreements with its neighbour Ventimiglia. Nice's most famous son is Garibaldi, founder of the Italian state, and the Italian flavour of the city is distinct.

In the 1980s the oil boom brought Arab money to the coast. Now it's the turn of the Russians, and Cyrillic script frequently appears in the menus of restaurants looking for a share of the wads of dollar bills that spill from the pockets of nouveaux riches Russians. In the restaurants of the Côte d'Azur, particularly in Nice and Antibes, English is frequently the majority language, as Britons make up the largest foreign resident population on the coast.

Immigration of retirement populations in search of warm winters, both from northern Europe and the rest of France, has given towns like Menton and Beaulieu the reputation of being France's *costa geriatrica*. But it also means that hill villages that were deserted half a century ago have been brought back to life and there is at least some work – building, maintenance, gardening – in the quieter months of the year.

Provence being home to a number of food and drink groups, including Pernod-Ricard, Nestlé and Coca Cola. As well as fruit and vegetables, Provence is an important producer of wine in the Vaucluse and the Var – the Côtes de Provence is one of the few areas of French wine production that is actually flourishing. Other less expected industries include salt in the Camargue, perfumes and food flavourings in Grasse, bauxite around Brignoles, nuclear research at Cadarache, and oil refining and petrochemicals companies around the Etang de Berre. People like to do business in Provence, and the large congress centres in Cannes and Nice are always popular.

Economy

The services industry is by far the largest employer, but technology companies, with a turnover of around four billion euros, now bring in the same amount of revenue as tourism. The high-tech industries are centred on Sophia Antipolis near Cannes, and there is a burgeoning electronics industry near Aix-en-Provence, where a quarter of all France's components are produced. The pharmaceuticals sector is expanding, too. Agriculture and the food and drink sectors are major employers,

Zaha Hadid's 33-storey glass CMA-CGM tower for a French shipping container company is set to dominate the waterfront in Marseille's Euroméditerranée development zone.

Marseille, France's second city and the Mediterranean's largest port, has been undergoing a dramatic revival. This boom city of the 19th century that suffered so badly in the war, and long held a reputation as France's

LEFT: girls about town in St-Tropez.
ABOVE: village life in the Provençal hinterland.

crime capital, is now a lively cultural focus and a magnet for service industries and advertising and creative agencies. These are moving in to replace the traditional port industries. Marseille's massive Euroméditerranée urban renewal programme, intended to create 35,000 jobs, includes the Joliette port district, with new passenger terminal, offices in converted warehouses, museums and cultural facilities, and the Belle de Mai Media Park, dedicated to film, TV and hi-tech media industries. Other large urban development projects are set for Nice along the River Var on the western side of town and Toulon.

Marseille may no longer be the crime capital of France, but it is not entirely redeemed. In fact, this whole region is spotted with dark areas where reputations are not always squeaky clean. Municipal corruption surfaces now and then in allegations, prosecutions and occasional shootings. Greedy property developers have been suspected to be behind the outbreaks of summer fires. Monaco continues to resist efforts by France to eliminate money laundering by making its banking rules more transparent. Its 45 banks produce a third of the nation's revenues, and fears have been voiced that these may fall under mobsters' control.

There are gangland killings over drugs and prostitution in the cities, and racketeering reverberates around slot machines. There are rich pickings for burglars along the coast, while the Cannes Film Festival and other glamorous events attract conmen and assorted small-time thieves. The gentlemen burglars of the Riviera are a breed that has passed.

Urbanisation

One would have thought that the authorities had learnt the lessons of *bétonisation*, the concreting-up of the coast at the risk of ruining the environment and the special beauty of the Riviera. But judging from the number of hoardings announcing new developments of "Grand Standing", it still seems as if nobody cares if all the land is cluttered up by unsightly apartment blocks, villas and garages, as long as everyone can have a glimpse of the sea.

Incessant urbanisation threatens to make the coast between Cannes and Menton one continuous conurbation. It puts up prices and excludes locals who can no longer afford the rents. Elsewhere the demand for holiday homes and second residences has seen a new sprawl around rural villages, while villas in the tinder-dry woods of the Var add a further fire risk to an already charred landscape. Fire is aided when there is little water to quench it, and the risk of drought increases as expanding urban areas tap the finite reserves.

Sun and wind

One thing that all the *départements* share is dazzling light from a potent sun. There is twice as much sunshine here as in Paris, even if out of season the climate is not always perfect. Winter has its share of cool or cold days, and there are often spectacular thunderstorms at the end of August.

The months of hot weather appeal not only to tourists; farmers and gardeners delight in the long growing season, and painters revel in the magical glow that surrounds the land. Another unifying characteristic is the infamous mistral. This wild, indefatigable northern wind sweeps across the region between late autumn and early spring, although the western and central sections, particularly down the Rhône valley and between Marseille and Toulon, are generally the worst hit. Its

Tourism

Coastal resorts and picturesque hill villages swing between seasonal extremes, from the summer, when populations increase tenfold, to winter, when it's quiet and there's little to do but watch the birds fly by. This has created a seasonal pattern of employment and many who come here to work cannot afford to stay all year round.

The growth of cheap flights, high-speed TGVs and the French 35-hour working week all help to extend the tourist season. Aix, Avignon, Marseille and Nice are ideal for out-of-season breaks. There have been efforts, too, to tempt visitors away from the crowded hot

violent, chilling gales are created whenever a depression develops over the Mediterranean.

High winds and a dry, hot climate mean forest fires are a real hazard, and access routes and walking paths are closed at times of high risk. Every summer thousands of hectares are destroyed by forest fires, making them especially susceptible to erosion from the mistral. The valuable top soil, rich in nutrients, is then lost, making the land less fertile and therefore less productive.

Left: Forville market in Cannes. **Above:** French veterans in St-Tropez. **Right:** glass maker in Biot, the medieval hill village renowned for its bubble glass products.

spots and lead them towards cultural centres and the developing "green tourism". The latter comprises activity holidays, often involving hiking, climbing and white-water rafting, in the less frequented inland areas, such as the Var, the Gorges du Verdon and the Parc National du Mercantour. Monaco is trying to regain its reputation as a cultural centre with its new art museum (two villas comprise the New National Museum of Monaco), and even along the crowded coast, in the Calanques, Cap Bregançon or along the Corniche des Maures, you can still find glorious unspoilt natural beaches.   ❑

Comment monsr sanit loys print la second fois la croix pour
aler oultremer : & son tresms : vlt chappie.

l'année dessus…
mil Ct loy…
Le bon Roy Ct…
loys qui toute sa vie auoit

este amenu et ententif de
cueur : & prisee de huir
a dieu : Aduenu que la tir
sainte auoit besoing de

THE MAKING OF PROVENCE

Like most regions of France, Provence is a well-defined area with a history of independence and a strong identity. The Romans gave it shape by establishing Provincia, and it drew its colour from Renaissance troubadours, alternative popes, a cosmopolitan seaport and a dazzling coast

Through the ages, Provence's strategic position and climate have drawn wave upon wave of settlers and colonisers. Ligurians, Celts, Greeks, Romans, Visigoths, Franks and Arabs have all left their mark here.

Prehistoric rock carvings in the Grottes de l'Observatoire in Monaco, made over a million years ago, provide the earliest evidence of human habitation in the region, and are among the oldest carvings of their kind in the world. For thousands of years, Neanderthal hunters occupied the area, until modern man (*Homo sapiens*) made an appearance in 30,000 BC. Ancient sites all along the coast show significant traces of primitive settlements in the form of skeletons, rock carvings and paintings, standing stones and drystone dwellings. Among the most fascinating of these are the thousands of Bronze Age petroglyphs of the Alpine Vallée des Merveilles at the foot of Mont Bégo.

Between 1800 and 800 BC the area was inhabited and cultivated by Ligurians, an extremely tough people, who lived in small, disparate settlements and enjoyed a considerable degree of autonomy until the arrival of the Greeks.

Greeks and Romans

It could be argued that Marseille was the birthplace of Western civilisation on the European continent. It was to this marshy bay that Greeks from Phocaea in Asia Minor set sail in the early 6th century BC. The peaceable Phocaeans

formed a happy alliance with the locals and quickly set up a successful trading post. Their new colony, Massilia, soon became the most important commercial centre along the coast and a flourishing republican city-state in its own right. During its heyday in the mid-4th century BC, the Phocaean presence spread throughout the area. Among the cities founded were Nikaia (Nice), Antipolis (Antibes), Citharista (la Ciotat), Olbia (Hyères) and Athenopolis (St-Tropez). The Greeks introduced the olive tree and techniques for cultivating vines.

By the 3rd century BC, however, the indigents' ties with Greece were weakened, as a budding relationship with Rome developed. The

LEFT: scenes from the life of saintly king, Louis IX.
RIGHT: the founding of the town Massalia (Marseille) by the Phocaeans, c.600BC.

friendship with Rome initially proved beneficial. The warlike Celts, Ligurians and Celto-Ligurians in the north of the region had been watching the prosperous Phocaeans with envy, and banded together in 125 BC to seize the Massilian riches. Overwhelmed, the Phocaeans turned to the Romans for help, and, in response, the warrior Caius Sextius Calvinius brought in an entire Roman army. After a vicious three-year war the victorious Roman consul established the city of Aquae Sextiae (Aix-en-Provence).

Before long, the Romans had replaced the Phocaeans as lords of the region, which they called "Provincia Romana". Massilia, however, continued to thrive and to operate with a fairly high degree of autonomy. Now no longer just a trading post, the city became famous as an intellectual centre, with universities rivalling those of Athens.

During Rome's civil war though, Massilia made the fatal error of siding with Pompey against Caesar. After Caesar's victory, in 49 BC, the dictator punished the city by making it a Roman vassal. He further crushed the colony by strengthening the port of Arelate (Arles), strategically located on the Via Aurelia – the Roman road linking Italy with Spain – and recruiting its inhabitants to besiege Massilia. With the fall of Massilia, Arles became capital of the Roman province, with a secondary city

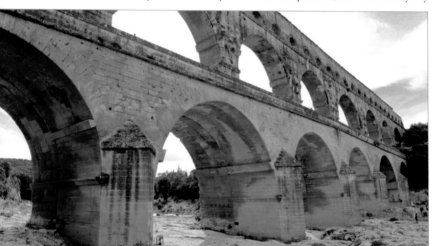

COUME VAI?

Today there are few speakers of Provençal, the language bequeathed by the Romans to this corner of their empire. In various dialects this Occitan language developed right across southern France from the Atlantic into Italy, unaffected by words from visiting Saracens or northern tribes.

The earliest surviving complete works in Provençal are poems designed to be sung, written by William IX, duke of Aquitaine (1071–1126). In fact, most of our knowledge of the development of the language comes through song, particularly through the ballads of troubadours who gathered at courts such as Les Baux *(see page 125)*. This medieval period saw the flowering of the language.

Although few people speak Provençal today, it has been making something of a comeback. It is possible to study Provençal for the baccalaureat, while various associations offer courses in the language, songs and traditional instruments. Street signs in old towns are often bilingual: look for the Nissart *carrièra* or Provençal *carriero* meaning *rue* or street, and *castelét* or *castelar* for *château* or castle. Troubadour revivalists continue to reinterpret the medieval music, and world music performers have even tried mixing it with reggae.

In answer to the question *coume vai?* (how are you?), you might say *balin-balan* (so-so).

at Cimiez, just north of Nice.

The Romans remained in Provence for a further 600 peaceful and prosperous years, uniting the disparate trading posts and building roads, temples, bridges, aqueducts, baths and amphitheatres. One sign of this growing unity was the emergence of a regional language, Provençal, which was derived from Latin and is still spoken in the region *(see panel on opposite page)*.

The arrival of Christianity

According to legend, Provence was converted to Christianity in the 1st century after the miraculous landing of the boat from Judaea – the so-called Boat of Bethany – carrying, among

Invaders and marauders

With the fall of the Western Empire, chaos reigned once again. The territory was invaded and occupied by Vandals, Visigoths, Burgundians, Ostrogoths and finally the Franks, who took control of the territory in 536. For the first two centuries under Frankish rule, Provence fared pretty well commercially. But the Franks ruled with an iron fist. Anti-Frankish rebellions in Marseille, Arles and Avignon between 732 and 739 were brutally quashed. Great numbers of Provençals were slaughtered, and whole cities, including Avignon, were razed.

In the 8th and 9th centuries more marauders came from the sea. The Saracens, origi-

others, Mary Magdalene, Martha and Martha's resurrected brother Lazarus. This saintly company landed on the shores of a town that is now called Stes-Maries-de-la-Mer. Mary Magdalene found a cave up in the hills of Ste-Baume where she lived as a hermit until her death 30 years later. When the Western Roman Empire fell in AD 476, the entire region had been converted to Christianity, with important centres of monasticism at the Abbaye St-Victor in Marseille and the Iles de Lérins.

nating from North Africa and the eastern Mediterranean coast, appear to have been exceptionally violent, and devastated great swathes of the Mediterranean coastline. The terrified inhabitants were forced to flee to the hills where they set about building the *villages perchés* – fortified hill villages – Provence is so famous for. Not until 974 did Guillaume le Libérateur drive the Saracens from Provence once and for all, beating back the Arab forces at their fortress in La Garde Freinet. The providential hero took the title of marquis, thereby inaugurating the first Provençal dynasty, and at the same time marking a new era of prosperity for the region.

LEFT: Pont du Gard, Nîmes. **ABOVE:** early 19th-century painting on glass of Mary Magdalene. Legend has it that she lived in a Provençal cave and was fed by angels.

Feudal Provence

The lack of a strong central authority in the region promoted the rise of the feudal system. Towns such as Arles, Avignon, Nice, Grasse, Tarascon, Les Baux and Marseille became independent, self-governing forces. Grandiose castles were built, and the church started a major expansion campaign. The construction of Romanesque churches and chapels was also inspired by Roman building techniques. The arts found patronage within the various courts, and throughout the area cultural creativity reached unprecedented heights.

Agriculture developed and trade increased, and through the interplay of expedient mar-

> *In 1297 a new dynasty was born when François Grimaldi seized the rock of Monaco disguised as a monk.*

Two years later Louis IX (St Louis) set out from Aigues-Mortes on the Seventh Crusade which bolstered economic activity back home.

The popes in Avignon

In 1274 Comtat-Venaissin on the lower Rhône (roughly Carpentras and its Vaucluse hinterland) was ceded to Pope Gregory X in Rome. In 1309, Pope Clement V, a native French-

riages, control of the area was divided between the counts of Toulouse, who ruled the north, and the counts of Barcelona, who ruled the southern area stretching from the Rhône to the Durance and from the Alps to the sea, known as the Comté de Provence. Raimond Bérenger V in particular did much to unify the province, and took up residence in Aix, by now the regional capital. After his death in 1245, his daughter Béatrice was married off a year later by the cunning Blanche of Castille to ambitious Charles of Anjou (brother of the French king, Louis IX) who became count of Provence. From that day onwards, the destiny of Provence was linked to that of the Angevins and, increasingly, to France.

man, decided that he had had enough of the anarchy that had gripped Rome, and when King Philippe the Fair of France invited him to return home, he transferred the papal court to Avignon. What had been a small provincial backwater suddenly swelled into an important centre for diplomats and pilgrims, holy ecclesiastics and very unholy courtiers, who brought with them a sophisticated and *mondaine* way of life. Six more popes were to follow, and a period called "the second Babylonian captivity of the Church" began. The third Provençal pope, Benedict XII, had a reputation for being avaricious, egotistical and uncharitable. He instigated the construction of the vast Palais des Papes, as a symbol of the absolute power of the Church. Benedict's successor, Clement VI – who had bought Avignon from the reigning countess Jeanne of Provence for 80,000 gold florins – added a more ornate section to the palace, and had the Pont d'Avignon built in 1350.

The popes stayed in Avignon for almost 70 years. In returning to Rome, however, they started the "Great Schism" (1378–1417), when there were two popes: one in Avignon and one in Rome. This bitter rivalry continued for several decades. The popes in Rome and the antipopes in Avignon excommunicated each other with monotonous regularity, and each of the powers in Europe chose their papal cham-

pion according to their current interests. The Schism was finally brought to an end in 1417 by the Council of Constance, which deposed the antipopes.

Good King René

Meanwhile, the rest of Provence had degenerated into a state of constant civil war. The area was already reeling from the devastation of the first great plague in 1348. A semblance of peace and order was restored by Louis II, a capable

LEFT: Giovanna, heiress queen of Naples, visits Pope Clement VI in Avignon, to surrender her lands.
ABOVE: Good King René (1409–80).

ruler. Louis fathered the most beloved count of Provence, René d'Anjou, popularly known as Good King René. René ushered in a new era of prosperity. A self-styled philosopher and humanist, he devoted himself to promoting the economic revival of Provence and its ports and to reinstating interest in the arts. He was a tolerant, amicable leader, whose steady control allowed cultural life to flourish.

After René's death in 1480, Provence passed to his nephew and heir, Charles III du Maine, who in 1481 bequeathed the entire region to Louis XI, king of France – a distant cousin – although the Savoy-controlled Comté of Nice remained outside France, making the River Var an important frontier, marked by a line of fortresses. The conditions he attached for Provence's independence were confirmed by the Constitution Provençale in 53 "chapters", which the central government in Paris increasingly ignored. This caused constant friction between Provence and the French government, and there were numerous rebellions and attempts to secede. François I further curtailed the region's independence by strengthening the control of the hated Parlement over the local judiciaries and declaring French the official language, supplanting the native Provençal dialect. Although the ancient dialect was not wiped out, the new law initiated its decline.

The Provençals fight back

Despite the repression by France during the early 16th century, noble Provençal families continued to thrive. Numerous chateaux were built, and small fortunes were amassed. Concerned that these wealthy inhabitants might try to rival the French nobility, the Parlement turned its Gallic eye towards their belittlement. Deciding that the chateaux, with their rounded corner towers, were potentially aggressive as well as presumptuous, they commanded that all towers be truncated to the level of the main roof. The stunted leftovers are still visible, dubbed *poivrières* ("pepper pots") by the locals.

However, the arts continued to flourish. There was a revival of native literature, mostly in the form of religious mystery plays; the period is sometimes called the "Provençal Renaissance". Many of the writers were scientific pioneers. Among them was the physician and astrologer Nostradamus (*see panel, page 26*). A less sensational Provençal was Adam de Craponne (1527–76). Born in Salon-de-Provence amid the dry plains of the Crau, de Craponne designed the irrigation canal that diverts water from the Durance River through the Lamanon gap, bringing water to the region.

War, rebellion and plague

The brutal Wars of Religion between the Catholics and the Protestants, brought on by the Reformation, lasted for much of the mid- and late 16th century. A particularly bloody campaign was wielded against the Vaudois sect in the Luberon (*see page 86*), which was disbanded in 1545. Countless other atrocities took place

in the region, notably in Orange, Nîmes, where three-quarters of the population was Protestant and Vence, where the people threw out a reformist bishop. However, in 1598, the first Bourbon king, Henri IV, issued the Edict of Nantes, which granted religious tolerance to Protestants and calmed the situation. Under Richelieu, the Catholic church fought back with Counter-Reformation Baroque churches. When the Edict was subsequently revoked by Louis XIV in 1685, thousands of Huguenots emigrated from Nîmes.

New dissension against the French emerged in the form of the Provençal Fronde, which pitted itself against royal absolutism. The Fronde

was suppressed in 1653, but discontent persisted in Marseille. The defiant city revolted in 1659, only to be stripped of all its remaining rights after its defeat the following year.

In 1660, Louis XIV made one of his rare visits outside the royal palace, coming with great pomp to Marseille, whose strategic importance he recognised. His objective was to win over the opposition and anchor Marseille on his side. He ordered the construction of Fort St-Nicolas, from which both the town and port could be closely monitored, expanded the urban area threefold and encouraged the growth of maritime trade by making it a free port. In a period of constant wars with Spain,

Louis XIV's military engineer Vauban also built new star-shaped fortifications at Toulon and Antibes.

In all likelihood, it was the expansion of Marseille port which caused the third and deadliest of all the plagues to hit Provence. The epidemic that struck in the early 1720s was carried on trading vessels from the east, and more than 100,000 people – 38,000 from Marseille alone – died. Traces of a vast wall built in the desperate effort to contain the disease can still be seen near Fontaine de Vaucluse.

The French Revolution

The people of Provence embraced the Revolution with open arms and an extraordinary excess of blood-letting. Their interest in the new constitution stemmed not so much from a desire for social reform as from the hope that it might offer a chance to regain lost powers. A revolt against the church as well as monarchy, churches as well as chateaux were ransacked and confiscated as state property. Marseille was an enthusiastic adherent. Before long, a guillotine graced la Canebière, the city's main street, and the cobblestones ran red with spilt blood.

On 11 April 1789, the Société Patriotique des Amis de la Constitution was formed on the rue Thubaneau in Marseille, and it was there that Rouget de Lisle's *Le Chant des Marseillais* – now the bloody national anthem for all of France – was sung for the first time. It was from the small nearby town of Martigues that the *tricolore* (now France's national flag) originated. Martigues consists of three boroughs, each with its own standard. Ferrières's is blue, Ile St-Genest's white, and Jonquières's red. United, they form the red, white and blue flag adopted by the Revolutionaries.

The Revolution did not, however, restore the autonomy Provence had enjoyed in earlier centuries. Instead, the region lost what little independence it had been able to retain. The local government was completely dissolved in 1790, and the region was divided into three *départements*: the Bouches-du-Rhône, the Var and the Basses-Alpes. The Vaucluse was added in 1793, after the French annexation of the

papal territory in the Comtat-Venaisson, as was Nice, conquered by revolutionary troops.

Napoleon

Although the Provençals had embraced Napoleon the military genius, they were much less enthusiastic about Napoleon the emperor. This same people, such eager participants in the early years of the Revolution, soon became staunch supporters of the returning Bourbon monarchy. Blood flowed again in the streets, as those suspected of being anti-royalist were slaughtered with the same intensity as the anti-Revolutionaries had been under Jacobinism.

The Provençal antipathy towards Napoleon

proved to be justified, for his ever-escalating wars resulted in the ceding of much of the eastern territory (including Nice and the land as far north as the Var River) to Sardinia during the Congress of Vienna in 1814–5, after Napoleon's defeat. It was not until 1860 that these lands were returned to France.

The 19th Century

Nonetheless, the 19th century was probably the most peaceful period Provence had ever experienced. The French revolutions of 1830 and 1848 and the new regimes they heralded aroused little interest in the southern regions. With the Second Empire (1852–70) came a Provençal

LEFT: carts laden with the dead, outside Marseille town hall, during the plague of 1720.
RIGHT: *The Marseillaise*, by Gustave Doré, 1870.

revival, led by Nobel Prize-winning poet and local hero, Frédéric Mistral. With a group of Provençal poets, he founded the Félibrige, a cultural and literary organisation that encouraged the local language and traditions, promoting literary works written in Provençal. He used his Nobel Prize money to found the Provençal museum in Arles.

Agriculture remained the economic mainstay, but the Industrial Revolution, which came fairly late to France, did not leave Provence untouched. Between 1876 and 1880 alone, the rural *département* of the Vaucluse lost some 20,000 inhabitants to the cities.

Aix-en-Provence languished through most of the 19th century as a provincial, if distinguished, backwater. Marseille, on the other hand, grew dramatically in size. Almost all trade with the French Maghreb (Algeria, Tunisia and Morocco) passed through the city, and the new industries it engendered drew waves of immigrant workers from Algeria, Armenia, Spain and Italy.

Another thriving new industry came in the form of tourism. A small community of English aristocrats had begun wintering on the Côte d'Azur in the late 1700s, but it wasn't until Lord Brougham took a fancy to the town of Cannes in 1834 that tourism on the "French Riviera" really took off (see page 233). The area became very popular with the aristocrats of Victorian Eng-

THE GLITTERING COAST

The "French Riviera", as the Italians dubbed this Mediterranean strip, was not always considered glamorous. When the Scottish novelist Tobias Smollett (1721–71) came to Nice in 1764 to cure his bronchitis, he wrote that it was a land of rude peasants and persistent mosquitoes. He did, however, admit that the gentle climate was remarkable. This praise encouraged a few brave Brits to visit, but the French stayed away, preferring fashionable Normandy.

In 1834, Lord Brougham, the English Lord Chancellor, and his daughter were detained in Cannes while a bout of cholera spread through their favourite Italian winter playground. Eight days after his arrival in the tiny fishing village,

he bought land and ordered a villa to be constructed. The rage had begun. Within a year, a small but extant winter colony had sprung up in Cannes. Within three years, 30 new villas had been built, and the following year the harbourside avenue now called La Croisette was created. Five years later, the Promenade des Anglais was constructed in Nice for the newcomers' morning constitutionals.

In the second half of the 19th century the Côte d'Azur went into full swing. Any halfway fashionable Briton wintered in Nice, Cannes, Menton or Beaulieu. The elaborate Belle Epoque villas for which the Côte is still famous were built along the coast, and immortal glamour was assured.

land and European royals. Rich French, American and Russian tourists followed. Railway lines and roads were extended along the coast, and grand neoclassical buildings mushroomed.

The extraordinary quality of the light and intense colours of the landscape were captured on canvas by Monet, Renoir and Van Gogh, who were drawn to Provence, and by Cézanne, a native of Aix *(see pages 35–8)*.

In the 1890s, Queen Victoria stayed several times in Nice, travelling as Lady Balmoral and visiting the town with a donkey and trap.

Between the wars

Although thousands of soldiers conscripted from the south were killed in World War I, Provence was far from the battlefields of the north and remained unscathed. Post-war recovery was rapid. The period between the wars saw a boom in the tourist industry, particularly along the coast. In the 1920s and '30s Cannes and Nice became the playground for the rich and famous. The Scott Fitzgeralds, Noël Coward, Wallis Simpson and Gertrude Stein all made their mark on the Côte d'Azur, their hedonistic and liberal lifestyles centred on the casinos, jazz clubs, villas and outdoor pools. Sunbathing had been famously introduced by Coco Chanel, and the first nudist colony opened on the Ile de Levant. With the introduction of paid holidays in 1936, the south of France was no longer the preserve of the rich. French workers began flocking to the south, many of them to see the sea for the first time.

Provence continued to flourish as a centre of the avant-garde. Matisse, Picasso, Le Corbusier and other cutting-edge artists and architects continued to find inspiration here.

World War II

The Depression and World War II brought this carefree period to an end. Occupation by Italy in 1940 was followed by German occupation in 1942–3. When the Allies landed in North

Africa in the winter of 1942, the Germans marched on Toulon and Marseille. Eager to get in on the deal, the Italians took over the Côte d'Azur. After the collapse of the Italian regime ten months later, the Germans took possession of the entire area. The Provençals were swept into the thick of things. Those who had not already been conscripted into the French army banded into fierce local Resistance groups. Particularly active in the mountainous regions, their guerrilla tactics brought relentless reprisals from the occupying forces. Meanwhile, the US Air Force began to mount counter-attacks against the Germans, causing additional damage to once peaceful towns and destroying

many historical monuments.

Finally, General de Lattre de Tassigny's 1st French and General Patch's 7th US armies landed on the Dramont beaches just east of St-Raphaël on 15 August 1944. By 15 September, most of Provence had been freed from the occupying forces, and by April the following year, the enemy had been totally eliminated.

Post-war Provence

Glamour and optimism returned to the Riviera soon after the war. The first international film festival at Cannes in 1946 delivered Hollywood to the sunny Mediterranean shores, as the arrival of the likes of Clark Gable, Humphrey

LEFT: La Croisette, Cannes, in the 1920s.
RIGHT: an Allied soldier and local demoiselle.

Bogart and Rita Hayworth heralded a return to the star-spangled tradition of the Côte d'Azur. Artists and writers continued to take up residence in the area. Picasso moved to Antibes in 1946 and spent the rest of his life in Provence. Parisian bohemian stars like Juliette Greco and the writer Françoise Sagan followed in the footsteps of Colette and Anaïs Nin, and basked in the simple, sunny pleasures of the little port of St-Tropez. By the late '50s, with the arrival of the bikini and the Brigitte Bardot phenomenon, the quiet fishing village had been transformed into a "metropolis of illicit pleasures".

Until the war Provence's economy had been almost entirely based on agriculture. After the war, farmers were encouraged to modernise their operations. The small-scale Provençal farms tried to adapt, going into debt to invest in modern machinery, but without any form of government support many were unable to survive. By the early 1980s only 10 percent of locals worked the land, compared to 35 percent 40 years earlier.

The 1960s were characterised by industrial expansion and the embracing of new technologies. Nuclear power stations developed along the Rhône and at Cadarache. Hydroelectric plants were built on the banks of the Durance, and the area around the Berre Lagoon was turned into a huge petrochemical zone and industrial port with tanker docks and oil refineries. The traditional jobs of boat-building and fishing available to the locals were replaced by less interesting jobs in the industrial plants.

In 1969 the high-tech Sophia-Antipolis Science Park, north of Cannes, was inaugurated. Hailed as Europe's answer to California's Silicon Valley, this centre for new technologies has been expanding steadily since its foundation. It now has 1,100 companies occupying an area a quarter the size of Paris, and is one of the most sought-after business locations in Europe. More traditional heavy industry continues on more than 7,000 hectares bordering the port of Marseille and Fos, which remains the country's main chemical and petrochemical centre.

ET DIEU... CREA LA FEMME

Immigration and the far right

Following the creation of the Fifth Republic, General de Gaulle, its first president, set about tackling the unrest in the French colonies, negotiating independence with Algeria in 1962. Algerian independence was followed by a wave of immigrants from North Africa. Tens of thousands of *pieds noirs* (literally "black feet") – French settlers from Algeria – flooded into France, many settling in the large southern cities like Marseille and Nice. A steady flow of immigrant workers (legal and illegal) from the former colonies added to the ethnic mix, creating significant Muslim communities in towns across the region.

With economic recession and growing unemployment at the end of the 20th century, the extreme right Front National party gained enormous popularity in the region among those less than content with the growth of a multiethnic society. Its xenophobic leader, Jean-Marie Le Pen, was not born in Provence, nor does he embody any particularly Provençal attributes, yet he found a remarkably large following in the region, polling 22 percent in the elections in 2004. However, formerly Front National municipalities in Toulon and Orange have since returned to right or independent status.

The 21st century

It has taken a while for Provence, which for so long has been deeply rooted in agricultural life, to come to terms with modernisation. However, prosperity in the region is now growing, and unemployment continues to fall. The European

to Nice (due to open in 2023).

Tourism continues to dominate the economy. An increase in the number of low-cost flights is bringing more and more visitors to Provence – and not just to the big cities and coast. The more rural, further-flung corners are attracting increasing numbers of tourists looking to escape the crowds. The rural economy is experiencing a significant boost, with foreigners buying and renovating run-down farmhouses and other properties. Whole villages have been rejuvenated as a result of well-to-do British and German tourists buying holiday homes in the countryside, while multi-millionaires, particularly Russian

Fund for Regional Development is currently involved in supporting scores of minor rural enterprises and agricultural projects which benefit the regional economy. The TGV has been extended to Avignon, Nîmes, Marseille and Aix-en-Provence, making Provence only a comfortable three-hour journey from Paris. Property prices in the region have boomed, and plans have been confirmed to extend the track

oligarchs, have pushed up prices so dramatically in the Côte d'Azur that a lot of old French money is moving out.

Provence also continues to be the most popular holiday spot for the French themselves. They make up 80 percent of the 34 million visitors who bring 10 billion euros to the region's economy and account for 11 percent of its GDP. Such an influx obviously creates ecological problems, both on land and in the sea. Global warming brings the increased risk of summer fires, and many hiking trails are now closed during high-risk periods, but by and large the region continues to look after its visitors very successfully. ❏

LEFT: Roger Vadim's *And God Created Woman*, shot the director's then wife, Brigitte Bardot, to fame.
ABOVE: Cannes' beach and old town. **ABOVE RIGHT:** the marina in the Baie des Anges, the "Bay of Angels" which lies between Nice and Cannes.

Decisive Dates

Prehistoric times
Evidence of human habitation in the Gorges de Verdon, the Vallée des Merveilles, Terra Amata, Nice, and caves near Cassis and Monaco.

1800 BC
Ligurians occupy the Mediterranean coast.

600 BC
Marseille is founded by Greek traders.

121 BC
Romans conquer southern Gaul and establish Aquae Sextiae (Aix-en-Provence).

27 BC–AD 14
Reign of Caesar Augustus. Provence flourishes.

AD 3rd–5th centuries
Christianity spreads.

395
Arles becomes the administrative capital of the western provinces (Gaul).

476
Fall of the Western Roman Empire. Vandals, Visigoths, Burgundians, Ostrogoths and Franks invade.

8th–10th centuries
Provence becomes part of the Carolingian Empire. Arabs from Iberian peninsula invade, but are expelled 200 years later in 974.

1032
Provence annexed to the Holy Roman Empire.

1178
Frederick I (Barbarossa) is crowned king of Provence in Arles.

1274
Comtat-Venaissin (east of Avignon) is ceded to the pope.

1297
François Grimaldi, disguised as a monk, takes the Monaco rock.

1316
Pope John XXII moves papacy to Avignon.

1348
Pope Clement VI buys Avignon. Plague strikes.

1377
Papacy returns to Rome.

1388
Eastern Provence (the Comté de Nice) falls under the rule of the House of Savoy (Italy).

1409
University of Aix is founded.

1471
Good King René (1434–80) moves to Aix.

1481
Provence becomes part of the French kingdom.

1501
The founding of the parliament in Aix.

1539
French replaces Provençal as the official language.

1545
Massacre of the Vaudois heretics in the Luberon.

1598
Under the Edict of Nantes, the Huguenots are granted

the right to worship in freedom, ending the Wars of Religion.

1660
Pilgrimage by Anne of Austria to Apt and Cotignac in thanks for the birth of her son, the future Louis XIV.

1685
The Edict of Nantes is revoked, and thousands of Huguenots emigrate, especially from Nîmes.

1691
The French conquer Nice, but the town is handed back to Savoy in 1715 after the Spanish War of Succession.

1718
Nice becomes part of Sardinia.

1720
Plague spreads from Marseille into Provence and over 100,000 people die.

1789
Start of French Revolution.

1790
Provence is divided into three *départements*: Basse-Alpes, Bouches-du-Rhône and Var.

1791
France annexes Avignon and the Comtat-Venaissin.

1793
End of the siege of Toulon, which sparks Napoleon Bonaparte's rise to glory.

1815
Napoleon lands at Golfe Juan on escaping from Elba; the English aristocracy begins to winter in the south of France.

1854
Mistral founds the Félibrige, a cultural association to promote the Provençal language.

1860
Nice votes to return to France.

1869
Suez Canal opens. Marseille

LEFT: detail from the *Burning Bush* triptych, showing Good King René and his wife. Painted by Nicolas Froment, it can be found in Cathédrale St-Sauveur in Aix-en-Provence. ABOVE: Napoleon.

gains in importance as a Mediterranean port.

1887
The term Côte d'Azur is coined by the writer Stephen Liégeard.

1929
Monaco holds its first Grand Prix.

1939
The Cannes Film Festival is inaugurated but World War II causes the first festival to be delayed until 1946.

1940
Italians annex Menton and occupy Alpes Maritimes.

1942
German troops occupy southern France.

1944
The Allies land between Toulon and the Estérel, recapturing Toulon and Nice.

From 1945
Mass tourism. The coastal strip no longer attracts only the rich and famous.

1956
American film star Grace

Kelly marries Prince Rainier III of Monaco. Brigitte Bardot hits St-Tropez, starring in the film *And God Created Woman*.

1962
Many French Algerians settle in Provence after the Algerian war of independence.

1972
The Provence-Alpes-Côte d'Azur region is created with the reorganisation of local government.

1990
Jacques Médecin, mayor of Nice for 25 years, flees to Uruguay to avoid trial for corruption.

1999
The Front National is split by internal feuding and an extreme-right breakaway party forms.

2001
High-speed TGV rail network reaches Marseille, cutting journey times to the Riviera.

2003
Heatwave and fatal forest fires create major problems for the region.

2005
Prince Rainier of Monaco dies, Prince Albert II enthroned. Avignon and Nice affected in nationwide riots.

2010
Marseille wins French football championship. Floods in the Var cause 25 deaths.

ARTISTS IN PROVENCE

"The whole future of art is to be found in southern France," Van Gogh told Gauguin. He was right. With such intense light, inspirational landscapes and azure bays, no other part of the world has had such a dramatic effect on modern art

Our image of Provence has been largely created by modern artists, and they in turn have given the history of modern art a distinctly southern flavour. Familiar images include Cézanne's *Montagne Ste-Victoire*, Van Gogh's tortured olive trees, Picasso's nymphs and sea urchins, the iron tracery of Matisse's balconies and Bonnard's red-tiled roofs and palm trees, seen through an open window.

Today Provence and the Côte d'Azur are among the best places in the world to see modern art in the setting in which it was created, whilst enjoying the sensual pleasures and luminous light that inspired Cézanne, Van Gogh, Matisse and Picasso.

Van Gogh

Vincent Van Gogh (1853–90) was one of the first artists to be inspired by the intense bleached light and brilliant colours of the south. Today

> *"The Midi fires the senses, your hand is more agile, your eye sharper, your brain clearer..." wrote Van Gogh to his brother.*

his image and work are slapped on everything from wine bottles to ash trays, but few people wanted to know him when he arrived in Arles in 1888 at the age of 35. Yet this was where, in just three years, all his great paintings were executed. Here he found a power and vitality that

LEFT: *Café Terrace, Place du Forum, Arles*, by Van Gogh, 1888. **RIGHT:** Renoir painting in his garden, c.1910.

inspired him almost beyond endurance.

"The Midi fires the senses, your hand is more agile, your eye sharper, your brain clearer..." he wrote in one of his many letters to his brother, Theo. Interiors, sunflowers, irises, night skies and the harvest fields all charged his brush with colour – "The olive trees look like silver, at times bluer, at times greener, bronze-coloured, whitening on a soil that is yellow, purple or orange pink or even deep ochre red."

Van Gogh had been painting for only six years before he arrived in Arles. He was born in the Netherlands, the son of a Protestant pastor, and although he began work as an art dealer, he became obsessed with evangelical Christianity.

Determined to become a preacher, he spent a year living in poverty in a mining community in Holland. Slowly the inspiration to paint took over, and after training in Antwerp, he went to Paris where Theo worked as an art dealer at Goupil & Cie. Inspired by what he saw of the Impressionists, he then headed for Provence and immediately began working furiously. Wanting to share his experience, he wrote to his friend Paul Gauguin, saying "The whole future of art is to be found in southern France."

In preparation for Gauguin's arrival, he rented four rooms in the Yellow House at 2 Place Lamartine in Arles as a studio and began painting sunflowers. Impoverished, his health was deteriorating and he was drinking excessively. When Gauguin arrived he found Vincent impossible to tolerate and they fell out. This was the cause of Van Gogh slicing off part of his ear lobe, which he wrapped in newspaper and gave to a prostitute in the local brothel, asking her to keep it safely.

A series of mental breakdowns followed as epilepsy and syphilis took their toll, exacerbated by heavy drinking and a meagre diet. Finally he entered the Asylum for the Alienated in St-Rémy-de-Provence, and although he suffered further breakdowns, he continued to paint, producing more than 150 works, among them some of his best paintings. He then travelled to

THE SCHOOLS OF AVIGNON AND NICE

The patronage of the papal palace helped to establish a school of Avignon painters led by Simone Martini of Siena, who arrived in 1335, and his successor Matteo de Giovanetti from Viterbo. They worked on the palace and in surrounding secular buildings, and some of their frescos can still be seen. One of the finest works to emerge from the school is the *Avignon Pietà* (1457) by Enguerrand Quarton, now in the Louvre; there are more works of his at Villeneuve-lès-Avignon and the Musée du Petit Palais in Avignon. Nicolas Froment (1435–86), another member of the Avignon school, was court painter to Good King René. He came from northern France, where he had been

a follower of Jan van Eyck, and both he and Quarton are credited with infusing French art with Flemish naturalism. Froment's major surviving work is the triptych in the cathedral of St-Sauveur in Aix, which depicts René in the left-hand panel.

In the 15th and 16th centuries a painting school flourished in the county of Nice, where many churches and even the humblest chapels were decorated with murals. The school's principal painter was Louis Bréa (1450–1523), the "Provençal Fra Angelico", who provided the altarpiece for Monaco cathedral and three fine works for the Franciscan monastery in Cimiez.

Auvers-sur-Oise just outside Paris to consult a physician recommended by Pissarro. Here he ended his life by shooting himself, even though by this time he was becoming appreciated as a major talent. The only original Van Gogh to be seen in Provence is in Avignon, but around the Asylum *(see page 124)* you can follow a trail to see the scenes that he painted. The landscape that inspired him remains largely unchanged, and it is hard to see it all without feeling moved.

Cézanne and Braque

Although many painters came to Provence, one of the most famous was born there. Paul Cézanne (1839–1906) was the son of a banker

standing of the "depth of reality".

In 1870 Cézanne returned to Aix, where he lived until his death in 1906. He painted the Provençal landscape, the park and gardeners at the family home Le Jas de Bouffon (now open to the public) and, above all, countless versions of his beloved Montagne Ste-Victoire, determined to capture the structure of nature on canvas. "To paint a landscape well", he wrote, "I must first discover its geological characteristics."

You can tour Montagne Ste-Victoire and, in Aix, visit Cézanne's atelier *(see page 117)* as well as the Musée Granet *(see page 117)*, which shows eight of his works including *Les Baigneurs (The Bathers)*.

from Aix-en-Provence, where he went to college with his friend the novelist Emile Zola. In spite of a desire to paint he struggled for a while to become his father's successor. Eventually his family realised that it would be better to allow him to pursue his painting, and in 1863 he went to join Zola in Paris. Once there, Cézanne's distaste for the "old school" led to his association with the revolutionary group of painters now known as the Impressionists. But he eventually went his own way, believing that the Impressionists' work lacked an under-

Cézanne was highly influential. His paintings of the bay and sea at l'Estaque, just outside Marseille, inspired Georges Braque (1882–1963) to visit the port in homage to the master. The Cubist's key painting *Les Maisons de l'Estaque* (*Houses at l'Estaque*, 1908) was the result. Although the port is now overwhelmed by industry, the little houses that were transformed into revolutionary blocks and planes of colour can still be seen.

Renoir

The Impressionists came to Provence and the Côte d'Azur, fascinated by what Claude Monet (1840–1926) described as "the glaring, festive

LEFT: *Avignon Pietà*, by Enguerrand Quarton, 1457.
ABOVE: *Montagne Ste-Victoire*, by Cézanne, 1900.

light", which made colours so intense that he claimed no one would believe that they were real. In 1883 Monet brought Pierre Auguste Renoir (1841–1919) on his first visit to the area; Renoir returned increasingly often to paint the filtered golden light, the olive trees and the soft terracotta roofs that are characteristic of Provençal villages.

Suffering from arthritis, he settled in the south for his health, buying up a 500-year-old olive grove and building a house, Les Colettes, there for his family. This proved the ideal setting for Renoir's final period; he had a glassed-in studio built among the olive trees, with curtains to control the light, providing a perfect solution

to the choice between working from nature and in a studio. He even found the strength, with the help of an assistant, to sculpt. "Under this sun you have a desire to see marble or bronze Venuses among the foliage," he said. And here among the olives you can still see his bronze *Venus Victrix*. Today Les Colettes is a museum *(see page 242)*, surrounded by the magnificent shady olive grove. Inside the house are 10 original paintings as well as the master's studio, with chair, easel and palette just as he left them.

Picasso and his influence

The south of France belongs in large part to Pablo Picasso (1881–1973), and nowhere is his

THE APPEAL OF ST-TROPEZ

Although many of the ports and coastal towns beyond Marseille, such as Toulon, La Ciotat, Cassis and Hyères, became favoured destinations for artists, St-Tropez had the greatest pull. Paul Signac (1863–1935), a keen sailor, was one of the first artists to move here, although the place was then only accessible by sea. In 1892 he bought a villa just outside St-Tropez, which at that time was no more than a tiny fishing port. He invited many of his fellow artists, including Georges Seurat (1859–91), Maurice Utrillo (1883–1955), André Derain (1880–1954) and Raoul Dufy (1877–1953), who all painted the little harbour, the ochre cottages and the shimmering sea. Henri Matisse visited

Signac in St-Tropez in 1904, producing his own experiment with pointillism – *Luxe, Calme et Volupté (Luxury, Calm and Delight)* – and the liberation from traditional techniques that led him to Fauvism. In 1909 Pierre Bonnard (1867–1947) also rented a villa in St-Tropez. He too was stunned: "Suddenly I was hit with a Thousand and One Nights; the sea, the yellow walls, the reflections which were as brightly coloured as the lights..."

The work of many of these artists, including Signac's *St-Tropez au Soleil Couchant (St-Tropez at Sunset)* and Matisse's *La Gitane (The Gypsy)*, is on show at the Musée de l'Annonciade in St-Tropez *(see page 197)*.

presence more palpable than the Musée Picasso (*see page 239*) in Antibes.

Picasso's love affair with the Riviera began in 1920, when he spent the summer in Juan-les-Pins, and he became a frequent visitor to the coast over the following summers. When World War II broke out in 1939, he was in Antibes, painting *Pêche de Nuit à Antibes (Night Fishing at Antibes)*, a luminous nocturnal seascape inspired by watching the fishermen and their boats illuminated by white acetylene lamps. The painter returned to Antibes in 1946 with Françoise Gilot, whom he had met in 1943, and he was given the chateau – then the local archaeological museum – to use as a studio.

also has a large collection of work by Russian-born Nicolas de Staël, who lived in Ménerbes in the Luberon before moving into a house in the Antibes ramparts before his death in 1955. Works by César, Yves Klein and Joan Miró, as well as more recent Antibes resident Hans Hartung, can also be seen.

In Vallauris Picasso single-handedly revived the town's pottery industry. In Cannes he painted the *Las Meninas* series (1957), after Velázquez's painting of the Spanish court. The pleasure he took in the environment is particularly evident in the wonderful dove paintings, *Els Colomins* (1957), which feature exuberant yellows and oranges with views of turquoise

After the grim war years in Paris, Picasso was inspired by the light, colour and antiquity of the Mediterranean; his nymphs, centaurs, goats, sea urchins and monumental women running on the beach have a pagan innocence that expresses the inspiration the painter derived from the hard shadows and bright colours of sea, beach and mountains. These paintings and drawings resulted in a major work, *Joie de Vivre (Joy of Life)*, the gem of a collection that includes paintings, drawings, sculpture, engravings and ceramics. The Musée Picasso

sea and black-and-purple palm trees.

Droves of painters followed in Picasso's footsteps, including Fernand Léger (1881–1955), whose interest in developing large architectural ceramic sculpture and murals attracted him to Biot. Along with Vallauris, this town became the centre of a revival of ceramic art. Shortly before Léger died in 1955 he bought a plot of land just outside Biot on which to build a studio, and his wife subsequently created the Musée National Fernand Léger (*see page 241*). The museum houses his personal collection, and its exterior is dominated by his massive, brilliantly coloured ceramic panels.

LEFT: *The Harbour at St-Tropez*, by Paul Signac, c.1905.
ABOVE: Picasso's *Joy of Life*, 1946.

Matisse

Henri Matisse (1869–1954) spent much of his life on the Côte d'Azur. After early visits to St-Tropez and L'Estaque, he settled in Nice in 1917. For a year he lived in the Hôtel Beau Rivage, painting the great sweeping bay of the Promenade des Anglais, before buying an apartment on the Place Charles Félix, where he painted his famous *odalisques* – harem slaves – framed by shuttered windows and flowers, capturing forever the voluptuous ease of the Riviera.

One of the most moving examples of his work is the Chapelle du Rosaire *(see page 208)*, just outside Vence, an exquisite blue-and-white chapel designed and decorated by Matisse at

the end of his life. The tiled roof, the blue-and-yellow stained glass, and the appliquéd vestments are all a poignant testimony to the artist's genius. He once observed that if there was

> Matisse on Nice: "What made me stay are the great coloured reflections of January, the luminosity of daylight."

a heaven, he would want it to be "a Paradise where I paint frescos". The Musée Matisse *(see page 230)* in Nice houses paintings, drawings and sculptures from every period of Matisse's

working life, as well as his vases, masks, pots, shell furniture and Moroccan wall hangings.

Chagall, Dufy and Cocteau

The Russian artist Marc Chagall (1887–1985) settled on the Côte d'Azur towards the end of his career, finding inspiration in the light and colour of the south. The Musée Chagall in Nice *(see page 230)* is home to the largest collection of Chagall's work; it was built to house his Old Testament series, the *Message Biblique (Biblical Message)*. There are mosaics by Chagall in the cathedral in Vence and the Chapelle Ste-Roseline near Les Arcs.

Raoul Dufy (1877–1953) often came to the south of France, and his sensual paintings convey the delights of the region – the food, wine, palm trees and grand hotels – perhaps more than those of any other artist.

Jean Cocteau (1889–1963) was another frequent visitor, both to the grand villas of St-Jean-Cap-Ferrat and to the seedy sailors' bars of Villefranche-sur-Mer. In Villefranche, the candy-coloured Chapelle St-Pierre has an interior designed by Cocteau, and Menton has the Musée Jean Cocteau *(see page 248)*, which houses the artist's self-portraits, abstracts, the *Inamorati (Lovers)* painting series, mosaic floors and pottery. The Salle des Mariages in Menton's town hall, which he decorated with murals, is a seriously recherché wedding location.

Nouveaux Réalistes and beyond

In the 1950s Nice produced its own school of artists, the Nouveaux Réalistes. They are well represented at the Musée d'Art Moderne et d'Art Contemporain in Nice, and include Yves Klein (1928–62), Arman (1928–2005), Martial Raysse (*b.*1936), all from Nice, and César (1921–98), born in Marseille. These artists' fascination with everyday material surfaces, packaging and industrial waste is evident in Arman's transparent containers packed with rubbish and flock of birds created from pliers. There are many works by Klein, who took the inspiration of the Riviera to its limit with his startling blue paint IKB (International Klein Blue). The Fluxus artist Ben (*b.*1935), whose 1985 piece *Il y a Trop d'Art (There is Too Much Art)* is reproduced all over Nice, may have a point. ❏

LEFT: Jean Cocteau seated by one of his paintings.

Architecture

From Roman arenas to modern art galleries via Renaissance elements in hill towns – Provence contains a veritable multitude of architectural styles

It was the Romans who set Provence's building style. Nowhere outside Italy is there such a collection of Roman remains – arenas, theatres, temples, cemeteries and triumphal arches. The great gladiatorial arenas at Nîmes and Arles, the theatre at Orange and the Pont du Gard demonstrate how the Romans displayed their power through their buildings. They also invented the arch, and nowhere can its function be better appreciated than in the three tiers supporting the vast Pont du Gard aqueduct.

From the Romans' rounded arches and barrel vaults came Romanesque, the style of medieval church architecture that combines spaciousness with bulk. Great ecclesiastic buildings were constructed in this style, some in secluded surroundings like the Abbaye du Thoronet. Others were highly ornamented; the figures on the façade of St-Trophime in Arles and the abbey church of St-Gilles-du-Gard are exquisite examples. Gothic style arrived late in Provence but can be seen at the Eglise St-Jean-de-Malte in Aix or the cathedral in Grasse.

A Renaissance flair embellishes the streets of many *villages perchés*, fortified hill towns, where from the late 16th century onwards, mansions were built side by side. An additional flourish was the ironwork belltower, a speciality of Provence. Castles, too, such as the Château de Lourmarin, Château Grimaldi at Cagnes-sur-Mer and the Palais des Papes at Avignon, were built in, or adapted to, the Renaissance style.

Grand classical town houses in the 17th and 18th centuries were built where life prospered, notably in the Cours Mirabeau in Aix, while wealthy parlementarians erected country bastides. In the 19th century, Marseille and Toulon gained Parisian-style apartment blocks. The Belle Epoque resulted in a lavish casino and splendid hotels in Monaco and the Côte d'Azur, injected with a touch of fantasty in the mock castles, neoclassical mansions and Mauresque villas built by wealthy European aristocrats.

The early 20th century saw avant-garde villas such as Mallet-Stevens' Villa Noailles in Hyères and Eileen Gray's villas at Cap Martin and Menton, while Le Cor-

busier's Unité d'Habitation in Marseille saw the beginnings of modern architecture for the masses.

Adventurous design is rare in a region where strict planning laws are in force, but Norman Foster has snuck in with a glass art gallery in Nîmes, and the world's largest museum of prehistory in the Gorges du Verdon. Provence has its own star architect in Bandol-based Rudy Ricciotti who, after rehabilitating the Abbaye de Montmajour, is behind the radical Pavillon Noir dance venue in Aix, the future museum in Marseille and the new Cocteau museum in Menton. ❏

RIGHT: grand-scale buildings: the Pont du Gard aqueduct and Le Corbusier's Unité d'Habitation.

PROVENÇAL WINE AND CUISINE

The secret to Provençal cooking, one of the simplest, yet most flavoursome of French cuisines, is its total reliance on fresh, natural ingredients and the fragrant herbs that are so abundant in this fertile region

If there's one thing that truly distinguishes Provençal cuisine it's the sheer wealth and variety of local produce. To get an idea of what's best at the moment, head to one of the food markets that take place in almost every town and village, where you'll find countless varieties of tomatoes, different colours and shapes of courgettes, bundles of purple artichokes, cherries, Cavaillon melons and figs in summer, wild mushrooms, pumpkins and even truffles in winter, as well as appealing displays of cheeses, sausages, olive oil and much more.

The magic ingredients

The real essence of Provençal cuisine is based on simplicity and quality, the respect for seasonal produce and recipes that maximise individual flavours, plus an emphasis on vegetables and fish that are perfectly adapted to today's demands for healthy eating.

The region's fruits are made into all sorts of sweet treats, from the candied fruits of Apt and calissons of Aix to the marrons glacés of Collobrières and stripy berlingots of Carpentras.

Cooking here is characterised by the use of olive oil – with none of the rich butter and cream sauces of northern France – and herbs. This may

be a *herbes de Provence* mix (various combinations of rosemary, thyme, marjoram, sage, savory and bay leaves) but is often just a single herb chosen to go with a specific ingredient: *daurade* (sea bream) or *loup de mer* (sea bass) baked with fennel, rabbit or lamb roasted with rosemary, a meaty *daube* infused with thyme and bay leaves, chicken roast with whole heads of garlic, even crème brûlée flavoured with lavender.

Although many restaurants, especially tourist-oriented ones, continue to perpetuate age-old recipes, a new generation of young chefs is busy revitalising southern cuisine, intelligently dusting off old recipes, experimenting with new techniques and foreign influences.

LEFT: olives are one of the cornerstones of Provençal cuisine. **RIGHT:** Porcini mushrooms (cèpes in Provence).

A cornucopia of vegetables

Tomatoes, aubergines, courgettes, onions and peppers all get into the classic Provençal ratatouille. Elsewhere one vegetable is privileged: *tomates à la provençale* are simply tomatoes halved horizontally, topped with a sprinkling of chopped garlic and breadcrumbs, and baked in a slow oven until succulent and almost caramel sweet. Red peppers are grilled and served cold marinated in olive oil. Small purple artichokes are braised *à la barigoule*, or sliced thinly and served raw dressed with olive oil and lemon. Courgettes and aubergines are baked as *tians*, gratins named after the rectangular earthenware dish in which they are cooked. A speciality

of Nice are the *petits farcis* – assorted vegetables each with their own stuffing (variants on rice, leftover meat and onion bound with egg or bread), served lukewarm as a starter, legacy of a long frugal tradition of using up leftovers.

A hearty rustic speciality found around Grasse and St-Paul-de-Vence is *lou fassum*, cabbage stuffed with a mixture of sausage meat, rice, swiss chard and onion and boiled in a *fassumier*, a sort of cotton net, to hold it together. More refined are courgette flowers, either stuffed or dipped in egg and deep fried.

A variety of *crudités* (chopped raw vegetables) might be served with an *anchoïade* (or *bagna caouda*), to be dipped in a warm

---

The Phocaeans are believed to have introduced the olive tree to Provence around 600 BC, and harvesting and milling methods have changed little since then. Whole olives are milled and repeatedly pressed, producing about a litre (1¾ pints) of oil per 5kg (11 lb) of fruit. Only the results of initial pressings may be called virgin oils (look for "huile d'olive extra vièrge, première pression à froid" on the label). The cooking qualities and health benefits of this precious golden liquid have made it one of Provence's most prized exports. Varying from pale gold to deep green in colour, some olive oils are produced from just one variety of olive, others are blends of several varieties.

The main Provençal production areas with their own *appellation contrôlée* are in the Alpilles around Les Baux-de-Provence, in the Alpes-Maritimes around Grasse, Opio and Sospel, near Aix-en-Provence and around Nîmes. With the harvest beginning at the end of September, pressing generally takes place between November and February, but many of the area's mills and co-operatives have shops open all year round. Table olives are rinsed and soaked in lye (a brine solution), then stored for up to a year prior to consumption, to be served with aperitifs, pounded into purées and *tapenades*, cooked in stews or baked in bread.

anchovy, garlic and olive oil sauce, while all sorts of vegetables accompany the *grand aioli*, the classic Friday feast of salt cod, whelks and lashings of garlic mayonnaise.

Today's chefs make the most of this vegetable bounty. For example, for a tomato tartare, Reine Sammut of La Fenière in the Luberon uses no fewer than six different varieties of tomato grown in her own vegetable garden.

Fish and shellfish

Ugly *rascasse* (scorpion fish), tiny *girelle* (wrasse), *rouget de roche* (red mullet) and silvery *congre* (conger eel) are just some of the *poissons de roche* (literally "rock fish") that hide in the themselves on the quays to get the pick of the night's catch.

Other species include prized *loup de mer*, *daurade* and its cousins *pagre*, *pageot* and *sarde*, and shoals of sardines and anchovies. Shellfish include *langouste* (spiny lobster), little crabs, sea urchins collected by divers off the Côte Bleue west of Marseille and mussels cultivated in the bay of Toulon. Today the region's top restaurants often reserve the best of the artisanal catch, but overfishing of the Mediterranean means that much of the fish served in restaurants may well come from Brittany or the Channel ports.

At its best, fish may be simply chargrilled at a beach-side restaurant – the waiter will

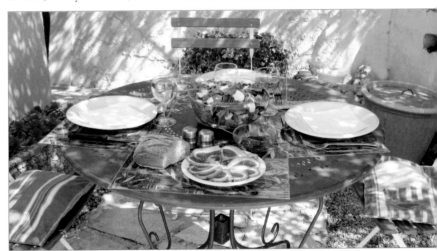

shadows of the indented Mediterranean coastline, caught at night from the little wooden boats called *pointus*. In Marseille, locals jostle for position and are prepared to pay high prices for the still flapping fresh fish at the daily fish market on the Vieux Port. In towns such as Beaulieu-sur-Mer, where the fishing fleet caters to at least a dozen restaurants, the competition is fierce; restaurant chefs position

---

FAR LEFT: the market area of cours Saleya in Nice. Fruit, vegetables and flowers are for sale here every day except Monday. **ABOVE LEFT:** locally caught fish at Forville market in Cannes. **ABOVE:** freshly baked bread and local wine are perfect ingredients for a rustic-style lunch.

BOUILLABAISSE

Bouillabaisse is *the* dish of Marseille, and you'll find it all along the Riviera coast. Several types of fish (in particular gurnard, scorpion fish, john dory and conger eel) are simmered with onion, leek, tomatoes and saffron, with mussels and potatoes added just before the end. It is traditionally served in two courses, first the broth accompanied by *rouille*, toasted baguette and grated cheese, then the pieces of fish and potatoes.

Originally a humble dish made by fishermen from the leftovers of the catch they couldn't sell, bouillabaisse is now a luxurious – and expensive – dish; be prepared to fork out at least €45 for a good one *(see page 100)*.

Young Chefs and Baby Bistros

Provence has witnessed a surge in the popularity of low-key, more informal restaurants run by up-and-coming chefs

A generation of cosmopolitan young chefs has been revitalising Provençal cooking, revisiting regional recipes, rediscovering seasonal produce and rare varieties of vegetable or injecting interna-

tional influences and the foams and suspensions of molecular cuisine. While the south still has its share of very grand restaurants, many of these chefs have also been changing the style of restaurant-going, eschewing the formality of squadrons of suited waiters and silver cutlery for a more informal (and usually more affordable) atmosphere where the emphasis is very much on the food. Chefs might follow the Parisian trend for opening informal bistro annexes – such as Bruno Cirino who, alongside his elegant Hostellerie Jérôme at La Turbie, also has a roaring success with the Café de la Fontaine, a

village café which is now also a superb bistro – or strike out on their own, like Mathias Dandine. He left the luxurious Les Roches in Le Lavandou to return to Bormes-les-Mimosas where he opened a casual but still gastronomic bistro-épicerie on the main street in 2010.

One of the most astonishing recent arrivals has been Argentine-born Mauro Colagreco at Mirazur in Menton. He focuses on fruit and vegetables from his own kitchen garden, combining them with his impeccable technique and original cocktails that might include such ingredients as spinach. In Nice, Keisuke Matsushima (who trained with Ferran Adria in Spain) brings influences from his native Japan to create picture-perfect Franco-Asian dishes, with a stylish, minimalist restaurant setting to match.

Lionel Levy opened his Marseille restaurant, Une Table au Sud, in 1999, after working as Alain Ducasse's number two at Parisian world food pioneer Spoon, Food & Wine. His cooking is light, creative and fun. While inspired by his adopted home Marseille, elements of his native southwest creep in, such as *espelette* pepper, foie gras or *piperade*. Sometimes surprising associations might include a foie gras crème brûlée, grey mullet and ginger crumble, or a dessert of strawberry and black olive tart. The technique is impeccable, but the style of the restaurant has also adapted to today's lifestyles, with its contemporary setting and an atmosphere that is convivial and relaxed. He is also behind the informal, inexpensive bistro La Virgule, further along the port, in the hands of his young protégé Christophe Pareda.

Jean-Luc Rabanel has an expanding empire in Arles, where alongside his Michelin-starred Atelier de Jean-Luc Rabanel, a restaurant he describes as "a gallery of culinary expression", he has also opened the less expensive Bistro A Côté, which reinterprets traditional dishes, a table d'hôtes and a cookery school. ❑

LEFT: Mauro Colagreco on the terrace of his restaurant Mirazur in Menton.

often present a basket of fresh fish for you to select the one you like the look of, which will then be paid for by weight. Other preparations include sea bream stuffed with fennel, red mullet cooked with basil or fish baked *à la provençale* (with white wine and tomatoes), and the famous bouillabaisse of Marseille *(see box on page 45)*. Inland, freshwater trout is the speciality at Fontaine-de-Vaucluse and in the fast-racing mountain torrents of the Mercantour.

Meat and game

Provence's quintessential meat dish is the *daube de boeuf*, chunks of beef marinated overnight in red wine and cooked slowly with bay

olives as *gardiane de boeuf*. The Camargue bull meat is France's only meat to carry an AOC, meaning it has to come from a geographically designated area. The best lamb comes from Sisteron in the Alpes de Haute-Provence, where *transhumance*, the twice-yearly moving of the flocks between summer and winter grazing, is still an important ritual. The animals' tough mountain lifestyle gives lean meat with an incomparable herby flavour. Another widely used meat is rabbit, simply baked with herbs or stewed with white wine, tomatoes and herbs. In winter, the Mercantour and Maures yield plentiful game, such as sanglier (wild boar).

leaves, thyme and a twist of orange peel until it is a deep, almost black colour; in Avignon, it is more usually made with lamb, and in Nice, the leftovers go to stuff ravioli. The rustic dish of *alouettes sans têtes* are not the headless skylarks the name might suggest but beef or veal olives – slices of meat stuffed and rolled up. In the Camargue and nearby Nîmes and Arles you'll find *viande de taureau*, the meat of the area's little black bulls. It can be grilled as steaks or on skewers or stewed with wine and

ABOVE: the *transhumance*, when thousands of sheep are herded through St-Rémy to summer pastures. The Fête de la Transhumance occurs in late May.

Départemental differences

Within the region, different *départements* or even different villages proudly cling on to their own specialities. The cuisine of Nice reflects its Italian past. Here you'll find gnocchi, pasta and ravioli – which the Niçois like to claim originated here – typically filled with rich, meaty *daube de boeuf*, minestrone-like *soupe au pistou* and the street snacks of *socca* and *pissaladière*. Another Niçois speciality is *estocaficada* (stockfish), made from dried cod, soaked in water for several days, then cooked with onions, leeks and tomatoes (and similar *stocafi* in Monaco). In Nîmes, *brandade* is a speciality: salt cod is soaked and then beaten up into a purée with lashings of olive oil and a little milk and served piping hot, often with croûtes. *Pieds et paquets* is a dish typical of Marseille: stuffed sheep's tripe stewed with sheep's feet.

Cheese, fruit and desserts

Provence is not a major dairy region, but you can find local cheeses mainly made from goat's or sheep's milk. Banon, produced in the mountains around Forcalquier, is easily recognisable: the creamy goat's cheese is wrapped in a chestnut leaf, which gives it a distinctive tangy flavour. Other goat's cheeses vary from moist fresh cheeses to mature, hard *crottins*; they may

be rolled in herbs or marinated in olive oil.

Brousse is a soft, ricotta-like fresh cheese made from goat's or sheep's milk depending on the season, the best coming from Rove near Marseille, which is stirred into soups or sweetened with honey and nuts for dessert.

Desserts – served after the cheese course in France – make the most of the region's wonderful fruit. St-Tropez's *Tarte Tropézienne* is brioche filled with vanilla cream and strawberries or raspberries. Menton's lemons go into lemon tart, with or without a meringue topping. In late summer fresh figs come into their own, to accompany cheese or ham, or are stewed or baked in gratins.

As for crêpes Suzette – crêpes flambéed in orange liqueur and named in honour of 19th-century actress Suzanne Reichenberg, a mistress of the Prince of Wales – they supposedly arose from a culinary mishap at the Café de Paris in Monte-Carlo: a face-saving exercise when famous chef Auguste Escoffier (or one of his kitchen boys) accidentally set a crêpe on fire.

Destination restaurants

In small villages the best place to eat may well serve as shop, newsagent and tobacconist as well as restaurant, but still be packed with diners hungry for genuine home cooking and local gossip. In recent years, there has been a trend for top chefs to open less expensive annexes. Globe-trotting chef-entrepreneur Alain Ducasse is at the head of an empire that includes the renowned Louis XV at the Hôtel de Paris in Monte-Carlo, as well as simpler (yet sophisticated) country inns, the Bastide de Moustiers, Abbaye de la Celle and Spoon Byblos in St-Tropez. Others who have opened less formal offshoots include Bruno Cirino of the Hostellerie de Jérôme in La Turbie, who transformed traditional fare at a village café.

> Great wines aren't restricted to haute-cuisine restaurants. Try Chez Serge at Carpentras for the very best from the Mont Ventoux and southern Rhône appellations.

For the best restaurants you may have to book weeks ahead; even for simpler places it's worth ringing in advance, especially in high season. It's often easier to get a table at lunch than dinner, and lunch can also be a good time to sample a top chef's style for a fraction of the dinner price, as many offer excellent-value lunch menus.

Lunch is generally served from noon to 2pm. After 2pm, you may find it difficult to get served, except in cafés and brasseries. Dinner is served from around 8pm to 9.30pm, and often later in big cities and trendy resorts. ❑

LEFT: browsing the cours Saleya market in Nice.

Regional Wines and Spirits

The sheer variety and quality of wine in Provence, also home to the famous red blend Châteauneuf-du-Pape, means you'll be spoilt for choice

Vines were introduced to Provence by the Phocaeans when they established trading posts up the Rhône valley some 2,600 years ago. The high-living Avignon papacy gave winemaking a further boost when it established its vineyards around its summer residences at Châteauneuf-du-Pape and in the Luberon. Today, most of the wines in the Vaucluse and Bouches-du-Rhône fall within the numerous appellations of the southern Côtes du Rhône. These include the illustrious, full-bodied reds of Châteauneuf-du-Pape, grown on flat pebble-covered terrains and made from a complex variety of grape cépages, dominated by Syrah, Mourvèdre and Cinsault. Other wines grown around Orange include Gigondas, Vacqueyras, Rasteau, Lirac and Côtes du Ventoux, while further south you'll find the Côtes du Luberon, Coteaux de Pierrevert and Costières de Nîmes. Look out also for the rarer but highly regarded white Châteauneuf-du-Pape, the rosés of Tavel and the sweet white dessert wines of Beaumes-de-Venise, made with the tiny Muscat grape.

The wines of Les Baux-de-Provence have a growing reputation. Cultivated by a dozen or so vignerons in tiny vineyards scattered around the white limestone Alpilles hills beneath Les Baux, most are produced according to organic or even biodynamic principles, a holistic philosophy that involves the whole ecological system and the phases of the moon and planets. The red wines have the appellation AOC Les Baux-de-Provence, but white wines come under the neighbouring

RIGHT: bottles of golden Beaumes-de-Venise, a fine dessert wine.

Coteaux d'Aix-en-Provence label. The white wines of Cassis, east of Marseille, are perfect for drinking with fish.

In the Var, by far the largest Riviera appellation is the Côtes de Provence, principally producing vast amounts of easily quaffable dry rosés, but also small quantities of white and some good-quality reds. The main vineyards are concentrated around La Londe-des-Maures, around Ramatuelle on the St-Tropez peninsula, where they grow virtually up to the sea, and inland around Les Arcs-sur-Argens and Draguignan. Further west, you'll find the Coteaux Varois around Brignoles and

the St-Baume massif. Bandol, produced in eight communes around the seaside resort of Bandol, is the département's most prestigious appellation, notably for its excellent though pricey reds, made using the Mourvèdre grape. The only wine appellation in the Alpes-Maritimes *département* is the ancient but tiny Bellet appellation outside Nice, with just 60 hectares of vineyards under cultivation, producing white, red and rosé wines.

Another famous Provençal tipple is pastis, a strong aniseed-flavoured spirit created in Marseille in the 1930s. It's served with ice and a carafe of water for mixing. ❑

Provence

PLACES

In this detailed guide to the region, the principal sites are cross-referenced by numbers to the maps. A supplementary touring map inside the back cover describes eight scenic routes through the region

This guide covers the south of France from the delta of the River Rhône to the Italian border. Most of this falls within the modern administrative region of Provence-Alpes-Côte d'Azur (commonly abbreviated to PACA), and it includes the *départements* of Alpes-de-Haute-Provence, Alpes-Maritimes, Bouches-du-Rhône, the Var and the Vaucluse. It also sneaks across the Rhône into the Gard *département* in order to take in Nîmes, for without this glorious Roman city and its extraordinary aqueduct, the story of Provence would be incomplete.

The vigour with which Provence clings to its traditions means that each region is distinct. In the Camargue you will find bullfights to remind you of Spain; in Nice you will eat ravioli to make you think of Italy (although the Niçois claim they invented it here); in Avignon you will feel yourself on the world stage in the papal palace; in Les Baux you will hear lute strings in the wind and imagine troubadours of medieval times, and in Marseille you'll discover a dynamic multicultural city where urbanism meets sparkling sea views.

Getting around is no problem. Motorways swoop through the region, as does the high-speed TGV, but there are also local buses and trains. You don't need a car if you make a city the base of your visit, but a vehicle is essential

for exploring the interior of wild mountains and hill villages. At every twist and turn the landscape changes, villages come and go, vistas open and close; the extraordinary light moves through ilex, oak, the silver olive and dark cypress, and the heady scrub of lavender and rock roses, thyme and rosemary intermingle with the rich ochres and glinting granites of this harmonious land. The landscape is clearly labelled: Van Gogh's sunflowers, Cézanne's Montagne Ste-Victoire, Picasso's Antibes, Matisse's Nice. The familiarity adds comfort to a sense of well-being. Stop for roadside water melons, peaches, or honey, to have a drink or to watch an unfolding game of *pétanque*. The routes on the enclosed touring map take in the best of the region. ❑

PRECEDING PAGES: Cannes' beach; Tourrettes-sur-Loup. **LEFT:** backstreets of Les Baux-de-Provence. **ABOVE LEFT:** sunflowers in Les Alpilles. **ABOVE RIGHT:** town square of Aigues-Mortes.

AVIGNON

Glowering within a ring of serrated city walls, Avignon preserves something of the air of the independent city state it was from its time as capital of Christendom in the Middle Ages to after the French Revolution. However, a thriving student population and the theatre festivals in July keep things lively

Strategically situated at the confluence of the Rhône, Sorgue and Durance rivers, Avignon was established by the early Gauls as a tribal capital, and it was known to the Greek traders of Marseille. During the Roman period, however, it became overshadowed by Orange and Arles. Avignon's moment of glory came when French-born Pope Clement V fled to France in 1309 to escape the papal power struggles in Rome, eventually settling in Avignon. It was the start of 70 years of the "second Babylonian captivity of the Church", which saw the city ruling Christendom under nine successive popes *(see box page 62)*. Even after the popes returned to Rome, Avignon continued to be governed by papal legates and, although it had lost its glory, remained an important trading centre with strong links to Italy, seen in some of the fine mansions built by Italian families.

Punctuated by 39 towers and seven gates, Avignon's 4.3km (2½-mile) ramparts still enclose its inner core: a cornucopia of historic mansions, shady cloisters, churches and palaces. French writer Rabelais called Avi-gnon *"la ville sonnante"* because of the number of steeples that adorned its skyline. Less poetic are the views of the modern suburbs which fan outwards. This is where the majority of the city's 90,000 inhabitants live, although pretty much everything you want to see lies within the city walls.

Orientation

It's best to explore the town centre on foot, leaving your car outside the ramparts or in one of the underground car parks by the Palais des Papes, Place

LEFT: Le Pont St-Bénézet – the Pont d'Avignon of nursery-rhyme fame.
RIGHT: the Palais des Papes, seen from across the Rhône.

TIP

"Palais Secret" (Sept–May) is a guided visit through hidden corridors and private papal apartments that are normally off limits to the public. The tour finishes with brunch and a glass of wine on the grand terrace. Or you can join one of the "nocturnal promenades" (June, August, early September) which visit the Pont St Bénézet and hidden corners of the Palais des Papes by night, culminating in a medieval banquet. For reservations, tel: 04 9027 5000.

Pie or cours Jean-Jaurès. If you arrive by train, the main station is at the Porte de la République, south of the centre; the new TGV station outside the city has shuttle buses that depose you inside the walls.

From the station, the plane tree-lined cours Jean Jaurès, home to the tourist office at No. 41, and its continuation, the rue de la République shopping street roughly divides the town through the middle, leading into the **place de l'Horloge**. A lively brasserie-filled square sitting on the site of the original Roman forum, this is still the epicentre of town life. On it stand the **Hôtel de Ville**, with the 14th-century clock tower that gives the square its name, and the ornate **Théâtre Municipal**. Behind the square looms the **Palais des Papes**.

The Palais des Papes

As the local saying goes, all roads lead to the **Palais des Papes Ⓐ** (Papal Palace; www.palais-des-papes.com; tel: 04

9027 5000; daily summer 9am–7pm, winter 9.30am–5.45pm, with exceptions; charge), the monumental symbol of papal Provence. The original city walls, built by popes Innocent VI and Urban V, were not strong enough to ward off attack by the bands of wandering knights that plagued the countryside, so the palace was designed to double as a fortress.

Step through the **Porte des Champeaux** and into the **Cour d'Honneur** and you get an instant sense of the palace as a city within a city. It's a veritable labyrinth of vaulted halls, echoing assembly rooms, small chapels and narrow staircases, illustrating the palace's multiple functions as residence, place of worship, fortress and administrative centre.

The palace is divided into two sections: the "old" palace (**Palais Vieux**), built by Pope Benedict XII between 1334 and 1342, and the "new" palace (**Palais Neuf**), begun under Benedict's successor, Pope

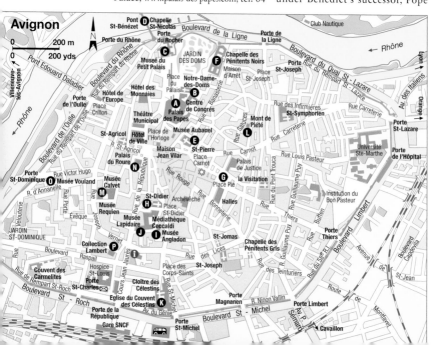

Clement VI, and completed in 1348. The old palace has a monastic simplicity and austerity that reflects the minimalist tastes of Benedict XII. The new palace, on the other hand, is brightly decorated with elaborate frescos and flamboyant ceilings, the hallmarks of Clement VI, patron of the arts and lover of the high life.

The first rooms, beginning with the **Grande Trésorie**, present the history of the building and some of the papal bulls and other artefacts discovered here. Frescos by the Sienese artist Simone Martini, originally from Notre-Dame-des-Doms, now hang in the **Salle du Consistoire**, where the pope held assemblies with his cardinals or received kings and ambassadors. The sheer size of the vaulted **Grande Audience** and **Grande Chapelle** is awe-inspiring. The frescos in the **Chambre du Pape** and **Chambre du Cerf** were painted by Matteo Giovanetti in 1343 and reveal the sumptuous tastes of Clement VI. These lively scenes of hunting, fishing, falconry and youths picking fruit give valuable insight into life at the papal court during the 14th century.

Around the place du Palais

In contrast to the grand Palais des Papes, Avignon's cathedral, **Notre-Dame-des-Doms** Ⓑ (daily 8am–6pm), is a more sombre affair. This 12th-century building has undergone many structural changes over the years, but despite the 19th-century addition of a gilded Madonna to the tower, it retains its original spiritual simplicity. Rising behind the cathedral overlooking the Rhône, the **Jardin des Doms** crowns the rocky promontory that saw Avignon's Neolithic beginnings. A vineyard was planted here at the end of the 1990s, symbolising Avignon's status as capital of Côtes du Rhône wines.

Across the place du Palais, the façade of the **Hôtel des Monnaies** (the old mint) is lavishly sculpted with swags of fruit and birds that look more like turkeys than eagles; long home to the municipal music school it is being turned into a luxury hotel. At the north end of the square, the former bishops' palace contains the **Musée du Petit Palais** Ⓒ (tel: 04 9086 4458; Wed–Mon 10am–1pm, 2–6pm; charge). The Gothic

Avignon's main square, the place de l'Horloge, is a hub of social activity. It is named after the 14th-century Gothic Tour de l'Horloge, the last remnant of the original town hall.

BELOW: the Palais des Papes.

palace, built around 1318 for Cardinal Bérenger Frédol the Elder, later became the bishops' palace and was given an elegant Renaissance façade. Today it houses a well-presented collection of medieval and Renaissance Italian and Provençal painting and sculpture, including a *Madonna and Child* by Botticelli.

Next to the Petit Palais you can take a footpath down to the **Pont St-Bénézet ⓓ** the celebrated Pont d'Avignon *(see box page 66)*.

Behind the Palais des Papes, a fine cardinal's palace, now the Hôtel de la Mirande, and the **Eglise St-Pierre ⓔ** (Thur 2–5pm, Fri–Sat 2–6.30pm) with its pyramidal spire, Gothic facade and carved walnut doors, are further testimonies to the wealth and power of the church. The richly decorated interior of the **Chapelle des Pénitents Noirs ⓕ** (Sat 2–5pm, plus Fri in summer) on rue de la Banasterie is rarely open, but worth a detour to see the façade, which has an exquisite sculpted relief of cherubs bearing the head of John the Baptist on a dish – the emblem of this charitable brotherhood which tended prisoners sentenced to death and the mentally ill.

Southeast of place de l'Horloge towards place Pie and place St-Didier, is a semi-pedestrianised area of ancient narrow streets, many of which contain crumbling former noble residences. **Place Pie ⓖ** is home to the city's covered market (every morning except Monday), topped by an unsightly multi-storey car park – partially disguised by a "vegetal wall" by botanist Patrick Blanc. Further east towards the Porte St-Lazare lies the **university quarter**.

On shady **place St-Didier**, the Gothic **Eglise St-Didier ⓗ** (daily 8am–6.30pm), consecrated in 1359, contains an imposing pulpit in the centre of the church and an early Renaissance work by Francesco Laurana in the first chapel. Near by discover the **Médiathèque Ceccaldi** (Mon–Fri 12.30–6pm, Sat 10am–6pm) on rue Laboureur, a 14th-century cardinal's palace, now the municipal library, which still has original frescos and painted wooden ceilings. Across the street, the **Musée Angladon ⓘ** (5 rue Laboureur; www.angladon.com; tel: 04

The Papal Legacy

In 1348 pope Clement VI bought Avignon from Jeanne, countess of Provence. The popes built not only the massive Palais des Papes; they also built cardinals' palaces, enlarged churches and gave the city an extensive new set of city walls. A lavish court grew up and cultural life flourished around the poet Petrarch and painters such as Matteo Giovanetti and Simone Martini. From 1378, during the Great Schism there were two popes – one in Rome, and one the "anti pope" in Avignon – the last, Benedict XIII (or Benoît XIII), was besieged in the Palais des Papes for five years before escaping one night in 1403.

Even after the popes returned to Rome, Avignon retained its independent status ruled by a papal legate – along with the nearby Comtat-Venaissin. The paper, publishing and textile industries flourished, the city's prosperity evident in fine residences put up in the 17th and 18th centuries. Avignon was reunited with France only in 1791 after the French Revolution. It remained an intellectual centre, where the Félibrige, the movement founded by Mistral and likeminded poets to preserve the Provençal language, printed its newspaper, *Aioli*.

9082 2903; summer Tue–Sun 1–6pm, winter Wed–Sun 1–6pm; charge) has a fine collection of 17th-century Dutch oils and furniture, and Post-Impressionist and modern French art. The only painting by Van Gogh in Provence, *Les Wagons du Chemin de Fer*, hangs alongside works by Modigliani, Cézanne, Picasso and Degas. From here rue Frédéric Mistral leads back to rue de la République, where a former Jesuit chapel with sculpted Baroque facade contains the **Musée Lapidaire** ❼ (27 rue de la République; www.fondation-calvet.org; Wed–Mon 10am–1pm, 2–6pm; charge), the town's archaeological collection. The Egyptian, Greek, Roman and Gallic antiquities include carved sarcophagi, Roman glass, painted Greek vases and the 1st-century Tarasque de Noves, a statue of the mysterious amphibian beast that once terrorised the region.

On place des Corps-Saints stands the unfinished **Eglise du Couvent des Célestins** ❻ – the apse and transept were completed but the nave was hurriedly truncated and shored up at the end. In summer the square is filled with café terraces. East of here,

picturesque **rue des Teinturiers** was once the dyers' street supplying local weavers, and is lined with mill wheels along a branch of the River Sorgues that flows down one side. At No. 8, the **Chapelle des Pénitents Gris** (daily 3.30–5.30pm), which still belongs to a penitent order, has paintings by Parrocel and Nicolas Mignard.

Another oddity is the **Mont de Piété** ❿ (6 rue Saluces; tel: 04 9086 5312; Mon–Fri 8.30–11.30am, 1.30–5pm; free), a charitable institution which functioned as the local pawnshop, offering credit to the city's poor. Its history is recounted in this small museum alongside an exhibition on the silk-conditioning industry.

Around rue Joseph Vernet

West of rue de la République, the circular sweep of **rue Joseph Vernet** contains Avignon's smartest shops, along with the Musée Calvet and other elegant mansions housing trendy restaurants. At the northern end of the street, towards the Rhône, is a quiet district with antiques shops and the venerable **Hôtel de l'Europe** on place de Crillon. The **Musée**

From afar, the admirable city... has something of the form of Athens. Its walls, whose stone is golden like the august ruins of the Peloponnese, have a touch of Greek beauty. Like Athens, Avignon has its acropolis. The château of the popes is its Parthenon.

VICTOR HUGO, 1839

BELOW: rue des Teinturiers.

Avignon Festival and the fringe festival "Off"

Avignon Festival – too hybrid and highbrow or a melting pot of performances with something to appeal to everyone?

For three weeks each July, Avignon becomes the capital of French theatre – as it has ever since 1947, when Jean Vilar of the Théâtre National Populaire first put on a production in the grandiose outdoor setting of the Cour d'Honneur in the Palais des Papes. Originally just three shows and an art exhibition, it marked the birth of the Avignon Festival. In the spirit of post-war idealism, Jean Vilar's ambition was to bring first-rate adventurous theatre to the people of the provinces.

The Festival is still renowned for its adventurous theatre productions, often by leading international directors and with big-name actors, as well as some first-rate contemporary dance. Jeanne Moreau, Michel Piccoli, Isabelle Huppert, Kristen Scott Thomas and Denis Podalydès have all performed here, not just in the Cour d'Honneur but also in the Chapelle des Pénitents-Blancs or the Lycée St-Joseph.

How much it is still a festival for the people is a contentious issue. Debate rages as to the artistic quality and intended audience. Often accused of elitism, the festival seems caught in a conflict between accessibility and the highbrow avant-garde. Many recent productions have been criticised as being too "hybrid" – interdisciplinary mixes removed from the classic theatre of its origins. In 2003 the festival was cancelled at the eleventh hour when the *intermittents du spectacle* (the union of performing artists and backstage staff) went on strike. Since 2004, the festival has been in the hands of young directors Hortense Archambault and Vincent Baudriller, joined each year by a guest "associated artist" – French playwright Olivier Cadiot and Swiss director Christophe Marthaler in 2010; French dancer-choreographer Boris Charmatz in 2011 – intended to attract new blood.

However, what really makes the streets of Avignon buzz is the more spontaneous "Off" – the offshoot and self-financed fringe festival created in 1963 by André Benedetto, which has long since outgrown its parent: in 2010 some 900 companies presented 1,100 shows in over 120 venues. During the Off, posters are plastered on every available lamp-post and railing; the streets are full of actors, comedians and street acts handing out flyers to advertise their shows. The sheer choice of acts, mostly French but also from foreign companies, is incredible, performed in every available small theatre, old church or café. You can easily watch five or six different shows a day, ranging from stand-up comedy to musicals to Molière, children's shows to risqué reviews or political satire. Some of the most popular acts return annually, for others Avignon is a springboard for transfers to theatres in Paris or Lyon.

For Avignon Festival details: www.festival-avignon.com; tel: 04 9014 1460. For Festival Le Off: www.avignonleoff.com; tel: 04 9085 1308. ❏

LEFT: street theatre performer at Avignon Festival, with some of the numerous flyers as a backdrop.

Calvet (www.fondation-calvet.org; tel: 04 9086 3384; Wed–Mon 10am–1pm, 2–6pm; charge) is Avignon's museum of fine art, housed in a beautiful 18th-century mansion with a stunning forecourt paved in russet-coloured pebbles from the Durance. Jacques-Louis David, Théodore Géricault, Eugène Delacroix, Camille Corot and Edouard Manet are just a few of the painters represented here. There is also a good modern section, showing work by Chaïm Soutine, Alfred Sisley, Albert Gleizes, Maurice Utrillo, Raoul Dufy and Camille Claudel. Next door is the **Musée Requien** (Tue–Sat 10am–1pm, 2–6pm), a natural history museum founded around the local botanical specimens collected by Esprit Requin.

Near by, entered through a Gothic doorway, the **Palais du Roure** (3 rue Collège du Roure; tel: 04 9080 8088; guided visits Tue 3pm or by appointment) contains a library and research centre of Provençal culture. It is rather dry unless you are passionate about the battle to revive the Provençal language but the mansion of the Baroncelli family is unusual and the eclectic display includes Provençal furniture and costumes, the stagecoach which once transported Mistral and Daudet, the printing press on which Mistral and Co. printed their journal *Aioli*, and the American Indian costume donated by Buffalo Bill to would-be Camargue cowboy and Félibrige activist Falco de Baroncelli.

Keeping up the period atmosphere, the **Musée Louis Vouland** (17 rue Victor Hugo; www.vouland.com; tel: 04 9086 0379; Tue–Sun 2–6pm; charge) presents fine 18th-century furniture, faience from Moustiers and Marseille, and paintings by 19th-century regional artists.

Fans of contemporary art will delight in the cutting-edge **Collection Lambert** (Hôtel de Caumont, 5 rue Violette; www.collectionlambert.com; tel: 04 9016 5620; Tue–Sun 11am–6pm, daily 11am–7pm in July; charge). The beautifully renovated 18th-century *hôtel particulier* alternates between a revolving display from the private collection of Paris art dealer Yvan Lambert, which

BELOW: inside the Musée Calvet.

Both the Fort St-André and the Tour Philippe le Bel offer excellent views over the papal city. On a clear evening you can watch the mesmerising colours of twilight as the sun sets on Avignon's golden stone.

BELOW RIGHT: views from the Fort St-André.

includes such artists as Sol LeWitt, Jenny Holzer, On Kawara, Thomas Hirschhorn and Douglas Gordon, and temporary loan exhibitions.

Take a look also at the **Cloître des Célestins** on rue du Portail Boquier. The cloister with the mossy fountain in the centre is home to the Avignon Festival offices and an exhibition space, as well as the Hôtel du Cloître St-Louis, part in former monastic buildings, part in a modern extension by Jean Nouvel.

Villeneuve-lès-Avignon

Facing Avignon across the Rhône, attractive **Villeneuve-lès-Avignon** is much smaller yet nevertheless has a rich history of its own. The French king founded the town to keep a beady eye on what was going on in Provençal and later papal territory across the river. As the papal court increased in importance, the number of adjunct cardinals rose. Finding that Avignon had no more suitable space available, many of these cardinals chose to build their magnificent estates in Villeneuve.

Towering over the town is the 14th-century **Fort St-André** (west tower open daily 10am–1pm, 2–6pm, until 5pm in winter; charge), which guarded the frontier of France when Avignon was allied to the Holy Roman Empire. Inside the crenellated ramparts are the gardens of the **Abbaye St-André**, a restored Romanesque chapel, and the ruins of the 13th-century church (closed Jan and Mon; tel: 04 9025 5595; charge).

The **Chartreuse du Val de Bénédiction** (rue de la République; www.chartreuse.org; daily mid-May–mid-Sept 10am–1pm, 2–6.30pm, until 5pm mid-Sept–mid-May; charge) was founded in the mid-14th century by Pope Innocent VI (whose tomb lies in the chapel) and has a series of beautiful cloisters. A small vaulted chapel features frescos by Matteo Giovanetti. The Chartreuse now functions as a centre for playwrights.

The **Musée Pierre de Luxembourg** (3 rue de la République; tel: 04 9027 4966; closed Feb and Mon; charge) contains some wonderful works of art, including a carved ivory *Virgin and Child* and the *Coronation of the Virgin* (1453) by Enguerrand Quarton. ❑

Sur le Pont d'Avignon

Immortalised in the popular children's song "Sur le pont d'Avignon", the Pont St-Bénézet is one of the region's most famous landmarks. Hearing a voice from heaven, a young shepherd boy, Bénézet, left his mountains in the Ardèche and travelled to Avignon to build a bridge. At first the inhabitants mocked him, but when they saw him lift a massive rock and throw it into the river they were convinced that divine power was at work and helped to build the bridge between 1177 and 1185. The bridge was destroyed in 1226 during the Crusades but reconstructed in 1234. During the Avignon papacy, it provided a vital link between the town and the cardinals who had chosen to live across the river in less polluted Villeneuve. A chapel dedicated to St Nicholas, patron saint of sailors, was added on top of the Chapelle St-Bénézet, which stands halfway along the remaining structure. Unfortunately the Rhône's frequent floods took their toll and the bridge collapsed during the 17th century, leaving only four of its original 22 arches at the Avignon end and the Tour Philippe le Bel on the far bank.

BEST RESTAURANTS, BARS AND CAFÉS

Restaurants

Prices for a three-course meal without wine. Many restaurants have a less expensive lunch menu:
€ = under €25
€€ = €25–40
€€€ = €40–60
€€€€ = over €60

La Cantina
83 rue Joseph Vernet
www.lacantina-avignon.fr
Tel: 04 9085 9904. Open L & D Tue–Sat. €€
A trendy Franco-Italian restaurant housed in the cloister of a former Benedictine monastery. A stylish place for salads, pasta and simple bistro dishes at lunch. Afternoon tea in the courtyard.

Christian Etienne
10 rue de Mons
www.christian-etienne.fr
Tel: 04 9086 1650. Open L & D Tue–Sat (daily in July). €€€€
Avignon's top chef is renowned for his creative cuisine using different varieties of tomato or *épeautre* (wild wheat) and saffron from Mont Ventoux. Set in a splendid medieval residence.

Les Cinq Sens
18 rue Joseph Vernet
www.restaurantles5sens.com
Tel: 04 9085 2651. Open L & D Tue–Sat. €€€
The five senses is Avignon's latest gastro-nomic venue for Thierry Baucher's revisited classic cooking, such as his *cassoulet gastronomique* and a chocolate and black olive dessert; there's also a vegetarian menu.

L'Extramuros
44 boulevard St-Michel
Tel: 04 3274 2222. Open L Mon–Fri, D daily. €
A trendy address in an airily converted building just outside the city walls, serving steaks and other brasserie classics. Good cocktails and live jazz some evenings.

La Fourchette
17 rue Racine
Tel: 04 9085 2093. Open L & D Mon–Fri. Closed 3 weeks Aug. €€
This cheerful bistro is a local favourite for its good-value gastronomic take on *daube avignonnais*, *pieds et pacquets* and other traditional Provençal specialities.

Hiély Lucullus
5 rue de la République (1st floor) www.hiely-lucullus.com
Tel: 04 9086 1707. Open L Wed–Sat, D daily. €€
Opened in the early 1900s, this institution is now in the hands of chef Laurent Azoulay. The menu has kept Monsieur Hiély's *pieds et pacquets* and *marmite de pêcheur* from 1938, while also introducing new ideas.

La Mirande
4 place de la Mirande
www.la-mirande.fr
Tel: 04 9014 2020. Open L & D Thur–Mon. Closed Jan. €€€€
A magnificent tapestry-hung dining room and summer terrace are the setting for grand classical cuisine inspired by seasonal local produce, much of it organic.

Numéro 75
75 rue Guillaume Puy
www.numero75.fr
Tel: 04 9027 1600. Open L & D Mon–Sat (daily during Avignon Festival). €€
A fine *hôtel particulier* – this one used to belong to the pastis-producing Pernod family – is now the place for modern Med-wide cooking.

Bars and Cafés

Place de l'Horloge is awash with cafés: trendy designer **Opéra Café** is ideal for both a simple lunch and night-time DJs, the big brasserie **Le Forum** doubles as a theatre during Festival Off, and **Le Cid** is a popular gay haunt. On place du Palais, the **Café In et Off** has views of the Palais des Papes. Other favourites include **La Comédie** on place Crillon, while an arty intellectual crowd frequents **La Manutention** (4 rue Escaliers Ste-Anne). Studenty bars congregate around rue Carnot – find live music at the **Red Zone**.

RIGHT: La Mirande's grand interior.

ORANGE AND THE MONT VENTOUX

From sunbaked plains to deep river gorges, fields of purple lavender and windswept mountains, the northern Vaucluse offers plenty to discover from imposing Roman remains to the prestigious vineyards of the Côtes du Rhône villages

The northern Vaucluse stretches from the Rhône valley north of Avignon across the staccato peaks of the Dentelles de Montmirail to the bald summit of Mont Ventoux. There's plenty to see and do in this area, from exploring Roman remains and seeking out France's oldest synagogue to wine tasting and hill-walking.

Orange

Founded in around 35 BC by veterans of the Second Roman Legion, **Orange ❶** is famous for its two outstanding Roman monuments – the Arc de Triomphe and the Théâtre Antique (both Unesco-listed heritage sites). The second largest town in the Vaucluse, with a population of 30,000, Orange is busy all year round, and its proximity to the *autoroute* plus high-speed TGV trains direct from Paris make it a popular stopping-off point.

For centuries, Orange remained an independent principality, ruling over a domain about 12km (7½ miles) from north to south and 25km (15½ miles) east to west. By the 14th century, numerous religious foundations had been established, and the town had its own university. The city's name has nothing to do with the fruit but is a derivation of the

town's Roman name *Arausio*. It was subsequently adopted by the Dutch royal family, the House of Nassau, who inherited the city in 1559 (the Queen of Holland still bears the honorary title of Princess of Orange). The population of Orange was largely Protestant, making it a target during the Wars of Religion, when hundreds of Huguenots were massacred.

In the 1670s, when France was at war with Holland, ruled by William of Orange (later William III of England), Louis XIV ordered the destruction

Main attractions

THÉÂTRE ANTIQUE, ORANGE
VINEYARDS, CHÂTEAUNEUF-DU-PAPE
SYNAGOGUE, CARPENTRAS
ROMAN REMAINS, VAISON-LA-ROMAINE
MONT VENTOUX
LAVENDER FIELDS AT SAULT
GORGES DE LA NESQUE

LEFT: lavender fields, Sault.
RIGHT: walking through wine country.

St-Siffrein cathedral, Carpentras.

of the magnificent chateau built by Prince Maurice de Nassau in the 1620s on the hill behind the theatre. Its ruins in the **Colline St-Eutrope** now make pleasant grounds for a stroll. Control of Orange was finally ceded to France in 1713 by the Treaty of Utrecht.

Roman treasures

Orange's greatest Roman monument stands right in the heart of town, the **Théâtre Antique** (www.theatre-antique.com; tel: 04 9051 1760; daily 9am–7pm, winter 9.30am–4.30pm; charge), home to the renowned Chorégies d'Orange opera festival evey summer. Built in the 1st century BC, it is the best-preserved theatre of the ancient world, and the only one in Europe with an intact stage wall, a massive 37-metre-high structure that gives the theatre its distinctive acoustics. It was originally clad in marble of which just a few fragments remain. Time and the weather have taken their toll, but an ingenious high-tech glass-and-steel roof erected in 2006 protects the stage wall without weighing down the structure. Across the orchestra pit, semi-circular tiers of seating that once sat 10,000 are carved into the St-Eutrope hill.

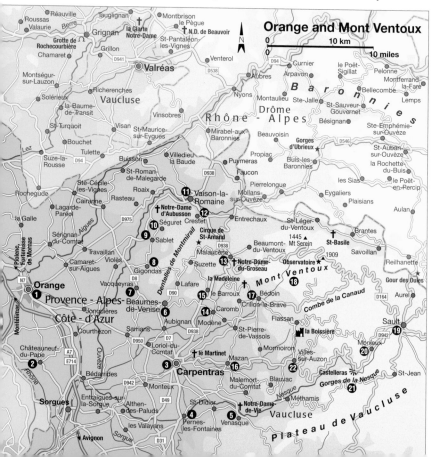

Housed in a fine 17th-century mansion opposite the theatre, the **Musée de l'Art et d'Histoire** (rue Madeleine Foch; tel: 04 9051 1760; daily 9.30am–6.30pm, winter 10am–4pm; charge included with Théâtre Antique) sheds light on Roman goverment policy in Gaul. The collection includes fragments of a marble tablet on which land holdings were recorded in AD 77. This early form of land registry not only reveals what areas were settled but also to whom the better plots belonged, providing insight into early property ownership and social dynamics. The museum also contains a reconstructed atelier demonstrating how the famous printed indiennes fabrics were once manufactured here. The museum's art collection contains portraits of members of the Royal House of Orange and some paintings by British artist Sir Frank Brangwyn.

Behind the museum the streets of the old town give way to pretty squares and fine architecture. **Place Clemenceau** (often called place de la Mairie), home to the Thursday morning market, is graced by the handsome 17th-century Hôtel de Ville with its wrought-iron belfry and arcades and, near by, the restored **Cathédrale Notre-Dame**.

Orange's second Roman treasure, the magnificent **Arc de Triomphe** that once straddled the Via Agrippa between Lyon and Arles, now stands at the centre of a roundabout on the N7 on the northern edge of town. Erected in 21 BC, the decorative friezes and carvings of battle scenes, enslaved Gauls and naval equipment, newly visible after recent cleaning and restoration, celebrate Roman supremacy on land and sea.

North of Orange up the N7, past the wine-producing village of **Piolenc**, the dramatic clifftop ruins of the **Forteresse de Mornas** (www.forteresse-de-mornas.com; tel: 04 9037 0126; mid-Mar–mid-Oct times vary; charge) come into view. Built by the Count of Toulouse and later a papal stronghold, today they appear to be defending little more than the motorway but were long a strategic eyrie over the Rhône valley. Some of the guided tours are accompanied by guides in medieval costumes. Below

Below: Châteauneuf-du-Pape vines are planted amid heat-absorbing stones.

Châteauneuf-du-Pape

The vineyards of Châteauneuf-du-Pape are planted with 13 different grape varieties, predominantly Grenache, followed by Mourvèdre, Syrah and Cinsault. The best wines achieve their complexity and character from skilful blends of these grapes. The end product is a supple, warm and full-bodied wine that goes well with strongly flavoured dishes such as game and red meat, as well as pungent cheese. The writer Alphonse Daudet (1840–97) praised Châteauneuf-du-Pape as "the king of wines and the wine of kings". This noble wine can be sampled at countless local vineyards that line the lanes around here.

Black Diamonds

Go on a truffle hunt, enrol on a course to learn how to cook them, savour the atmosphere of a truffle market or simply visit a restaurant with a special truffle menu

A delicacy prized by leading chefs – and in ancient times reputed to have aphrodisiac qualities – the pungent black truffle, known in Provence as the *rabasse* (also dubbed the "black diamond" or "black pearl of Carpentras") is the result of an unusual symbiosis between a tree, generally an oak, and the parasitic underground fungus *tuber melanosporum*, which lives on its roots. Although *tuber melanosporum* is also known as the truffle du Périgord, today 80 percent of French truffles come from southeast France, and of those 70 percent come from the Carpentras area.

The Foire St-Siffrein on 27 November heralds the start of the truffle season and augurs the weekly truffle auction held in Carpentras each Friday morning until March, near the Café de l'Univers on place Aristide Briand opposite Hôtel-Dieu. The auction itself is a somewhat cloak-and-dagger affair. Sellers discreetly unveil their precious black treasures from jute sacks, and bidding starts promptly at 9am. The Carpentras market serves as a reference to determine the weekly rate per kilogram for other truffle markets in the region, such as the Saturday market at Richerenches, the Tuesday market at Vaison-la-Romaine and the Wednesday market at Valréas.

Should you buy truffles yourself (there is also a small unregulated market for individuals), you are advised to keep them in olive oil or to store them with eggs in a closed box in the fridge, where they will help to perfume the eggs for a future *brouillard aux truffes* (scrambled egg with truffles).

Truffles were once so widespread that Parisians ate them as interval snacks at the opera, and even peasants could scoff them down as vegetables. But climate change and over-exploitation means that truffle yields have been declining in recent years.

The first conscious attempt to cultivate truffles – as opposed to simply finding them in appropriate woods – began in the 19th century with the deliberate planting of oak trees in suitably chalky soils.

Truffles often leave tell-tale rings in the ground under the trees where they might be found. But don't be tempted to go foraging for them yourself – truffle orchards are privately owned, and individuals pay high prices when truffle-collecting permits are auctioned every five years.

As to how truffle-hunting – or the art of *rabassage* – is done, both dogs and pigs have their fans. Pigs are the traditional method, as they will hunt truffles naturally, but they also adore eating them. Dogs have to be trained for the purpose, but are happier to relinquish their trophy.

The Office de Tourisme at Carpentras (97 place du 25 août; www.carpentras-ventoux. com; tel: 04 9063 0078) can provide information on truffle-hunting weekends, cookery courses and restaurants serving special truffle menus. ❑

LEFT: a truffle farmer and his truffle-sniffing pig forage for the prized *tuber melanosporum*.

the fortress, Mornas stretches along the foot of the cliff, with plane tree-lined cours, remnants of old fortified gateways and an upper village, where the square-towered Romanesque Chapelle Notre-Dame du Val Romigier, the former parish church, nestles between two mountain spurs.

Châteauneuf-du-Pape

As you approach **Châteauneuf-du-Pape ❷**, rows of green vines rise out of what looks like a pebble beach on either side of the road. In fact, this land was once washed by the waters of the Rhône. The stones are said to radiate back the heat from the sun, thus "cooking" the grapes on the vine. This curious landscape marks the beginning of a winegrowing area of 55 vineyards all classified under the Châteauneuf-du-Pape appellation *(see box on page 71)*.

Vines have been cultivated here since the Avignon papacy (bottles bear the papal coat of arms). The town is named after the summer palace built by Pope John XXII in the 14th century. Although the **Château des Papes** looks impressive

from afar when silhouetted against the sky at the top of the village, it now consists of little more than one facade and part of a tower. This is all that is left after centuries of being occupied and sacked and its near-total destruction in 1944, when German troops fought a battle against Resistance forces. From the ruins, however, there are fine views over the tiled rooftops and across vineyards towards Avignon. The main attractions of the village today are wine tasting and buying – almost every other house appears to be a wine producer. The **Musée du Vin Brotte** (D17, boulevard Pierre de Luxembourg; www.brotte.com; tel: 04 9083 7007; summer daily 9am–1pm, 2–7pm, winter 9am–noon, 2–6pm) is dedicated to the history and traditions of winemaking in the region.

Carpentras

Southeast of Châteauneuf-du-Pape, the market town of **Carpentras ❸** was also once part of the Comtat-Venaissin, the papal territory that roughly spanned the land between the Rhône, the Durance and Mont

When buying Châteauneuf-du-Pape wines, make sure the bottle carries either the crossed keys or the bishop's mitre design.

BELOW LEFT: drinking from one of Pernes-les-Fontaines' many fountains. **BELOW RIGHT:** Châteauneuf-du-Pape is renowned for its red wines.

TIP

On 27 November, every year since 1525, Carpentras has celebrated the feast day of St Siffrein with the Foire St-Siffrein, a huge agricultural and craft market with hundreds of stalls selling local produce and hand-crafted goods. There's also a horse fair and the first truffle market of the season.

BELOW: the prayer room, Carpentras' synagogue.

Ventoux. Before the Roman conquest, the settlement was the tribal capital of the Celto-Ligurian Memini. The conquest itself is recorded in the carvings on the monumental gate in the courtyard of the **Palais de Justice**. By the 4th century, Carpentras had become a bishopric. Between 1320 and 1797 it was capital of the Comtat-Venaissin and therefore part of the Holy See.

During the Middle Ages, a thriving Jewish community, known as the *juifs du pape* (papal Jews), enjoyed freedom of worship here. Behind the Hôtel de Ville, France's oldest **synagogue** (Mon–Thur 10am–noon, 3–5pm, Fri 10am–noon, 3–4pm, closed Jewish holidays) is a testament to this enclave of religious tolerance. It was founded in 1367, but rebuilt in the 18th century when the prayer room was given its lavish fake marble interior. Sadly, the Jewish cemetery outside town was desecrated some years ago.

Further evidence of the Jewish presence can be seen in the 15th-century **Cathédrale St-Siffrein** in the centre of the old town. The south portal is known as the Porte

Juive, probably because it was used by Jewish converts to Christianity.

One man who was less than tolerant of the Jewish population, however, was the Bishop d'Inguimbert. In the 18th century, he decreed that the Jewish community must remain segregated within their own ghetto. Intolerance aside, the bishop played a major role in the cultural and architectural development of Carpentras. He ordered the building of the Rococo **Chapelle Notre-Dame-de-Sainte** and founded the **Hôtel-Dieu** in 1750. The well-preserved pharmacy of the former hospital is lined with faience jars and decorated with panels by court painter Duplessis. The rest of the building is being restored to house an ambitious new cultural centre (due to open in 2012), incorporating most of the town's museums.

Most notable among Carpentras's museums is the **Musée Comtadin et Duplessis** (234 boulevard A. Durand; summer Wed–Mon 10am–noon, 2–6pm, winter by appointment; charge). It covers the customs and history of the region and features

The Papal Jews

When Jews were expelled from France in the 13th century, they were allowed to remain in Avignon and the Comtat Venaissin, which were subject to papal rule rather than that of the French crown. The ancient Jewish populations of cities like Marseille and Aix took refuge in the papal territories. This tolerance has given Provence a Jewish heritage unique in France. Gradually the laws became stricter: Jews were excluded from practising many trades or owning land, and they were forced to live cramped together in the carrière or ghetto, which was locked by gates at night. By the 17th century, the Jewish communities were concentrated in four ghettos in Avignon, Carpentras, Cavaillon and L'Isle-sur-la-Sorgue. Nonetheless, the Jews enjoyed a certain prosperity, especially during the 18th century, as the rules relaxed and merchants often had the freedom to trade in neighbouring towns.

It was the French Revolution that brought an end to the official exclusion of Jews from France, allowing them full citizenship, and the ghetto disappeared. Two beautiful synagogues survive at Carpentras and Cavaillon.

works by Hyacinthe Rigaud, Joseph Vernet and local painters. Across the courtyard is the magnificent **library**, bequeathed by Bishop d'Inguimbert, which contains more than 150,000 volumes, including some rare editions of works by Petrarch.

The **Musée Sobirats** (rue du Collège; summer Wed–Mon 10am–noon, 2–6pm, winter by appointment only; charge) preserves the atmosphere and furnishings of an 18th-century mansion.

Every Friday, an excellent **market** takes over the town centre. Local specialities include strawberries and the stripy caramel sweets called *berlingots*, but Carpentras is most famous for its truffles (*see page 72*).

Pernes-les-Fontaines and Venasque

Baking on the plain 6km (4 miles) south of Carpentras, the lively little agricultural town of **Pernes-les-Fontaines** ❹ preceded Carpentras as capital of the Comtat-Venaissin from 1125 until 1320. With its ramparts and fortified gateways, it's like an Avignon in miniature. The town boasts a medieval tower, the **Tour Ferrande** (visits booked through the tourist office; tel: 04 9061 3104), decorated with vivid frescos depicting the victory of Charles II of Anjou over the Emperor Frederick II near Naples in 1266. But the most remarkable thing about Pernes is its multitude of sculpted fountains, most installed in the 18th century. Among the most beautiful of these is the "Gigot" next to the Tour Ferrande and the Cormoran by the covered market.

A few kilometres further up the Nesque River, perched on a rocky spur and bordered to the east by a dense forest, stands **Venasque** ❺, the very first capital of the Comtat-Venaissin and one of the prettiest villages in the region. From its strategic position, it offers commanding views of the Carpentras plain. At one end are the impressive remains of medieval **ramparts**. The other historic highlight is **the baptistery** within the Eglise de Notre-Dame. Founded in the 6th century and remodelled during the 11th, it is one of France's oldest religious buildings.

Poppies frame a view of Venasque.

BELOW: the Théâtre Antique, Orange.

Nine scenic colour-coded wine routes cross the Côtes du Rhône wine region: the Azur route takes in vineyards and co-operatives around Avignon and Châteauneuf-du-Pape, the Indigo route meanders between Orange and Vaison-la-Romaine, and the Turquoise route covers Beaumes-de-Venise and the Dentelles de Montmirail (www. vins-rhone.com).

BELOW: the Dentelles de Montmirail.

Wine villages

North of Carpentras, the D7 links a string of picturesque wine-producing villages. Take a short detour along the D90 to **Beaumes-de-Venise ⑥**, famed for its sweet white dessert wine made from the tiny Muscat grape, before heading to the hamlet of **Vacqueyras ⑦**, home of the troubadour Raimbaut de Vaqueiras, who died while on Crusade.

The beautiful medieval village of **Gigondas ⑧** has fragments of ramparts and modern sculpture dotted around the streets. The best wines here fetch high prices, but there are several lesser-known *caves de dégustation* where you can pick up a bottle or two without breaking the bank.

Continuing along the D7 will take you towards the prototypically Provençal village of **Sablet ⑨**, which in turn leads into **Séguret ⑩**. The latter is a charming village, with steep paved streets, an old gateway, a fountain, lavoir, belltower, Romanesque chapel and, high above the village, some castle ruins.

The sharp limestone peaks that frame the area are known as the **Dentelles de Montmirail**. The jagged forms that pierce the clear blue sky present an irresistible challenge to climbers. More accessible pathways through the hills make this an excellent area for gentle rambles through the surrounding pine and oak woods.

Vaison-la-Romaine

The Vaucluse's second great Roman town, **Vaison-la-Romaine ⑪**, grew up on the east bank of the Ouvèze River, 28km (17 miles) northeast of Orange. Vaison divides into two distinct parts: the animated modern town, which developed around the Roman remains, and the medieval Haute Ville (upper town) on the other side of the river. With the fall of the Roman Empire, the villagers no longer found it safe to live on the exposed riverbank and retreated to the more easily defensible hill.

Two archaeological sites have been excavated and although the ruins are less spectacular and less well known than those at Orange, Arles or Nîmes, the extensive traces of villas, shops and baths give a particularly good impression of everyday life under

Roman rule. The upper site, known as the **Quartier Puymin** (summer daily 9.30am–6.30pm; winter 10am–noon, 2–5pm; charge), is a pleasant park dotted with cypress trees and the excavations of several Roman buildings, most notably the House of Laureled Apollo, where a marble head of Apollo was unearthed, the House of the Messii, a patrician villa, a colonnade known as Pompey's Portico and a nymphaeum. Reproductions of statues housed in the adjacent museum decorate the park's promenade.

The **Musée Théo Desplans** has a helpful map of the province of Gallia Narbonensis and a varied collection of mosaics, jewellery, weapons, coins and ceramics. The imposing statue of Tiberius and two larger-than-life marbles of the Emperor Hadrian and Empress Sabina speak volumes about the power and arrogance of Rome.

Built into the hillside at the top of the Puymin site, the 1st-century **Théâtre Antique** could seat 6,000 spectators and is now the main venue for the town's summer arts festival, Vaison Danses.

Southwest of the Puymin site, and separated from it by a road, the **Quartier Villasse** (summer daily 10am–noon, 2.30–6.30pm, until 5pm winter, closed Jan; charge) contains the extensive ruins of two Roman villas, a bathing complex and the rue des Boutiques, a paved Roman street lined with shops, which leads to the arch of a former basilica.

Near the exit of the Villasse site, the **Cathédrale Notre-Dame-de-Nazareth** has a fine 12th-century cloister (daily 10am–12.30pm, 2–6.30pm, until 5pm in winter, closed Jan; charge), featuring pillars with beautifully decorated capitals.

Cross the **Pont Romain** (Roman Bridge), heavily restored following severe flood damage in 1992, to reach the picturesque Cité Médiévale or **Haute Ville** (upper town). From the fortified gate, a cobbled street climbs to a dilapidated church and ruined chateau that was once the country seat of the counts of Toulouse. Looking east from the top of the upper town will give you one of the best views over the valleys and foothills that lead to Mont Ventoux.

Each autumn the villages around Vaison-la-Romaine get all souped up for the Festival des Soupes. This is when the Confrérie des Louchiers (brotherhood of ladlers) elects the best soup from a panoply of veloutés, potages *and* bouillons. *Tastings and recipes for all. Visit http://soupes84.free.fr*

Below: Quartier Puymin, Vaison-la-Romaine.

A Roman bridge in Vaison-la-Romaine.

BELOW: Bédoin.

Hill villages

One of the simplest and best pleasures of touring Provence is persevering along a tortuously winding road, for the reward of seeing a tranquil village perched at the crest of a hill. **Crestet** ⓬, set above olive groves south of Vaison-la-Romaine, is one of many such villages tucked away in the Dentelles de Montmirail. A climb up the cobbled alleyways brings you to a 12th-century church and, after a further ascent, to the castle. The former residence of the bishops of Vaison-la-Romaine is now privately owned, but there are some stunning views across the valleys and to the peak of Mont Ventoux.

Further south the D938 will take you to the small town of **Malaucène** ⓭, a good base for hiking and biking in the nearby Mont Ventoux. The lively main street bustles with cafés and restaurants.

Heading west from here towards Mont Ventoux will take you along the very route that Petrarch followed in 1336 when he undertook to climb the mountain. First, however, you might want to make a scenic detour by D938 and D13 south to **Caromb** ⓮, another medieval hilltop village. Long famed for its vines, its well-preserved exterior walls enclose another typical feature of the area: a church topped with a wrought-iron cage, designed to protect the bell from the fierce mistral. The interior is decorated with frescos and woodcarvings.

The base of Mont Ventoux is surrounded by many other attractive villages. Fortified **Le Barroux** ⓯, with its chateau and fine Romanesque church, **Mazan** ⓰, where the former chateau of the de Sade family is now a comfortable hotel, **Crillon-le-Brave**, **St-Pierre-de-Vassols** and **Bédoin** ⓱, a popular starting point for hikes up Mont Ventoux, all have their individual charm.

Mont Ventoux

Rejoin the D974 at Malaucène for the best route to **Mont Ventoux** ⓲, the "Giant of Provence" that dominates the landscape. The road passes through lavender fields and meadows dotted with cedars of Lebanon. You can take a refreshment stop at the waterfall and café beyond the

Chapelle Notre-Dame du Groseau, before beginning the climb to the Observatory. It's possible to drive all the way to the top except when the road is blocked by snow. The temperature drops dramatically as you climb and there are often strong winds – hence the mountain's name, meaning "windy mountain".

En route you'll doubtless pass cyclists doing it the hard way. Mont Ventoux is frequently included as one of the stages in the Tour de France cycle race, and it was on these steep slopes that the English rider Tommy Simpson suffered a fatal heart attack in 1967. Countless amateurs attempt to follow in the tracks of the professionals *(see right)*. Words of encouragement are painted in white on the road surface.

If you've time and energy it's perfectly possible to walk to the summit (detailed information on the best routes can be obtained from the tourist office in Bédoin).

Below the ski resort of Mont Serein, the lower slopes of the mountain are ferny and forested. As you approach the wind-blown summit

(the peak is snowcapped for at least two-thirds of the year), the greenery gives way to harsh white limestone, where nothing grows. When the sun reflects off the bald white top, the glare is blinding. From this elevated point, at 1,909 metres (6,263ft), it is easy to appreciate why the Vaucluse has always been such an important crossroads. On a clear day – although mist and haze are more typical – you can see the Rhône, the Alps and the Mediterranean. Some people even claim to have caught sight of the Pyrenees from this spot.

Once below the tree line, the drive downhill on the D164 in the direction of Sault takes you through a nature reserve of particular interest to botanists. The Mont Ventoux has been designated a "Réserve de Biosphère" by Unesco for the rarity and diversity of its flora, ranging from Mediterranean to Alpine species as the altitude mounts; panels at various stopping points indicate some of the flora and fauna found here. Pine trees give way to oak, followed by fields of wild thyme and, in the lower valleys, rolling fields of lavender.

BELOW: ascending Mont Ventoux the hard way.

The Association des Routes de Lavande (www.routes-lavande. com) proposes five itineraries through the main lavender-producing areas of southeast France, with information on lavender distilleries to visit, restaurants, places to stay and traditional lavender fairs and parades.

BELOW: Gorges de la Nesque; the summit of Mont Ventoux.

Sault and the Gorges de la Nesque

Sault , on the flanks of Mont Ventoux, is the capital of the largest area of true lavender *(lavande vraie)* production in Europe (at its colourful best in June and July). It is also at the heart of the revival of *épeautre*, a sort of hardy, primitive wild wheat that has been rediscovered by many of Provence's leading chefs and is brewed here in a *bière blanche* (white beer). The only remnants of the town's former glory as a baronial seat are the towers of a 16th-century castle. The Romanesque Eglise de St-Sauveur (also known as Notre Dame de la Tour) stands guard over the town, which acts as a marketplace for the surrounding lavender distilleries.

South of Sault between Mont Ventoux and the Plateau de Vaucluse, the drive along the D942 (towards Carpentras) to the lively hillside village of **Monieux** is lush, green and lined with fields of lavender.

Monieux marks the start of the **Gorges de la Nesque** , which offer breathtaking views and a sensational display of colours, with plenty of opportunities for climbing and hiking. The river itself is often dry, but the scrub-covered limestone gorges – also part of the Mont Ventoux biosphere – are impressive, a breeding ground for eagles, falcons and rare salamanders, plunging in some spots to depths of over 300 metres (984ft). A couple of kilometres along, the **Castelleras** belvedere looks across to the **Rocher du Cire**, a steep, wax-covered rock climbed by Frédéric Mistral in 1866 to collect honey. The belvedere is the starting point for one of several footpaths down to the medieval chapel of St-Michel de Anesca at the foot of the gorges.

The Nesque Gorges are sprinkled with attractive villages, surrounded by vineyards, olive groves and cherry trees. **Villes-sur-Auzon** has had its fair share of disasters in the form of invaders, sieges and plagues; it now lives off the vineyards that surround the town. Stop at one of the town's *caves de dégustation* to sample the local Côtes du Ventoux, best drunk when young. To the south, **Méthamis** is dominated by its surprisingly large Romanesque church. ❑

RESTAURANTS AND BARS

Restaurants

Prices for a three-course meal without wine. Many restaurants have a less expensive lunch menu:

€ = under €25
€€ = €25–40
€€€ = €40–60
€€€€ = over €60

Carpentras

Chez Serge
90 rue Cottier
www.chez-serge.com
Tel: 04 9063 2124. Open L & D daily, in winter Mon–Sat **€€**
Serge Ghoukassian is a local personality and his tastefully decorated restaurant near the cathedral is a fashionable venue for both the cooking and wines. The exceptional selection of wines concentrates mainly on the Rhône. Local truffles are a speciality, with the prized *tuber melanosporum* in winter and the little-known nutty-flavoured *tuber aestivum* in summer appearing in dishes such as asparagus soup with summer truffles, and foie gras and duck magret tart.

Monteux

Saule Pleureur
145 chemin de Beauregard
www.le-saule-pleureur.com
Tel: 04 9062 0135. Open L & D Tue–Fri and Sun, D Sat. Closed 1–15 Nov. **€€€**
Provençal native Laurent Azoulay has worked for many of the top chefs in France and shows off his talent with dishes like a *barigoule* of langoustines, sea bream with artichokes and anchovies, rabbit prepared in four different ways, or a dessert combining raspberries and red peppers. A good-value weekday lunch menu introduces you to his style.

Orange

La Table Vigneronne
Palais des Vins, RN 7
Tel: 04 9051 7650. Open L Mon–Sat. **€€**
Located at the motorway exit just south of town, the Palais des Vins was created by a group of independent wine producers. In addition to the restaurant serving Provençal dishes, a shop stocks around 600 different wines from 150 domaines in the Côtes du Rhône. Wine courses are available.

Le Yaca
24 place Silvain
Tel: 04 9034 7003. Open L Thur–Tue, D Thur–Mon. Closed Nov. **€**
Tasty dishes are offered at a good price in attractive, wood-beamed surroundings near the Théâtre Antique. Offers a friendly welcome.

Séguret

Le Mesclun
rue des Poternes
www.lemesclun.com
Tel: 04 9046 9343. Open L & D Tue–Sun. **€€**
Sit on the shady terrace with a view over the vineyards or in one of the dining rooms of this attractive 16th-century house. Young chef Christophe Bonzi's artistically presented creations draw on both Mediterranean and local traditions. Irresistible desserts.

Vaison-la-Romaine

Bistro du'O
rue Gaston du Gévaudan, Cité Médiévale
Tel: 04 9041 7290. Open L & D Tue–Sat. **€€**
Fresh modern bistro cooking in the hands of a haute-cuisine chef. Menu focuses on a small choice of seasonal produce that changes frequently. Set in the stylishly converted vaulted former castle stables.

Hostellerie Le Beffroi
rue de l'Evêché, Cité Médiévale
www.le-beffroi.com
Tel: 04 9036 0471. Open L Sat & Sun, D daily. Closed Nov–Mar. **€€**
This picturesque hotel-restaurant in the medieval upper town serves proficient Provençal and French classics.

THE LUBERON AND PLATEAU DE VAUCLUSE

With its sensuous landscape of wooded limestone hills, rolling vineyards and orchards, peppered with picturesque hill villages, historic châteaux and country farmhouses, the Luberon has become one of the most fashionable areas of the Vaucluse

The Luberon is the quintessential rural Provence of most people's imaginings. An area protected as a regional nature park since the 1970s, an authenticity mixes with the good life and a certain cosmopolitan chic. It's hardly surprising that this area is a favourite with France's champagne socialists, American actors and international tourists in search of the idyllic corner of France evoked by the English expat Peter Mayle's best-selling book, *A Year in Provence*. But the area's wealthy second-homers remain a more discreet breed than those on the show-off Riviera. A dedicated local population ensures that it remains a lived-in area, with an economy based on agriculture – notably fruit-growing and respectable wines – as well as tourism.

This area of the Vaucluse has gone through several waves of fortune. It was decimated by the Black Death and ravaged by the Wars of Religion, but later prospered as a centre for silkworm farming and the paper, glass, ochre and faience industries. Severely depopulated after World War I, it was rediscovered by writers and artists (among them Camus, De Staël and Vasarely), who helped restore and repopulate its historic villages.

Orientation

The regional park stretches between Cavaillon in the west and Manosque in the east, taking in villages such as Gordes and Roussillon on the Plateau de Vaucluse, as well as the main mountain ridge.

Two main roads run either side of the Montagne du Luberon: the D900 to the north and the D973 along the Durance valley to the south. The D943 runs from Cadenet and Lourmarin along the Aigue Brun River

Main attractions

SYNAGOGUE AND CATHEDRAL, CAVAILLON
CHÂTEAU DE LOURMARIN
VILLAGE OF CUCURON
PERCHED VILLAGES OF MÉNERBES AND BONNIEUX
SATURDAY MARKET AT APT
ANTIQUES MARKETS, L'ISLE-SUR-LA-SORGUE
LA SOURCE, FONTAINE-DE-VAUCLUSE
VILLAGE DES BORIES, GORDES
COLORADO DE RUSTREL

LEFT: Apt market. **RIGHT:** shady viewpoint at Bonnieux, a typical Provençal hill village.

through the Combe de Lourmarin gorge. It is the only road that crosses the massif, dividing it into the Petit Luberon to the west and the Grand Luberon to the east, and forks to Apt (D943) and Bonnieux (D194).

The Luberon offers plenty of opportunities for walking, cycling, riding and rock-climbing, and is crossed by numerous footpaths, including stretches of the GR4, GR6 and GR9 long-distance footpaths.

Cavaillon

Cavaillon ❶, the main town on the western edge of the Luberon, is known as the melon capital of France. Melon-growing here dates back to the days of the Avignon papacy, when cantaloupe melons were introduced from Italy and flourished thanks to irrigation from the medieval Canal St-Julien (*see left*).

Although the modern town sits on the heat-baked plain, its history began on the hill up above – the **Colline St-Jacques**. A footpath ascends the hill from behind a Roman triumphal arch on place du Clos (Cavaillon was an important Roman settlement), past traces of ramparts to the hilltop, where there is an ancient hermit's chapel and a fine view over the plain.

On Monday morning a lively **market** fills the town centre, but the more serious business goes on at the edge of town, where the daily wholesale fruit-and-vegetable market (not open to the public except on guided tours by the tourist office) is one of the most important in France.

The melon is not the only thing that is legendary in this town. Popular mythology suggests the area around Cavaillon was once flattened by a monster called the "Coulobie". Basically an oversized lizard, he was chased away by St Véran, a hermit from nearby Fontaine-de-Vaucluse and later bishop of Cavaillon. The Coulobie is the subject of a painting that hangs in the **Cathédrale Notre-**

Dame-et-St-Véran (2.30-6.30pm) on place Joseph d'Arrard, worth visiting for its altarpieces and the lovely Romanesque cloister. Go round the side of the cathedral to see its unusual octagonal tower and carved sundial, and the fine old houses on shady **square Philippe de Cabassole**. From here a covered passage leads to the elegant 18th-century **Hôtel de Ville** (town hall).

The **Musée Archéologique de l'Hôtel-Dieu** (Porte d'Avignon; tel: 04 9076 0034; Wed–Mon 2.30–6.30pm; charge), a collection of local archeological finds, is housed in the chapel of the former hospital.

As part of the papal Comtat Venaissin, Cavaillon, like Carpentras, "tolerated" a significant Jewish community when Jews were being expelled from the rest of France (see page 74). The present **synagogue** was built in 1772, a time of prosperity and increasing freedom for the Jews. It has a splendid interior in pastel pink and blue with fine Rococo carving and a beautiful wrought-iron gallery. Below the prayer room, the former bakery houses the small **Musée Juif-**

Comtadin (rue Hebraïque; tel: 04 9076 0034; guided tours of museum and synagogue every hour, 2.30–6.30pm, May–Sept Wed–Mon, Oct–Apr Wed–Fri and Mon), containing Jewish prayer books, tombstones and Torahs, as well as the original bread oven. Outside, an archway across the street marks the former gate into the ghetto, which was locked at night.

Gorges de Regalon and the Mérindol memorial

About 13km (8 miles) east of Cavaillon on the D973, a lane leads to the **Gorges de Regalon ❷**. The high walls of the limestone gorge make this a refreshing walk in summer. Note that it is closed after heavy rain.

Modern **Mérindol ❸** has little of interest, but the town remains the symbol of the horror of the religious massacres of 1545 (see box on page 86). A memorial footpath climbs amid olive trees, rosemary and evergreen oak through the still partly ruined old village to the top of the hill, where a simple memorial plaque on the battered castle ruins remains extraordinarily evocative. From here there is

TIP

In summer, classical music festivals abound in the Luberon, often providing an opportunity to see inside its churches and chateaux.

BELOW LEFT: Cavaillon melons. **BELOW:** inside the synagogue.

Busy markets are held on different mornings around the Luberon: Monday in Cadenet and Cavaillon, Tuesday in Cucuron, Gordes, Lacoste and La Tour d'Aigues, Thursday in Roussillon, Friday in Bonnieux, Lourmarin and Pertuis, Saturday in Apt and Manosque. Expect printed Provençal fabrics and pottery, fruit and veg, goats' cheeses, dried sausages, olives and tapenades.

BELOW RIGHT: Château de Lourmarin.

good access to several footpaths over the Petit Luberon, and an orientation table points out the views stretching to the Alpilles, the Montagne Ste-Victoire and the Sainte-Baume.

Lourmarin

Chic but not showy, **Lourmarin ④** is a pleasant place to stop off, with a choice of good restaurants, lively cafés and an unusual semi-buried pathway ringing the village centre. Existentialist author Albert Camus (1913–60) bought a house here in 1958 and is buried in the cemetery outside the village.

At the opposite edge of the village, the **Château de Lourmarin** (www. chateau-de-lourmarin.com; tel: 04 9068 1523; summer daily 10–11.30am, 2.30–5.30pm; 10am–6pm July–Aug; winter 10–11.30am, 2.30–4pm, Jan Sat and Sun afternoons only; charge) bridges the period between medieval fortification in the 15th-century "old" wing and the new, more comfortable lifestyle of the 16th-century Renaissance wing – seen in the large mullioned windows, Italianate loggia and cantilevered staircase. Note the unusual fireplace with carved Corinthian columns below and column figures of Native American Indians above, inspired by the recent discovery of the Americas.

The chateau was rescued from dilapidation in the 1920s and turned into an arts foundation with residences for writers and musicians in summer, when it is also used for classical concerts.

Nearby **Cadenet ⑤** is a more workaday village, with a good market on Mondays. It was once a centre of *vannerie* (basket-making), using willows from the nearby river bank.

South from Cadenet, across the Durance River, is the austerely elegant **Abbaye de Silvacane ⑥** (tel: 04 4250 4169; Apr–Sept daily, Oct–Mar closed Tue; charge). Completed in 1144, it is considered the finest of three Cistercian abbeys in Provence (the others are Sénanque and Le Thoronet), although the least visited, and is one of the venues for the prestigious Roque d'Antheron international piano festival.

East of Lourmarin, a web of lanes runs through vineyards and olive

The Massacre of Mérindol

The Vaudois or Waldensian sect was founded in Lyon in 1180 by Pierre Valdes, who preached the virtues of poverty. The Vaudois took refuge in the Alps of Savoie and northern Italy, then spread to the Luberon, encouraged by local landlords looking to repopulate the area after the Black Death. Then came the Reformation and its subsequent condemnation by the Catholic Church. Being associated with Protestantism, the Vaudois suffered a brutal repression that was particularly violent in the Luberon. The Wars of Religion split the region in two: some villages such as Mérindol, Lourmarin and La Motte d'Aigues had large Vaudois populations; others, such as Cucuron, Bonnieux and Oppède, remained staunchly Catholic. On 16 April 1545, Jean de Meynier, Baron of Oppède, sent in his troops to implement the Decree of Mérindol, which condemned the Vaudois as heretics. Within six days 22 villages were pillaged and burnt and an estimated 2,500 people were killed. Mérindol was razed to the ground. The route des Vaudois climbs up through the still partly ruined village to the top of the hill, where the bleak ruins of the citadel, now bearing a memorial plaque, are a potent reminder of the bloodshed.

groves under the eastern flank of the Montagne du Luberon. At tiny **Vaugines** ❼ many of the houses are built into the rock. Several footpaths lead up from here to Mourre Nègre, the Luberon's highest point at 1,125 metres (3,690ft).

There's much more to explore at **Cucuron** ❽. At the foot of the pretty village you'll find the **Moulin à Huile Dauphin** (tel: 04 9077 2617), whose olive oil is used by many of the area's top chefs, and the Etang, a rectangular pool of water, around which the weekly market is held on Tuesday mornings. Above, still contained within fragments of ramparts and fortified gateways, the old village is scattered with fine doorways, fountains and traces of medieval and Renaissance windows, and even remnants of a Roman kiln in one of the shops. The large Eglise Notre-Dame de Beaulieu, a bastion of Catholicism when much of the area was Protestant, has a fine Baroque altarpiece.

Further east beneath the ridge, small, sleepy villlages like **Cabrières d'Aigues** and **La Motte d'Aigues** with tall houses, painted shutters and narrow alleyways, seem to be have been bypassed by the fashionable revival of much of the Luberon.

Ansouis and the Tour d'Aigues

The D56 south of Cucuron heads to the village of **Ansouis** ❾, which spirals up around a small hill to the impressive **Château d'Ansouis**. It has an elegant 16th-century classical façade overlooking terraced gardens with topiaried hedges. The interior likewise reflects different periods, including the panelled dining room, the chapel and the big old-fashioned kitchens. After belonging to the Sabran-Pontevès family for 800 years, the château changed hands in 2008 and is gradually being refurnished (guided tours Apr–Oct Wed–Mon 2.30pm, 3.45pm, 5pm; Tue 3pm, 5pm; charge).

In one old village house, the **Musée Extraordinaire de Georges Mazoyer** (rue du Vieux Moulin; Mar–Dec Wed–Mon 2–5pm; charge) is a somewhat eccentric one-man show created by a painter with a passion for marine life and now run

The Luberon à Velo is a 235km (146-mile) cycle route taking in many of the area's prettiest villages. It runs between Cavaillon and Forcalquier, via Oppède-le-Vieux, Lacoste and Apt on the north side of the Montagne du Luberon, and Manosque, Lourmarin and Lauris by the southern route.

BELOW LEFT: Cucuron.
BELOW: the chapel, Château d'Ansouis.

by his widow. It includes a recreated underwater cave in the cellars.

The third of the great chateaux of the southern Luberon at **La Tour d'Aigues** ❿ (www.chateau-latourdaigues. com; Apr–Oct daily 10am–6pm, Nov–Mar Mon–Fri 1.30–5pm, Sat–Sun 10am–noon, 1.30–5pm; charge) is only a shadow of its former self. The pedimented entrance with its crisply carved friezes and the remains of the central pavilion and two towers only hint at what must have once been the finest Renaissance chateau in the Luberon if not all Provence, until it was pillaged by the revolutionary mob in 1792.

Towards Pertuis, the **Château Val Joanis** (www.val-joanis.com; tel: 04 9079 2077; gardens open July–Aug daily 10am–7pm; rest of year times vary; free) is known both for its wines and its imaginative modern formal gardens.

From La Tour d'Aigues, the D956 continues northeast across the eastern flank of the Luberon towards Manosque and Forcalquier, through unspoilt villages such as **Grambois** and the **Bastide-des-Jourdans**.

The northern villages

A string of old villages runs along the northern side of the Petit Luberon. At the western end, the quiet villages of **Taillades** and **Robion** were once important for stone-quarrying. Taillades' castle and houses are strangely perched on rectangular blocks of rock; an imposing 18th-century watermill stands at the foot of the village.

Further east, **Oppède-le-Vieux** ⓫ is a symbol of the Luberon revival. Largely deserted in the 19th century when the population moved to a new village on the plain, Oppède has since been resettled, often by writers, craftsmen and artists, who have restored some of its ancient houses and the village church. A footpath climbs up a cobbled street to the **Collégiale Notre-Dame d'Alidon** (July and Aug daily 10am–7pm, Easter–June, Sept–Oct Sat–Sun 10am–7pm, closed Nov–Easter), a fine Romanesque church where gargoyles leer from a hexagonal belltower. Above it is the ruined château of mercenary Baron Meynier d'Oppède who ordered the massacres of the Vaudois in 1545 *(see box on page 86)*.

Starting from the car park below the village, a footpath has been created through the vineyards, with panels explaining the soils and different grape varieties cultivated here.

Back down on the plain, **Coustellet** ⓬ is known for its farmers' market held in the main square beside the D900 on Sunday mornings (May–Nov) and Wednesday evenings (June–Sept). The **Musée de la Lavande** (Lavender Museum; www.museedelalavande.com; tel: 04 9076 9123; daily July–Aug 9am–7pm, June, Sept 9am–noon, 2–7pm, Oct–May 9am–noon, 2–6pm; charge) has a collection of lavender stills, archive photos and a film explaining the distillation processes. Near by, Beaumettes is a curiosity for its troglodyte homes carved into the rock.

BELOW: characteristic wrought-iron belltower, Lacoste.

Ménerbes

Today the village of **Ménerbes** ⓑ is particularly associated with Peter Mayle as the central focus of his best-seller *A Year in Provence*, but it was long renowned for its impregnable fortress. During the Wars of Religion, Protestants captured the stonghold in a surprise attack in 1573, holding out until 1578 when it fell back into Catholic hands after an 18-month-long siege.

Walk along the main street following signs for the Mairie, past the fine 18th-century house that belonged to Picasso muse and companion Dora Maar from 1944 to 1997, and is now used for residencies by American writers and artists. At the top of the hill is a small square where you'll find the elegant town hall, the church and clocktower with wrought-iron campanile and the 17th-century Hôtel d'Astier de Montfaucon, recently restored as the **Maison de la Truffe et du Vin** (tel: 04 9072 3837; Apr–Oct daily 9am–noon, 3–6pm, Nov–Mar times vary). Here you can join a truffle and wine-tasting workshop or visit the *Oenothèque*, which has an excellent selection of the three wine appellations found in the Luberon (Côtes du Luberon, Côtes du Ventoux and Coteaux de Pierrevert) arranged by village. The truffle museum is fairly limited, with a collection of old prints, photos and documents about truffles and truffle hunting, but the house itself has vaulted ceilings and an impressive grand staircase, and is also used for painting exhibitions. There's a café on the terrace, serving truffle-rich snacks and salads.

Just outside the village, the **Domaine de la Citadelle**, which produces some of the Luberon's best wines, is home to the surprisingly interesting **Musée du Tire-Bouchon** (www.domaine-citadelle.com; tel: 04 9072 4158; Apr–Oct daily 10am–noon, 2–7pm, Nov–Mar 9am–noon, 2–5pm; charge), a vast collection of corkscrews ranging from historic items to novelty pieces.

East of Ménerbes, the scenic D109 passes the remote **Abbaye St-Hilaire** (www.prieuresainthilaire.com; daily July–

The cross in front of Ménerbes' church.

Below: tranquil street scene in Ménerbes.

Apt is known for two distinctive styles of faience: the historic creamy yellow monochrome wares, and the more modern Aptware, characterised by the swirling multi-coloured patterns that result from mixing white, red, ochre and green clays. If you're interested in buying some faience visit Atelier du Vieil Apt, 61 place Carnot, tel: 04 9004 0396; www. atelierduvieilapt.com

mid-Nov 10am–8pm, Easter–June, 26 Dec–1 Jan 10am–7pm), the remains of a 13th-century Carmelite priory, lovingly restored by its owners as a residence, and listed as a historic monument. You can visit the chapel, a typical example of Provençal late Romanesque architecture, the cloister and chapter house.

Lacoste and Bonnieux

Lacoste ⑭ sits beneath the imposing ruins of the castle that once belonged to the notorious Marquis de Sade, who lived here from 1771 until his arrest in 1778 for sodomy and other nefarious deeds. The castle now belongs to veteran fashion designer Pierre Cardin, who has established a summer opera festival here.

The village itself is an intimate place, with a ruined gateway leading to some tastefully restored houses and an overgrown tangle of old arches and stairways. Despite the increased glamour quotient some semblance of ordinary village life continues, where the inevitably named Café de Sade is still the sort of place where you can pick up a newspaper, stop by for a *plat du jour* and eavesdrop on local gossip.

Zigzagging up a hillside further east, Bonnieux ⑮ is an archetypal Provençal hill village. It was once a property of the Knights Templar and later part of the papal enclave and home to a powerful clergy. Several elegant carved doorways and two churches hint at a village that was rather grander than it is today.

From Bonnieux you can head south towards the Combe de Lourmarin, or north towards the D900 via Pont Julien, a well-preserved Roman bridge from the 1st century BC, or northeast towards Apt.

One detour worth making is to Buoux ⑯. Its crags are popular with rock-climbers, and at the valley entrance are the scattered ruins of the Fort de Buoux, a Protestant stronghold until dismantled under the orders of Cardinal Richelieu. The main attraction, however, is the quiet valley of L'Aigrebrun, where there is a simple hotel with friendly buvette bar. This is a good starting point for several walks up towards the Mourre-Nègre or across to the isolated hamlet of Sivergues.

BELOW: bird's-eye view of Bonnieux.

Apt

Apt , the Roman city of Apta Julia and an ancient bishopric, is the main town of the northern Luberon, and headquarters of the regional park. Apt comes to life on Saturday mornings, when its food market, one of the best in Provence, fills the old town from place de la Bouquerie up to the **Ancienne Cathédrale Ste-Anne** (Mon–Fri 9am–noon, 2.30–6pm, Sun 2.30–6pm). For centuries, this curious Baroque and Gothic structure was a place of pilgrimage due to the relics of St Anne, mother of the Virgin Mary, supposedly buried in the crypt. There are, in fact, two crypts, one dating from the 4th century where you can see the niches left by ancient tombs and a later 11th-century one with medieval tombs. In 1660 the Baroque Royal Chapel was added when Anne of Austria, wife of Louis XIII, came here to give thanks for the birth of her son Louis XIV.

Apt's past prosperity came from the three industries of faïence, ochre production and crystallised fruit (*fruits confits*). Its history is traced in the interesting **Musée de l'Aventure Industrielle** (summer Mon, Wed–Sat 10am–noon, 3–6.30pm, Sun 3–7pm, winter Mon, Wed–Sat 10am–noon, 2–5.30pm; charge), housed in a converted crystallised fruit factory just behind the cathedral. Near by, an 18th-century *hôtel particulier* contains the **Maison du Parc** (place Jean Jaurès; tel: 04 9004 4200; Mon–Fri 8.30am–noon, 1.30–6pm) which focuses on the Luberon's fauna, flora and geology.

Four km (2½ miles) southwest of Apt, **Saignon** sits on a magnificent escarpment, with a cluster of fine houses under some impressive crags, a Romanesque church and a rocky belvedere with the ruins of a castle.

L'Isle-sur-la-Sorgue

Watery **L'Isle-sur-la-Sorgue** , 12km (7 miles) north of Cavaillon, was once a marshy island in the middle of the Sorgue River. The old town was built on piles in the 12th century, and the river's numerous branches were channelled to surround it in a double – in places triple – ring of canals. Countless waterwheels remain from the mills

The Sorgue River is a popular spot for kayaking.

BELOW: festival at L'Isle-sur-la-Sorgue.

TIP

The D25 between L'Isle-sur-la-Sorgue and Fontaine-de-Vaucluse gets extremely busy in summer. There's much less traffic if you arrive at Fontaine-de-Vaucluse by the D100a from the east via Lagnes or Cabrières-d'Avignon.

that once supplied silks, wools and paper to the Avignon court.

Today L'Isle-sur-la-Sorgue is famous for the biggest antiques and flea market (Sat–Mon) outside Paris *(see box)*, but the old centre, sprinkled with Renaissance doorways and old town houses, is worth exploring. On a square in the centre stands the church of **Notre-Dame des Anges**. Its stern Romanesque exterior is in marked contrast to the exuberant Baroque interior, awash with cheerful angels.

Fontaine-de-Vaucluse

Seven km (4 miles) up the Sorgue River, **Fontaine-de-Vaucluse ⓳** is named after the mysterious spring that surges out of the bedrock into an incredibly deep pool a few minutes' walk from the village in the Vallis Clausa (closed valley) that has given its name to the Vaucluse *département*. Despite diving trips and exploratory robots, no one has yet discovered the base of the pool, which is fed by rainwater that drains through the Vaucluse Plateau. In winter and spring the flow rate can be so great that water does

BELOW RIGHT: antiques fair, Isle-sur-la-Sorgue.

indeed bubble out like a fountain.

Although full of souvenir shops and tourist restaurants, the village is spectacularly situated, beneath the ruins of a castle surrounded by rocky cliffs, and dotted with the remains of paper and glass factories that once flourished here.

The spring, a 10-minute walk from the centre, is well worth the visit. Along the footpath, the **Monde Souterrain de Norbert Casteret** (tel: 04 9020 3413), dedicated to a famous potholer, has displays of potholing and cave systems, and attempts to explain the Fontaine-de-Vaucluse phenomenon. Further along, curiously situated at the end of a shopping mall, you can watch fine handmade rag paper still being made at the village's last water-powered paper factory, **Vallis Clausa Moulin à Papier** (open daily; tel: 04 9020 3414). On the other side of the footpath, the **Musée d'Histoire Jean Garcin 1939–1945 l'Appel de la Liberté** (tel: 04 9020 2400; June–Sept Wed–Mon 10am–6pm, days and times vary rest of year; charge) traces life in the Vaucluse during World

The Antiques Trail

Ever since a *brocante* was first held in L'Isle-sur-la-Sorgue in 1966, antiques dealers, bric-a-brac-ers and cosmopolitan collectors have been arriving to give the town the largest concentration of antiques dealers in France outside Paris. There are four main arcades open Monday to Saturday. Le Quai de la Gare (4 avenue Julien Guigue), by the station, and Hôtel Dongier (9 place Gambetta), an 18th-century coaching inn, are rather upmarket. Many items reflect the south – carved Beaucaire mirrors, faience from Apt and Moustiers, marriage wardrobes and elaborate openwork bread cupboards. The Village des Antiquaires de la Gare (2bis avenue de l'Egalité), in a ramshackle old carpet factory, and the Isle-aux-Brocantes (7 avenue des Quatre Otages), reached across its own canal, are more bohemian in mood. The goods tend more towards 20th-century items and collectables, such as Art Deco furniture, vintage toys, garden furniture and old bar and hotel fittings. Every Sunday, the permanent shops and arcades are joined by a flea market that sprawls along avenue des Quatre Otages. For the big Easter and 15 August fairs, stalls take over the local park and meadows as well.

War II and the maquisards of the Resistance movement.

Near the village entrance, the Romanesque **Eglise de St-Véran** is dedicated to the 6th-century bishop of Cavaillon, who is said to have freed the area of the Coloubie monster *(see page 84)*, and who is buried in the crypt. It has an unusual 11th-century open altar table made from an antique tombstone.

Fontaine-de-Vaucluse is also associated with Italian poet and scholar Petrarch, who lived here from 1337 to 1353, where he composed his famous sonnets to the love of his life, Laura. He is commemorated by the tall column near the bridge on place de la Colonne, and in the **Musée Bibliothèque Pétrarque** (quai du Château Vieux; tel: 04 9020 3720; Apr–Oct Wed–Mon 10am–12.30pm, 1.30–6pm, closed Nov–Mar; charge). A narrow road runs out of Fontaine-de-Vaucluse over a bleak mountainside to Cabrières d'Avignon. One curiosity here is the fragments of the **Mur de la Peste**, a drystone wall built in 1721 in an attempt to keep out the plague.

Gordes and the Plateau de Vaucluse

With its pristine drystone walls and renovated houses, smart hotels and interior-decoration shops, **Gordes ⓴** epitomises the Luberon's social rise. During the summer, the town is one of the most popular tourist spots in the Vaucluse. It's dominated by its **Château** (tel: 04 9072 0275; daily 10am–noon, 2–6pm; charge), a medieval castle transformed during the Renaissance, which houses the tourist office and an exhibition of paintings by Belgian artist Pol Mara.

The majority of tourists, however, come here to see the **Village des Bories** (tel: 04 9072 0348; daily 9am–sunset; charge), a cluster of 20 restored beehive-shaped *bories* (drystone huts) that lies below the town. The wind-resistant dwellings are believed to date from the 16th to 19th centuries, but may have replaced much earlier structures. Similar drystone huts are found throughout the area, some used as sheep pens, others as holiday homes.

The winding D177 Vénasque road leads from Gordes across the plateau to the **Abbaye de Sénanque ㉑** (www.

One of the drystone huts in Village des Bories.

BELOW: Abbaye de Sénanque.

Map on page 84

> **TIP**
>
> Visits to the l'Occitane factory to see the production of traditionally made perfumes, soaps and cosmetics using natural ingredients can be arranged through L'Occitane, ZI St-Maurice, Manosque, tel: 04 9270 1900, www.loccitane.com.

BELOW RIGHT: the library in Jean Giono's house, Lou Parais.

senanque.fr; tel: 04 9072 0572; Feb–Dec, guided visits in French only, but leaflet in English available, hours vary, reservation advised; charge). One of the three great 12th-century Cistercian abbeys of Provence (along with Thoronet and Silvacane), it is a typically austere structure, sitting in calm isolation amid lavender fields.

Ochre country

With its colourful ochre-washed houses, the hill village of **Roussillon** ㉒ is the most visible reminder of the ochre industry that once thrived here, thanks to a 50km (30-mile) seam of ochre-bearing rock that runs through the area. The only industrial-scale mine still in operation is in Gargas. Roussillon's economy is now driven by tourism, and it can get suffocatingly overrun in summer. On the edge of the village is the **Sentier des Ochres** (charge), a waymarked trail through the reddish landscape.

Even more spectacular than Roussillon, though more difficult to find (look for signs from the D22), is the **Colorado de Rustrel** ㉓, situated south of the village of Rustrel to the

northeast of Apt. From the car park, footpaths lead through a surreal landscape of orangey-red rocks sculpted into chimneys, turrets, bowls and narrow valleys, by a combination of ochre-quarrying and natural erosion.

Manosque

At the eastern edge of the Luberon, just into the *département* of Alpes-de-Haute-Provence, is the town of **Manosque** ㉑. This once sleepy town has become a thriving economic axis. Agriculture in the Durance valley (Manosque is known for its peaches) is blossoming, the proximity of the Cadarache nuclear research centre has drawn scientists to settle here, and the global success of skincare group Occitane means it is now the town's largest employer.

The central core of Manosque, ringed by busy boulevards that replaced the ancient ramparts, has changed little from the "tortoiseshell in the grass" described by the town's own Jean Giono (*see box below*). Two imposing gateways – **Porte Saunerie** and **Porte Soubeyran** – stand guard at either end of the **Vieille Ville**. ❑

Jean Giono

Writer Jean Giono (1895–1970) was a lifelong resident of Manosque. An ecologist and pacifist, he was imprisoned by the Nazis for his beliefs at the start of the occupation, and by the French at the end of the war because his philosophical love of nature had been twisted to support Nazi propaganda. He made his name with a series of novels on village life in the Alpes-de-Haute-Provence, including the swashbuckling *Hussard sur le Toit*. Giono's Provence has little in common with the sunny region of Pagnol or even Daudet. His main themes were the abandonment of the mountain villages, the destruction of the traditional patterns of rural life and the rough sensuality of man's communion with nature. A plaque marks the writer's birthplace at 14 Grande Rue, above his parents' shoe shop. Outside the old town, the **Centre Jean Giono** (tel: 04 9270 5454; Tue–Sat 2–6pm; charge) puts on temporary exhibitions and has a permanent display about the writer's life and work. Giono's house, **Lou Parais** (Montée des Vrais Richesses; tel: 04 9287 7303), north of the Old Town, is open for guided visits by appointment on Friday afternoons.

RESTAURANTS AND BARS

Restaurants

Prices for a three-course meal without wine. Many restaurants have a less expensive lunch menu:
€ = under €25
€€ = €25–40
€€€ = €40–60
€€€€ = over €60

Bonnieux
Le Fournil
5 place Carnot. Tel: 04 9075 8362. Open L & D Tue–Fri and Sun, D only Sat. Closed Dec–Jan. **€€**
This troglodyte restaurant draws a fashionable set with its good-value updated Provençal food.

Cavaillon
Restaurant Pantagruel
5 place Philippe de Cabassole. Tel: 04 9076 1198. Open L & D Tue–Sat, D only Mon. **€€**
You're in for a Rabelaisian feast at this laid-back restaurant. In winter meat is cooked on the open fire.

Coustellet
Maison Gouin
N100. Tel: 04 9076 9018. Open L & D Mon, Tue, Thur–Sat. **€€**
Small bistro within an upmarket butcher and deli. More elaborate menu by night.

Cucuron
La Petite Maison
place de l'Etang

www.lapetitemaisonde
cucuron.com
Tel: 04 9068 2199. Open L & D Wed–Sun. **€€€**
Chef Eric Sapet worked at several top restaurants in Paris and the Luberon before taking over this pretty bistro, where he puts his gourmet touch on fresh market produce.

Fontaine-de-Vaucluse
Philip
chemin de la Fontaine
Tel: 04 9020 3181. Open L Apr–June & Sept, L & D July–Aug. Closed Oct–Mar. **€€**
Last stop on the footpath towards the spring, with a terrace overlooking the rushing torrent, Philip serves traditional Provençal cuisine at lunch, including the local speciality of river trout, and ice creams and sandwiches in the afternoon.

Goult
Café de la Poste
place de la Libération
Tel: 04 9072 2323. Open L Tue–Sun. **€**
An institution where local families, second-homers and international tourists pile in for no-nonsense home cooking.

L'Isle-sur-la-Sorgue
Le Jardin du Quai
91 avenue Julien Guigue
Tel: 04 9020 1498. Open L & D Thur–Mon. **€€**

Reputed chef Daniel Hébert serves simple bistro fare at lunch and more complicated gastronomic cuisine at night.

Lourmarin
Auberge La Fenière
route de Cadenet
www.reinesammut.com
Tel: 04 9068 1179. Open L Wed–Sun, D Tue–Sun. Closed mid-Nov–mid-Dec & Jan. **€€€€**
Chef Reine Sammut produces stylish food at this modern *mas* between Cadenet and Lourmarin. Near by, La Cour de la Ferme serves a less expensive *menu du jour* and spit-roast meats.

Ménerbes
Café Véranda
avenue Marcellin Poncet
www.café-veranda.com

Tel: 04 9072 3333. Open L & D Tue–Sat. **€€**
The trio behind this excellent new bistro previously had a restaurant in the Dordogne, so don't be surprised to find southwestern touches on the menu, which changes regularly, and might include delicate salmon ravioli.

Vaugines
Hostellerie du Luberon
cours St-Louis
www.hostellerieduluberon.com
Tel: 04 9077 2719. Open L Thur–Tue, D daily. Closed Dec–Jan. **€€**
Family-run hotel-restaurant where menus feature personalised Provençal dishes, such as squid with broad beans.

WILD PROVENCE

If you wish to escape the crowded cities and coast, the countryside isn't far away. Here, among mountains and rivers, you can seem miles from civilisation

This swallowtail butterfly is a common visitor to Provence and is just one small component in the colourful landscape which runs from the salt marshes and brackish lagoons of the Camargue in the Rhône delta, pink with flamingos and home to countless waterfowl and waders, to the Alpine summits along the Italian border. It includes seven nature parks and 20 nature reserves. The *maquis* scrub of rock rose and lavender, myrtle and thyme is the enduring attraction of the region, typified by the Luberon, with its evergreen oak, abundance of wild flowers and herbs, and beavers busy in the Durance and Calavon rivers. Eagles and vultures gaze down on the spectacular limestone Gorges de Verdon. The Valensole plateau, also in the Parc Naturel Régional du Verdon, is the place to head for in June and July to see and smell the lavender fields and buy honey. Mushroom- and boar-hunting take place in autumn, which also sees chestnut-gatherers roam the Maures Massif. Wildest of all is the Mercantour National Park *(see below)*, with its glaciated landscape of mountains and lakes.

LEFT: Swallowtail butterfly.

ABOVE: cornflowers and poppies, which flower between March and June, in an Alpine meadow.

LEFT: glimpse chamois in Mercantour National Park, on steep slopes in forested areas and Alpine pastures.

LEFT: this prehistoric ammonite fossil comes from near Dignes.

GET OUT AND GET ACTIVE

Provence's wonderful landscape provides endless opportunities to enjoy the outdoors. For the sedate and leisurely, it's great walking country, while for the more energetic there are well-marked long-distance routes *(grandes randonnées)*, or strenuous challenges such as the Sentier Martel in the Gorges de Verdon or the Vallée des Merveilles in the Mercantour. Cycling can also be leisurely or demanding. The Luberon is a popular place for bikers, while Mont Ventoux is one of the arduous climbs on the Tour de France. The local rivers run swiftly, particularly the Verdon *(above)*, making canoeing, kayaking and white-water rafting a possibility, and because its gorge is so deep you can go bungee jumping from bridges. The rivers also offer a chance for trout-fishing. Mountains and escarpments present opportunities for climbing at every level, and of course there are the ski resorts of the Alps *(see page 283)*. There are few more evocative places to go horse-riding than the Camargue, where the local horses are perfect for a day's hack in the marshes. Equestrian centres *(centres équestres)* can be found throughout the region.

ABOVE: the famed white horses live wild in the marshy delta of the Rhône. Each year they are rounded up and the foals are branded.

ABOVE: diving at Freighter le Donateur off the coast of Ile de Porquerolles, one of the islands off the coast of Hyères.

BELOW: heathland and stone pine woodland in the Ribeirotte Valley, in the Var.

ABOVE: the bee eater, relative of the kingfisher, is often seen around vineyards and meadows. Look out for roller birds and, near woodlands, hoopoes.

MARSEILLE AND THE CALANQUES

France's oldest and second-largest city is a gloriously gutsy multicultural port, where tower blocks jostle with historic monuments. A city in evolution, it is redeveloping its docklands and gearing up for its role as European cultural capital in 2013

France's oldest city and leading port, **Marseille ①** is a magnificent mix of urban and marine, the grandiose and the intimate. With 2,600 years of history, the town abounds in historic monuments, fine churches, old fortresses, interesting museums and some icons of modern architecture. It is a city of 860,000 inhabitants, where ancient tenements, fishermen's cottages, Haussmannian boulevards, Belle Epoque villas and modern tower blocks alternate with docks, beaches and tiny coves. In one district you'll find luxury fashion boutiques, in another North African grocers and backstreet mosques. Some 40km (25 miles) of seaboard stretch from the fishing port and industrial suburb of L'Estaque in the north, past the docks, ferry terminal, fishing inlets and the long expanse of the Prado beach to tiny Les Goudes. Even the remote, fjord-like Calanques which stretch east between Marseille and Cassis largely fall within the urban limits of Marseille.

Birth of a city

It was 2,600 years ago that Greek sailors from the Ionian city of Phocaea first sailed into the harbour at Marseille, establishing a prosperous trading post called Massilia. The new settlement set up a string of outposts including Hyères, Antibes and Nice, and was also a thriving intellectual centre, home to one of the principal universities of the Greek Empire. Later a major Roman port, Marseille was an early centre of Christian monasticism around the important abbey of St-Victor. The city briefly set itself up as an independent republic in 1214, until it was taken by Charles d'Anjou in 1256. Along with the rest of Provence, the city became part

Main attractions
VIEUX PORT
ABBAYE DE ST-VICTOR
LE PANIER
LA VIEILLE-CHARITÉ
MUSÉE CANTINI
NOTRE-DAME-DE-LA-GARDE
VALLON DES AUFFES
PLAGES DU PRADO
CITÉ RADIEUSE
CASSIS HARBOUR
LES CALANQUES

LEFT: Marseille's Vieux Port.
RIGHT: the tranquil beauty of the Calanques.

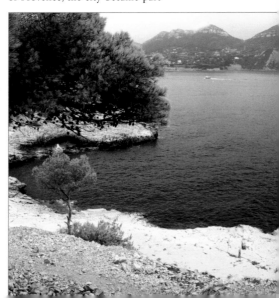

BELOW:
selling the daily catch.

of France in 1481. As a vital part of Louis XIV's maritime strategy, he built the star-shaped Fort St-Nicolas and enlarged Fort St-Jean, on either side of the Vieux-Port, as much to control the unruly citizens as to protect the port.

In 1720, an outbreak of the plague – the worst of several epidemics that hit the city – wiped out half the population, and despite efforts to isolate the city, spread to the rest of Provence.

Unsurprisingly, the Marseillais were active in the Revolution. In 1792, 600 Marseillais *fédéralistes* marched towards Paris singing the song that has since become France's national anthem, known as la Marseillaise. In the 19th century Marseille became the most powerful port on the Mediterranean, serving the expanding French Empire, its wealth reflected in the construction of grand hotels, the Docks de la Joliette, the new cathedral and Palais du Pharo.

Today the city is still a major port, and adminstrative capital of the Bouches-du-Rhône *département* and the Provence-Côte d'Azur region. This is one of the most invigorating cities in France: a place where most of the city's residents proudly consider themselves Marseillais before being Provençal, with a take it or leave it attitude to tourists – although it now receives more than 4 million visitors annually.

The arrival of the TGV high-speed train in 2001, bringing Marseille within three hours of Paris, and massive investment in urban regeneration have tranformed the city's image; facades have been cleaned and the city has gained a sleek new tramway. The refurbishment of the 19th-century Joliette docks, flagship of the larger Euroméditerranée redevelopment project, illustrates the transformation of the local economy, as design and advertising agencies and service companies replace shipping ones and the dockworkers of old. Marseille has long been an entry point for immigrants – Italians, Greeks, Spanish and, more recently, North and West Africans have all contributed to a melting pot where France's often uneasy racial mix for once largely seems to work.

The Vieux-Port

Any visit to Marseille should begin at the **Vieux-Port** Ⓐ (old port), the heart of the city, with its yachts, fishing boats and café-lined quays framed by forts at either end. There's a lively fish market each morning along the quai des Belges; this is also where boats leave for trips to the Calanques, the Château d'If and the Iles du Frioul (see page 107). A tiny passenger ferry runs across the Vieux-Port between the quai du Port and quai de Rive Neuve.

The Quai du Port was heavily bombed by the Germans during World War II, but was sensitively rebuilt in the 1950s by architect Fernand Pouillon. His tinted reinforced concrete housing frames one of the rare buildings to survive, the ornate 17th-century **Hôtel de Ville** Ⓑ (town hall). From here various stairways lead up to Le Panier district. Just beside the Hôtel de Ville, terraced gardens climb up to the **Hôtel-Dieu**,

the city's old hospital, designed in the 18th century by Mansard, and currently being refurbished as a luxury hotel. On the other side of the town hall stands the **Maison Diamantée** Ⓒ, built in the 16th century and one of the oldest surviving houses in Marseille, so called because of the unusual diamond-faceted façade.

A little further along the quai, look in on the **Musée des Docks Romains** Ⓓ (place du Vivaux; www. marseille. fr; Tue–Sun June–Sept 11am–6pm, Oct–May 10am–5pm; charge), which shelters relics of Roman docks on the site of their excavation. The open amphorae once stored grain, olives and wine. On the esplanade just before Fort St-Jean, a blockhaus contains the **Mémorial des Camps de la Mort** (quai Louis Branquier; tel: 04 9190 7315; charge), where texts and photos recall the deportations and internment camps of World War II. At the end of the quay, Fort St-Jean will form the centrepiece of the

First created in 1781 in Le Four des Navettes, navettes are biscuits flavoured with orange-flower water. They are the special mark of the Fête de la Chandeleur on 2 February.

BELOW:
sunset over the port.

future **MuCEM** (Musée National des Civilisations de l'Europe et de la Méditerranée; www.mucem.eu; tel: 04 9613 8090; opens 2013), an ethnographic and folk art collection centred on Mediterranean cultures.

On the opposite side of the Vieux-Port, the quai de Rive Neuve has lively bars and cafés amid ships' chandlers. The former fish market at No.33 is now Marseille's highly renowned **Théâtre National de la Criée**.

The quai leads towards the star-shaped Fort St-Nicolas (now occupied by the French Foreign Legion) and the **Jardins** and **Palais de Pharo**, the palace built for Napoléon III. The gardens, much loved by Marseillais, offer great views of boats coming in and out of the port.

Behind the quai, **place Thiars**, place aux Huiles and cours d'Estienne d'Orves are busy with restaurants, fashion boutiques and galleries, many of them in converted warehouses and arsenal buildings. Parallel to the quai, long rue Sainte has an enclave of Marseillais tradition, the Four des Navettes bakery at No 136, which has been baking *navettes –*

biscuits flavoured with orange-flower water cooked in the shape of the boat that is said to have brought Mary Magdalene to the shores of Provence 2,000 years ago – since 1781.

Rue Sainte ends at the **Abbaye de St-Victor** (tel: 04 9611 2260; daily 9am–7pm; charge for crypt), an ancient basilica that looks as much like a fortress as a church. It was built on the site of an ancient burial ground in the 5th century and is named after local martyr St Victor, patron saint of sailors, millers (Victor was ground to death between two millstones) and Marseille. Throughout the Middle Ages, the abbey's power was felt across the Mediterranean as it set up daughter houses from northern Spain to Italy. What remains is the extraordinary two-storey fortified church – the original 5th-century church in the crypt and the lofty 11th- to 13th-century church above. In the crypt, ancient sarcophagi, some hidden in candlelit alcoves, line the walls; in the centre stands the sombre tomb of two slain martyrs over which the basilica was built. In a rocky alcove is the 3rd-century tomb of St Victor.

Le Panier

Climbing up the hill behind the quai du Port, bordered to the east by the 19th-century apartment buildings of rue de la République, is the picturesque **Quartier du Panier**. Characterised by leaning colour-washed houses, narrow streets, flights of steps and little squares, it holds a small morning market on the site of the original Greek agora. Traditionally the immigrant quarter, it has recently been colonised by artists, craftsmen and Parisians in search of a southern pied-à-terre.

At the heart of Le Panier is **La Vieille-Charité** (2 rue de la Charité; Tue–Sun June–Sept 11am–6pm, Oct–May 10am–5pm; charge). Erected as a charity hospital in the

17th century, it is the masterpiece of Marseille-born architect and sculptor Pierre Puget (1620–94), who also created several sculptures for Louis XIV at Versailles. The three storeys of galleried arcades are amazingly serene and beautiful for a building originally destined to round up beggars, fallen women and other social rejects. The restored buildings now contain the **Musée d'Archéologie Méditerranéenne** (www.marseille.fr), which features local archaeology and a small but well-presented Egyptian collection, and the **Musée d'Arts Africains, Océaniens et Amerindiens** (www.marseille.fr), particularly strong on American Indian art and artefacts. At the centre of the courtyard, the **Chapelle**, which has an unusual oval dome, makes a striking setting for temporary exhibitions.

More contemporary art can be found down the hill at the gallery of the **FRAC-PACA** (Fonds Régional d'Art Contemporain Provence-Alpes-Côte d'Azur, 1 place Francis-Chirat; tel: 04 9191 2755; open during exhibitions Tue–Sat 2–6pm; free). It is due to move into an adventurous new building by Kengo Kuma in La Joliette in 2013. Looming over the coast is the stripy neo-Byzantine **Cathédrale de la Major** ❶ (Tue–Sun 9am–noon, 2–5.30pm). Built 1852–93, its interior is a riot of coloured marble and porphyry. Adjacent to la Major is the 11th-century Romanesque Ancienne-Major, the earlier cathedral, which was undermined by the construction of the new cathedral and the flyover below it, and is closed for restoration.

Euroméditerranée

Stretching north along the seaboard from Fort St-Jean and inland as far as the Gare St-Charles train station is Marseille's ambitious 480-hectare Euroméditerranée urban regeneration district. The beautiful 19th-century brick warehouses of the **Docks de la Joliette** ❶ have been restored as offices and restaurants. On the waterfront the future FRAC artspace will join the MuCEM and Le Silo, a vast 1920s concrete grain silo rehabilitated as a music venue. Inland, the rundown Belle de Mai

BELOW: streets in the Quartier du Panier, Marseille's oldest quarter.

district, centred on the arty **Friche de Belle de Mai** (41 rue Jobin; www.lafriche.org; tel: 04 9504 9504; Mon–Sat 9am–midnight), a former tobacco factory converted into artists' studios, a local radio station and dance and theatre companies, is becoming a new focus for media, TV and film companies. The Gare St-Charles station has also been renovated with a bright glass shopping mall extension and paved esplanade leading to Marseille's main university district.

Around La Canabière

Running inland from the Vieux-Port is **La Canabière** , Marseille's equivalent of the Champs-Elysées. It was laid out in 1666 as part of Louis XIV's expansion of the city, but its heyday came in the 19th century when its smart hotels, banks, cafés and department stores were a symbol of Marseille's booming port economy at the height of the French Empire.

Near the port, at No. 4 is the tourist office. Almost opposite, the Palais de la Bourse – the ornate 19th-century maritime stock exchange (note the ship carvings on the façade) – con-

tains the **Musée de la Marine et de l'Economie de Marseille** (9 La Canabière; tel: 04 9139 3333; daily 10am–6pm; charge), which documents Marseille's maritime history.

Between here and the Vieux-Port, excavations during the construction of the Centre Bourse shopping centre in the 1960s unearthed Greek and Roman fortifications, wharfs, wells and a road, dating from between the 3rd century BC and the 4th century AD. These now lie exposed in the **Jardins des Vestiges**. The adjoining **Musée d'Histoire de Marseille** (1 square Belsunce; www.marseille.fr; July–Aug Tue–Sun 11am–6pm, Sept–June Mon–Sat 10am–5pm; charge) presents some of the finds and the city's subsequent history.

Behind here, running north of La Canabière, is the **cours Belsunce**, a broad promenade laid out in the 17th century. It has a souk-like atmosphere with its stalls, street traders and oriental patisseries. A recent arrival is the striking new municipal library. The street continues into rue d'Aix, leading up to a busy road junction crowned by the Porte d'Aix triumphal arch.

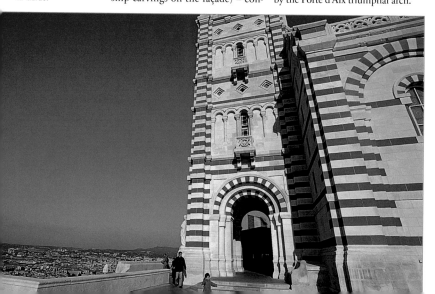

Rue Beauvau leads to Marseille's **Opéra** , reconstructed in Art Deco style behind an 18th-century classical facade after the original caught fire in 1919. It is used for both opera and ballet. Near here, amid Marseille's smartest shops on rue Paradis, rue St-Ferréol, rue Francis Davso and rue Grignan, is the **Musée Cantini** (19 rue Grignan; www.marseille. fr; Tue–Sun June–Sept 11am–6pm, Oct–May 10am–5pm; charge). This notable collection has Fauve, Surrealist, early abstraction and post-war art, including paintings and sculptures by Derain, Signac, Léger, Kandinsky, Ernst, Arp, Brauner and Bacon. At the end of pedestrianised rue St-Ferréol is the grandiose Préfecture. Behind here rue Edmond Rostand is the focus of a small antiques district. On the other side of rue de Rome, rue d'Aubagne is lined with North African grocers, with sacks of couscous, spices, nuts and dates. Steps climb up the hill to Notre-Dame-du-Mont and the colourful **cours Julien** with its fountain, cosmopolitan restaurants, morning produce market (Mon–Sat), book and record shops and music venues.

Palais de Longchamp

Crowning the top of boulevard de Longchamp, the **Palais de Longchamp** is a glorious confection of fountains and waterfalls, with a winged colonnade around a central fountain. It is in fact a grandiose water tower that celebrated the arrival of a much-needed drinking-water supply to the city in 1869. The pavilions on either side house two museums: the **Musée des Beaux-Arts** (closed for renovation until 2013) has sculptures by Pierre Puget and old master paintings, while **Muséum d'Histoire Naturelle** (www.museum-marseille.org; tel: 04 9114 5950; Tue–Sun June–Sept 11am–6pm, Oct–May 10am–5pm; charge) features a variety of zoological and geological exhibits.

A little way down the street is the **Musée Grobet-Labadié** (140 boulevard de Longchamp; www.marseille.fr; tel: 04 9162 2182; Tue–Sun June–Sept 11am–6pm, Oct–May 10am–5pm; charge), the restored private mansion of a couple of avid 19th-century collectors, filled with the treasures they amassed: Northern and Italian Renaissance paintings, French

The brasserie La Samaritaine on the Vieux-Port is a Marseille institution. It celebrated its centenary in 2010.

BELOW: relaxing in cours Julien.

Cafés and Bars

Naturally the Vieux-Port is first port of call if you're pausing for a drink or a snack. Elegant **La Samaritaine** (2 quai du Port), with its corner vantage point, is a favourite meeting place; the **OM Café** (3 quai des Belges) is the rallying point for supporters of Olympique de Marseille football team. **Le Crystal** (148 quai du Port), with its '50s decor and terrace, is a cocktail hotspot, as is **La Caravelle** (34 quai du Port), on the first floor of the Hôtel Bellevue. Across the harbour, the **Bar de la Marine** (15 quai de Rive Neuve) is a local classic. Up the hill east of the Canabière, place Jean Jaurès and the bars and music venues around cours Julien draw a younger, bohemian set.

18th-century paintings, Provençal furniture and faience and a unique array of Flemish, Beauvais and Gobelins textiles.

The Good Mother

Perhaps the best-loved site in all Marseille is the church of **Notre-Dame-de-la-Garde** Q (tel: 04 9113 4080; daily summer 7am–7pm, winter 7.30am–5.30pm), dubbed "la Bonne Mère" (the Good Mother) by the Marseillais. Erected on a bluff of 162 metres (530ft), no matter where you go in Marseille, you can't miss the extravagant 19th-century basilica with its stripy marble walls and massive gilded statue of the Virgin atop the campanile. Inside, the two-storey church glitters with neo-Byzantine mosaics and white marble ex-votos offering thanks for recovery for everything from shipwrecks to armed hold-ups. The terrace in front offers the best view over the city. Supposedly a lookout post since prehistoric times

and later a fort, it also became a place of worship for seafarers.

Along the corniche

The Château du Pharo and the tiny plage des Catalans, a small sandy beach and little harbour of the Anse des Catalans, mark the start of the **corniche Président-J.-F.-Kennedy**, the 5km (3-mile) stretch of road that follows the coastline east of the Vieux-Port. Take a short detour up the picturesque **Vallon des Auffes**, with its colourful *pointu* fishing boats, old fishermen's *cabanons* and renowned bouillabaisse restaurants.

The road eventually leads to the **Plages du Prado**, a large area of lawns, sports facilities and mainly pebble beaches on artificial land created with landfill from the construction of the Marseille metro system. The beach here has been split into two parts, the first half being pebble and the second sand, and the water is quite clean. This area is a lively

Marseille and the Calanques

0 ——— 10 km
0 ——— 10 miles

MEDITERRANEAN SEA

and chic place to dine at night.

On the avenue du Prado, **Parc Borély** is Marseille's largest park, with its landscaped *jardins à l'anglaise*, French formal gardens, botanical garden with tropical greenhouse and racetrack, laid around the Château Borély, most elegant of all the *bastides*. A huge 18th-century neoclassical country house put up by the Borély family in 1766, it is now used for cultural events and exhibitions. Near here, Château Pastre, built by a wealthy 19th-century ship owner, houses **Musée de la Faïence** (Earthenware Museum; 157 avenue de Montredon; www.marseille.fr; tel: 04 9172 4347; June–Sept Tue–Sun 11am–6pm, Oct–May 10am–5pm; charge). Pride of place goes to Provençal faience from Moustiers, Apt, Tour d'Aigues and, of course, Marseille, but the collection ranges from ancient Neolithic pottery to ceramics by contemporary designers.

The coast road continues past the **Plage de la Pointe Rouge**, a sandy beach that is known for its restaurants and watersports facilities, notably windsurfing and water-skiing, past

La Madrague de Mondredon to finish at Les Goudes and tiny Callelongue. You're still technically in Marseille, but with the bare white rock, glittering blue sea and whirling seagulls you could well be on a Greek island.

Modern monuments

Heading inland up avenue du Prado from the beaches, past the giant replica of Michelangelo's *David* on boulevard Michelet, are two modern shrines. At No. 3, the **Stade Vélodrome**, the stadium of Marseille's much-loved football team, Olympique de Marseille, is set to be expanded for the European cup in 2016. At No. 280, a must-see for modern architecture enthusiasts is the **Cité Radieuse ®** by the Modernist architect Le Corbusier. Built in 1947–52, the block illustrated Le Corbusier's principles of mass housing with its reinforced concrete structure built on *pilottis*, clever duplex apartments with balconies and built-in furniture, use of colour, and sculptural roof. As well as 337 apartments, it contains a supermarket, rooftop theatre, gym and infant school. It

Although locals nicknamed it the Maison du Fada (madman's house), Le Corbusier's Cité Radieuse is much loved by its residents.

BELOW LEFT: Château d'If.

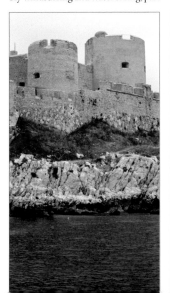

Château d'If and the Iles du Frioul

The Iles du Frioul, a rocky archipelago off the shore of Marseille, are just minutes from the frenetic Vieux-Port activity, yet miles away in mood. Regular boat trips leave from the quai des Belges out to the tiny Ile d'If, site of the Château d'If (summer daily 9.30am–6.30pm, winter Tue–Sun 9.30am–5.30pm; charge), France's version of Alcatraz. It was built by François I in the 1520s to keep an eye on the unruly Marseillais, and later used for the internment of Protestants and political prisoners. Its most famous inmate was fictional – Edmond Dantès, hero of Alexandre Dumas's novel *The Count of Monte-Cristo*. As well as visiting the fortress, you can enjoy a great view of the city, and even take a swim off the rocky shores.

You can combine the trip with a visit to the Iles de Frioul, two rocky, sparsely vegetated islands linked by a causeway. There are a few cafés and apartments near the quay, and some little creeks for swimming. Climb the hill to see the ruins of the Hôpital Caroline, an 18th-century quarantine hospital, today used for Les Nuits de Caroline outdoor theatre festival in July.

Les Calanques

Explore the fjord-like Calanques on foot or by boat and find unspoilt nature in an area that appeals to divers, birdwatchers, rock-climbers and walkers

Stretching for 20km (12 miles) south-east of Marseille, between Cap Croisette and Cassis, lies a stunning landscape of rocky inlets, sheer white cliffs, sparse *garrigue* vegetation and tiny beaches, offering superb opportunities for walking, rock-climbing, birdwatching and swimming. Although most of the area is within the city limits of Marseille, it remains a haven of unspoilt nature, largely because most of it is accessible only by foot or boat – and from 2011 will gain further protection as a Parc National. Often compared to the Norwegian fjords, the Calanques are technically *rias* – valleys flooded by the rising sea level at the end of the Ice Age some 10,000 years ago. Over 700 species of plant, including 14 types of orchid, grow here; birdlife includes the rare Bonelli's eagle, the peregrine falcon and huge colonies of seagulls.

You can reach the Calanques by taking boats from the Vieux-Port in Marseille and the harbour in Cassis, or by walking along the GR98 footpath between Marseille and Cassis. Certain roads offer access out of season and at night for those with restaurant reservations. Note that from July to mid-September, access is severely restricted due to fire risk. Most footpaths are closed; only the GR98 remains open. The rest of the year, the Marseille tourist office organises walks in the Calanques on Friday afternoons and Saturday mornings (reserve on 04 9113 8900). If walking alone, be sure to take a good map, sun cream and water.

The Marseille coast road ends just beyond Les Goudes at Calanque de Callelongue, a starting point for the GR98, which follows the coast to the Calanque de Cortiou and the series of little Calanques of the Massif de Marseilleveyre. The broad Calanque de Sormiou, with its small beach, and Morgiou, with its fishing harbour, are two of the most picturesque, still lined with some old *cabanons* – simple rickety shacks built by fishermen or as weekend homes by the ordinary workers of Marseille –that are now considered part of the region's architectural heritage. Further east, Sugiton, accessible by foot from Luminy in the north-east of Marseille, sits under a sheer cliff face favoured by rock-climbers, while its flat, waterside rocks attract nude bathers.

From Cassis the first inlet, the only one reachable by car, is Port-Miou; this is dedicated to harbouring yachts. The second is Port-Pin, so named for the shrubby pines that decorate its rocky walls, with a small sandy beach. The breathtaking Calanque d'En-Vau, about an hour's walk further on, has a difficult descent at the end, where white cliffs fall into water of the deepest blue-green imaginable. A sandy white beach adorns one end.

The Grotte Cosquier, an underwater cave covered with prehistoric paintings, is closed to the public, but diving expeditions can be organised from Marseille and Cassis to other underwater caves and shipwrecks. ❑

LEFT: Port-Miou, first inlet on the route from Cassis.

AIX-EN-PROVENCE

Elegant, aristocratic Aix-en-Provence is the former capital of Provence. Seat of a prestigious university, the home town of Emile Zola and Paul Cézanne is still a delightful place to visit with its handsome town houses, bubbling fountains, smart shops and lively café society

Roman spa and garrison town, former capital of the counts of Provence and historic university city, **Aix-en-Provence** is still the epitome of civilised aristocratic Provence. The Romans first founded Aquae Sextiae – so named for its hot springs – in 122 BC, after conquering the nearby Ligurian settlement of Entremont. It was overshadowed, however, by Marseille and Arles until the 15th century when "Good" King René, count of Provence and Anjou, made it his city of preference, and a cultural as well as political capital. René's death brought Provence under the rule of the French crown, and Aix was made the seat of a parliament designed to keep the region under Gallic control.

Much of Aix's renowned architecture dates from this period of prosperity, as the parliamentarians and wealthy burghers built themselves fine town houses and lavish country *bastides*. During the Industrial Revolution, Aix fell back under Marseille's shadow. In the 20th century, however, new industries managed to find a niche here: the city remains the European capital for prepared almonds, but it also has a growing high-tech industry and the region's main law courts. Whole new university, business and residential districts have grown up around the historic centre. Today, Aix is particularly renowned as a university town (of its 150,000 inhabitants around 40,000 are students).

Cours Mirabeau

The best place to begin exploring the city is the **cours Mirabeau** Ⓐ, which marks the dividing line between Vieil Aix (Old Aix), the commercial heart of the city, and the aristocratic Quartier

Main attractions

COURS MIRABEAU
MORNING MARKET ON PLACE RICHELME
RUE GASTON DE SAPORTA
CATHÉDRALE ST-SAUVEUR
MUSÉE GRANET
ATELIER PAUL CÉZANNE
BALLET PRELJOCAJ - PAVILLON NOIR

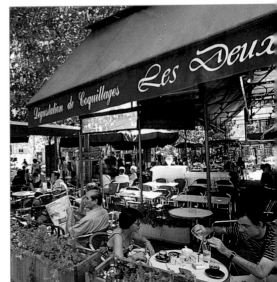

LEFT: handsome architecture in Aix.
RIGHT: Les Deux Garçons, cours Mirabeau.

TIP

Aix's culinary speciality is the white diamond-shaped *calisson d'Aix*, made out of a mixture of sugar, almonds and preserved melon. You'll find them at most patisseries and chocolate shops.

Mazarin. Laid out in the 17th century as a carriageway on the trace of the old ramparts, the tree-lined avenue is flanked by café terraces and punctuated by fountains: the Fontaine du Roi René with a 19th-century sculpture of the king by David d'Angers, the Fontaine des Neuf Canons, the Fontaine d'Eau Chaude, which burbles out water at a constant 34°C (93°F), and at the western entrance to the avenue, the ornate **Fontaine de la Rotonde 𝐁**, on place du Général de Gaulle. You'll also find the tourist office here. West of La Rotonde, beyond the new Allées Provençales pedestrian shopping street, a modern arts district has been developing *(see box on page 117)*.

About two-thirds of the way up the cours, the **Café des Deux Garçons**, affectionately dubbed "les Deux Gs", is an Aix institution, an intellectual hub since 1792; the café's terrace is still the ideal place for people-watching. Just a couple of

doors up at No. 55 once stood the *chapellerie* – hat shop – of Cézanne's father Louis Auguste, where Paul Cézanne lived when a child.

Vieil Aix

North of cours Mirabeau, the largely medieval narrow streets of **Vieil Aix** are the beating heart of the city: a tangle of small squares and ancient buildings, many with carved heads looming over doorways, and busy with fashion shops and snack stalls.

On rue Espariat you can see the Baroque church of St-Esprit and the belfry of a former Augustinian monastery. At No. 6, the **Musée d'Histoire Naturelle 𝐂** (tel: 04 4227 9127; daily 10am–noon, 1–5pm; charge for over 25s) is located inside a 17th-century *hôtel particulier*, built according to the Parisian fashion with the main building at the rear of a fine entrance courtyard. The collection's star attraction is the thousands of dinosaur eggs found on Montagne Ste-Victoire.

BELOW: busking on the Place de l'Hôtel de Ville.

Aix-en-Provence

0   200 m
0   200 yds

Almost opposite is the delightful semicircular **place d'Albertas** 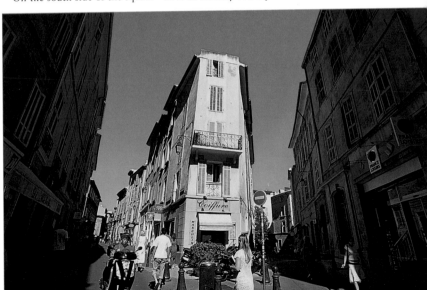. When the parliamentarian Albertas built his home in the 1720s, he also bought all the land in front of it – to "protect his view". The four contiguous buildings that now enclose the square were not constructed until 1740. Near by, **rue Aude** and **rue Fabrot** are home to many of Aix's most fashionable stores. Rue Aude runs into **place Richelme** 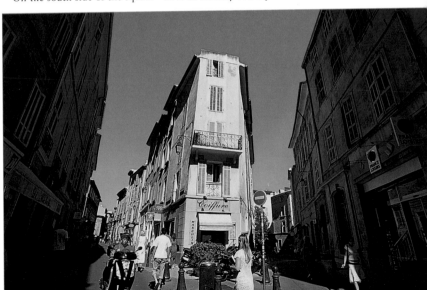, with an excellent morning fruit-and-vegetable market, which adjoins the more genteel **place de l'Hôtel de Ville** 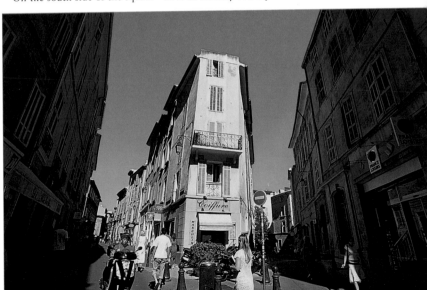, a good place to stop and have a drink or a bite to eat.

On the western side of this square is Aix's **Hôtel de Ville** (town hall), built 1655–78, originally the regional assembly of the Etats de Provence. If you go into the town hall, glance up at the beautiful wrought-iron gateway, which fans out in a representation of the sun. Inside, an elegant staircase leads up to the Salle des Etats de Provence, where regional taxes were voted, hung with portraits and mythological paintings.

On the south side of the square is **la Poste** (post office), built in the 18th century as the splendid corn exchange. Note the cavorting figures, intended to represent the Rhône and Durance rivers, that drape themselves around the pediment.

East of the town hall, small streets lead towards the place de la Madeleine, with its central gigantic obelisk, and the large Baroque church of **Ste-Marie Madeleine**, containing an *Annunciation* attributed to 15th-century Flemish painter Barthélemy Van Eyck.

On the north side of the Hôtel de Ville is the whimsical **Tour de l'Horloge**, dating from 1510. This clocktower houses four statues, each of which marks a season: in the summer, you'll see a woman holding wheat; autumn shows the wine harvest; winter has a wood-bearer, and spring appears as a woman carrying fruit and a young salmon. Originally part of the city wall, the tower marked the division between the count's city and that of the clergy around the cathedral to the north. Continue up rue Gaston de Saporta with its string of 17th-century *hôtels particuliers*.

Every Tuesday, Thursday and Saturday morning the Marché d'Aix takes over the centre of town, joining the daily fruit and vegetable stalls of place Richelme. The food and produce heart is on place de la Madeleine. Stalls of household goods, textiles and second-hand goods take over streets and squares towards the Palais de Justice and flower stands are by the Hôtel de Ville.

BELOW: Vieil Aix.

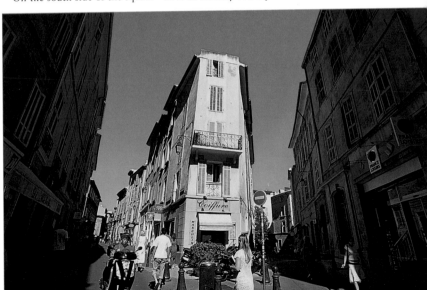

BELOW: Cathédrale St-Sauveur. **RIGHT:** detail from one of the tapestries depicting Don Quixote's exploits, Musée des Tapisseries.

Several of them are linked to the university or theatres, so you can often wander in on weekdays to see the magnificent entrance stairways.

At No. 17, the Hôtel Estienne de St-Jean contains the **Musée du Vieil Aix** (tel: 04 4221 4355; Tue–Sun 10am–noon, 2.30–6pm, until 5pm in winter; charge). The collection focuses on local folk art, including an array of mechanised puppets.

The **Cathédrale St-Sauveur** (place de l'Université; tel: 04 4221 1051; open daily but closed to tourists during services; cloister closed Sun) is an eclectic structure. Its façade combines the 12th century with the 16th, the belfry belongs to the 15th, and there are three naves in Romanesque, Gothic and Baroque styles. The highlight inside is Nicolas Froment's 15th-century triptych, *Le Buisson Ardent (The Burning Bush)*. Off the right-hand nave is the 5th-century **baptistery**, one of the rare surviving Merovingian baptisteries in Provence (others being in Fréjus and Riez).

The Baroque **Palais de l' Ancien Archevêché** (Archbishop's palace) contains the **Musée des Tapisseries** (Tapestry Museum; Wed–Mon summer 10am–6pm, winter 1.30–5pm; charge), which includes a rare series depicting the adventures of Don Quixote, from 1735. There's a section dedicated to performance arts, and the opera festival in particular. The courtyard is used for the most prestigious opera productions in Aix's Festival d'Art Lyrique *(see left)*.

Rue du Bon Pasteur leads towards the **Thermes Sextius** , now a luxury glass-and-marble spa but originally a series of 1st-century BC Roman baths (these can be seen to the right of the present entrance), fed by the water from the *Source Impériatrice*. The baths were expanded in the 18th century, and a fountain from this period is still on view to visitors.

The Quartier Mazarin

Back across the cours Mirabeau, the Quartier Mazarin was a speculative property venture laid out in the 17th century on a geometric grid plan. It still has a calmer, more discreet residential atmosphere than Vieil Aix, with its 17th- and 18th-century *hôtels particuliers*, now often housing antique shops, as well as Aix's most important museum. The **Musée Granet** (place St-Jean-de-Malte; www.museegranet-aixenprovence.fr; Tue–Sun June–Sept 11am–7pm, Oct–May noon–6pm; charge), in the former monastery of the Knights of Malta, recently reopened after restoration; it has one of the best fine art collections in Provence. Archaeological finds from the Oppidum at Entremont and from Roman Aix, 18th-century statues and portrait busts are on display, along with French paintings from the 16th to the 20th centuries, and Dutch, Flemish and Italian art, including Ingres' extraordinary and disturbing *Jupiter and Thetis*. Although the original curator spurned Cézanne, the collection now includes eight paintings by the artist, as well as a recent Philippe Meyer donation of modern art, which includes superb works by Bonnard, Mondrian, Picasso and Giacometti.

Next door is the 13th-century **St-Jean-de-Malte**. The long single-naved building was one of the first Gothic structures in Provence; note the Maltese cross carved over the

door. Further down the street at No. 41 is the Collège Mignet (then Collège Bourbon), where Cézanne went to school and became friends with the young Emile Zola.

West down the rue Cardinale lies the **Fontaine des Quatre-Dauphins** ⬤. Dating from 1667, it was the first fountain in Aix to be placed in the middle of a street rather than against a wall, giving it an unprecedented decorative purpose.

The **Musée Paul Arbaud** ⬤ (2 rue du Quatre-Septembre; tel: 04 4238 3895; Mon–Sat 2–5pm; charge) has a fine collection of Provençal faience (pottery) from Moustiers, Marseille and Apt.

Just beyond the Thermes Sextius, past a remaining turret of medieval wall, is another architectural gem, the **Pavillon Vendôme** (*see right*).

Cézanne and Vasarely

Up chemin des Lauves, north of Vieil Aix, is the **Atelier Paul Cézanne** ⬤ (9 avenue Paul-Cézanne; www.ateliercezanne.com; daily July–Aug 10am–6pm, Apr–June and Sept 10am–noon, 2–6pm, Oct–Mar until 5pm; charge),

The Pavillon Vendôme (Wed–Mon summer 10am–6pm, winter 1.30–5pm; charge). Louis de Mercoeur, duke of Vendôme and governor of Provence, built this home in 1665 so he could meet his lover here in secret.

BELOW: in the courtyard of the Atelier Paul Cézanne.

Artistic Aix

New districts are transforming the area south of the station and Vieil Aix, where university buildings, a landscaped esplanade and several important arts buildings are giving new all-year facilities to a city long dominated by its summer festival. Marked by a sculpture of a giant open book, the **Cité du Livre** (tel: 04 4291 9888) is a vast complex of library, cinema, performance and exhibition spaces, housed in a converted match factory. Next door stands the striking black concrete and glass skeletal structure of the **Ballet Preljocaj – Pavillon Noir** dance venue and the tiered structure of the **Grand Théâtre de Provence** concert hall.

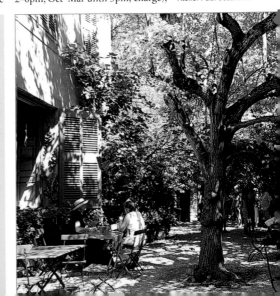

TIP

A terrible episode of Provençal history can be traced at the **Mémorial des Milles** (tel: 04 4239 1711, www. campdesmilles.org), a former tile factory to the south of the city which was used as an internment camp during World War II. Thousands of Jewish and foreign prisoners passed through here on the way to concentration camps; the refectory is painted with moving murals made by the prisoners showing the daily atrocities of internment.

BELOW: Fondation Vasarely gallery.

built by the artist in 1902; it was here that Cézanne painted his last works. The scrupulously preserved studio is an atmospheric place, still cluttered with easels, palettes and objects familiar from Cézanne's still lifes (see page 120). A steepish 15-minute walk further up the hill brings you to the plateau where Cézanne painted many of his views of the distant Montagne Ste-Victoire – or "the motif" as he called it.

The manor house at **Jas de Bouffan** (www.aixenprovencetourism.com; closed Jan–Mar; reserve at tourist office) gives a sense of the country residence it was when bought by Cézanne's father in 1859. Cézanne had a studio in the attic and painted many works directly on the walls, all since dispersed to museums around the world. Here you have to make do with a multimedia presentation in their place, but outside you can still recognise the long avenue of chestnut trees from his paintings.

Another artist who left his mark on Aix was Hungarian-born Victor Vasarely. The **Fondation Vasarely** ❶ (1 avenue Marcel-Pagnol; www.

fondationasarely.fr; tel: 04 4220 0109; Tue–Sat 10am–noon, 1–6pm; charge; take bus No. 8 from la Rotonde), on the Jas de Bouffan, is unmistakable, with its bold black-and-white Op Art architecture that is itself a piece of kinetic art.

The Montagne Ste-Victoire

East of Aix is the Montagne Ste-Victoire, ringed by the D10 road to the north and D17 to the south, which makes a pleasant excursion from Aix. Along the D10, you come to the **Barrage de Bimont** dam ❽, with its dramatic waterworks and nature reserve. Several footpaths lead to the Barrage Zola, designed by Emile Zola's father in 1854. Further along the D10 is the pretty village of **Vauvenargues** ❾, famous for its Renaissance chateau (not open to the public), bought by Picasso in 1958, where he died aged 91 in 1973. A footpath leads up onto the mountain, more accessible from this side than the vertiginous southern crags. On the D17 back towards Aix is Le Tholonet, where Cézanne rented a room to paint at the Château Noir. ❏

BEST RESTAURANTS, BARS AND CAFÉS

Restaurants

Prices for a three-course meal without wine. Many restaurants have a less expensive lunch menu:
€ = under €25
€€ = €25–40
€€€ = €40–60
€€€€ = over €60

Antoine Côté Court
19 cours Mirabeau
www.antoine-cote-court.com
Tel: 04 4293 1251. €€
With its conservatory-style setting in a courtyard, this long-standing local favourite draws a fashionable crowd for plentiful Italian food.

Bistro Latin
18 rue de la Couronne
Tel: 04 4238 2288. Open L Tue–Fri, D daily. €
This small-scale bistro in Vieil Aix serves real cooking at remarkable prices. Try southern dishes like pork fillet with honey, and a trio of *tapenade*, chickpea terrine and *brousse*, accompanied by decent Coteaux d'Aix wines.

Brasserie Léopold
2 avenue Victor Hugo
Tel: 04 4226 0124. Open L & D daily. €€
A classic brasserie near la Rotonde with excellent old-fashioned service. Vintage photos reveal that the Art-Deco interior was once a garage.

Chimère Café
15 rue Brueys
Tel: 04 4238 3000. Open D daily (except on Sun in Aug). €€
This fashionable old-town haunt has a colourful Baroque interior and a star-spangled cellar for market-inspired cooking.

Le Clos de la Violette
10 avenue de la Violette
www.closdelaviolette.com
Tel: 04 4223 3071. Open L & D Tue–Sat. €€€€
At Aix's long-standing gastronomic address, chef Jean-Marc Banzo offers light and healthy Provençal cuisine and some exceptional desserts. Dine in the garden under the chestnut trees.

Les Deux Frères
4 avenue de la Reine Astrid
www.les2freres.com
Tel: 04 4227 9032. Open L & D daily. €€
The success story of the Bouchérif brothers, this restaurant has a pared-back contemporary design, spacious terrace and a screen on which images of the excellent modern Mediterranean food are projected.

Le Formal
32 rue Espariat
www.restaurant-leformal.fr
Tel: 04 4227 0831. Open L & D Tue–Fri, D Sat. €€€
Hidden in a cool cellar in Vieil Aix, haute cuisine-trained chef Jean-Luc Le Formal modernises classic ingredients with real flair.

Le Passage
10 rue Villars
www.le-passage.fr
Tel: 04 4237 0900. Open L & D daily. €€
Reine Sammut, one of France's leading female chefs, is behind fashionable Le Passage, located in a converted sweet factory. The accomplished modern Provençal cooking is based on first-rate ingredients.

Bars and Cafés

All the great and good from Cézanne to Colette to Churchill have frequented **Les Deux Garçons** (53 cours Mirabeau), or "les Deux Gs". This intellectual hub, founded in 1792, has a perfect people-watching terrace for an aperitif and a Consular-period interior for brasserie food. Almost as venerable is **Café Grillon** at No. 49, with another fine terrace and an elegant dining room. The laid-back **Le Verdun** on place de Verdun near the Palais de Justice is very popular with the town's student population, as are the small bars on rue de la Verrerie in Vieux Aix. **La Rotonde** is a *branché* cocktail haunt with a cosmopolitan menu, overlooking the Rotonde fountain.

RIGHT: Aix's many patisseries are irresistible.

CÉZANNE

Paul Cézanne, born in Aix-en-Provence in 1839, was a post-Impressionist painter whose work laid the foundations for Cubism and modern art

Cézanne's work is inextricably linked with the landscape of his native Provence, and above all the countryside around Aix-en-Provence. In the 1860s and '70s he alternated between Paris, Auvers-sur-Oise and Aix, meeting Pissarro and forming part of the circle of Impressionists, with whom he exhibited in 1874 and 1877. Paradoxically though, for an artist seen as one of the forerunners of modern art, Cézanne mistrusted modernity and industrialisation.

Cézanne's favourite *motif* or subject was the Montagne Ste-Victoire. A tireless walker, he spent many hours on the mountain, first as a schoolboy with his friend Emile Zola, later carrying up his easel and bag. He depicts it in over 80 oils and watercolours, searching the key to its structure: "To paint a landscape well, I must first discover its geological characteristics," he wrote. In the mountain, Cézanne found the geometrical ordering of nature – "Nature must be treated by the cylinder, the sphere, the cone..." – that would lead him towards a new concept of perspective. Moving away from the Impressionists' moulding through light and colour, he developed a relationship with landscape that approaches abstraction and prefigures the Cubism of Braque and Picasso.

ABOVE: his studio at chemin des Lauves, north of Vieil Aix, which has been scrupulously preserved.
LEFT: Pissarro and Cézanne.
BELOW: *The Sea at l'Estaque*, 1878.

LEFT: his celebrated *Card Players* portrays two of the gardeners at his family's estate, Jas de Bouffan.

ABOVE: Montagne Ste-Victoire, the barren, limestone peak that dominates the Aixois landscape from afar, in a painting from 1900.

ABOVE: the painting *Bathers* became an inspiration for the nascent Cubist movement; Picasso and Matisse took a strong interest in it.

LEFT: *Pears and Peaches.* Cézanne altered traditional perspective, expressed in terms of successive planes of depth, by emphasising the foreground.

THE CÉZANNE TRAIL

A Cézanne trail around Aix picks out numerous spots associated with the artist. Take a leaflet from the tourist office (2 place du Général de Gaulle; tel: 04 4216 1161; www.aix enprovencetourism.com) or follow the brass medallions inserted in the pavement. You'll see the building where he was born on rue de l'Opéra, the site of his father's hat shop on 55 cours Mirabeau where he lived as a small child, the Café des Deux Garçons at No. 53, where he would often stop for an aperitif, the Collège Mignet (then Collège Bourbon) where he went to school, and the Hôtel de Ville where he got married in 1886.

The Jas de Bouffan, the family estate bought by his father, is also open to the public *(see page 118)*, and although now surrounded by modern housing you can still see the chestnut trees painted by the artist.

The Carrières de Bibémus, atmospheric disused quarries, can also be visited (reserve at tourist office) with a route taking you past views depicted by Cézanne, and the simple drystone cottage he rented to store his materials.

BELOW: *Chestnut Trees at the Jas de Bouffan, c.1885-7.* The long avenue of chestnut trees can still be seen at Jas de Bouffan.

St-Rémy and les Alpilles

Les Alpilles may not reach Alpine heights, but the jagged crags and ravines of these miniature mountains are nonetheless impressive. It was here, amid the dazzling limestone, pine woods and olive groves, that Van Gogh was inspired to paint some of his best-known works

The limestone Alpilles form the backdrop for elegant St-Rémy-de-Provence, the dramatic ruins of Les Baux-de-Provence and a cluster of chic villages, while along the Rhône, impressive castle remains serve as a reminder that this was once the frontier between France and Provence.

St-Rémy-de-Provence

The mini-capital of the Alpilles, **St-Rémy-de-Provence ❶**, makes a good base for exploring the area with its combination of archaeological remains, fine architecture and a thriving café society that gives the town a distinctly Parisian air. As in many Provençal towns, the dense network of narrow streets that makes up the old city is ringed by broad, plane tree-shaded boulevards which trace the line of the former ramparts.

On boulevard Marceau, the cavernous **Collégiale St-Martin** was rebuilt in neoclassical style in 1821 after the previous church collapsed. An enormous organ dominates the interior (recitals every Saturday at 5.30pm, July–Sept).

Behind here lies the old town, full of cafés, art galleries, smart interior-design shops, and some remarkable Renaissance houses. The 16th-century

Hôtel Mistral de Mondragon, on the corner of the main thoroughfare, rue Carnot, is home to the **Musée des Alpilles** (place Favier; Mar–Oct Tue–Sat and first Sun of month 10am–noon, 2–6pm, July–Aug until 7pm, Nov–Feb Tue–Sat and first Sun of month 2–5pm; charge). The superb Renaissance mansion has an ornate façade decorated with Ionic pilasters, carved friezes and a tower with rams' and lions' heads. An arcaded courtyard is graced by a bust of Van Gogh by Zadkine. The museum focuses

Main attractions

MUSÉE DES ALPILLES, ST-RÉMY-DE-PROVENCE
LES ANTIQUES, ST-RÉMY-DE-PROVENCE
LES BAUX-DE-PROVENCE
CHÂTEAU DU ROI RÉNÉ, TARASCON
ZOO DE LA BARBEN

LEFT: Les Baux-de-Provence.
RIGHT: Daudet's windmill.

A numbered walking trail follows the main sites in St-Rémy painted by Van Gogh, illustrated with 21 of his canvases reproduced on enamel plaques. It starts near St-Paul-de-Mausole and finishes at the Centre d'Art Présence Van Gogh. See www.saint remy-de-provence.com.

on local history and folk art, with displays on quarrying in the Alpilles, agriculture, pottery and tile-making, and collections of *santons*.

The elaborate Renaissance facade of the **Hôtel de Sade** across the square and the **Mairie** (town hall), housed in a former convent, are also worth a look. On Tuesday and Thursday evenings in summer, a craft market is held beneath the arcades fronting the square. An 18th-century residence, formerly the Centre de Présence Van Gogh, now contains the **Musée Estrine** (rue Estrine; May– Sept Tue–Sun 10.30am–12.30pm, 2– 7pm, all day Wed; Oct–Apr Tue– Sun 2–6pm, closed Dec; charge). It focuses on 20th-century art, including several paintings by Cubist artist Albert Gleizes, who lived in St-Rémy in 1939–53, and works by Alechinsky, Leroy and Rebeyrolle, although there is still an annually changing audiovisual and documentary presentation about Van Gogh.

The Van Gogh trail

Many people come to St-Rémy on the trail of Vincent Van Gogh, who checked himself into the local asylum on 8 May 1889, after an argument with Gauguin in Arles during which he sliced off part of his ear. The Dutch artist spent a year here, painting some 150 canvases. These included many of his most famous works, including *Irises* and *Starry Night*. Follow the avenue Vincent Van Gogh south of the centre to the **Monastère St-Paul-de-Mausole** (daily Apr–Sept 9.30am–7pm, Oct– Mar 10.15am–5.15pm, closed Jan; charge), the medieval monastery that houses the clinic where he stayed, which is still a psychiatric home. The pretty cloisters and the Romanesque chapel can be visited, as can a reconstruction of Van Gogh's room. Today, art plays a part in the therapy received by the psychiatric patients, whose works are displayed in the chapterhouse.

Glanum

Ancient **Glanum** lies just south of St-Paul-de-Mausole en route to Les Baux. Marking the entrance are two particularly well-preserved monuments, an arch and a mausoleum, known collectively as **Les Antiques** ❷. The **triumphal arch** straddles what was once the Via Domitia, the Roman road connecting Spain to Italy. It was built during the reign of Augustus to mark the entrance to the city of Glanum, and decorated with reliefs illustrating Caesar's conquest of Gaul. The **Mausolée de Jules**, dated 30–20 BC, is a three-tiered funereal monument built by members of a powerful Roman family in honour of their ancestors.

Slightly further up the road is the archaeological site of **Glanum** ❸ (www.monum.fr; tel: 04 9092 2379; Apr–Aug daily 9.30am–6.30pm, Sept–Mar Tue–Sun 10.30am–5pm; charge). A Celto-Ligurian sanctuary city built beside a sacred spring was succeeded during the Gallo-Greek era by a flourishing Phocaean trading post that served as a commercial and religious centre. This role continued under the Romans, until the city was virtually destroyed by invaders in the 3rd century.

The remains of baths and villas around a paved main street have been unearthed, as has a separate district of temples, where a couple of facsimile columns provide a sense of scale. Even if it is not easy to work out what the different remains represent, the setting – a hollow in the mountains – is remarkably beautiful.

Les Baux-de-Provence

For a change of scenery, take the D5 south from St-Rémy and then the D27A, climbing up through wooded hills and the award-winning vineyards of the Mas de la Dame towards spectacularly situated **Les Baux-de-Provence** ❹. The name Baux comes from *baou*, Provençal

for rocky spur, and gave its name to bauxite, the reddish ore, which was discovered near here by geologist Pierre Berthier in 1821.

Although Les Baux has been inhabited for 5,000 years, its fame derives from the period between the 11th and 14th centuries when the arrogant lords of Baux made their presence felt throughout the region. Today, more than 1½ million tourists a year come to see where the lords raged and troubadours once roamed. In July and August Les Baux resembles a theme park, its streets thronged with coachloads of tourists, and souvenir shops and ice-cream parlours spill out of old buildings. Visit in early spring, autumn or on a crisp winter's day, and you can appreciate this extraordinary place in relative calm.

The site divides into two parts: the "Château", which contains the ruins of the feudal court, and the partially ruined "Village" below it, an attractive mixture of shops and galleries set in medieval and Renaissance houses. One well-restored house contains the **Musée Yves Brayer** (Hôtel Porcelet, rue de l'Eglise; www.yvesbrayer.

TIP

St-Rémy is a good place to come for those interested in herbalism and aromatherapy. There are many charming shops selling essential oils, soaps and more. The boutique Florame also has a small museum, the Musée des Arômes, a collection of perfume bottles and alambics. Find it at 34 boulevard Mirabeau; tel: 04 3260 0518; www.florame.com

BELOW: Glanum.

The feudal life of Les Baux presents a fascinating paradox. Here, amidst these "impregnable fortresses, inhabited by men whose roughness was only matched by that of their suits of armour, the 'Respect of the Lady' and ritual adoration of her beauty was born." The patronage of the troubadours by these lords gave rise to the chivalric code, and a tradition of romantic poetry emerged from the bloody citadel.

com; Apr–Sept daily 10am–12.30pm, 2.30–6.30pm, Oct–Mar Wed–Mon until 5.30pm, closed Jan–mid-Feb; charge) with paintings of the region by the popular landscape artist (1907-90). The **Fondation Louis Jou** (Hôtel Brion, Grande Rue; tel: 04 9054 3417; Apr–Dec Thur–Mon 11am–1pm, 2–6pm; charge) offers guided tours of typographer and publisher Louis Jou's collection of antiquarian books, engravings, presses and woodblocks.

Best-preserved of all the monuments in the old city is the **Eglise St-Vincent**, which has a central nave dating back to the 12th century and stained glass that is a striking *mélange* of ancient and modern. Across the road is the lovely 17th-century **Chapelle des Pénitents Blancs**, painted with Nativity scenes by Brayer in 1974.

The castle and its ramparts

The "Cité Morte" or **Château des Baux** (www.chateau-baux-provence.com; daily summer 9am–7.30pm, winter 9.30am–5pm/6.30pm; charge), stronghold of the lords of Baux, is entered through the rectangular Tour de Brau, dating from the late 14th century. Beside it lies a small modern cemetery filled with lavender, and the 12th-century **Chapelle de St-Blaise**. Press on to the highest point of the ruins, where a round tower stands. The view from here is incredible: on one side, the crags of the Alpilles, on the other, a sheer drop to the rolling vineyards and olive groves. Much of the Château is a big open space, dotted with reproductions of a giant catapult and other siege warfare machines, which are put into action four times a day between April and September. By the northern ramparts, investigate what is left of the 15th-century castle, the 10th-century keep and the Paravelle tower, as well as some troglodyte dwellings.

For more breathtaking views head northwards out of Les Baux on the D27, which winds along a perilous precipice overlooking the **Val d'Enfer** (valley of hell), said to have inspired Dante's *Hell*. Just outside Les Baux, stop off at the **Cathédrale d'Images** (rte de Maillane; www.cathedrale-images.com; tel: 04 9054 3865; Mar–Dec daily 10am–6pm, Apr–Sept until 7pm;

charge), a vast former quarry where a sophisticated *son et lumière* show, which changes annually, is projected onto the rocky walls.

Olive country

Head south of Les Baux and you're in vine and olive country. Gentrified **Maussane-les-Alpilles** ❺ and more workaday **Mouriès** ❻ vie for the title of the village with the most olive trees in France, and both have reputable olive mills. Others swear by the olives of **Aureille** ❼, a half-forgotten town a little further east, with a friendly central bar and the ruins of an 11th-century castle rising above it on a hill that is only accessible on foot.

North of here, **Eygalières** ❽ provides some of the prettiest perspectives in the Alpilles with its cluster of old houses climbing up a small hill and, 1 km (½ mile) outside the village, the quaint Romanesque Chapelle St-Sixte, ringed by cypresses.

Daudet's Windmill

Towards Arles and west of Maussane-les-Alpilles, the picturesque town of **Fontvieille** ❾ is notable for its series of modest oratories, erected in 1721 in thanksgiving for an end to the plague. The town's primary attraction is the **Moulin de Daudet**, immortalised in Alphonse Daudet's (1840–97) *Letters from My Windmill*. The fact that the windmill actually belonged to Daudet's friends and witnessed little penmanship has done little to deter the hordes of tourists that crowd its tiny interior. The mill does enjoy a picturesque location and contains some interesting features, such as a circular ceiling inscribed compass-fashion with the names of the winds that sweep the hill. However, the narrow underground museum is rather disappointing.

Tarascon

Bordering the Rhône, 14km (6 miles) west of St-Rémy, the historic town of **Tarascon** ❿ became the stuff of

Provençal legend in AD 48 when its resident monster, the Tarasque, was tamed by St Martha *(see page 128)*. By the Middle Ages the town had become an important place of pilgrimage thanks to the saint's relics, which are held in the crypt of the **Collégiale Ste-Marthe**. The church also contains some of the countless paintings of Martha and the Tarasque that exist, while a marble Tarasque de Noves sculpture sits in the archaeological museum in Avignon.

The feudal **Château du Roi René** (daily June–Sept 9.30am–6.30pm, Oct–Jan until 5pm, Feb–May until 5.30pm; charge) on the banks of the Rhône is a grandiose affair. The castle was begun in 1400 by Louis II d'Anjou and completed by his son Good King René, who turned it into a sumptuous Renaissance palace. The building proudly rivals the Château de Beaucaire on the opposite bank, built from the same white limestone. The interior of the Château du Roi René is mostly empty, apart from six magnificent 17th-century Flemish tapestries and the reconstructed interior of an old pharmacy.

TIP

Olive oil AOC Les Baux-de-Provence is made from a blend of oils. Two mills making high-quality oil according to traditional methods are the 17th-century Moulin Jean-Marie Cornille (rue Charloun-Rien, Maussane-les-Alpilles; tel: 04 9054 3237; open Mon–Sat), and the recently constructed Moulin de Calanquet (vieux chemin d'Arles, St-Rémy-de-Provence; tel: 04 3260 0950; open daily).

BELOW: olive grove, Vallée des Baux.

According to legend a scaly amphibious monster had for years terrorised the people of Tarascon, drinking the Rhône dry and devouring villagers. In the 1st century, Martha, member of the saintly boat from Bethany crew (see page 23) tamed the beast, then converted the grateful and hitherto pagan Tarasconnais to Christianity. Tarascon celebrates the legend with the annual Fête de la Tarasque.

Architectural highlights in the old town itself include the three fortified gateways, the Renaissance cloisters of the former Couvent des Cordeliers and the arcaded rue des Halles. On rue Proudhon, the Hôtel d'Aiminy now contains the **Musée Soleïado** (www.souleiado.com; tel: 04 9091 5011; Mar–Dec Mon–Sat 10am–12.30pm, 2.30–6pm/7pm; charge), with a collection of woodblocks, printed *indiennes*, costumes, pottery and objects belonging to the Tarascon textile house *(see box below)*.

Beaucaire

Across the Rhône, Tarascon's twin and historic rival **Beaucaire** ⓫ grew up as a stop on the Via Domitia. The town is dominated by the ruined stronghold of the medieval counts of Toulouse – and later of the French king from where he could keep an eye on Provence. The massive **castle ruins** (tourist office 04 6659 2657; mid-Mar–Oct, closed Tue, times vary; free) are used as a site for eagle and falconry displays, and there's a small archaeology museum. The castle was destroyed on the orders of Richelieu

in 1632 when it was a Huguenot stronghold but the town continued to prosper in the 17th and 18th centuries when wealthy merchants built themselves fine houses, thanks to its river port and 10-day-long annual fair, the Foire de la Madeleine. Beaucaire's importance as a port was confirmed with the construction of the Canal du Rhône à Sète in the 19th century, and the town still has a lively port at its heart, with numerous quayside cafés, moored barges and companies offering boat trips on the Rhône to the Camargue or along the canal to Sète.

On a hill just north of Beaucaire, the **Abbaye de St-Roman** (www.abaye-saint-roman.com; July–Aug daily 10am–1pm, 2–7pm, Apr–June and Sept Tue–Sun 10am–1pm, 2–6pm, Mar, Oct Tue–Sun 2–5pm, Nov–Mar Sun only except during school hols; charge) is a fascinating ancient troglodyte abbey. Allow a 15-minute climb from the car park to explore the remains of individual cells and chapel carved out of the rock between the 5th and 14th centuries by hermits and Benedictine monks.

Provençal Textiles

Today no Provençal hotel or restaurant seems to be without its colourful Provençal print curtains and tablecloths, still called *indiennes* after the woodblock-printed textiles first imported from India in the 17th century. The prints soon became a craze adopted by the latest fashions and copied by local manufacturers in kaleidoscopic floral and geometric patterns. Although Louis XIV's minister Colbert banned their production in France in 1686 to protect the Compagnie des Indes, and local manufacturers moved to Orange within the Comtat Venaissin, production in Provence flourished again when the law was repealed in 1759. The original Indian designs were gradually replaced by the classic Provençal motifs of lavender, olives, sunflowers, cicadas, mimosas and lemons.

Two companies continue to produce quality traditional *indiennes*, although even they are no longer printed by hand: Les Olivades, at St-Etienne-des-Grès in the Alpilles, produces fabrics from both modern designs and those based on 17th- and 18th-century fabrics, and Soleïado, which uses motifs from its huge archive of old woodblocks and is based in Tarascon *(see above)*.

The Petite Crau

Between Avignon and St-Rémy, **Châteaurenard** is a quiet Provençal town – except during its colourful horse-drawn wagon parades *(see page 146)* – set amid a network of 17th-century canals that turned the Petite Crau plain into a major centre for market gardening.

You may want to make a quick sweep through **Noves** ⓭, to the east. The town today has little to attract tourists (all that remains of its chateau are segments of the 14th-century ramparts), but it was here that Petrarch first laid eyes on his beloved Laura, about whom he would later write some of the world's most famous love poems. The wine grown on the neighbouring hillsides is called the *Cuvée des Amours* (love's vintage).

Another town of literary significance crops up on the D5 between St-Rémy-de-Provence and Graveson. **Maillane** ⓮ was both the birth and burial place of Frédéric Mistral *(see page 28)*. The house where the poet lived from 1876 until his death in 1914 has been turned into a museum.

The **Musée Frédéric Mistral** (11 avenue Lamartine; tel: 04 3261 9386; Tue–Sun times vary; charge), contains his desk and gloves just as he left them, while the house, Maison du Lézard, where he lived earlier with his mother now contains the tourist office and public library. He is buried in the cemetery down the street.

Salon-de-Provence

South of the Alpilles, the landscape changes radically as you cross the Grande Crau plain, an area of sheep pasture and hay cultivation centred around the market town of **St-Martin-de-Crau** ⓯. Here, a small **Ecomusée** (Mon–Sat 9am–noon, 2–6pm; free) in an old sheepfold explains the local habitat and agriculture.

Situated on the eastern edge of the Crau, the sprawling, dusty traffic-filled **Salon-de-Provence** ⓰ has been dubbed the "crossroads of Provence" for its central location. Its role in the olive oil trade, aided by the arrival of the railway in the late 19th century, turned it into the heart of the soap industry. A few of the elaborate villas built by the soap barons survive,

Transhumance *is the moving of sheep flocks between their winter grazing on the Crau plain and summer grazing up in the Alps. The practice is celebrated each year with a festival in St-Rémy.*

Below: horse-drawn wagon parade in Châteaurenard.

Nostradamus died in Salon in 1566. His tomb is marked with a plaque which reads: "Here lie the bones of Michel de Nostradame, alone at the judgement of humans worthy of knowing the stars of the future. He lived 62 years, 6 months and 17 days."

BELOW:
Château de l'Emperi.

mostly on and around rue de la République, though only two companies still make soap. **Marius Fabre** (148 avenue Paul Bourret) has been in operation here since 1900. You can see how the soap is made on tours of the factory (10.30am every Mon and Thur, Mon–Fri in July–Aug). There is also a small **museum** (www.mariusfabre.fr; tel: 04 9053 8275; Mon–Thur 8.30am–noon, 2–5pm, Fri 8.30am–noon, 2–4pm; free).

The town is dominated by the forbidding turrets of the **Château de l'Emperi**, built between the 10th and 16th centuries as a residence of the bishops of Arles. Inside, the **Musée de l'Emperi** (Wed–Mon 10am–noon, 2–6pm, with exceptions; charge) showcases one of France's largest collections of militaria, dating from 1700 to 1918. Several rooms are dedicated to the Napoleonic era, with the diminutive general's short blue bed among the treasures.

The hub of the town is the cours Gimon, where you'll find the 17th-century Hôtel de Ville and tourist hotspot, the **Maison de Nostradamus** (13 rue Nostradamus; Mon–

Fri 9am–noon, 2–6pm, Sat–Sun 2–6pm; charge), where the renowned physician-turned-astrologer wrote his famous book of predictions. It has been turned into a waxworks experience, with ten scenes recounting episodes from his life.

Also in the old town is the beautiful early Gothic Eglise St-Michel, dating from 1220 to 1239. Lying outside the old town walls is the grander Eglise St-Laurent, built in characteristically sombre Provençal Gothic style. In the Lady Chapel is the tomb of Nostradamus, who died in Salon in 1566, marked with a plaque which reads: "Here lie the bones of Michel de Nostradame, alone at the judgement of humans worthy of knowing the stars of the future. He lived 62 years, 6 months and 17 days."

A second famous inhabitant of Salon, Adam de Craponne, the 16th-century engineer who transformed the dry Crau plain by constructing an irrigation canal from the Durance River, is commemorated by a statue in front of the Hôtel de Ville.

Château de la Barben

Six km (4 miles) east of Salon-de-Provence on the D572/D22, the impressive **Château de la Barben** ⑰ (tel: 04 9055 2541; guided visits daily 11am, 2pm, 3pm, 4pm, plus 5pm and 6pm in July–Aug; charge) is yet another of Good King René's castles. Its formal gardens were laid out by the landscape gardener of Versailles, Le Nôtre. In the centre is a fountain in which Napoleon's sister, Pauline Bonaparte, liked to bathe *au naturel*.

Outside the chateau, the **Zoo de la Barben** (www.zoolabarben.com; daily July–Aug 9.30am–7pm, Sept–mid-Nov and mid-Feb–June 10am–6pm, mid-Nov–mid-Feb 10am–5.30pm; charge) is the largest zoo in the region, where some 120 species of animal have the run of the grounds. ❑

RESTAURANTS AND BARS

Restaurants

Prices for a three-course meal without wine. Many restaurants have a less expensive lunch menu:
€ = under €25
€€ = €25–40
€€€ = €40–60
€€€€ = over €60

Les Baux-de-Provence
Hostellerie de la Reine Jeanne
Grande Rue
www.la-reinejeanne.com
Tel: 04 9054 3206. Open L & D daily. €
Les Baux's chic eateries hide out in the hills, but if you want to eat in the village itself, then this place offers reliable traditional Provençal cooking and lovely views. Garlicky lamb from the Alpilles is a speciality.

L'Oustou de la Baumanière
Val d'Enfer
www.oustoudebaumaniere.com
Tel: 04 9054 3307. Open L & D daily (closed Wed and L Thur in winter). Closed Feb.
€€€€
The luxurious *bastide* of Jean-André Charial is the place for a gastronomic splurge and draws a jet-set clientele from heads of state to film stars, for cuisine based on home-grown vegetables and a magnificent wine list.

Talented chef Sylvestre Wahid, previously chez Ducasse, produces dishes like gently spiced spider crab.

Eygalières
Chez Bru
route d'Orgon
www.chezbru.com
Tel: 04 9090 6034. Open L Wed–Sun, D Tue–Sun (closed D Sun in winter). Closed Jan–mid-Mar. €€€€
Flamboyant Belgian chef Wout Bru has moved to stylish new premises amid vineyards 4km outside the village. His trademark is a light, inventive blend of flavours and textures and sweet-and-sour mixes. Book well ahead.

Fontvieille
Villa Regalido
rue Frédéric Mistral
www.laregalido.com
Tel: 04 9054 6022. Open L & D Tue–Sat, L Sun. €€
Grand classic cuisine is served in the vaulted dining room of a restored olive-oil mill. Dishes such as monkfish in Châteauneuf-du-Pape wine sauce are a culinary and aesthetic treat.

La Paradou
Bistrot La Petite France
55 avenue de la Vallée-de-Baux. www.lapetitefrance.info

Tel: 04 9054 4191. Open L & D Fri–Tue, D only Wed. Closed mid-Oct–early Dec.
€€
In a pretty beamed stone farmhouse, simple home-cooked dishes like garlicky lamb, Camargue bull stew, Ventoux pork and sea bream in *beurre blanc* sauce make the most of local produce.

St-Rémy-de-Provence
Alain Assaud
13 boulevard Marceau
Tel: 04 9092 3711. Open L & D Mon–Tue and Fri–Sat, D only Thur, Sun. €€
It may look like no more than a stone-walled café, but don't be deceived – the food here is surprisingly

sophisticated. Try the *aioli* with fresh cod and leave room for the excellent desserts and sorbets.

Bistrot Découverte
19 boulevard Victor Hugo
www.bistrotdecouverte.com
Tel: 04 9092 3449. Open L Tue–Sun, D Tue–Sat. €€
Wine sommelier Claude and wife Dana opened this attractive little bistro in 2005. The menu might include dishes such as an accomplished risotto with *girolles*, the fish of the day or roast veal with seasonal vegetables, accompanied by well-chosen wines. The cellar contains a wine shop and can be used for tastings.

RIGHT: an artisan bakery.

ARLES AND THE CAMARGUE

The Rhône delta city of Arles is a delightful maze of
Roman remains, Romanesque churches, noble
town houses and sun-dappled cafés. Arles is
also gateway to the Camargue, an area of
desolate beauty, famed for its white horses,
pink flamingos, black bulls and cowboys

Nice
Marseille

Despite its grand past and impressive architectural heritage,
Arles ❶ still has an intimate,
villagey atmosphere that makes it
easily accessible to the visitor. While
the Arlesiens are fiercely proud of
their past and dedicated to upholding
Provençal and, especially, Camarguais
traditions, the town also has an active
cultural scene. Home to a world
music festival and one of France's
most respected publishing houses,
Actes Sud, it also hosts the annual
Rencontres de la Photographie.

Arles in its heyday

Founded by the Massilians as a trading post in the 6th century BC, Arles'
position at the crossroads of the
Rhône and the Via Aurelia made it
a natural choice for development by
the Romans. The town grew slowly
for several hundred years, cementing
its position as a river and maritime
port. Then, during the struggle for
power between Caesar and Pompey,
Arles got its lucky break. Marseille
made the fatal error of showing
friendship towards Pompey, and
Caesar turned to Arles, known for its
skilled boatbuilders, with the request
that 12 war vessels be built for him
within 30 days. The city complied,

and Arles' good fortune was sealed.
Caesar designated Arles the first city
of Provence, leading to the construction of temples, baths, the theatre,
amphitheatre and circus.

The city continued to prosper, and
was briefly capital of the 10th-century
kingdom of Bourgogne-Provence.
Although its predominance waned
over the following centuries, Arles
enjoyed a new period of prosperity in
the 16th and 17th centuries, reflected
in the fine Renaissance and classical
town houses of local landowners. It

Main attractions

SATURDAY MARKET ON BOULEVARD
  DES LICES, ARLES
CLOÎTRE ST-TROPHIME, ARLES
PLACE DU FORUM, ARLES
ARÈNES, ARLES
LES ALYSCAMPS, ARLES
ETANG DE VACCARÈS, CAMARGUE
MARAIS DU VIGUEIRAT,
  CAMARGUE
AIGUES-MORTES

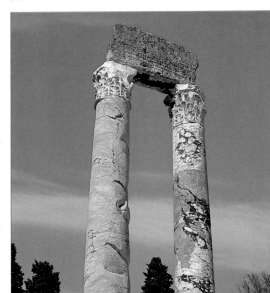

LEFT: riding is an excellent way to experience
the Camargue. **RIGHT:** Théâtre Antique, Arles.

TIP

If you're planning to do a lot of sightseeing, invest in the Pass Monuments, which gives access to all the ancient monuments and museums in Arles. Available from the tourist office, museums and monuments. For more information see www.arlestourisme.com.

remained a key maritime and river port right until the advent of the steam engine. With the construction of the Marseille-Avignon railway (later the Paris-Lyon-Marseille line) in the 1840s, Arles' economy took a new direction. It became a centre for the construction and repair of locomotives that employed generations of workers until the SNCF ateliers closed in 1984.

The Vieille Ville

At the heart of Arles is the **Vieille Ville** (old town), an attractive maze of narrow stone streets where crumbling Roman edifices mingle with sturdy medieval stonework and elegant classical town houses. The old town is bordered to the south by the wide boulevard des Lices, to the east by the remnants of ancient ramparts and to the north and west by the grand sweep of the River Rhône.

Most visitors will arrive in Arles via the boulevard des Lices. If you have a car, it's a good idea to leave it in the car park on the street's south side. Almost all of the main sights are within easy walking distance. Although often traffic-clogged, the boulevard des Lices is a lively spot with numerous cafés and the tourist office (esplanade Charles de Gaulle; www.tourisme.ville-arles.fr; tel: 04 9018 4120). Its high points come during the huge produce market on Saturday morning and the flea market on the first Wednesday of the month.

Eglise St-Trophime

The cobbled rue Jean Jaurès will bring you to the spacious **place de la République Ⓐ**, with an ancient obelisk in the middle and the 17th-century **Hôtel de Ville** (town hall) at one end, which was built following designs by Jules Hardouin-Mansart, the architect of Versailles. The most impressive building in the square, however, is the **Eglise St-Trophime Ⓑ** (daily 9am–noon, 3–7pm), named

BELOW:
portal sculptures,
St-Trophime.

after the saint credited with bringing Christianity to Provence. The richly carved doorway is a glorious example of the Provençal Romanesque style. Built between 1152 and 1180, its intricate tympanum shows the Last Judgement overseen by a barefoot and crowned Jesus, while dozens of winged angels soar over the archway. The barrel-vaulted nave is, at over 20 metres (60ft), the highest in Provence. To the left of the entrance, a 4th-century sarcophagus serves as a baptismal font. Further in, the life of the Virgin is depicted on a huge 17th-century Aubusson tapestry.

St-Trophime's 12th- to 14th-century **cloisters** (daily summer 9am–6.30pm, winter 10am–4.30pm; charge), Romanesque on two sides, Gothic on the other two, are a feast of intricately carved capitals, crowded with stylised figures, some depicting biblical scenes, others the life of St Trophime. The rooms above are the setting of the annual Salon des Santonniers (mid-Nov–mid-Jan), a display of traditional and contemporary nativity-scene figurines (*santons*) typical to Provence. Take a look too at the courtyard of the adjacent **Palais de l'Evêché** (bishop's palace), now part of the university, which is used for exhibitions during the Rencontres event.

Museon Arlaten

A couple of blocks down rue de la République, the **Museon Arlaten** Ⓒ (closed for renovation until 2014; www.museonarlaten.fr) occupies an imposing Renaissance mansion built over Roman remains, some of which jut up in the courtyard. Regional poet Frédéric Mistral founded this ethnographic museum and funded it with the money he was awarded when he won the Nobel Prize for literature in 1904, with the proviso that it be dedicated to all things Provençal. All the labels are in Provençal (as well as French) and the staff are dressed in traditional costume. One hall is filled with costumes, others feature amulets and charms, musical instruments, nautical and agricultural equipment, wall hangings and paintings.

The *museon* is not the only mark left on the city by the poet. A formidable **bust of Mistral** looks down over the **place du Forum** Ⓓ, once the

Traditional Arlesienne dress is still worn for local festivals and for the féria, *when Arlesiennes parade around the arena prior to the bullfighting. Fine examples can be seen at the Museon Arlaten.*

BELOW: old town, Arles.

BELOW:
bullfighters waiting to enter the arena.

commercial heart of the Roman city. A couple of columns from an ancient temple can be spotted in the façade of the Grand Hôtel Nord-Pinus. Much of Arles' nightlife is concentrated on this lively square. Several cafés, including the Café de la Nuit, done up in homage to Van Gogh's painting, make it a great place to enjoy a drink or a laid-back meal. Bullfighting aficionados frequent the Tambourin, whose walls are lined with autographed photos of local champions.

Towards the river

If you continue towards the river, you will come to the **Thermes de Constantin ❶** (rue Dominique Maisto). These 4th-century baths were once the largest in Provence, but not much remains. The **Musée Réattu ❶** (10 rue du Grand Prieuré; www. museereattu.arles.fr; July–Sept Tue–Sun 10am–7pm, Oct–June 10am–12-.30pm, 2–6.30pm; charge) across the street is far more interesting. Many of the rooms are devoted to historical paintings by Jacques Réattu (a local artist who bought the former priory in 1790) and his collection of

17th-century paintings. Much more worthwhile, however, are the collections of modern sculpture – including works by Zadkine, Richier and Toni Grand – photography, and the Picasso Donation, a collection of 57 Picasso sketches and two paintings.

The Arènes and Roman Arles

At the very heart of the old city, the **Arènes ❶** (rond-point des Arènes; tel: 04 9049 3686; daily May–Sept 9am–7pm, Mar–Apr and Oct 9am–6pm, Nov–Feb 10am–5pm, closed during féria; charge) is another place to chase Roman ghosts. It is now used for bullfights and concerts, though on summer afternoons they also put on gladiator shows. This vast amphitheatre measures an impressive 136 by 107 metres (440 by 345ft) and holds more than 20,000 spectators. Built in the 1st century AD, it is larger and older than its counterpart in Nîmes. A climb up one of the remaining medieval towers offers a view over the red-roofed expanse of the old city, its modern environs, the Rhône and the Alpilles hills beyond.

Follow the Arènes round and you'll come across another trace of ancient Arles, the neighbouring **Théâtre Antique ❶** (rue de la Calade; tel: 04 9049 3674; daily May–Sept 9am–7pm, Mar–Apr and Oct 9am–6pm, Nov–Feb 10am–5pm, closed on concert days; charge). By day, this 1st-century BC theatre equates to little more than a few piles of rubble, worn stone seating and two half-standing columns, but it makes a romantic setting for summer evening concerts.

Van Gogh in Arles

Visitors who come to Arles with the intention of making a pilgrimage to Van Gogh's old haunts may be disappointed. The Maison Jaune where he and Gauguin lived, worked and argued no longer stands, and the Café de la Nuit on place du Forum is a reconstruction. However, you can visit the **Fondation Van Gogh** (Palais de Luppé, 24 bis rond-point des Arènes; tel: 04 9049 9404; Apr–Sept daily 10am–6pm, July–Aug until 7pm, Oct–Mar Tue–Sun 11am–5pm; charge), which has a collection of works by contemporary artists in tribute to Van Gogh.

The **Espace Van Gogh** ❶ (place du Docteur Félix Rey; tel: 04 9049 3805; daily 9am–6pm; admission varies) is housed in the 16th-century hospital building where Van Gogh was treated, restored to look as it did when the artist was there. The building, set around a courtyard garden, incorporates a bookshop, library and temporary exhibition space.

Museum of Roman Arles

Once you've seen the monuments, you can learn about the former splendour of Roman Arles at the **Musée de l'Arles et de la Provence Antique** ❶ (avenue de la Première Division Française Libre; www.arles-antique.cg13.fr; Wed–Mon 10am–6pm; charge), outside the old town. Inside the striking blue triangular building, designed by Henri Ciriani, models of Roman Arles complement ancient statues, jewellery and richly carved marble sarcophagi. Among highlights are a bust of Julius Caesar and statue of Neptune recently discovered in the bed of the Rhône. Outside is the partially excavated **Circus**, used by the Romans for chariot-racing.

Also outside the centre, **Les Alyscamps** ❶ (avenue des Alyscamps; tel: 04 9049 3687; daily summer 9am–6.30pm, winter 10am–5pm; charge), an atmospheric ancient necropolis, still looks very much as it did when Van Gogh painted it in October 1888. The cemetery was begun by the Romans, but by the 4th century had been taken over by Gallic Christians. As you walk down the lane, lined with stone sarcophagi, look for the plaque that reads: "Van Gogh. Here, struck by the beauty of the site, he came to set up his easel." There is a solemn tranquillity under the poplars that makes it a favourite place for afternoon walks.

Just north of here, or an easy walk from the town centre along avenue

Four separate colour-coded walks around Arles allow you to discover different aspects of the town's heritage: blue for ancient Arles, green for medieval Arles, red for Renaissance and classical Arles, and yellow for Van Gogh. Pick up a brochure at the tourist office.

BELOW:
the Espace Van Gogh.

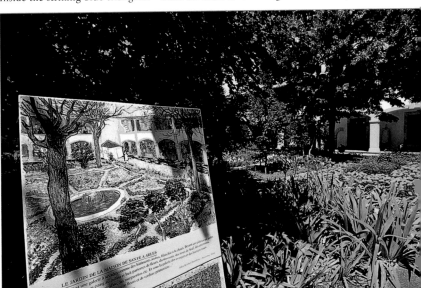

Although many major names have shown at Rencontres, including Nan Goldin, Peter Lindberg, Paolo Reversi, Hans Peter Feldmann and Martin Parr in recent years, the event is also about discoveries, with the pick of the year's graduates from Arles' Ecole National Supérieure de la Photographie, the SFR Jeunes Talents show and the Discovery Award.

BELOW: the flat plains of the Camargue.

Victor Hugo, is the **Parc des Ateliers** . The huge complex of abandoned SNCF railway repair sheds, some still with trade union graffiti on the wall and rails running across the floor, is now one of the main venues of the Rencontres Photographiques *(see margin)* and an interesting testimony to Arles' industrial past. In future the site will also contain the Fondation Luna, designed by Frank Gehry, housing studios, gallery and research facilities intended to turn the town into a year-round centre for photography.

Arles' annual summer **Rencontres de la Photographie** (www.rencontres-arles.com) brings together photographers from around the world for a panorama of exhibitions. Many take place in the historic monuments, chapels, deconsecrated churches and museums of old Arles. While the sixty or so exhibitions last until mid-September, the opening week in early July lives up to the festival's name (encounters) with a packed programme of debates, lectures, workshops and presentations, and parties with DJs and VJs. Most of the event is devoted to art and documentary photography but the *Night of the Year* pays tribute to photo-journalism.

Abbaye de Montmajour

Just 5km (3 miles) northeast of Arles, the **Abbaye de Montmajour** ❷ (route de Fontvieille; www.monum.fr; May–Aug daily 10am–6.30pm, Sept–Apr Tue–Sun 10am–5pm; charge) was founded in the 10th century by Benedictine monks who turned the island refuge, surrounded by marshland, into an oasis, by draining the swamp and building an abbey. By the Middle Ages it became rich with the thousands of pilgrims who flocked here to buy pardons. However, the abbey fell on hard times in the 18th century, when the head abbot, Cardinal de Rohan, became embroiled in a scandal involving Marie Antoinette. In the 1790s, the property was bought and stripped by antique dealers. Restoration didn't begin until 1872. The enormous 12th-century **Eglise de Notre-Dame** is a Romanesque masterpiece. The central crypt forms a perfect circle, and the restored cloister has some remarkable capitals carved with beasts, plants and little figures. For stunning views, climb to the top of the 14th-century tower.

The Camargue

Arles is the gateway to the Camargue, a mysterious, flat wild area of lagoons and marshes, rice fields and salt flats, cowboys riding white horses, herds of black bulls and thousands of flamingos that turn the waters pink in summer. Bordered to the west by the Petit-Rhône, which flows to the sea past Stes-Maries-de-la-Mer, and to the east by the Grand-Rhône, which runs down from Arles to Port St-Louis, the marshlands of the Rhône delta form an unusual natural environment that has helped shape the Camargue's unique history. The setting for one of France's greatest wildlife reserves also provides a spiritual home for the country's gypsies, stages a national windsurfing championship, and offers a range of historic towns and churches to visit as well as the joys of riding across beaches and salt plains.

The celebrated horizons that inspired the poet Frédéric Mistral and the light that fascinated Van Gogh

have also encouraged an onslaught of tourism resulting in pseudo-rustic hotels, brash campsites, and piles of debris generated by holidaymakers. In places you'll have to get around by boat, in a 4WD, on horseback or by bicycle. Some areas are best discovered on foot. Even if you spend only a few days in the region, visits to two or three well-chosen spots can reveal an amazingly rich variety of wildlife.

Getting to know the area

For a good introduction to the area, take the D570 southwest from Arles to the **Musée de la Camargue** ❸ (Mas du Pont du Rousty; tel: 04 9097 1082; Apr–Sept Wed–Mon 9am–12.30pm, 1–6pm, Oct–Mar Wed–Mon 10am–12.30pm, 1–5pm; charge). This sheep farm-cum-regional museum contains an exhibition illustrating the history, agriculture and traditional way of life of the Camargue and its different natural habitats.

A signposted footpath to the rear leads to the beginning of the marshes. The walk will take you about an hour and give you a feel for these strange flatlands and the chance to see a wide

The white horses of the Camargue, like white horses everywhere, are not born white. They are born dark brown or black and change colour as they become older.

BELOW: *gardian rounding up bulls.*

Cowboy Country

The Camargue cowboys (*gardians*) cling passionately to their traditional way of life, herding the small black bulls destined for the arenas of Nîmes or Arles, and riding their beautiful white horses in costume – flat black hat, leather chaps, high leather boots and shirts in Provençal fabric. Many still live on *manades* (bull-breeding ranches) in the Camargue, in traditional low white cabins with reed-thatched roofs and rounded north ends as protection against the blasts of the mistral wind. If you enquire about the *manades* that offer horse-riding or demonstrations, you will be able to see *gardians* at work. They can also be seen before the bullfights and *féria* in Arles and Nîmes.

TIP

Because of the lay of the land, exploration of the Camargue inevitably entails a certain amount of zigzagging, so it's worth considering basing yourself at its edge, in or near Arles, and making a series of day trips. Bear in mind it is not always possible to wander off the main track without a permit. If you hate crowds, avoid July and August, when the mosquitoes are also out in force.

variety of birds: the black-winged stilts with their long pink legs, herons, and all sorts of wading birds. Spring is the ideal season for birdwatching, as this is when the migrating birds visit the Camargue on their journey back north.

Once you've left Mas du Pont du Rousty, continue along the D570 through paddy and wheat fields, towards the Camargue's main town, Stes-Maries-de-la-Mer. En route, you'll pass numerous advertisements for roadside ranches which run half- or full-day pony-trekking and trips into the marshes. Just before Stes-Maries, the information centre at **Ginès ❹** has an exhibition about the indigenous flora and fauna. Next door is the **Parc Ornithologique de Pont de Gau** (ornithological park; tel: 04 9097 8262; daily Apr–Sept 9am–7pm, Oct–Mar 10am–5pm; charge), where you can see regional bird species in aviaries and follow birdwatching trails.

Stes-Maries-de-la-Mer

Situated at the southern tip of the Camargue, **Stes-Maries-de-la-Mer ❺** resembles a mirage after the flat landscape. The flourishing resort owes its name to a group of travellers that landed on this shore. According to legend, these early Christians had set out to sea from Palestine around AD 40 in a small boat without sails. They were miraculously washed ashore, safe and sound, at this spot. Among the saintly company were Mary Jacoby (sister of the Virgin Mary), Mary Magdalene, Mary Salome (mother of Apostles John and James), Martha and the miraculously resurrected Lazarus, along with their Egyptian servant Sarah. After their deaths, the two Marys who had stayed in the Camargue gained a cult following among newly Christianised gypsies and nomads. The town has been a place of pilgrimage ever since.

In the 9th century, the **Eglise de Notre-Dame-de-la-Mer** replaced

Arles and the Camargue

the simple chapel that existed on the site and was fortified against invading Saracens. Excavations beneath this structure, begun in 1448 at the behest of Good King René, led to the discovery of a well and a spring filled with "the fragrances of sweet-scented bodies". The remains of the saints were uncovered in this same spot and their tomb was placed in the church's Chapelle de St-Michel. The stones on which the bodies had rested are kept below in the crypt and have become "miracle" stones, said to have the power to cure infertility and heal sore eyes. Climb to the roof of the church for stunning panoramic views across the sand dunes to the sea.

Stes-Maries-de-la-Mer is a thriving summer resort, with numerous inexpensive hotels and campsites, and places where you can rent horses and boats, swim or play tennis. The little **Musée Baroncelli** (tel: 04 9097 8760; summer daily 10am–noon, 3–8pm) contains material on bullfighting and Camargue traditions donated by Marquis Folco de Baroncelli-Javon, aristocratic champion of the *gardians*.

The beaches close to town can get very busy. Frédéric Mistral, who set the tragic end of his famous work *Mireille* (*Mireio* in Provençal) on these sandy shores, would no longer be able to write of it "no trees, no shade and not a soul". There are some quieter beaches west of Stes-Maries-de-la-Mer if you brave the weathered tracks off the main road to reach them. Or you can escape the bustle with a boat trip along the Petit-Rhône. Excursions leave at regular intervals from the landing stage near Baroncelli-Javon's tomb and offer the opportunity to get close to Camargue wildlife.

Marshes and lagoons

If you turn off the D570 at Albaron, eastwards onto the D37 and then the D36, you skirt around the **Etang de Vaccarès ❻**, a huge brackish lagoon, and head into the regional park. Travelling in this direction offers excellent sightings of flamingos and other waterfowl, even from a car. On foot, a sharp eye should be able to spot beavers, turtle or lime-green tree frogs. Remember that the lagoon is a protected area. Hunting, fishing and the picking of plants and flowers are prohibited.

In May, gypsies flock to Stes-Maries-de-la-Mer to celebrate the cult of Sarah (see page 140), and on the last Sunday of October, the feast day for Mary Salome is commemorated by colourful processions around the church (above).

BELOW: flamingos on the marshland bordering Stes-Marie-de-la-Mer.

The black bulls of the Camargue also roam here, and sometimes (but not as often as postcards may have you believe) you will see a *gardian* astride his white horse. Twilight is particularly lovely here, when the setting sun casts its colours over the lagoon.

To get a closer look at the famous white horses of the Camargue, you may want to check in at one of the Camargue's "ranches", where the *gardians* take you out on horseback for a tour of the marshes. The *mas* belonging to Paul Ricard (of pastis fame) at **Méjanes** ❼, (www.mejanes.camargue.fr; tel: 04 9097 1010) is especially well publicised. Around the fortified medieval buildings of a Templar *commanderie*, you will find an efficient pony-trekking centre, and some particularly knowledgeable *gardians* willing to show off their skills, such as calf-branding.

Two further areas of protected marshland, managed by the Conservatoire du Littoral (the French coastal conservation trust) are open to the public, with footpaths and observation posts. The **Marais du Vigueirat** ❽ (www.marais-vigueirat.

reserves-naturelles.org; tel: 04 9098 7091; office and shop open Feb–Nov daily 10am–5pm, footpaths accessible sunrise–sunset) at Mas Thibert sits at the junction of two remarkable ecosystems: the marshy Rhône delta and the Crau plain; it receives numerous bird species, including storks, egrets and nine types of heron. Access is free, but ring ahead if you want to join one of the guided walks, visit in a horse-drawn cart or fish for crayfish. Located on the eastern bank of the Grand-Rhône, it is most easily reached by the D35 from Arles, although you can cross the river by the Bac de Barcarin (*see tip*) at Salin-de-Giraud.

Around Salin-de-Giraud

Southeast of the Etang de Vaccarès along the D36, the landscape changes to one of powdery white hills and salt pans. This corner of the Camargue, around **Salin-de-Giraud** ❾, a town of red-brick workers' housing, is the French capital for salt production. Over half of the country's supply comes from here, providing both table salt and road salt in winter. From March to October you can visit the salt flats

BELOW: Aigues-Mortes.

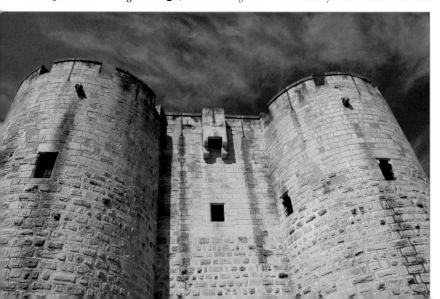

by tourist train, the last stop being the **Ecomusée du Sel** (tel: 04 4008 1404; daily July–Aug 9.30am–12.30pm, 2–7pm, Mar–June and Sept–Oct 10.15am–12.15pm, 2–6pm; museum free, charge for tours by train).

On the edge of the salt flats, southeast of Salin-de-Giraud along the D36D, the **Domaine de la Palissade** ❿, (tel: 04 4286 8128; daily 9am–5pm) is rare in that it subsists in its quasi-natural state. Continually affected by the tides, it has never been controlled by the dykes that separate the Rhône from the sea nor cultivated for agriculture, disturbed only by hunters and grazing horses. Again, several footpaths and bridleways have been created, and the reed beds and remains of dunes that trace the former coastline provide a habitat for rare plants, eels, herons and egrets.

This area is also the gateway to the Camargue's dune-backed beaches: the **Plage de Piémanson** is a well-known "clothing optional" beach, drawing an anarchic community of tents, caravans and cabanons each summer, and the even wilder, remote white sands of the **Plage de Beauduc**.

The western Camargue and Aigues-Mortes

West of the Petit-Rhône, the D58 takes you across the plain of Aigues-Mortes, a part of the Camargue that has hardly changed in decades. Every so often an authentic *cabane de gardian* comes into view – a single-storey whitewashed cabin with a thatched, mistral-defying roof. At the end of the D58, the **Tour Carbonnière** ⓫ offers a splendid view to the foothills of the Cévennes in the northwest, the Petite Camargue in the east and across the salt flats of Aigues-Mortes to the south. Built as a watchtower for the garrison of Aigues-Mortes during the Crusades, the tower was long a tollhouse guarding what was the only route in and out of town.

Aigues-Mortes ⓬ itself was built in the middle of the marsh in 1241 by King Louis IX (St Louis), who wanted a port on the Mediterranean from which to launch the Seventh Crusade in 1248. Laid out on a square grid plan, the new town was named for its location (Aigues-Mortes means "dead waters") as it contrasted with the town of Aigues-Vives ("living

TIP

All year round, a system of *bacs* (miniature ferries) carries both vehicles and horses across the Rhône. The Bac de Barcarin crosses the Grand Rhône between Salin-de-Giraud and Port St-Louis-du-Rhône; the Bac du Sauvage crosses the Petit-Rhône near Stes-Maries-de-la-Mer.

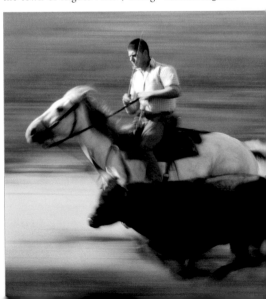

BELOW: practising for the course *camarguaise*.

Course Camarguaise

The *course camarguaise*, in which the bull is chased but not killed, is the style of bullfighting practised in towns and villages all over the Camargue and the nearby Crau and Alpilles. It is more light-hearted than Spanish-style bull-fighting (although you will also find the latter at the big *férias* in Arles and Nîmes). The *course* began as a game with lions, dogs, bears and men chasing bulls. Now the real competition is between the *manades* (bull-breeders), who raise the bulls, and the *raseteurs*, who take the animals on. In Arles, the fighting season starts with the April *féria*, when the Queen of Arles is crowned. It ends at the beginning of July with the awarding of the *Cocarde d'Or*.

Plage d'Arles, one of the Camargue's beaches, leads into Plage de Piémanson, the nudist beach along the same stretch of coast.

waters") in the hills about 20km (12 miles) further north. Aigues-Mortes flourished under its royal patronage, but the incorporation of Marseille and Provence into the French kingdom and the recession of the sea meant it didn't last long as a major port – although it is still connected to the sea by a canal that leads to the fishing village and beach resort of le Grau-du-Roi.

Today Aigues-Mortes is still contained within its remarkably intact city wall, punctuated by 20 defensive towers. Once you've passed through the gateway, narrow streets crisscross the town. They lead to place St-Louis, the main square, lined with cafés and restaurants – although you will get a better meal by wandering down the more secluded side streets in search of local specialities, such as *gardiane de taureau* (a delicious beef stew with olives) or seafood.

Dominating the town is the circular **Tour de Constance** (www.monum.fr; tel: 04 6653 6155; daily May–Aug 10am–7pm, Sept–Apr 10am–5.30pm; charge). The defensive keep, built by Louis IX, served

as both watchtower and lighthouse. It looks over the Renaissance Logis du Gouverneur, which replaced the royal palace burnt down in the 15th century. Later, the tower became an infamous prison where Protestant women were held during the 16th-century Wars of Religion. Visiting the tower also gives you access to the walk along the ramparts.

Aigues-Mortes is still a centre for salt production, vine-growing and the cultivation of asparagus and carrots. In summer, the **Salins du Midi** (route du Grau du Roi; www.salins.com; tel: 04 4286 7020; daily 10am–5pm with variations) organises tours in a little train around the crystallisation tables and evaporation basins, as well as longer expeditions in 4WD vehicles through the salt marsh.

Back inland towards Arles, **St-Gilles-du-Gard** ⑬, a busy little agricultural town hemmed in by canals, is also worth visiting, chiefly for the carvings on the western front of the town's 12th-century abbey church – a masterpiece of Provençal Romanesque architecture with a fine stone spiral staircase.   ❑

RESTAURANTS AND BARS

Restaurants

Prices for a three-course meal without wine:

€ = under €25
€€ = €25–40
€€€ = €40–60
€€€€ = over €60

Aigues-Mortes

Restaurant Marie-Rose
13 rue Pasteur
Tel: 04 6653 7984. Open D daily. €€
A lively restaurant in an old presbytery, with dishes such as rabbit with *tapenade* or little fillets of sole with *pistou*, to be accompanied by local *gris de gris* wine.

Arles

L'Apostrophe
7 place du Forum
www.lapostrophe-arles.com
Tel: 04 9096 3417. Open L & D daily. €€
A funky modern bar and brasserie with a big terrace. Food includes inventive summery salads and updated brasserie classics.

L'Atelier de Jean-Luc Rabanel
7 rue des Carmes
www.rabanel.com
Tel: 04 9091 0769. Open L & D Wed–Sun. €€€€
Innovative chef Jean-Luc Rabanel's elegant modern restaurant serves the most inventive food

in town, designed like artworks in what Rabanel calls his "gallery of culinary expression". He has also opened the simpler Bistro A Côté, which reinterprets traditional dishes, and a cookery school.

Café de la Nuit
place du Forum
Tel: 04 9096 4456. Open L & D daily. €
This brightly painted re-creation of the café immortalised by Van Gogh has a lively atmosphere and a good terrace on the square. Decent food includes pasta and Camargue bull *daube*. Touristy but fun.

La Caravelle
1 place Constantin
www.la-caravelle.net
Tel: 04 9096 3909. Open D Wed–Mon (plus L during *feria*). €€
Expect cosmopolitan dishes and a trendy young crowd at this restaurant and cocktail bar opposite the Thermes de Constantin. Food ranges from local oysters to ostrich steak.

Le Sambuc

La Chassagnette
route du Sambuc
www.chassagnette.fr
Tel: 04 9097 2696. Open L & D Thur–Tue (daily in July & Aug). Closed Wed except in July

and Aug. €€€
This spacious, stylishly converted barn southeast of Arles serves creative cuisine from Ducasse-trained young chef Armand Arnal. The dishes are inspired by the organic produce from the restaurant's own kitchen garden, along with local fish and meat from the Camargue.

St-Gilles

Le Cours
10 avenue François Griffeuille
www.hotel-le-cours.com
Tel: 04 6687 3193. Open L & D daily. Closed mid-Dec–mid-Mar. €
With its shady terrace under the plane trees

and good-value menus, the restaurant at this friendly Logis de France hotel is very popular.

Stes-Maries-de-la-Mer

Hostellerie du Pont de Gau
route d'Arles
www.pontdegau.camargue.fr
Tel: 04 9097 8153. Open L and D daily (closed Wed in winter). Closed Jan–mid-Feb. €€
Right next to the bird reserve is this serious restaurant, serving expertly prepared classic and regional dishes. Expect the menu to feature foie gras, eel stew, local bull's meat and hare, plus wild boar and other seasonal game.

RIGHT: Café de la Nuit.

FESTIVALS

Merrymaking activities take place across Provence all year round. Everything is celebrated, from saints and cowboys to lavender and lemons

Though religious observance has declined, the Christian history of Provence still influences the *fêtes* that are part of the cultural life of every village. Christian tradition is particularly obvious in the *fêtes* on Christmas Eve, when the Nativity is enacted by members of the village (one of the best-known of these is in the village of Séguret in the Vaucluse) or in the Christmas feast which ends in 13 symbolic desserts. In many cases, though, the Christian foundations of a festival have been forgotten or overlayed with new meaning, and the *fête* has become a popular celebration. The rowdy Bravades of 16 May in St-Tropez, originally to commemorate its martyred patron saint, is one example; another is the gypsy *fête et pèlerinage* to Stes-Maries-de-la-Mer. The 700-year-old pilgrimage to the town where the Boat of Bethany (carrying Mary Magdalene) landed is now famous for its energetic two-day festival *(see right)*.

Summer arts festivals abound: Avignon is known for its theatre festival, Aix-en-Provence for its prestigious opera festivals and La Roque d'Antheron and Menton for classical music. Jazz festivals are held in Nice, Ramatuelle and Juan-les-Pins, dance at Vaison-la-Romaine, and world music in Vence.

ABOVE LEFT: people on floats throw flowers into the crowds, Nice carnival. **ABOVE RIGHT:** Tarascon's dragoness La Tarasque, *c.*1910.

ABOVE: Châteaurenard's Fête des Charrettes Ramées in July is a horse-and-cart parade, part of the festival of St Eloi, patron saint of farriers.

LEFT: Maceo Parker performs during Jazz à Juan in Juan-les-Pins.

ABOVE: Roma in the Saint Sarah (patron saint of the gypsies) pilgrimage to Stes-Maries-de-la-Mer, where a two-day festival is held.

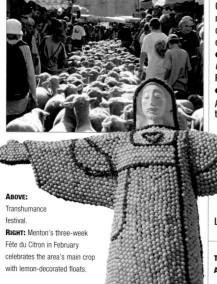

ABOVE: Transhumance festival.

RIGHT: Menton's three-week Fête du Citron in February celebrates the area's main crop with lemon-decorated floats.

FOOD AND WINE

Countless festivals across the region celebrate the richness and variety of Provençal produce: truffles, rice, mushrooms, olives, chestnuts, cherries and lemons, not to mention the many Provençal wines. All are fêted with parades, bands, fairs, fireworks and, of course, plenty of eating and drinking. Most of these festivals take place around harvest time. Some of the best:

● *Mid-September: Prémices du Riz, Arles.* Annual rice festival.
● *October: Fête de la Châtaigne, Collobrières.* Celebration of the chestnut harvest. Takes place on the last three Sundays of the month.

● *End October–early November: Journées Gourmandes, Vaison-la-Romaine.* Five-day festival of feasting on regional specialities.
● *Mid-November: Festival of the Côtes du Rhône primeurs, Avignon.* Celebration of the first wines of the year, with lots of opportunities for tasting.
● *December–February : Les Oursinades, Carry-le-Rouet.* Tastings of sea urchins and other shellfish that thrive in the shallow waters of la Côte Bleue.
● *December: Fête du Millésime, Bandol.* Lively wine festival. First Sunday of the month.

TOP: L'Isle-sur-la-Sorgue's floating market takes place every August.
ABOVE RIGHT: Truffle Mass Sunday in Richerenches, Vaucluse.

NÎMES AND THE PONT DU GARD

Nîmes is a far-sighted city which combines the ancient with the avant-garde. Alongside the 2,000-year-old amphitheatre stands Sir Norman Foster's Carré d'Art, a steel-and-glass tribute to Roman architectural flair. The nearby Pont du Gard aqueduct is another unmissable marvel on the Roman trail

Main attractions

LES ARÈNES
LA MAISON CARRÉE
LE CARRÉ D'ART
LES HALLES
MUSÉE DU VIEUX NÎMES
JARDIN DE LA FONTAINE
PONT DU GARD

BELOW:
the Pont du Gard.

Nîmes may rival Arles as the ancient Rome of France, but far from being a museum city, here ancient monuments – some of the best-preserved in Europe – co-exist with Renaissance lodgings, high-tech architecture and contemporary works of art typical of a modern multicultural city. Its lively streetlife mingles Provençal traditions with a Spanish-tinged love of bullfighting. During *féria* time the whole town resounds with flamenco music and outdoor *bodegas* set up on the boulevards. High unemployment and some dodgy housing estates have given the outskirts a slightly rough reputation, but new biotechnology companies are bringing employment opportunities and sensitive rehabilitation, while ongoing renovation programmes are keeping the old centre alive.

Nîmes' three principal Roman monuments, the Arènes, the Maison Carrée and the Tour Magne, can all be visited using one combined ticket. Visit www.arenes-nimes.com for details.

The tourist office can be found on 6 rue Auguste (www.ot-nimes.fr; tel: 04 6658 3815).

The Arènes

Originally, Nîmes was a Celtic settlement around the spring Nemausus. It then became a staging post on the road to Spain, and was the first French city to be colonised by the Romans. Almost the first thing you'll see if you arrive by train is the vast elliptical amphitheatre, the **Arènes ●** (boulevard des Arènes; www.arenes-nimes.com; tel: 04 6621 8256; daily July–Aug 9am–8pm, Mar–June, Sept–Oct 9am–6pm, Nov–Feb 9.30am–5pm, hours vary during *féria* and concerts; charge). It was built between AD 90 and 120, roughly at the same time as the Colosseum in Rome, for gladiatorial combat (*see box on page 152*). Today the amphitheatre has been restored to something approaching its former glory, and a clever glass-and-steel roof, removable in summer, allows the arena to be used for a variety of activities all year round. Most famous are the bullfights,

both the traditional Spanish *corrida* (in which they do kill the bull) and the more light-hearted, Provençal-style *course camarguaise* (in which they don't).

Several shops selling bullfighting souvenirs and toreadors' costumes can be found in the streets around the arena. The **Musée des Cultures Taurines ●** (6 rue Alexandre Ducros; tel: 04 6636 8377; Tue–Sun 10am–5.30pm; charge) contains an eclectic array of posters, costumes and miscellaneous *tauromachie* – bullfighting memorabilia.

The Maison Carrée

Behind the amphitheatre, the heart of old Nîmes lies within the shield-shaped ring, known as the escutcheon, formed by boulevards Victor Hugo, Gambetta and Amiral Courbet. Nîmes' second-most important Roman sight is the **Maison Carrée ●** (www.arenes-nimes.com; tel: 04 6621 8256; daily July–Aug 10am–8pm, Apr–June and Sept 10am–6.30pm, Oct–Mar times vary; charge), further up boulevard Victor Hugo on the western side of the old town.

The most important of Nîmes' férias is the Féria de la Pentecôte, held on Pentecost weekend in June, when bodegas fill the streets, the sangria flows and the whole town is in high festive spirits.

BELOW: rue des Arènes is in the very heart of Nîmes.

Norman Foster's Carré d'Art complements the form of the Roman temple opposite.

Known as the "square house" despite being twice as long as it is wide, the 1st-century BC structure is generally considered to be the best-preserved Roman temple in existence. It is entered up a flight of tall steps and surrounded by a set of fluted columns with carved Corinthian capitals.

Its original dedication has long been debated – some say it was dedicated to Juno, others cite Jupiter or Minerva. Like the amphitheatre, it underwent several incarnations, serving as a stable, the town hall and a monastery church temple. Inside, a 3D film presents daily life in ancient Nîmes, medieval Nîmes and during the *féria*.

Statues, frescos and other Roman and Iron Age archaeological finds can be seen at the **Musée d'Archéologie** ❶ (13bis boulevard Amiral Courbet; tel: 04 6676 7454; Tue–Sun 10am– 6pm; charge) housed in an old Jesuit college.

A superb Roman mosaic, uncovered here in 1883, holds centre stage amid the eclectic painting collection of the **Musée des Beaux-Arts E** (20–22 rue de la Cité Foulc; tel: 04 6667 3821; Tue–Sun 10am–6pm; charge).

The Carré d'Art

Facing the temple is the **Carré d'Art F** (place de la Maison Carrée; tel: 04 6676 3570; Tue–Sat 10am–6pm; permanent collection free, charge for exhibitions), a contemporary art museum and public library in a glass-and-steel building designed by the British architect Sir Norman Foster, which brilliantly echoes the form of the ancient temple. The collection focuses on European art since 1960, with particular emphasis on movements such as Arte Povera and New Realism, and work by French and Mediterranean artists. Artists well represented include Martial Raysse, Christian Boltanski and Arman.

This mix of the ancient and the modern is typical of Nîmes. There are commissioned artworks all over the city, notably a Philippe Starck bus stop (Abribus on avenue Carnot) and crocodile fountain by Martial Raysse in the place du Marché.

The origins of denim

From the Maison Carrée, rue du Général Perrier leads to Les Halles, Nîmes' excellent covered market (mornings daily). At the far end of the market, rue Nationale follows the traces of the Via Domitia to **Porte Augustus G** on boulevard Gambetta, which was one of the city's original Roman gates. It has two large arches that provided a dual carriageway for chariots, while the two smaller arches took pedestrian traffic. South of the market, explore the old town with its mix of 18th-century facades, Renaissance courtyards and medieval vaults.

On the place aux Herbes, the elegant 17th-century former bishops' palace now houses the **Musée du Vieux Nîmes H** (Tue–Sun 10am–6pm; free), which has rooms furnished with regional furniture, pottery and paintings. It also features an interesting display on the famous hard-wearing, blue cotton serge "de Nîmes" that has since conquered the world under the name of… denim.

BELOW: the 1st-century BC Maison Carrée.

BELOW RIGHT: walking on the Pont du Gard.

The neighbouring **Cathédrale** was severely damaged during the Wars of Religion, particularly violent in this town which was a major centre of Protestantism in the 16th century. The town's Protestant heritage can still be seen in the imposing Grand Temple and Petit Temple in the **Îlot Littré**, the former dyers' district situated near the tourist office.

Jardin de la Fontaine

Just west of the old town, the quai de la Fontaine leads along a canal lined with patrician houses to the lovely **Jardin de la Fontaine** (open daily). The park was laid out in the 18th century with gravel paths, canals, terraces and sculptures and is still a favourite place for the Nîmois to promenade. On one side is the so-called Temple de Diane, the ruins of a mysterious Roman sanctuary. At the top of Mont Cavalier, the **Tour Magne** watchtower (www.arenes-nimes.com; daily July–Aug 9.30am–8pm, Sept–June 9.30am–1pm, 2–6pm; charge) was built by the Celtic Volques tribe and later enlarged and incorporated within the Roman ramparts.

The Pont du Gard

The extraordinary three-storey **Pont du Gard** dates from around 50 AD and stands 27km (17 miles) northeast of Nîmes. A testament to the Romans' engineering prowess, it remains in excellent condition and stood firm against devastating floods in 1988 and 2002, when several nearby bridges collapsed. The structure spans the Gardon valley and was part of an aqueduct built to bring water along a 50km (31-mile) -long channel when the growing city's water requirements were no longer met by the Nemausus spring. At 360 metres (1,200ft) long and 48 metres (157ft) high, it was the tallest bridge that the Romans ever built.

The aqueduct is at its most stunning early in the morning or at dusk. Car parks (daily 6am–1am; charge) are on both banks. A visitor centre (www.pont dugard.fr; tel: 08 2090 3330; daily summer 9.30am–7pm, winter 9.30am–5.30pm, closed Mon morning and two weekends in Jan; charge), complete with museum, cinema, café and Ludo, an activity centre for 5- to 12-year-olds, is located on the left bank. ❏

The Arena – 2,000 Years of History

Slightly smaller than its counterpart in Arles, the two-tier arcaded oval amphitheatre could originally seat nearly 24,000 spectators, with a complex system of stairways providing access to the tiers of seats and *vomitoria* (exit tunnels). The structure was used for gladiatorial combat, wild-animal shows and the public executions of Christian martyrs, condemned slaves and foreigners, who would be thrown into the arena with wild beasts. It could also be flooded for aquatic events. The seating plan respected the social hierarchy: the lower tiers were reserved for notables, with citizens in the middle and the populace and slaves far up at the top.

Over the centuries, the amphitheatre was subjected to a variety of indignities. Visigoths substantially altered its form for use as a fortress, and it suffered further changes to accommodate a village for 2,000 poor people, with many houses and a chapel added. In the 19th century, when attempts were finally begun to unearth the original structure, it was by then concealed under 8 metres (25ft) of rubble. It now once again echoes with the sound of thundering hooves when summer bullfights are held.

RESTAURANTS, BARS AND CAFÉS

Restaurants

Prices for a three-course meal without wine. Many restaurants have a less expensive lunch menu:
€ = under €25
€€ = €25–40
€€€ = €40–60
€€€€ = over €60

La Bodéguita
3 boulevard Alphonse Daudete www.royalhotel-nimes.com
Tel: 04 6658 2829. Open L & D daily. €€
The trendy restaurant of the arty Royal Hôtel serves up grilled fish and Spanish specialities in its restaurant and tasty tapas in the bar by night, accompanied by both Nîmois and Spanish wines. A *feria* hotspot.

Le Chapon Fin
3 place du Château Fadaise
www.chaponfin-restaurant-nimes.com
Tel: 04 6667 3473. Open L & D Mon–Fri. €€
This popular, convivial bistro, plastered with Bardot posters, is a Nîmes stalwart. The traditional food includes *brandade de morue*, regional dishes and a smattering of south-western classics, such as *cassoulet*. The same team also runs Le Petit Chapon Rouge wine bar at 5 rue Vouland.

Le Ciel de Nîmes
3rd floor, Carré d'Art, 16 place de la Maison Carrée
www.lecieldenimes.fr
Tel: 04 6636 7170. Open L Tue–Sun, plus late May–Sept D Fri & Sat . €
The café at the top of the Carré d'Art is a stylish relaxed place and has the benefit of an outdoor terrace with a superb view of the Maison Carré. Light dishes are served for lunch, with cakes and desserts all afternoon. In summer it's also open for dinner, with a DJ adding to the loungey atmosphere.

Le Jardin d'Hadrien
11 rue de l'Enclos Rey
www.lejardindhadrien.fr
Tel: 04 6621 8665. Open D Tue, L & D Wed–Sat, L Sun. €€
This well-reputed restaurant has a new chef at the helm, presenting a modern take on French cuisine, served in the spacious beamed dining room. In summer, you can opt to dine outside in the lovely courtyard garden.

Le Lisita
2 boulevard des Arènes
www.lelisita.com
Tel: 04 6667 2915. Open L & D Tue–Sat (plus D Mon & Sun in July & Aug). €€€
Nîmes' gastronomic destination of choice is a collaboration between young chef Olivier Douet and sommelier Stéphane Debaille. Douet's stylishly presented modern French dishes are colourful works of art based on fresh market produce. Good selection of regional wines.

Aux Plaisirs des Halles
4 rue Littré
www.auxplaisirsdeshalles.com
Tel: 04 6636 0102. Open D Mon, L & D Tue–Sat. €€
An upmarket establishment where chef Sébastien Granier turns out excellent modern Mediterranean fare, with dishes such as scorpion fish with black olives, and meats and fish grilled *a la plancha*.

Restaurant Nicolas
1 rue Poise
Tel: 04 6667 5047. Open L & D Tue–Fri, D Sat, L Sun. €
This totally unpretentious, family-run bistro offers home cooking at prices that add up to good-value dining. Dishes are served amid exposed stone walls festooned with the obligatory bullfighting photos.

Bars and Cafés

Place aux Herbes, place du Marché and the western side of place de la Maison Carrée buzz with café life, while the Arènes is ringed by classic brasseries.

THE GORGES DU VERDON

France's very own Grand Canyon – the deepest gorges in Europe – provides spectacular views of dramatic cliffs and sheer drops to the blue-grey River Verdon below. This is a favourite area for hiking, white-water sports, paragliding and birdwatching

utting through the limestone, the River Verdon leaves a breathtaking, sweeping gorge in its wake. It flows from its source near the Col d'Allos at 2,200 metres (7,220ft) into the Durance River, 175km (108 miles) further west near Gréoux-les-Bains, marking the boundary between the *départements* of Alpes-de-Haute-Provence to the north and the Var to the south. Despite the rise in tourism, many of the villages here retain a rustic authenticity, and there are opportunities aplenty for walking, rock-climbing and white-water sports.

Grand Canyon du Verdon

The most spectacular section of the gorge is the **Grand Canyon du Verdon ❶**, the area roughly between Aiguines and Rougon. Statistics only hint at the Grand Canyon's magnificence. Around 21km (12½ miles) in length and up to 700 metres (2,300ft) deep, the vertiginous limestone cliffs were gouged out by the Verdon River when the Mediterranean receded some five million years ago. Cave dwellings, ruined castles and abandoned farms show that the gorges have been inhabited for thousands of years but by the early 20th cen-

tury the canyon was largely deserted. In the late 1940s the construction of the Corniche Sublime provided easy access. Tourism has now moved in wholesale, and the area is best avoided in August, when the roads become clogged with tour buses. Out of season, most of the restaurants and hotels will be closed, but you'll have the views and wildlife pretty much to yourself. Autumn puts on a particularly breathtaking display, when the ochres and russets of nearby trees contrast dramatically

Main attractions
GRAND CANYON DU VERDON
MOUSTIERS-STE-MARIE
CASTELLANE
MUSÉE DE LA PRÉHISTOIRE,
QUINSON
GRÉOUX-LES-BAINS

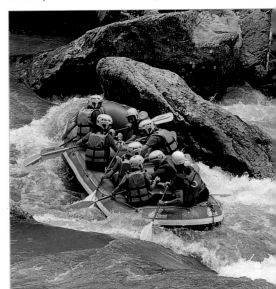

LEFT: Grand Canyon du Verdon.
RIGHT: white-water rafting.

With a wingspan of 2.5–2.8 metres (8–9ft), the griffon vulture is an impressive sight as it glides on the air currents high above the Gorges du Verdon. Easily recognisable by its white ruff and buff plumage with darker wing tips, the bird was once widespread in the mountains of southern France, but had died out. It has now been successfully reintroduced, with the 90 birds released in the Verdon Regional Park between 1999 and 2004 having formed a breeding colony.

with the turquoise waters. Whenever you travel it's worth checking with the tourist board which route they recommend, as the roads on either side of the Canyon are regularly closed for maintenance.

Moustiers-Ste-Marie

First stop on the Canyon trail is **Moustiers-Ste-Marie** ❷, where an astonishing backdrop of craggy cliffs offers a taste of what's to come. Moustiers is an attractive small town perched above a narrow torrent on the sides of a ravine. High up behind the town, the two sides of the ravine seem held together by a massive chain 225 metres (740ft) long from which a man-sized gilded star is suspended. The story goes that it was placed there by a knight fulfilling a religious vow on his return from the Crusades. The star has been replaced on a number of occasions after being blown down during storms, most recently in 1957.

During the 16th century, tanneries, paper mills and potteries flourished here. Moustiers' major claim to fame, however, is its faïence (*see box, opposite*). Established in the late 17th century by Antoine Clérissy, the recipe for the white tin glaze was believed to have come via an Italian monk from Faenza. The village streets are crammed to bursting with shops and studios producing this decorative glazed pottery, though quality is highly variable. The **Musée de la Faïence** (tel: 04 9274 6164; Apr–Oct Wed–Mon 10am–12.30pm, 2–6pm, daily until 7pm July–Aug, Nov–Mar Sat, Sun and school hols 2–5pm; closed Jan; charge), on the ground floor of the Mairie (town hall), has a good collection of historic wares by the Clérissy and Olerys families, on whom Moustiers built its reputation.

It's an energetic walk to the chapel of **Notre-Dame de Beauvoir** high above the village. The approach is from the eastern side of the stream, up 365 steps punctuated by a couple of ancient oratories and the 12 Stations of the Cross.

On the other side of the river, crossed by a small bridge, the village church on the main square has a three-storey Romanesque belfry and fine carved choir stalls.

Less than 3km (2 miles) south of Moustiers, a fork in the road offers a choice of two routes along the Grand Canyon du Verdon. Both have their virtues and require at least a half-day trip – the distance may not be long but the roads are narrow and winding.

The Corniche Sublime

Along the southern route, the D957 first skirts the man-made **Lac de Ste-Croix** ❸, an 11km (7-mile) stretch of azure water created in the 1970s by the installation of a hydroelectric dam. It is now a popular spot for hiring pedalos and canoeing and sailing, and has several beaches where you can bathe in summer. The small village of **Les Salles-sur-Verdon** was submerged by the creation of the lake and reconstructed on its eastern edge.

The D19 then dog-legs east via the village of Aiguines, continuing along the D71 to follow the southern ridge of the canyon, known as the **Corniche Sublime**. The village of **Aiguines** ❹ itself is a tranquil spot, where houses and narrow *ruelles* cluster around an attractive turreted chateau. There are many opportunities near by for climbing and rafting.

The Corniche Sublime offers consistently spectacular views, most notably those at the **Balcons de la Mescla** ❺, where the Verdon converges with the smaller canyon formed by the Artuby River. The single-span, concrete **Pont de l'Artuby** (Artuby Bridge) is a favourite spot for bungee jumpers.

East of here you can opt either to quit the Verdon and go south towards Draguignan, or head back towards the Verdon via the village of **Trigance** ❻, which sits under a vast 11th-century fortress, now a romantic hotel.

La Palud-sur-Verdon

Alternatively, the northern route along the Grand Canyon snakes along the old road to Castellane

TIP

Tourist information
Castellane: rue Nationale; tel: 04 9283 6114; www.castellane.org
Gréoux-les-Bains: 5 avenue des Marronniers; tel: 04 9278 0108; www.greoux-les-bains.com
Moustiers-Ste-Marie: place de l'Eglise; tel: 04 9274 6784; www.moustiers.eu

BELOW LEFT: Moustiers-Ste-Marie.

Faience

Moustiers-Ste-Marie has been a centre of faience (or tin-glazed earthernware) since the 16th century, when the technique was introduced by an Italian ceramicist. The industry prospered for the next 200 years, counting Madame de Pompadour among its clients.

Competition from porcelain and English bone china brought about its decline in the 19th century, and the art was not revived until the mid-1920s.

The finest indigenous clays are formed in moulds or turned on a wheel, biscuit-fired, then covered with a white tin glaze and given a second firing, resulting in a hard opaque finish, before the decoration is painted on using pigments made from various metal oxides. The most characteristic motif of the "Moustiers style" is inspired by the engravings of Jean Berain, which represent fantastic monsters, donkey musicians, monkeys and plumed birds.

The best-known of all the hiking trails is the Sentier Martel, which descends to the bed of the Grand Canyon between the Chalet de la Maline and the Point Sublime. The 15km (10-mile) trail takes around seven hours and is for experienced walkers only. Invest in a detailed map and check weather conditions before you set off.

BELOW: driving the Corniche Sublime.

(the D952). On the plain between the gorges and the Montdenier and Mourre de Chanier ridges, 19km (11 miles) from Moustiers, the village of **La Palud-sur-Verdon ❼** is a popular stop-off for hikers. It offers a few cafés and a sturdy chateau housing the **Maison des Gorges de Verdon** (www.lapaludsurverdon.com; tel: 04 9277 3202; mid-June–mid-Sept Wed–Mon 10am–1pm, 4–7pm, mid-Mar–mid-June and mid-Sept–mid-Nov Wed–Mon 10am–1pm, 4–6pm; charge), which focuses on the natural history, early inhabitants and village life of the region, as well as providing information on walks and nature trails (*see margin right*).

For the best views of the canyon, continue east out of La Palud on the D952, then turn right on the D23, the scenic **Route des Crêtes**, which brings you back in a clockwise zig-zagging loop, past a series of belvederes, to La Palud. Here you can park your car to admire the views of the gorges below and perhaps spot the impressive griffon vultures that were reintroduced here at the end of the 1990s (*see margin, page 156*).

Just before you get back to La Palud, the **Chalet de la Maline** (where there's a popular restaurant), marks one of the main routes for serious hikers down to the canyon floor, starting point for the Sentier Martel (*see left*). Back on the road to Castellane, a footpath off the D23a side road leads to the aptly named **Point Sublime ❽**, a dizzying belvedere 180 metres (600ft) above the river.

Castellane

Visitors to the gorges and traffic taking the north–south route along the Route Napoléon converge at **Castellane ❾**. Another spectacularly situated small town, Castellane, like Moustiers, has its own miracle-rendering Virgin to whom the chapel of **Notre-Dame-du-Roc**, perched on a cliff above the town, is consecrated. Count on a 30-minute walk up to the chapel, past fragments of the old ramparts. The current chapel, filled with ex-votos, dates from the 18th century, but the shrine has been a place of pilgrimage for centuries.

Napoleon paused in the town for lunch at what was then the Mairie, now the **Conservatoire des Arts et Traditions Populaires** (34 rue Nationale; tel: 04 9283 1923; Easter–Oct Tue–Sat 10am–1pm, 3–6pm, daily July–Aug; charge), a small museum of local crafts and traditions. Across the street, a fortified gateway-cum-clocktower leads into the attractive pedestrianised old quarter, where the place de l'Eglise is the scene of the annual *Fête des Fétardiers*. Held on 31 January, it commemorates the lifting of a Huguenot siege in 1586.

Back on the main street below the old quarter, arcaded place Marcel-Sauvaire is home to a lively market on Wednesday and Saturday mornings, as well as the curious **Musée des Sirènes et Fossiles** (tel: 04 9283 1923; Apr, July–Aug and Nov school hols daily 10am–1pm, 3–6.30pm, May–June and Sept Wed, Sat, Sun 10am–1pm, 3–6.30pm; charge). Run by the Geological Reserve of Haute-Provence, it is devoted to Sirenians, a group of herbivorous aquatic vertebrates, linked in mythology to mermaids. Ancestors of the sea cow and manatee that lived 40 million years ago in the nearby Vallée des Sirènes, (8km/5 miles northwest

of Castellane on the Route Napoléon, now D4085), some of their fossils can still be seen in situ on a waymarked footpath from the Col de Lèques.

Castellane has plenty of shops selling climbing equipment and organising kayak and rafting trips. For more information, contact the tourist office (*see margin, page 157*).

Quinson and the Basses-Gorges

Southwest of Moustiers the gorges are less dramatic; here you cross a sparsely inhabited landscape where little seems to have changed for centuries. One recent arrival, however, is the brilliantly presented **Musée de la Préhistoire des Gorges du Verdon** (www.museeprehistoire.com; tel 04 9274 0959; July–Aug daily 10am–8pm, Feb and Mar, Oct–mid–Dec Wed–Mon 10am–6pm, Apr–June and Sept Wed–Mon 10am–7pm; closed mid-Dec–Jan; charge) at **Quinson ⑩**, a spectacular, half-buried elliptical building designed by Sir Norman Foster. A ramp leads you back one million years as you work your way through time, past arrowheads, bones, pottery and other

TIP

If the Sentier Martel is too daunting or you are with children, the Maison des Gorges du Verdon at Le Palud-sur-Verdon sells a booklet of short waymarked walks that are easily accessible, such as the Sentiers de la Découverte du Lézard, indicated by a lizard symbol. It also organises guided walks that explore different aspects of the area. www.lapaludsur verdon.com

BELOW: the River Verdon gouges its way through the limestone rock.

Next to the village of Esparron-de-Verdon, the small man-made Lac d'Esparron is used for sailing and canoeing.

archaeological finds from some 60 sites in the region. About 500 metres outside the museum, a village has been constructed based on archaeological evidence, with dwellings from different epochs of prehistory.

You might well ask why such an ambitious museum has been created in such a tiny hamlet. The answer lies a little further down the River Verdon, where the cave known as the **Grotte de la Baume Bonne** (guided visits as part of a 3½-hour walk on Wed and Sat mornings, reserve at the museum) was discovered in 1946. First inhabited 500,000 years ago, bones of bouquetin, horses, bison, marmots and even rhinoceros and lions have been excavated here.

From Quinson a choice of roads cross the plateau, either rejoining the Verdon at **Esparron-de-Verdon** ⓫, a small village built around a chateau and next to the pretty **Lac d'Esparron** (*see left*), or heading north on the D15 to **Allemagne-en-Provence** ⓬. The L-shaped **Château** (tel: 04 9277 4678; guided visits July–mid-Sept Tue–Sun, 4pm, 5pm, Easter–June,

mid-Sept–Oct Sat–Sun 4pm, 5pm; charge) reveals both a medieval fortified aspect with its crenellations, and another, Renaissance one. The interior is noted for its fanciful moulded stucco chimneypieces.

Gréoux-les-Bains

Twelve km (8 miles) west of here, **Gréoux-les-Bains** ⓭ has been a spa town since Roman times, later a Templar stronghold. The castle courtyard is used for theatre, concerts and outdoor film screenings in summer, while exhibitions are held in the former guardroom. In the new quarter on the road towards Riez are the baths themselves. The 42°C sulphate- and magnesium-rich water still draws plenty of elderly devotees, though a modern establishment built in the 1970s has replaced the baths frequented by Pauline Bonaparte and the king of Spain in the early 1800s. Children might enjoy **Le Petit Monde d'Emilie** (16 avenue des Alpes; Apr–Oct Mon–Fri 4–7pm; charge), a small museum of period dolls and toys arranged in scenes around the rooms of an old house.

Plateau de Valensole

Sweeping northeast of Gréoux, the flat **Plateau de Valensole** ⓮ is France's leading centre for the production of lavender, but this has not always been the case. The cultivation of lavender is only a 19th-century phenomenon, important to both the fragrance and honey industries (in fact the almond trees that blossom here so spectacularly in early spring are a much more ancient mainstay of the economy). Summer is the time to see the Valensole in all its purple magnificence. On the cusp of July and into August, the dusky violet rows stretch away to the horizon and their intoxicating scent fills the air.

The few villages that huddle on the plain, surviving the winter lashings of wind and hailstorms, are for the most part unremarkable. The exception is **Riez** ⑮, 15km (10 miles) west of Moustiers on the D952, where four Corinthian columns – remains of a Roman temple of Apollo – standing alone in a field on the edge of town recall its foundation by the Emperor Augustus in the 1st century BC. Gaining enough importance in later years to become a bishopric, Riez's other "sight" is the **Merovingian baptistery** (tel: 04 9277 9909; guided visits only, 15 June–15 Sept Tue, Fri, Sat 6pm; charge), built in the 5th century reusing masonry from a Roman baths complex. The town has an appealingly scruffy old quarter, reached through two fortified gateways. Several fine houses on Grande Rue, notably the Renaissance Hôtel de Mazan, bear witness to its more illustrious past.

East of Castellane

The Verdon River keeps its luminous colour in the northern reaches. In the Vallée du Haut Verdon (Upper Verdon Valley), the **Lac de Castillon**

⑯ is edged by odd, vertically grooved rock formations that alternate with white sand spits, providing pleasant spots for swimming in summer.

The D955 follows the lake round to the east. At **St-Julien-du-Verdon**, you can branch off towards **Annot** *(see page 169)*, passing through the dramatic Col de Toutes Aures (Pass of All Winds) which lies in the shadow of the 1,878m (6,160ft) -high Pic de Chamatte. This richly forested landscape contrasts sharply with the bleak beauty of the canyon region. Here, shaly, precipitous slopes are cloaked with sweeps of dark evergreens. Minuscule villages, such as **Vergons** and **Rouaine**, consist of little more than a handful of drystone houses.

In a valley of orchards and lavender fields, at the head of the lake, sits **St-André-les-Alpes** ⑰, a haven for windsurfers, hang-gliders and anglers, and a stop on the Train des Pignes line *(see page 262)*.

North of St-André, the Verdon valley becomes progressively more Alpine as it ascends towards Colmars and its source in the Sestrière. ❏

Hidden on a garrigue-covered hill southeast of Gréoux-les-Bains, the tiny chapel dedicated to Notre-Dame-des-Oeufs (Our Lady of the Eggs) was long believed to have the power of curing infertility. Women would climb to the church on Easter Monday with an egg in each hand, eating one egg and burying the other. If the buried egg was still intact on a second pilgrimage on 8 September, the woman would be able to have children.

RESTAURANTS

Castellane
La Main à la Pâte
2 rue de la Fontaine. Tel: 04 9283 6116. Open L & D daily. Closed mid-Dec–mid-Feb. €
Copious salads and pizzas are the speciality at this establishment, which has two cheerful beamed dining rooms and an outdoor terrace.

Moustiers-Ste-Marie
La Bastide de Moustiers
chemin de Quinson
www.bastide-moustiers.com

Tel: 04 9270 4747. Open L & D Apr–Oct daily, Mar, Nov–Dec Thur–Mon. Closed Jan–Feb. €€€
The restaurant at Alain Ducasse's lovely country inn serves up refined regional cuisine, as chef Alain Souliac finds inspiration in the Bastide's kitchen garden, as well as local lamb and pigeon.

Les Santons
place de l'Eglise
www.lessantons.com
Tel: 04 9274 6648. Open D Mon & Sat, L & D Tue–Fri &

Sun. Closed Nov–Feb. €€
This pleasant bistro next to the church puts a light touch on Provençal cuisine in tasty dishes such as tomato tatin and rabbit with rosemary.

La Palud-sur-Verdon
Bar-Restaurant de la Place
Tel: 04 9277 3803. Open L & D daily. €
Bar at the front, simple restaurant at the rear. Expect hearty dishes such as *haricot de mouton* (lamb with beans) or *boudin noir* with mashed potato. Popular with the rock-climbing fraternity.

Rougon
Auberge de la Point Sublime
D952. Tel: 04 9283 6035. Open Easter–Oct L & D Fri–Tue, D Thur (plus L Thur July–Aug). €
A busy family-run restaurant and hotel with good home cooking where you can make the most of the celebrated viewpoint.

Prices for a three-course meal without wine. Many restaurants have a less expensive lunch menu:
€ = under €25
€€ = €25–40
€€€ = €40–60

DIGNE AND THE SOUTHERN ALPS

A zone of transition between the Mediterranean and the Alps, this region shows the wild, rugged face of Provence, where forbidding citadels sit on top of clifftops, and the landscape switches from rolling fields of lavender to rocky Alpine terrain

t the border between Provence and the Alps, north of the Verdon gorges, the Alpes-de-Haute-Provence is a land of beautiful lakes, bizarre rock formations and inaccessible mountainous terrain. Stark citadels crown many towns, and villages are built to give maximum protection against the elements. Like its architecture, the region's cultural heritage is characterised by its simplicity and austerity. In common with the rest of inland Provence, many villages became depopulated over the 20th century as locals moved south to work along the coast. The Route Napoléon N85, supplemented by the A51 motorway between Aix-en-Provence and Gap, makes this area a through-route for summer holiday traffic attempting to avoid the Rhône corridor, bringing additional visitors in the process.

Digne-les-Bains

Digne-les-Bains ❶, last stop on the Train des Pignes *(see page 262)*, is a genteel spa town and administrative centre in the sparsely populated Pré-Alpes de Digne. It was here that Victor Hugo set the first chapters of *Les Misérables*. However, Digne is not simply a town of fictional unfortunates,

rheumatics and departmental officials. The shady boulevard Gassendi tempts with several pleasant cafés, and in August the town hosts the Corso de la Lavande, four days of revelry where flower-decked floats parade through the town.

Architecturally, Digne's greatest attraction is the **Cathédrale de Notre-Dame-du-Bourg** (15 June–15 Sept daily 3–6pm, rest of year Sun 3–5pm), north of boulevard Gassendi on the outskirts of town. Built in the Lombardy Romanesque style that

Main attractions

MUSÉE GASSENDI, DIGNE-LES-BAINS
CITADELLE, SISTERON
LES ROCHERS DES MÉES
PRIEURÉ DE SALAGON
ENTREVAUX
MEXICAN VILLAS, BARCELONNETTE

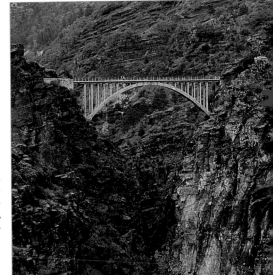

LEFT: Sisteron viewed from the citadel.
RIGHT: Gorge de Dalius.

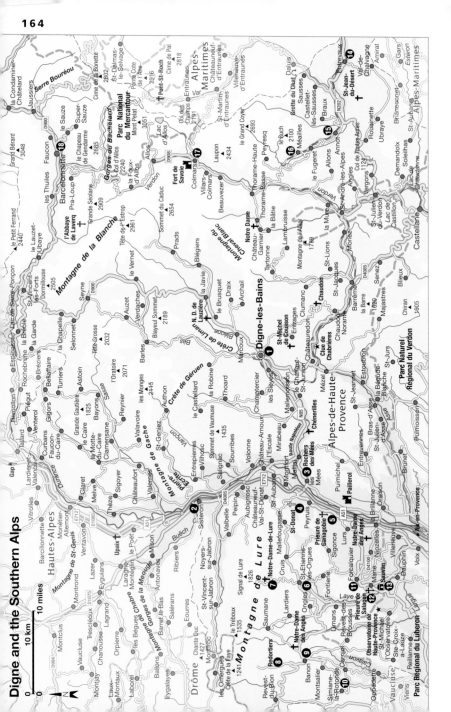

Digne and the Southern Alps

0 km 10
0 10 miles

continued to be employed in Provence long after northern France was well into the Gothic, it has a characteristic 13th-century portal in striking blue-and-white limestone guarded by two stone lions, and remnants of frescos inside. Traces of an earlier 6th-century church were revealed in recent excavations, now visible in a new archaeological crypt underneath the church (July–Sept Wed–Mon 10am–noon, 3–6pm; charge). In the later Middle Ages, a second church, the **Cathédrale St-Jérôme**, was built in the Gothic style.

Housed in a 16th-century hospice, the **Musée Gassendi** (64 boulevard Gassendi; www.museegassendi.org; tel: 04 9231 4529; Apr–Sept Wed–Mon 11am–7pm, Oct–Mar Wed–Mon 1.30–5.30pm, closed 25 Dec–1 Jan; charge) combines fine art and science and, since 2003, has reunited the two in an adventurous contemporary art project with the Réserve Géologique de Haute-Provence. Old master and regional paintings, natural history collections and the scientific instruments of 16th-century Digne-born astronomer, Pierre Gassendi, are displayed

alongside works by contemporary artists including Andy Goldsworthy *(see margin tip)*, Herman de Vries, Bertrand Plossu and Mark Dion.

Across the River Bléone, by the Pont des Arches, is the **Musée-Promenade** (www.resgeol04.org; July–Aug Mon–Fri 10am–1pm, 2–7pm, Sat–Sun opens 10.30am; Apr–June, Sept and Oct daily 9am–noon, 2–5.30pm, until 4.30pm Fri; Nov–Mar Mon–Fri 9am–noon, 2–5.30pm, until 4.30pm Fri; charge), part of the **Réserve Géologique de Haute-Provence**. Two footpaths lead from the car park through the Parc St-Benoît, past a waterfall and several outdoor works of art, and on to the museum at the top of the tufa knoll, where aquariums and a collection of fossils and prehistoric skeletons await you. Back near the car park, the **Cairn** is a centre for contemporary art exhibitions.

A particularly astonishing array of fossils can be seen at the **Dalle d'ammonites**, 4km (2½ miles) north of town on the D900A towards Barles, where over 1,500 giant ammonites protude out of what was the seabed 200 million years ago.

TIP

Refuges d'Art is a 10-day walking itinerary created by British land artist Andy Goldsworthy, starting at the *River of Earth*, a clay wall inside the Musée Gassendi, and following footpaths in the Réserve Géologique de Haute-Provence surrounding Digne. Goldsworthy has built cairn-like stone sentinels and restored abandoned farm buildings and an old chapel as *"refuges d'art"*, in some of which walkers can stop for the night. Information and reservations at Musée Gassendi.

BELOW:
Digne nestles amongst forested mountains.

Buddhist Retreat

On the outskirts of Digne is the Alexandra David-Néel Foundation (27 avenue Maréchal Juin; www.alexandra-david-neel.org; tel: 04 9231 3238; guided visits daily 10am, 2pm, 3.30pm; free). This cultural centre-cum-museum is named after a Parisian adventurer who spent much of her life travelling in remote parts of Asia. Seduced by the beauty of the Alpes-de-Haute-Provence, which she called a "Himalayas for Lilliputians", she bought a house in Digne in 1927 and named it Samten Dzong (the fortress of meditation). When she died in 1969, aged 101, David-Néel left the house and its contents to the city. The Foundation continues to attract visitors and Buddhist pilgrims.

Sisteron's citadel provides an atmospheric setting for Les Nuits de la Citadelle (www. nuitsdelacitadelle.fr), one of Provence's oldest arts festivals, founded in 1928. Each year from late July to early August it features top names in contemporary dance, theatre and classical music who perform outdoors.

BELOW:
Rochers des Mées.

Sisteron

About 40 km (25 miles) further up the Route Napoléon, **Sisteron ❷** occupies an impressive site on the Durance River, towered over by its impressive stonghold. **La Citadelle** (tel: 04 9261 2757; daily June–Sept 9am–7pm, Apr–May and Oct 9am–6pm, 1–11 Nov 9am–5pm; charge) was begun in the 13th century, then redesigned by Henri IV's military engineer Jean Erard during the 16th to double as a fortress and prison. Keeps and dungeons, watchtowers, a small chapel and crenellated battlements crowning mighty buttresses rise up on the massive rock that overshadows the town. It's a steep, sticky climb up to the fortress, so take the tourist train that runs from place de l'Eglise.

In 1944 the citadel was bombed by the Allies in an attempt to speed up the retreat of the German occupying army that had taken refuge there. More than 100 people died and the town was badly damaged. Fortunately, a good deal still remains of the **Vieille Ville** (old town), huddled at the foot of the fortress rock, including the large Romanesque Cathédrale

Notre-Dame des Pommiers and some fortified medieval towers. Most of the action takes place along rue Saunerie – where Napoleon stopped for lunch at the Auberge du Bras d'Or on 5 March 1815 on his triumphal return from exile in Elba – today busy with bistros and tourist shops. The numerous little streets and stairways running off to the side down to the Durance are known here as *andrônes* – from the Latin for "alleyway" or the Greek for "between two houses", depending on whom you ask. At the end of the street place de l'Horloge is home to a busy food market on Wednesday and Saturday mornings.

The Rochers de Mées

As the Durance snakes its way south and meets the Bléone flowing from the east, a sprawling collection of light industrial plants appears. Across the apex of the confluence, south of Château-Arnoux, the village of Les Mées itself does not tempt much, but the staggering **"Pénitents"**, or **Rochers des Mées ❸** do. The curious row of limestone pinnacles, some as high as 100 metres (330ft), rise out of a stunted forest – some alone, some clustered in groups – until they close ranks to form a single mini-massif, standing eerily over miles of fruit orchards and flat maize fields.

On the opposite bank of the Durance, the ruins of the early Romanesque **Eglise de St-Donat ❹**, reached by the narrow D101, sit isolated in oak woods. The retreat of St Donatus, a 6th-century monk, has eight mighty pillars supporting its ancient vaulting. A faded white apse, decorated with pale, terracotta-coloured stars, hints at its former glory.

More obviously impressive is the nearby medieval **Prieuré de Ganagobie ❺** (www.ndganagobie.com; Tue–Sun 3–5pm; free), famed for its lively 12th-century mosaics, in red, black and white, depicting knights, dragons and other mythical birds and beasts.

Montagne de Lure

The vast, forbidding **Montagne de Lure** is a continuation of lavender-covered Mont Ventoux to the west, and is bordered by the Luberon to the south. Its highest point, the **Signal de Lure** (1,826 metres/5,990ft) offers sweeping views as far as the Cévennes and Mont Ventoux. It can be reached from the north by the D946 that winds out of Sisteron, or from the south via the pretty village of **St-Etienne-les-Orgues ❻**. The prosperity of this pretty village was traditionally based on its medicinal remedies concocted from mountain herbs.

A road lined with lavender fields leads out of the village. Before long, the lavender gives way to the dense oak-and-fir forest of the mountain. Though seemingly deserted, this route becomes animated in August and September, as locals continue the centuries-old tradition of pilgrimage to the isolated **Chapelle de Notre-Dame-de-Lure ❼**, halfway to the summit. Also founded by the reclusive St Donatus, the chapel has none of the architectural distinction of the Eglise de St-Donat, but its setting is compensation enough.

The wild isolation of the Lure was the inspiration for many of Jean Giono's novels *(see page 94)*. It is widely believed that his fictional Aubignane is based on the ruined village of

A sad legend is connected to the strange rock formations known as the "Pénitents". The story goes that during the Arab invasions in the Middle Ages, a group of monks from the Montagne de Lure were bewitched by the beauty of some Moorish girls, whom they were unable to resist. As the cowled, disgraced figures were banished from the village, St Donatus turned them to stone as punishment for their impropriety.

BELOW LEFT: a welcoming mountain bistro.

Bistrot de Pays

Travel anywhere in France and you'll soon discover how vital a role the café plays as a focus of local life, not just as a place to eat and drink but also as a hub of gossip and social life. The Bistrot de Pays movement aims to help keep open or recreate the village café in small rural communities, where many of the shops and bars have closed, both to serve locals and to act as an ambassador for their area to tourists. The cafés and bistros sign a quality charter promising to provide snacks using local produce (many go much further, with full meals and regional specialities), to stay open all year, where possible to provide basic services not found elsewhere in the village, such as selling newspapers, cigarettes, vital groceries, or serving as a bread depot, to provide tourist information and to organise at least three cultural events a year, such as literary dinners, storytelling or musical evenings. First created in the sparsely populated area around Forcalquier and the Montagne de Lure, the concept has spread to remote rural districts in many corners of France, including the Haut-Var and Verdon (www.bistrotdepays.com).

Made from the milk of goats raised on the Montagne de Lure and the Plateau d'Albion, the small, round banon cheese, an ancient cheese dating back to at least the Middle Ages, is instantly recognisable, wrapped as it is in a dry chestnut leaf tied with raffia.

BELOW:
Simiane-la-Rotonde.

Redortiers ❽, just north of **Banon** ❾, worth a visit to sample its renowned goat's cheese. The remote village of **Simiane-la-Rotonde** ❿ is dominated by a strange 12th-century rotunda, actually the old castle keep. There are some fine period doorways and an old covered market here. Outside the summer months, however, its closed shutters and deserted streets make it a desolate place.

The Pays de Forcalquier

Rather livelier is **Forcalquier** ⓫, especially on Monday market day, when countless stalls groaning with local produce crowd the spacious **place du Bourguet** and the streets around it. The counts of Forcalquier once rivalled those of Provence, before the two dynasties were united when the Countess Gersande married Count Alphonse of Provence in 1195.

Forcalquier's main sight is the austere **Ancienne Cathédrale de Notre-Dame**, which has a wide triple nave and impressive organ loft. A wander through the narrow streets of the old town reveals fine stone doorways and arches decorated with chiselled plaques, scrolls and intricate reliefs, and there's a fine Gothic fountain on place St-Michel. Climb rue St-Mary to the grassy castle mound, now topped by a neo-Gothic **chapel** ringed by amusing sculptures of angels playing musical instruments.

South of Forcalquier on the D4100, just past the pretty village of Mane, is the beautiful medieval **Prieuré de Salagon** ⓬ (www.musee-de-salagon.com; tel: 04 9275 7050; daily June–Aug 10am–8pm, Feb–Apr 10am–6pm, May and Sept 10am–7pm, Oct–Dec Wed–Mon 10am–6pm; closed Jan; charge). The former priory buildings contain an ethnographic collection, including a blacksmith's forge, a tonnelier, a display about beekeeping and photographic archives of rural life in the Luberon; the simple chapel has modern windows by Aurélie Nemours. The most interesting aspect, though, is the series of themed gardens: a garden of medicinal plants used in local remedies, a perfume garden, and a medieval garden based on plants found in medieval manuscripts, including a kitchen garden, where the pulses and root vegetables that formed the staple diet in medieval times, before the arrival of tomatoes or aubergines, are a far cry from the typical Provençal cuisine of today. A couple of kilometres further on is the **Château de Sauvan** ⓭ (tel: 04 9275 0564; guided tours July–Aug daily 3.30pm, 4.30pm, Sept–June Thur, Sun 3.30pm; charge), an 18th-century neoclassical mansion, inspired by the Petit Trianon at Versailles and known locally as the *"Petit Trianon Provençal"*.

Entrevaux

On the eastern fringes of the *département*, the citadels fortified by Louis XIV's brilliant military architect, Sébastien Le Prestre de Vauban, give an indication of the strategic importance of this region – for a long time this was the border between Provence and what was then the Comté de Nice. The area is most easily reached by car (D6202 and D4202) from Nice or by the Train des Pignes.

The fairy-tale town of **Entrevaux** ⑭ is still surrounded by 17th-century ramparts, turrets, drawbridges and a deep moat formed by the Var River. Cars are firmly relegated to the busy Nice road on the opposite bank.

Like the ramparts, the majority of Entrevaux's tall stone houses date from the 17th century, as does the former **cathedral**. Its severe facade conceals a Baroque interior with a richly decorated high altar. The tiny main square, **place St-Martin**, has a pleasant café, a clutch of chestnut trees and a butcher who dispenses the local speciality, *secca de boeuf*, a type of dried salt beef best eaten with olive oil and lemon juice. The **citadel** (tel: 04 9305 4673; open daily 24 hours; take coins for entrance token or buy tickets at bureau d'accueil by drawbridge 10am–12.30pm, 2.30–6pm) bears testimony to the town's key strategic position.

Back into the modern age, the minuscule **Musée de la Moto** (Motorbike Museum; tel: 04 9379 1270; June– Sept daily 10am–noon, 2–6pm; free) is devoted to the history of the motorbike. Run by two enthusiasts, it houses over 70 vehicles, the oldest dating from 1901.

Annot

West of Entrevaux in the Vaire valley – and another stop on the Train des Pignes line – **Annot** ⑮ is typical of this area's dual aspect: the wrought-iron balconies and stone *lavoirs* are typically Provençal, but the majesty of the Alps comes through in the purity of the air and the steely grey streams that tumble through the town. In winter, the town sleeps under a thick blanket of snow. East of the main square, with its fine esplanade of ancient plane trees, the narrow streets of the picturesque old town climb steeply in medieval formation. Vaulted archways and carved stone lintels decorate the tall houses of the Grande Rue. At the top of the old town, the streets converge on a pretty square with the parish church and surrounding houses painted in a rainbow of pastel hues.

Entrevaux's citadel is reached by an ascending path of nine zigzag ramps, a remarkable feat of engineering that took 50 years to complete.

BELOW: Entrevaux.

The ski resorts of Pra-Loup and Super-Sauze are looking to the future. As well as 80 ski runs, Pra-Loup has opened the "Rider Space" for snow-boarding and freestyle activities, and provides floodlit night skiing and the chance to snowscoot (a type of snow cycling). Super-Sauze has 65 ski runs and the modern "Snow Park" aimed at daring snowboarders with a love of acrobatics. www.ubaye.com

BELOW: Villa Morélia, Jausiers, a hotel and prestigious restaurant.

Just outside the town to the south, a group of mammoth rocks known as the **Grès d'Annot** dots the hillside as if scattered there by giants. Locals have built houses directly beside them, often using their sheer faces as an outside wall. To this day, they are the subject of local legends which tell of troglodytes and primitive religions.

Those with stamina and sturdy boots can follow the spectacular hiking trails into the high-altitude **Val du Coulomp** near by. Alternatively, continuing north up the Vaire valley on the D908 towards Colmars will bring you to the mountain village of **Méailles** , before rejoining the upper Verdon valley.

Colmars

If Entrevaux seems uniquely untouched by its proximity to the Alps, **Colmars** ⓲, 50km (31 miles) to the north, could hardly be more Alpine. Colmars is crowned by two massive fortresses, and, like Entrevaux, is a former border post between Provence and Savoy. Inside the town ramparts, houses have been constructed with tidy wooden balco-

nies known as *solerets* (sun traps) and shop windows display amber bottles of *génépi* liqueur, made from Alpine flowers. Of the two castles, only the 17th-century **Fort de Savoie** (tel: 04 9283 4192; July–Aug daily 2.30–7pm, Sept–June visits by appointment; charge) is open to the public.

Barcelonnette and the Ubaye Valley

In the northwest corner of the Alpes-de-Haute-Provence, just north of the Parc National du Mercantour *(see page 216)*, **Barcelonnette** ⓲ squeezes into the glacial valley of the Ubaye, surrounded by towering peaks that draw skiers to the modern resorts of Super-Sauze and Pra-Loup. It owes its unlikely name to its 12th-century rulers, the counts of Barcelona. The Hispanic connection does not end there. Early in the 19th century, a period of emigration to Mexico began, prompted by the success of three local brothers who opened a textile shop there. Many followed, founding textile factories, department stores and banks. Having made their fortune, some of them returned to Barcelonnette to build the incongruous, so-called "Mexican" villas for which the town is famous. Set in large gardens around the edge of the old town, as well as in the nearby village of **Jausiers**, they were shaped by Italian craftsmen or took the forms of the new Art Nouveau style from Nancy. At 10 avenue de la Libération, the handsome 1870s Villa La Sapinière now contains the **Musée de la Vallée** (www.barcelonnette.com; tel: 04 9281 2715; mid-July–Aug daily 10am–noon, 2.30–7pm, rest of year Wed–Sat 2.30–6pm, plus Tue in school hols; charge), which traces the history of this emigration in documents and artefacts.

The "Mexican connection" continues today with the annual August Fêtes Latino-Méxicaines, cultural exchanges and a Mexican restaurant. ❑

RESTAURANTS AND BARS

Restaurants

Prices for a three-course meal without wine. Many restaurants have a less expensive lunch menu:

€ = under €25
€€ = €25–40
€€€ = €40–60
€€€€ = over €60

Barcelonnette
Villa Morélia
Jausiers.
www.villa-morelia.com
Tel: 04 9284 6778. Closed Nov–Dec and Apr. €€€€
Bruno Delamare, an ex of the restaurants in Le Negresco hotel in Nice, Le Bristol in Paris and The Ritz in London among others, is now the chef at this upmarket restaurant and hotel, located in one of the famous "Mexican" villas, with lovely gardens overlooking the Ubaye valley.

Château-Arnoux
La Bonne Etape
chemin du Lac.
www.bonneetape.com
Tel: 04 9264 0009. Open L & D daily (Nov–Apr Wed–Sun). Closed Jan–mid-Feb. €€€€
At this family-run hotel, part of the luxury Relais et Châteaux group, chef Jany Gleize combines local lavender and honey with luxury ingredients such as pigeon and lobster. A second, bistro-style restaurant, Le Goût du Jour (open daily, €€), serves up more rustic dishes, including *aioli*, pumpkin soup and *pieds et paquets* (sheep's feet and tripe).

L'Oustaou de la Foun
N85 route Napoléon.
www.restaurant-loustaou.com
Tel: 04 9262 6530. Open L & D Tue–Sat, L Sun (closed D Wed Jan–Mar). €€
An attractive stone farmhouse is the showcase for chef Patrick Chassy who creates wonderful regional fare and dramatic-looking desserts.

Digne-les-Bains
Le Grand Paris
19 boulevard Thiers.
www.hotel-grand-paris.com
Tel: 04 9231 1115. Open L Thur–Sun, D daily. Closed Dec–Feb. €€€
Noémie Ricaud has taken over from her father at this long-established restaurant housed in a former monastery. Expect lavish cooking in the classic mould with some modern touches.

Forcalquier
La Tourette
20 boulevard Latourette.
Tel: 04 9275 1400. Open L daily, D Wed–Sat. €
This relaxed, homely place on the main street near the cathedral has an inexpensive menu of Provençal staples, with dishes such as *daube*, lamb, rabbit and *caillettes* (little sausages with herbs, traditionally made the day a pig was slaughtered).

Lardiers
Café-Restaurant de la Lavande
place de la Lavande.
Tel: 04 9273 3152. Open L Thur–Tue, D Thur–Mon (Wed–Mon in July and Aug). Closed for 2 weeks in Nov and 2 weeks in Feb. €€
Prime example of a Bistrot de Pays (*see page 167*), with its bar, newspapers, literary evenings and menu based on local produce, such as truffles, figs, banon cheese and *petits farcis* (stuffed vegetables). It also has an excellent wine list, rare for these parts. Book ahead.

Sisteron
Grand Hôtel des Cours
place de l'Eglise.
www.hotel-lecours.com
Tel: 04 9261 0050. Open L & D Wed–Mon (also Tue in July and Aug). €€
A Sisteron institution for three generations. A lively atmosphere prevails, especially outdoors on the terrace in summer. Herby Sisteron lamb, raised on the pastures of the upper Durance valley, is a speciality.

RIGHT: Mexican flavours come to the Alps.

TOULON AND THE WESTERN VAR

Toulon's reputation as a gritty port town may not
entice those in search of Riviera glitz, but this vibrant,
historic city merits a visit. It offers good museums, a
great daily market, and ongoing restoration projects
are giving run-down quarters a new lease of life

The history of **Toulon** ❶ has
been determined by its natural
deep-water harbour, sitting in
the huge bay known as the Rade de
Toulon. When Provence became part
of France in 1481, Toulon inevitably
took on a key role in French naval
strategy. It was fortified by Henri IV,
Richelieu and Louis XIV's military
engineer Vauban, and home to the
naval arsenal and convict galleys, but
was then virtually destroyed in World
War II. The city is still home to
France's leading naval base today – a
massive town within the town, covering 268 hectares (662 acres) and
employing 12,000 people.

Many tourists bypass the city. Its
gritty reputation, busy through roads,
seedy alleyways, some disastrous post-
war reconstruction and a reputation
marred in the 1990s by extreme-right
politics offer little obvious entice-
ment to the casual visitor. However,
along with all the low-life trappings
of a major seaport, Toulon has its
own share of grand buildings, chic
boutiques, lively markets, an all-year
cultural scene that ranges from the
Belle Epoque opera house to modern
Oméga-Zénith concert venue, and a
cosmopolitan energy that is matched
in Provence only by Marseille.

Much of the town centre has been
renovated, as have several once seedy
hotels. Part of the motorway has been
funnelled underground and a new
coast path has been created. Even the
naval base is no longer completely
off limits to the public: as well as
an idea of its scale and glimpses of
docked naval vessels from boat trips
around the Rade, the small tourist
train which leaves from the port now
takes visitors inside the base (tel: 06
2077 4443; June–Aug, bring ID, no
photography allowed).

Main attractions

BOAT TRIP OF THE RADE DE
TOULON
MARCHÉ PROVENÇAL, COURS
LAFAYETTE, TOULON
BEACHES LE PRADET
MONT FARON, TOULON
TAMARIS
HARBOUR, BANDOL
BASILICA, ST-MAXIMIN-LA-
SAINTE-BAUME

LEFT: Sanary-sur-Mer's harbour.
RIGHT: on the waterfront, Toulon.

Toulon and the Western Var

```
0        10 km
0              10 miles
```

Central Toulon divides broadly into two districts: the Haute Ville, laid out in the late 19th century with expansive Hausmannian squares and avenues, and the Basse Ville leading towards the port, which incorporates the medieval alleys of the old town.

Haute Ville

Centrepiece of the Haute Ville is the **boulevard de Strasbourg**, which bisects the grid of tall apartment blocks, department stores and imposing administrative buildings that make up 19th-century Toulon. Admire the elaborate **Opéra de Toulon** on place Victor Hugo, with its sculpted facade and splendid gold-and-red interior, still used to stage dance, theatre and opera productions, and spacious **place de la Liberté**, with its palm trees, café terraces, ornate fountain and the sweeping façade of the former **Grand Hôtel**.

The neo-Renaissance **Musée d'Art** (113 boulevard du Maréchal Leclerc; tel: 04 9436 8101; Tue–Sun noon–6pm; free) has paintings by the Provençal school and a collection of contemporary art. Further down the road a fine 19th-century villa houses the **Hôtel des Arts** (tel: 04 9491 6918; Tue–Sun 11am–6pm, closed between exhibitions; free), which puts on contemporary art exhibitions, often with a Mediterranean emphasis.

Basse Ville

South of the Opéra lies the warren of narrow streets of the Basse Ville (Lower Town). Long insalubrious, it has been going through a major clean up, bringing back attention to its ancient buildings and numerous small squares with fountains. The attractive place Puget, with its pavement cafés, plane trees and a picturesquely overgrown fountain, draws elegant locals. Stalls laden with superb fish, vegetables and flowers under colourful umbrellas characterise the **Marché Provençal**

(Tue–Sun mornings) in the cours Lafayette. Here you'll also find the **Musée du Vieux Toulon** (69 cours Lafayette; tel: 04 9492 2923; Mon–Sat 2–5.45pm; free), which evokes Toulon's history. On a nearby side street is Toulon's **Cathédrale Ste-Marie des Seds** (place de la Cathédrale), begun in the 11th century, of which Romanesque sections remain, and expanded in the 17th, when it gained its Baroque facade and the altar sculpted by Pierre Puget's nephew and pupil Christophe Veyrier. At the end of cours Lafayette nearest the port is the pink Baroque facade of the Eglise St-François-de-Paule, with the tourist office opposite it.

The port

Much of the Basse Ville's bad press comes from the avenue de la République, a grubby roadway lined by a long concrete post-war housing block. Go through one of the archways to quai Cronstadt or quai de la Sinse, however, and the vision changes totally as you find yourself beside Toulon's lively marina and its quayside cafés and brasseries, such as the ever-fashionable **Grand Café de la Rade**, which are popular with locals for lunch or an early evening aperitif. Spot the doorway from the old town hall bombed in 1944 incorporated into the new town hall annexe, with its two muscular atlantes, sculpted in 1657 by Marseille sculptor Pierre Puget.

Boats leave from here for trips around the port and across the bay to La Seyne-sur-Mer, Tamaris and Les Sablettes, and to the Iles d'Hyères (in high season).

The original gateway to the arsenal, a rare relic of the old port, now forms the entrance to the **Musée de la Marine** (Place Monsenergue; www.musee-marine.fr; tel: 04 9402 0201; July–Aug daily; Feb–Dec Wed–Mon 10am–6pm; charge), housing historic ships' figureheads, model ships and marine paintings.

East of the port, the **Plages de Mourrillon** have a distinctly urban feel, drawing a local city population rather than tourists to their long stretch of sand, restaurants, lawns and playgrounds in the shelter of the circular Fort St-Louis, constructed in

Grand Hôtel on Toulon's spacious place de la Liberté.

BELOW: bird's-eye view of Toulon.

1696 at the entrance to the bay to warn of enemy ships. The corniche continues through Toulon's more upmarket suburbs to **Cap Brun**, where a coastal path leads to a series of little creeks, and the tranquil Anse de Méjean with its fishermen's shacks. Further east, Le Pradet has several pretty sandy coves, such as the Plage de la Garonne and Plage des Bonnettes.

Mont Faron

For a terrific bird's-eye view of Toulon, take a ride up to Mont Faron, the white limestone mountain that frames the city. You can reach it by car via a long and winding road, but the best way up is on the **Téléphérique** (www.telepherique-faron.com; tel: 04 9492 6825; Feb–Nov Tue–Sun, July–Aug daily, times vary, doesn't run in high winds; charge), which leaves from the Gare Inférieure on boulevard Amiral-Vence. Views from the cable car as you climb are stunning. At the top, amid a rocky landscape of parasol pines, evergreen oaks and maquis scrub, lie miles of footpaths, picnic areas, children's play areas, restaurants and the **Zoo du**

Mont Faron (tel: 04 9488 0789; daily 10am–6pm, closed on rainy days; charge), which specialises in breeding tigers, panthers, snow leopards and other wild cats.

Not far from the Téléphérique station is the Tour Beaumont, a 19th-century surveillance tower housing the **Mémorial du Débarquement** (tel: 04 9488 0809; summer daily 10am–noon, 2–5.30pm, closed Mon in winter; charge), a museum dedicated to the Liberation of Provence in August 1944.

La Seyne-sur-Mer

Rounding the bay west of Toulon, the first impression of **La Seyne-sur-Mer** ❷ is one of industrial dereliction. But this once important shipbuilding town hides some unusual gems. On the seashore, the 17th-century **Fort Balaguier** (924 corniche Bonaparte; tel: 04 9494 8472; Tue–Sun 10am–noon, 2–6pm, July–Aug Tue–Sun 10am–noon, 3–7pm; charge) now contains a museum which commemorates Napoleon's capture of Toulon and also has a display about the notorious penal colony, La Bagne.

The Naval Port

Though the city was a base for the royal navy as early as 1487, Toulon's era of major expansion occured in the 17th century. During the reign of Louis XIV, Toulon became the lynchpin of royal naval strategy against the Anglo-Spanish alliance (Marseille was favoured for commerce). The arsenal was expanded and the city's fortifications enlarged by the king's brilliant military engineer Vauban, who added the *darse neuve* (new dock), new forts and a set of star-shaped ramparts. The port was protected by over 20 new forts and towers, constructed both on the coast and on the surrounding hills.

A century later, the city took the side of the English against the Revolutionary government and was promptly brought to heel by a young Napoleon Bonaparte. The English fleet was defeated in 1793, ensuring that the general's name would never be forgotten. During World War II the French sabotaged their own fleet in 1942 to blockade the harbour and try to prevent the Nazis from taking the city, but in 1944 much of the town was razed by retreating Germans and advancing Allied troops.

Up on the Caire hill, the **Fort Napoléon** (Chemin Marc Sangnier; tel: 04 9487 8343, Tue–Sat 2–6pm; admission varies), built by Napoleon after his victory over the English, is today used for a summer jazz festival and other cultural events. But most fascinating of all here are the remains of **Tamaris**, an early seaside resort built in the 1890s by wealthy sailor and marine adventurer Michel Pacha, who made his fortune as director of lighthouses of the Ottoman Empire. Extravagant villas, hotels and a casino were built, most of them in a neo-Moresque style, as was his own vast chateau. Tamaris never quite made it big, and by the 1920s it had gone out of fashion. But it was bypassed rather than destroyed, and a number of buildings remain intact, including the classical-style **Villa Tamaris** (avenue de la Grande Maison; www.villatamaris.fr; tel: 04 9406 8400; Tue–Sun 2–6.30pm; free), now used for contemporary art shows, and the palatial Ottoman-style Institut Michel Pacha, a marine research institute on the sea front.

The **Baie de Lazaret** is used for mussel production, and is filled with mussel beds and picturesque mussel farmers' cabins on stilts (long known as *moules de Toulon*, you'll now find mussels on many menus referred to as *moules de Tamaris*). Sea bream and sea bass are also farmed in the bay.

From Tamaris you can cross a little isthmus to **Presqu'île de St-Mandrier ❸**, which has an attractive fishing port with numerous restaurants, or continue around the Six Fours peninsula to the sandy beaches of **Les Sablettes, Mar Vivo** and **Fabregas**.

At Cap Sicié, the southern point of the peninsula, the **Chapelle de Notre-Dame-du-Mai** sits on a high clifftop. The Fôret de Six-Fours is a protected natural habitat with a wide variety of pines, oaks, eucalyptus and aromatic plants. Its beauty is in sharp contrast to the downmarket hotels of sprawling Six-Fours-les-Plages down on the coast, whose beaches are popular with windsurfers.

Sanary and Bandol

Continuing westwards along the coast, the pretty pink-and-white

BELOW: Sanary-sur-Mer.

The vaulted nave in the Eglise Ste-Marie-Madeleine, St-Maximin-la-Ste-Baume.

BELOW: St Maximin-la-Ste-Baume basilica.

resort of **Sanary-sur-Mer** ❹ benefits from a sheltered position supplied by a rocky outcrop known as the Gros Cerveau (big brain). Family oriented and low key, with its pastel façades, palm trees along the promenade and a handful of wooden fishing boats in the harbour, Sanary has a timeless charm often lacking in more fashionable resorts.

Artists and writers began to flock to Sanary in the early 1930s, inspired by the presence of Aldous Huxley (1894–1963), who wrote *Brave New World* at his villa on Cap de la Gorguette in 1931. They were soon joined by a group of German intellectuals, headed by Nobel Prize-winning writer Thomas Mann (1875– 1955) and his novelist brother Heinrich (1871–1950), who fled here after Hitler's rise to power in 1933.

Screened from the ravages of the mistral by an arc of wooded hills, **Bandol** ❺ has attracted numerous visitors to its sandy coves and pleasant promenades since the arrival of the railway at the beginning of the 20th century. Among its more famous visitors were the New Zealand author Katherine Mansfield (1888–1923), who wrote *Prelude* in the quayside Villa Pauline in 1916.

Most modern-day visitors come for the town's sandy beaches and lively harbour. Another plus is Bandol's vineyards, spread over 1,000 hectares (2,500 acres) between the Ste-Baume Massif and the coast, around pretty medieval villages such as **La Cadière d'Azur** and fortified **Le Castellet**, which produce wines (particularly reds) that are rated among the best in Provence.

About 2km (1 mile) off the coast of Bandol lies the tiny island of **Bendor** ❻, which was enterprisingly transformed into a holiday village in the 1950s by the pastis magnate Paul Ricard. On the island is a hotel, a clutch of rather expensive cafés, and a re-creation of a Provençal fishing village. Though the island has an air of artificiality, its shady paths, lined with mimosa and eucalyptus, and tiny sandy beach are reason enough for a visit. Boats leave regularly from Bandol harbour for the seven-minute crossing (information from Bandol tourist office, tel: 04 9429 4135).

St-Maximin

On the western edge of the Var lies **St-Maximin-la-Ste-Baume ⑦**. Pilgrims have poured into this town since the 5th century to view one of the greatest Christian relics – the presumed bones of Mary Magdalene, which were discovered here in an ancient crypt. After the Boat of Bethany *(see page 140)* landed at Stes-Maries-de-la-Mer in the Camargue, its saintly crew dispersed to preach the word of God throughout Provence. Mary Magdalene is said to have made her way to the Massif de la Ste-Baume, where she lived in a cave for more than 30 years. She died in St-Maximin, where her remains were jealously guarded by the Cassianites.

In 1295 work began on the **Eglise Ste-Marie-Madeleine** (Place des Prêcheurs; tel: 04 4238 0178), founded by Charles II, king of Sicily and count of Provence, as a suitably magnificent receptacle for the relics. The result is the finest Gothic church in Provence, with its tall vaulted nave, Baroque high altar and elaborately carved walnut choirstalls. The well-preserved abbey buildings adjoining the church have been converted into a charming hotel, with a restaurant in the chapter house and cloister.

The Ste-Baume Massif

To the south of St-Maximin, in the heavily forested limestone mountain range of Ste-Baume, is the evocative, dank cave where Mary Magdalene is said to have spent her last years. From the village of **Nans-les-Pins**, the GR9 long-distance footpath follows the chemin des Rois, the pilgrimage path taken by popes and sovereigns for centuries. Reaching the cave's entrance involves a strenuous climb through towering beech trees and lush undergrowth (around 40 minutes from the Hôtellerie de la Baume, above the village of **Le Plan d'Aups-Ste-Baume**). Some 150 stone steps lead up to the cliffside cave. Inside,

the dark, dripping recess is filled with altars and saintly effigies. A final effort will bring you to **St-Pilon ⑧**, which is almost the highest point of the massif. Mary Magdalene was said to have been lifted up to this peak by angels seven times a day during her years of cave-dwelling.

Inhabited for thousands of years, the massif was used for sheep rearing, as well as a number of small industries including charcoal, slake lime and ice production. The main centre of ice production was the village of **Mazaugues ⑨** on the eastern side of the massif, which for centuries produced ice for Marseille and Toulon through a complex system of underground freezing reservoirs and ice stores. There's a small museum (Hameau du Château; http://museedelaglace.free.fr; tel: 04 9486 3924; June–Sept Tue–Sun 9am–noon, 2–6pm; charge). It is also possible to visit the restored **Glacière de Pivaut** (Aug–Sept Sat 2.30pm, tickets in advance from museum), an impressive 23-metre (75ft) -high stone cylinder, 7km (4 miles) from Mazaugues towards Le Plan.

The old quarter of Barjols (see page 180).

BELOW: the Ste-Baume massif.

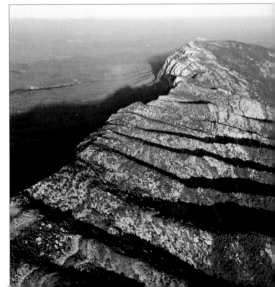

Brignoles and La Provence Verte

East of St-Maximin, **Brignoles** , once a mining centre for bauxite, has an attractive medieval quarter, containing the former residence of the counts of Provence, now home to the small **Musée du Pays Brignolais** (tel: 04 9469 4518; Wed–Sat 9am–noon, 2.30–6pm, Sun 9am–noon, 3–6pm; winter until 5pm; charge). It's devoted to local history, with an eclectic collection of paintings, fossils and an early Christian sarcophagus.

Brignoles sits at the heart of what is known as La Provence Verte (Green Provence), because of its verdant landscape watered by several rivers and underground springs. It is a popular area for walking, cycling and canoeing. The green tag has also taken on a double meaning because of the significant amount of organic produce grown in the area.

Twenty km (12 miles) north of Brignoles along the D554 is **Barjols**, dubbed the "Tivoli of Provence" – a small industrious town filled with streams, fountains and plane trees. What is reputedly the largest

BELOW: one of Barjols' 28 fountains.

plane tree in France, measuring an impressive 12 metres (40ft) in circumference, casts its shadow over the most celebrated of Barjols' 25 fountains, the vast moss-covered "Champignon" (mushroom) fountain, next to the Hôtel de Ville in the tiny place Capitaine Vincens.

Though the Tivoli tag attracts a good number of summer visitors, Barjols is more a workaday town than a tourist trap. Its prosperity was originally based on its tanneries, the last of which closed in 1986. Barjols is still, however, known for the manufacture of the traditional Provençal instruments, the *galoubet* (a three-holed flute) and *tambourin* (a narrow drum), which are played simultaneously by a single musician.

Barjols' old quarter, known as "**Réal**", is being extensively renovated. Low medieval archways stand in the dusty alleyways around the church of **Notre-Dame-de-l'Assomption**. An undistinguished square close to the church conceals one of Barjols's best treasures, the magnificent entrance to the Renaissance **Maison des Postevès**.	❏

RESTAURANTS AND BARS

Restaurants

Prices for a three-course meal without wine. Many restaurants have a less expensive lunch menu:
€ = under €25
€€ = €25–40
€€€ = €40–60
€€€€ = over €60

Bandol

Le Clocher
1 rue de la Paroissel
Tel: 04 9432 4765. Open D Mon & Thur, L & D Tue, Fri–Sun. €€
Revised Provençal specialities are served in an attractive setting on a pedestrianised street near the church.

Les Oliviers
Hôtel L'Ile Rousse, 25 boulevard Louis Lumièrel
www.ile-rousse.com
Tel: 04 9429 3300. Open L & D daily. €€€
Find elegant Mediterranean dining in this restaurant situated within a seaside spa hotel. The hotel has two private beaches.

Brignoles

Hostellerie de l'Abbaye de la Celle
place du Général de Gaulle
www.abbaye-celle.com
Tel: 04 9805 1414. Open L & D daily (Thur–Mon in winter). €€€€
Foodies make a beeline for Alain Ducasse's ele-

gant country inn and restaurant, 4 km (2½ miles) southwest of Brignoles. The 18th-century *auberge* adjoining a medieval abbey has a sophisticated restaurant run in partnership with truffle king Bruno Clémént. Ducasse disciple Benoît Witz puts a refined spin on regional dishes, most of them incorporating produce from the kitchen garden. Note that the Romanesque abbey church, which is currently being restored, is open for guided visits (daily; ring ahead for times on 04 9459 1905), as are the cloister and wine cellars.

La Cadière d'Azur

Hostellerie Bérard
avenue Gabriel Péri
www.hotel-berard.com
Tel: 04 9490 1143. Open D Tue, L & D Wed–Sun; bistro L & D Fri–Wed, D Thur. €€€€
Chef René Bérard and his son Jean-François marry classic and contemporary recipes, served in a stylish dining room looking out over the Bandol vineyards. There's also a simpler bistro. The inn consists of a number of houses in a medieval hill village.

St-Maximin-la-Ste-Baume

Hôtellerie le Couvent Royal
www.hotelfp-saintmaximin.com
Tel: 04 9486 5566. Open L & D daily. Closed D Sun. €€
Expect attractively presented classic French cuisine and regional wines. You can dine either in the lovely Gothic chapterhouse or out under the arcades of the cloister of this beautiful royal abbey.

Sanary-sur-Mer

Hôtel-Restaurant de la Tour
Port de Sanary
www.sanary-hoteldelatour.com
Tel: 04 9474 1010. Open L & D Thur–Mon (plus Wed in Aug). Closed Dec. €€

Sanary's most pleasant hotel also has an excellent restaurant with a terrace overlooking the port. The speciality is fresh fish and shellfish, perhaps baked in a salt crust or simmered in a bouillabaisse.

Toulon

Au Sourd
10 rue Molière
Tel: 04 9492 2852. Open L & D Tue–Sat. €€
Toulon's oldest restaurant was opened in 1862 by a soldier who had returned deaf (*sourd*) from the Crimean war. Today it serves high-quality fish straight from the local catch, whether grilled, as calamari or in bouillabaisse.

RIGHT: mussels are a menu staple in this coastal region.

INLAND VAR HILL VILLAGES

Picturesque hill villages and remote abbeys dot the interior of the Var, but much of this area still has a rural feel with densely forested hills and vine-covered valleys that make it good territory for walking and wine tasting

North of the A8 *autoroute*, the landscape of the inland Var progresses upwards in a series of tiers. Vineyards on the plain and lower valleys give rise to olive groves, then to densely forested hills – prowled by game-hunters, truffle-seekers and walkers – which open onto the sparse expanses of the Grand Plan de Canjuers, a high mountain plateau, most of which belongs to the French army.

Le Cannet and Le Luc

On the central Var plain, squeezed between the *autoroute* and the Maures, the wine-producing commune of **Le Cannet-des-Maures** has two distinct halves. Clustered around an 11th-century church, **Le Vieux-Cannet ❶** is a pretty hill village, while down on the plain the modern town developed with the arrival of the railway in the 1860s. Remnants of the Roman settlement of Forum Voconi, a halt on the Via Aurelia, have recently been excavated here. The nearby small market town of **Le Luc ❷** has as its centre-piece a 27-metre (90ft) -high hexagonal tower, built in the 16th century. Although rather overladen by traffic, Le Luc has a rich history as a Roman spa town and Protestant refuge,

which can be traced in the **Musée Historique du Centre Var** (tel: 04 9460 7451; 15 June–15 Oct Mon–Sat 3–6pm, rest of year by appointment; charge). It is located in the Château des Comtes de Vintimille along with the tourist office and a small museum devoted to stamps.

Abbaye du Thoronet

The main reason to pass through Le Cannet, however, is to access the Maures massif to the south (*see page 195*) or to visit the magnificent

Main attractions
ABBAYE DU THORONET
CHAPELLE STE-ROSELINE, LES ARCS
TOURTOUR
COTIGNAC
CHÂTEAU D'ENTRECASTEAUX
COLLECTION MAX ERNST DONATION DOROTHEA TANNING, SEILLANS

LEFT: the plane tree-shaded main square, Cotignac. **RIGHT:** vineyard near Draguignan.

Two summer music festivals are held in the lovely setting of the Abbaye du Thoronet. The first, in late July, focuses on medieval music. The Musique et Esprit festival in mid-August features classical and choral music. Obtain information from the Office de Tourisme, tel: 04 9460 1094.

Abbaye du Thoronet ❸ (http://thoronet.monuments-nationaux.fr; tel: 04 9460 4390; Apr–Sept Mon–Sat 10am–6.30pm, Sun 10am–noon, 2–6.30pm, Oct–Mar Mon–Sat 10am–1pm, 2–5pm, Sun 10am–noon, 2–5pm; charge). Thoronet is perhaps the finest of the Provençal trio of "Cistercian sisters", which includes the abbeys of Sénanque *(see page 93)* and Silvacane *(see page 86)*. Built in the 12th century to the ascetic precepts of the Cistercian Order, it is striking in its unadorned simplicity and masterful proportions. The abbey church is renowned for its fine acoustic, and you can also visit the cloister, dormitory, and olive press and cellars where monks made olive oil and wine.

Les Arcs-sur-Argens

Les Arcs-sur-Argens ❹, east of Le Cannet, is a focus for the Var's wine industry, and its **Maison des Vins** on the DN7 (www.caveaucp.fr; tel: 04 9499 5020) is a useful place to embark on a wine trail. It runs tasting courses, provides information on touring the vineyards, and has cellars containing over 800 Côtes de Provence wines. The town has an attractive old quarter, known as Le Parage, and the remains of a feudal castle destroyed after the Revolution.

Just east of Les Arcs, the **Château Ste-Roseline** (www.sainte-roseline.com; tel: 04 9499 5030; daily), a former Carthusian nunnery, is now one of Provence's best-known vineyards but for centuries was the focus of an ancient pilgrimage cult around local saint Roseline. You can visit the Romanesque **Chapelle Ste-Roseline** (Tue–Sun 2.30–6pm), where an ornate reliquary contains the "living" eyes of Roseline, who was born in 1263 in the castle at Les Arcs. According to legend, she was caught by her father in the act of giving away the rich family's possessions to the needy poor; when she opened up her apron, the items were miraculously transformed into roses. After her death, her body miraculously failed to decompose, and is now preserved in a glass sarcophagus. The chapel also has a mosaic by Chagall, stained glass by Ubac and Bazaine and church furnishings by Diego Giacometti (brother of Alberto).

Northwest of here, **Lorgues ❺**, a busy town with some fine 18th-century buildings and tiny medieval alleyways draws foodies to the restaurant of truffle king Clément Bruno.

Draguignan

Draguignan ❻, the main town in inland Var and home to a large garrison, is ringed by an unfortunate rash of supermarkets, some of which were badly damaged when the Nartuby River flooded in 2010.

After the Revolution, Draguignan became administrative capital of the Var from 1795 to 1974 (to punish Toulon which had supported the monarchy) gaining a set of broad boulevards laid out by Baron Haussmann, who was Préfet of the Var in the 1840s.

Within the boulevards is a compact but appealing old town and a superb market on place du Marché every Wednesday and Saturday morning. Housed in an old monastery, the **Musée des Arts et Traditions Populaires** (15 rue Joseph Roumanille; Tue–Sat 9am–noon, 2–6pm, Sun 2–6pm; charge) relays the social and cultural history of the community through reconstructed scenes. The venerable art museum, **Musée Municipal d'Art et d'Histoire** (rue de la République; Mon–Sat 9am–noon, 2–6pm; free), holds French and Flemish paintings, faience and furniture, in the former summer palace of the bishops of Fréjus.

At the top of the hill stands the Tour de l'Horloge, an impressive fortified clocktower built in 1663. Near by, on rue de la Juiverie, you can see remains of a synagogue façade, a relic of the sizeable Jewish community that thrived here in the Middle Ages.

An American military cemetery on the town's eastern edge is the legacy of a bloody battle fought here in August 1944. Five km (3 miles) west of Draguignan, pretty **Flayosc ❼** huddles around an 11th-century church. It is known for its excellent

The town of Draguignan is named after a dragon which was said to have terrorised the town in the 5th century, until vanquished by Hermentaire, bishop of Antibes. This mythical creature can be seen in stone crests on many of the old town's medieval gateways and houses.

BELOW: Draguignan's market square.

TIP

The Route des Ambassadeurs des Crus Classés takes in 13 Côtes de Provence wine chateaux with the prestigious *cru classé* status. Most are located along the Var coast or around Les Arcs in the central Var. Find more information at www.cruclasseprovence.com

olive oil; there's a working oil mill (Moulin du Flayosquet; tel: 04 9470 4145) just north of here in the hamlet of Flayosquet,

North of Draguignan on the D955 is the mysterious dolmen known as the Pierre de la Fée (Fairy Stone), a vast slab of rock on three stone legs, dating from 2500 to 2000 BC. Shortly after, you'll reach the **Gorges de Châteaudouble**, cut through by the River Nartuby. Perched dramatically above the gorges is the village of **Châteaudouble** and, upstream, **Ampus**, another picturesque village.

Tourtour and Villecroze

More gentrified but more spectacular is **Tourtour** ❽, "the village in the sky", with its medieval vaulted passageways that open onto breathtaking views. People congregate on the café terraces of place des Ormeaux, the main square. Sadly, the *ormeaux* – two elms planted to commemorate Louis XIV's birth – fell prey to disease and were replaced by olive trees.

Tourtour has two castles: the ruined old castle, and the square, four-towered Château Communal, now home to the tourist office and post office. The square outside has two bronze sculptures of a beetle and a butterfly by artist Bernard Buffet, who lived in the village until his death in 1999.

At neighbouring **Villecroze** ❾, mullioned Renaissance windows peer out of the red cliff face from troglodyte dwellings carved into the soft tufa rock. Below, the unusual Jardin de la Cascade was laid out in the 19th century, with pools and basins fed by water that cascades down the cliff.

Aups

Aups ❿ is an access point for the Grand Canyon du Verdon (*see page 155*) and a busy market town, famed for its truffle market on Thursday mornings in winter. The town is crowned by a fine 16th-century clocktower adorned with a sundial. Aups has a strong tradition of republican resistance, and was the scene of several popular uprisings during the mid-19th century. The portal of the town's Eglise de St-Pancrace bears the republican inscription: *Liberté, Egalité, Fraternité*.

BELOW: Aups.

Housed in an old Ursuline chapel, the **Musée Municipal Simon Segal** (tel: 04 9470 0195; 15 June–15 Sept daily 10am–noon, 4–7pm; charge) has a collection of works by the Russian-born painter and other artists associated with the Ecole de Paris in the 1920s.

Outside town, the **Musée de Faykod** (www.musee-de-faykod.com; tel: 04 9470 0394; July–Aug Wed–Mon 10am–noon, 3–7pm, Sept–June Wed–Mon 2–6pm, closed Nov; charge) is a sculpture garden of romantic white Carrara marble sculptures by Maria de Faykod, a Hungarian-born sculptor who carried out numerous commissions for public sculptures and religious works in France.

Salernes ⓫ is larger and more sprawling than Aups, with one of the best markets in the area, held on Wednesday and Sunday mornings on the central square. Above all, Salernes is known as the tile-making capital of Provence. Tiles have been made here for centuries, thanks to the combination of local clay, spring water and abundant forests for fuelling the kilns. Today it still has over a dozen tile workshops. The tiles range from the most traditional hand-moulded hexagonal unglazed floor tiles, known as *tommettes*, to hand-painted wall tiles and the contemporary glazed tiles and extravagant creations of Alain Vagh.

A few kilometres west of Salernes, **Sillans-la-Cascade** ⓬ has several remnants of its fortified town wall and an impressive waterfall, now sadly closed to the public after a landslide. Minuscule **Fox-Amphoux** crouches on a hill to the west, its pretty streets clustered round a Romanesque church.

The animated village of **Cotignac** ⓭ is set against the dramatic backdrop of a red cliff crowned with the remains of two fortified towers. It is popular with tourists, as the antique and gift shops testify, but it retains a workaday charm. South of town, the **Chapelle Notre-Dame-de-Grâce**, built after an apparition by the Virgin in 1519, was one of the three churches where the devout Queen Anne of Austria, wife of Louis XIII, made a vow, after a Parisian monk dreamt that the only way she could

BELOW: Draguignan's belltower.

Campaniles

Originally housing the bell that served as a warning in times of danger, located either on the town hall or the church, campaniles soon became far more than mere functional structures. With their fancy curlicues and finials, the elaborate wrought-ironwork became a way of proclaiming the village's identity and showing off the craftsman's skill, especially in the 18th century, when they were often added to much earlier structures. Countless campaniles can be found throughout Provence, but there are some particularly fine examples in the Var hill villages, including the clocktower gateway at Aups, the village churches at Flayosc and Le Vieux Cannet and the town belfry at Lorgues.

The ruins of a medieval fortress in the village of Bargème.

have a child was to carry out three novenas. The result was the birth of Louis XIV in 1638.

The D50 snakes east to **Entrecasteaux** , a delightful village overlooking the River Bresque, dominated by an imposing 16th- to 18th-century classical **chateau** (tel: 04 9404 4395; guided visit Easter–Oct Sun–Fri 4pm, plus 11.30am in Aug; charge). In 1974, the chateau was bought by painter, soldier and adventurer Ian McGarvie-Munn, a larger-than-life Scotsman who set about its restoration. The formal gardens (open daily) were designed by André Le Nôtre, creator of Louis XIV's gardens at Versailles.

Fayence and Seillans

Fayence ⓰, the largest town in the eastern Var and a big hang-gliding centre, has little overt charm, but is surrounded by a series of pretty satellite villages, such as Montauroux and Mons. On the edge of town, the **Ecomusée de Fayence** (Tue–Thur, and Sat 3–6pm; free) displays vine- and olive-growing equipment, wine presses and other traditional agriculture implements.

The Surrealist painter Max Ernst (1891–1976) spent the last 11 years of his life in **Seillans** ⓰, a pink-and-ochre village west of Fayence. A bronze cast of his *Génie de la République* stands on place de la République. The **Collection Max Ernst Donation Dorothea Tanning** (place du Valat; tel: 04 9476 8591; Tue–Sat 2.30–5.30pm; charge), containing lithographs and etchings he made while living in the village, and prints by his wife Dorothea Tanning, can be seen in a gallery above the Office de Tourisme. The countryside around Seillans is known for its igloo-shaped drystone *bories*.

Bargemon and Bargème

Bargemon ⓱, west of Seillans, with fragments of ramparts dating back to the 11th century, has medieval streets to wander and a good Thursday market. From here you can head south to **Callas** and the stunning landscapes of the **Gorges de Pennafort** or head 17km (10 miles) north, climbing in steep hairpin bends over the Col du Bel Homme pass, to tiny **Bargème** ⓲, the highest village in the Var. ❑

BELOW: Seillans.

RESTAURANTS AND BARS

Restaurants

Prices for a three-course meal without wine. Many restaurants have a less expensive lunch menu:
€ = under €25
€€ = €25–40
€€€ = €40–60
€€€€ = over €60

Les Arcs-sur-Argens
Le Relais des Moines
route Ste-Roseline
www.lerelaisdesmoines.com
Tel: 04 9447 4093. Open L & D July–Sept Tue–Sun, rest of year Tue–Sat. €€
In an historic stone farmhouse, *cuisine de terroir* is revisited with finesse by young chef Sébastien Sanjou. There's an excellent wine list, too.

Cotignac
Le Clos des Vignes
route de Montfort
Tel: 04 9404 7219. Open D Tue, L & D Wed–Sun. €€
In a rural setting outside town with a view over vineyards. Offers French classics (foie gras, game, *daubes*) and an interesting selection of wines.

La Table de la Fontaine
27 cours Gambetta
Tel: 04 9404 7913. Open L & D Tue–Sun. Closed Dec–Feb. €
This good-value little bistro with a terrace on Cotignac's main street is

a popular place for lunch after the Tuesday market or dinner in summer.

Flayosc
L'Oustaou
5 place Brémond. Tel: 04 9470 4269. Open L & D Tue, Thur–Sun, D Wed. €€
A well-regarded restaurant on the village square, where specialities include *daube* and local goat's cheese. Watch the world go by from the terrace.

Lorgues
Chez Bruno
route de Vidauban
www.restaurantbruno.com
Tel: 04 9485 9393. Open L & D daily (winter closed Sun D & Mon). €€€€
Expect extremely rich menus based around truffles and foie gras at this beautifully situated country *mas*, where larger-than-life character Clément Bruno, the truffle king, draws the sort of clientele who helicopter in for dinner.

Montauroux
Auberge Eric Maio
Quartier Narbonne
www.fontaines-daragon.com
Tel: 04 9447 7165. Open L & D Thur–Mon. Closed Jan. €€€
A rising name on the French culinary scene, owner-chef Eric Maio is

another fan of the truffle, which even appears in the ice cream.

Salernes
Chez Gilles
20 avenue Victor Hugo
www.chez-gilles.com
Tel: 04 9470 7280. Open L Fri–Sun, D Tue–Sun. €
A tiny, animated bistro, where chef Gilles makes the most of the Var's organic produce. Live music some evenings.

Seillans
Hôtel des Deux Rocs
1 place Font d'Amont
http://hoteldeuxrocs.pagesperso-orange.fr
Tel: 04 9476 8732. Open L & D Tue–Sun. €€€
This village house is a lovely characterful hotel

with an adventurous restaurant, where you can sample the personalised seasonal cuisine of chef David Carré, previously No.2 at the grand Lameloise restaurant in Burgundy.

Tourtour
La Bastide de Tourtour
Montée St-Denis
www.bastidedetourtour.com
Tel: 04 9810 5420. Open July–Aug L & D daily, rest of year D Mon–Fri, L & D Sat–Sun. €€
Modern French cuisine served in the elegant dining room of this upmarket hotel, or on the terrace with stunning views of the Haut Var.

RIGHT: La Bastide de Tourtour.

ST-TROPEZ, THE MAURES AND THE ESTÉREL

Glitzy St-Tropez, the star of the Var coast, is as fashionable as ever, but just beyond its boundaries is the surprisingly wild hinterland of the Massif des Maures and the Massif de l'Estérel. Sun-worshippers and nature-lovers are both well catered for here

rom Hyères to the Estérel, the Var coast provides some of the most spectacular colours in the south, with glorious sandy beaches set against mountain backdrops, where red rocks contrast with the azure seas and magnificent chestnut trees. The glamour of St-Tropez and busy resorts like Le Lavandou and St-Raphaël contrast starkly with the forested expanses of the Massif des Maures and the Estérel. Vineyards, fruit production and the steep terrain means that this area has been spared the worst of the concrete developments of the Alpes-Maritimes further east.

Hyères-les-Palmiers

Grandmother of the Riviera towns, **Hyères ❶** was the first resort to be established on the Côte d'Azur, setting a trend that spread rapidly east from the late 18th century onwards. The list of famous consumptives and pleasure-seekers drawn to its balmy winter climate reads like an international Who's Who: Queen Victoria, Tolstoy, Pauline Bonaparte, Aubrey Beardsley, Edith Wharton. Robert Louis Stevenson, though very ill during his stay, wrote: "I was only happy once – that was at Hyères."

By the 1920s, however, medical opinion had switched its allegiance to the curative properties of mountain rather than sea air. This and the arrival of the summer season soon relegated Hyères, sitting above the coast rather than down by the shore, to a distinctly unfashionable position.

In many ways, the town's air of faded gentility is now its most attractive quality. Its thriving agricultural economy centres around market gardening, cut flowers and palm trees, and the restoration of the Villa

LEFT: view across the rooftops of the Vieux-Port of St-Tropez.
RIGHT: traditional fishing boat.

Villa Noailles, a 1920s Cubist house visited regularly by members of the Dada and Surrealist movements.

Noailles has given it a cultural boost. Toulon-Hyères airport, located next to Hyères racetrack, also makes it a jumping off point for the Ile de Porquerolles and St-Tropez.

Amid the modern sprawl and a complicated one-way system lies the compact medieval **Vieille Ville** (old town). It is best entered through the Porte Mabillon, a fragment of the old city fortifications. From here rue Mabillon leads to the lively, café-filled place Mabillon where the square **Tour des Templiers** (Wed–Mon 10am–noon, 2–7pm, until 5pm in winter), the remains of a Templar

commanderie, is now used for exhibitions. Steps next to the tower lead up to the **Collégiale St-Paul**, a large, mainly Gothic church most notable for the array of naive ex-voto paintings on the walls.

Hyères' most interesting sight is the **Villa Noailles** (www.villanoailles-hyeres.com; tel: 04 9808 0198; Wed–Mon, hours vary; free), further up the hill below the castle ruins. In its heyday, this masterpiece of Modernist Cubist architecture, built in the 1920s by Robert Mallet-Stevens for aristocratic art patrons Charles and Marie-Laure de Noailles, was the

St-Tropez, the Maures and the Estérel

MEDITERRANEAN SEA

0   10 km
0   10 miles

ultimate expression of modern living and aesthetics, complete with indoor pool, gymnasium, guest rooms and garages. Buñuel, Giacometti, Stravinsky, Man Ray and other arty guests lounged on its sun terraces. Restored in the 1990s, the villa is now used for temporary exhibitions, with a fashion photography festival each spring and design festival in summer.

Above the villa, the road continues to the ruins of a 14th-century castle and the 19th-century Castel Ste-Claire, home from 1927 to 1937 of American novelist Edith Wharton, who planted the surrounding **Parc Ste-Claire** with numerous species from South America and Australia.

The modern town retains some of its 19th-century elegance in the stucco villas of avenue Joseph Clotis and the renovated Casino des Palmiers on avenue Amboise Thomas. Around the exotic **Jardins Olbius Riquier** are some notable examples of neo-Moorish architecture, dating from the 1870s.

Lower down, towards Le Capte, lies the **Site Archéologique d'Olbia** (www.monum.fr; tel: 04 9457 9828;

Apr–Sept 9.30am–12.30pm, 3–7pm; charge), the remains of the maritime trading post of Olbia founded by the Greeks in the 4th century BC.

Jutting out into the sea south of Hyères-Plage is the **Presqu'île de Giens ②**; on the sheltered eastern side of the isthmus, the beach road of La Capte is lined with cheap hotels and campsites. The road along the western side runs between the abandoned salt marshes of Les Pesquiers, now a nature reserve, and the long windswept Plage de l'Almanarre, a favourite with windsurfers. The Presqu'île itself is rather built up but is encircled by a lovely coast path which gives access to pretty creeks.

The Iles d'Hyères

Most people come to Giens to catch a boat from **La Tour-Fondue** – the remains of a fortress built by Richelieu – to **Porquerolles ③**, the largest of the Iles d'Hyères, also known as the Iles d'Or (Golden Islands), because of the mica or "fool's gold" that sparkles in the sand and rocks. Luxuriant Porquerolles was the inspiration for Robert Louis Steven-

Ile de Porquerolles, one of the unspoilt Iles d'Hyères off the Var coast. Boats to the islands are frequent in July and August, but limited the rest of the year (see tip, page 194).

BELOW: sunset over Porquerolles island.

TIP

TLV (tel: 04 9458 2181; www.tlv-tvm.com) operates ferries from Hyères to Port-Cros (1 hour) and Ile de Levant (1½ hours), and from La Tour-Fondue on the Presqu'île de Giens to Porquerolles (30 mins). **Vedettes Iles d'Or** (tel: 04 9471 0102; www. vedettesilesdor.fr) runs ferries from Le Lavandou to the Ile de Levant (35 mins; 1 hour via Port-Cros), and to Porquerolles in summer, as well as boats from Cavalaire.

son's *Treasure Island*. Its village was established as a small military base in the 19th century, and is more colonial than Provençal in character, with a large parade ground-like square surrounded by eucalyptus trees and several cafés. Above the village, the **Fort Ste-Agathe** (May–Oct 10am–12.30pm, 1.30–5pm; free) offers good views over the bay of Hyères. Numerous footpaths and cycle tracks traverse the island – bicycles can be hired near the harbour – but note that some parts may be out of bounds due to fire risk in summer. Major beauty spots include the lighthouse at Cap d'Arme, a small botanical garden, and the Plage d'Argent and Plage de la Courtade a short walk through pinewoods on either side of the village.

Rugged, mountainous **Port-Cros** ❹, reached by boat from Port de Hyères, Le Lavandou and Cavalaire, is a national park, and strict rules against smoking and fires must be observed. A small tourist centre, open in summer, provides maps and advice. Perhaps the most rewarding walk (around two hours for the

round trip) takes you along the Vallon de la Solitude, which cuts across the southern end of the island. Divers can follow an underwater "path" to see the marine flora and fauna.

The third island, **Levant** ❺, is inhabited by the French military and mostly out of bounds, except for the dramatic western tip which is occupied by Héliopolis, a nudist colony founded in the 1930s.

Bormes-les-Mimosas and the Corniche des Maures

West of Hyères, **Bormes-les-Mimosas** ❻ is a chocolate-box pretty medieval hill village perched above the coast, its streets overflowing with bougainvillea, mimosa and other exotic plants. Place Gambetta is the hub of Bormes life, with its restaurants and frequent live entertainment in summer; from here rue Carnot winds through the old village with stepped streets and covered alleyways leading off to either side. Look out for the painted sundial on the Eglise St-Trophime and the small **Musée d'Art et d'Histoire de Bormes** (103 rue Carnot; Tue–Sun except Wed am

BELOW: beach volleyball, Le Lavandou.

and Sun pm, June–Sept 10am–noon, 3–6.30pm, Oct–May 10am–noon, 2–5.30pm; free), which contains some terracottas by Rodin and neo-Impressionist paintings. Above the town, a road leads up to the remains of the Château des Seigneurs de Fos (private), offering magnficent views.

South of Bormes, linked to the exclusive promontory of Cap Bénat by a dyke, the sturdy medieval Fort de Brégançon, one of the official residences of the French president, sits proudly on its own peninsula. The fort cannot be visited, but **Cap de Brégançon**, planted with vineyards and pine woods, has some lovely unspoilt beaches, such as the Plage de Cabasson (parking fee), the Plage de l'Estagnol (open Easter–Oct; parking fee) and the Plage de Pellégrin (open Easter–Oct; parking fee).

Bormes' own modern beach suburb of La Favière, north of Cap Bénat, has a sandy beach, a marina, watersports facilities and numerous restaurants. Almost adjoining it is the popular resort of **Le Lavandou** ❼. Glitzy bars and discos make this a lively place by night, although there are also a few relics of the old fishing town behind the port, and a huge general market behind the promenade on Thursday morning. (This is also the best place for boats to Port-Cros and the Ile de Levant.)

Lavandou marks the start of the **Corniche des Maures** (D559), which winds around the coast past the Plage de St-Clair, the prettiest of Le Lavandou's beaches, the small Aiguebelle cove, the beach restaurants of Cavalière, and exclusive Cap Nègre. It then climbs up towards Le Rayol-Canadol and the wonderful gardens of the **Domaine du Rayol** ❽ (www.domainedurayol.org; tel: 04 9804 4400; daily 9.30am–5.30pm, until 7.30pm in summer; charge), laid out according to different tropical and desert habitats around the globe. After the big brash resort of Cavalaire-sur-Mer,

a side road leads to **Gigaro**, one of the landing beaches for the Liberation of Provence in August 1944.

The Massif des Maures

Only a couple of miles from jet-set St-Tropez, you'll find yourself in the steep, densely forested mountains of the Maures – the name comes from old Provençal *mauro*, meaning dark – an ancient massif made up of deep grey schist shot through with glittering mica and serpentine. It is wonderful walking country, traversed by numerous footpaths, including the long-distance GR51, GR9 and GR90, indicated by red-and-white striped markings, offering sea views and relative cool and solitude. Sadly, the area has often been ravaged by forest fires, sparked either by human carelessness or arsonists, so many of the footpaths may be closed in high summer, especially on windy days (www.cdg-var.org; call 04 9810 5541 for information in French).

The D98 main road follows the vineyard-filled valley via La Môle in the middle of the Maures, the most direct route between Hyères

TIP

The Office National de Forêts (ONF) organises a variety of guided walks in the Maures to discover flora and fauna, prehistoric remains or hidden chapels (Bormes-les-Mimosas tourist office; tel: 04 9401 3838; www.bormesles mimosas. com).

BELOW: Grimaud.

TIP

Delicious chestnut-based ice cream sundaes are served in summer at the Confiserie Azuréenne (tel: 04 9448 0720) in Collobrières. A small museum explains the process of making *marrons glacés*: chestnuts are harvested in autumn, peeled and cooked then soaked in syrup for seven days, coated in icing sugar, dried in the oven and individually wrapped.

and St-Tropez. To reach the heart of the mountains, however, it's better to take the narrow, sometimes hair-raisingly twisty D41 from Bormes-les-Mimosas, which climbs over the Col de Gratteloup and Col de Babaou passes (a good place to join the GR51 footpath), descending through magnificent chestnut woods towards Collobrières.

Collobrières ➒ is a refreshingly workaday place, dedicated to the timber trade and the cultivation and transformation of chestnuts – *marrons glacés* and *crème de marrons* are local specialities *(see left)* – with a pleasant low-key old town stretching along the Real Collobrier river. The chestnut harvest is celebrated with the Fête de la Chataigne on the last three Sundays in October.

Further east along the D14 towards Grimaud, turn off to the **Chartreuse de la Verne ➓** (http://la.verne.free.fr; tel: 04 9443 4541; Wed–Mon summer 11am–6pm, winter 11am–5pm, closed Jan; charge), an imposing fortress-like monastery hidden at the end of a remote valley. Built out of local schist edged with green serpen-

tine, the Carthusian monastery was founded in 1170. Abandoned after the Revolution, it is now home to a community of nuns, and you can visit the granary, church and one of the monk's cottages.

Grimaud ⓫ itself is a picturesque hilltop village with a maze of streets draped in bougainvillea and oleander. Wander along the rue des Templiers for its medieval arcades, then head up to the ruined castle.

Detour inland up the winding D558 amid cork oaks, chestnut trees and pines to **La Garde-Freinet ⓬**, an ancient Arab stronghold and, much later, a centre of cork production. By 1846, the town produced more than 75 percent of France's wine corks. Since the early 1980s, the industry has diversified into other uses of cork, and neatly stripped trunks of cork oaks line the massif's winding roads. In the town, the only obvious evidence of cork production are the cork bowls and ornaments on sale to tourists in the pricey shops of the rue St-Jacques, although the village still has some down-to-earth local cafés and stores, especially on place Vieille. North of the village, a climb to the ruins of **Fort Freinet** is rewarded with great views, although excavations have revealed more evidence of a medieval village here rather than the supposed Arab fortress.

Cogolin, 3km (1½ miles) south of Grimaud, is a small but lively town known for the manufacture of briar pipes and carpets.

St-Tropez

Once on the peninsula, you won't be able to resist the pull of **St-Tropez ⓭**, enduringly connected with the French sex symbol Brigitte Bardot. What had been a simple fishing village "discovered" by Guy de Maupassant and Paul Signac in the 19th century, and by the writer Colette in the early 20th century, was confirmed as the playground of the rich and

BELOW: red rooftops of La Garde-Freinet.

famous when Bardot starred in Roger Vadim's film *And God Created Woman* here in 1956. Although besieged by traffic jams in summer, "St-Trop" still has the allure of a Provençal fishing village (it even has a daily morning fish market on place aux Herbes behind the tourist office) combined with legendary nightlife, café society and designer shopping. It could all be ridiculous except that St-Trop gets away with it, and the rest of the year reverts to relatively normal small town status.

Whether you leave your car by the Nouveau Port or arrive by boat, the first essential port of call is the **Vieux-Port**, lined with tall rust-coloured houses and legendary café terraces, including Senequier, the Bar du Port and Café de Paris, from which to celebrity-spot and ogle the swanky yachts lined up along the quay. On the west side the **Musée de l'Annonciade** (place Gramont; tel: 04 9417 8410; July–Aug daily 10am–1pm, 3–7pm, Sept–June Wed–Mon 10am–noon, 2–6pm; charge) is a superb collection of modern art displayed in a deconsecrated chapel,

featuring many of the artists who visited St-Tropez at the beginning of the 20th century, including Signac, Bonnard, Marquet, Maillol, Matisse, Braque and Dufy.

Behind the port, **Château Suffren** is a remnant of the fortress built by Guillaume, first count of Provence, in 980. From here rue Portalet leads to the little cove of the Glaye, starting point of a coast path that winds its way round waterside houses, tiny coves and the old Port des Pêcheurs. Above the old town the 16th-century **Citadelle** (Montée de la Citadelle; tel: 04 9497 5943; daily Apr–Sept 10am–6.30pm, Oct–Mar 10am–12.30pm, 1.30–5.30pm; charge) boasts an impressive set of ramparts and bastions. The hexagonal keep houses the **Musée Naval de la Citadelle** (due to reopen in 2012 or later), containing souvenirs of Admiral de Suffren, model ships and diving equipment.

One of the best places to see the real St-Tropez is on the **place des Lices**, where there is a colourful market on Tuesday and Saturday mornings. At other times, the square serves as a terrain for boules (*pétanque*), where

It was the film And God Created Woman, *made in 1956 by Brigitte Bardot's then husband, Roger Vadim, that rocketed the overtly sexy actress to stardom, and put St-Tropez, where it was filmed, on the map.*

BELOW: the Vieux-Port, St-Tropez.

white linen-suited millionnaires, who've just jetted in that morning to the airstrip at La Môle, play at being Provençal villagers before retiring to one of its fashionable brasseries; you can even hire a set of boules from the famous Le Café. Across the square, the **Lavoir Vasserot** (rue Joseph Quaranta; times vary), an old wash house, is now used for art exhibitions. Narrow shopping streets run between the square and the Vieux-Port, and a small house contains the **Maison des Papillons** (9 rue Etienne Berny; tel: 04 9497 6345; Apr–Oct and Christmas hols Mon–Sat 2.30–6pm; charge), a display of over 4,500 butterflies collected by painter Dany Lartigue, son of the famous 1920s society photographer.

The main attraction of St-Tropez, however, is its glorious beaches, fringed with restaurants, and packed with sun-bronzed bodies all summer long. Those nearest to town are the Plage de la Bouillabaisse on the road in from Ste-Maxime and the Plage des Graniers and Plage des Salins to the east of town, but it is the fashionable **Plage de Pampelonne** that is

the main upholder of St-Tropez's sun, sea and sex image (see below).

Gassin and Ramatuelle

Many of St-Tropez's more glamorous residents actually hide out in discreet villas hidden among the vineyards of the St-Tropez peninsula. Perched up above are two gorgeous hill villages, **Gassin** and **Ramatuelle** ⓯, both offering chic restaurants and gorgeous views. Ramatuelle is well known for its summer jazz and theatre festivals. On a hill between the two villages are a group of ancient windmills, the Moulins de Paillas.

Port Grimaud and Ste-Maxime

Heading around the Golfe de St-Tropez towards Ste-Maxime, **Port Grimaud** ⓰ is a modern resort designed in the 1960s by the architect François Spoerry around a network of canals to resemble a miniature Venice, with space for boats to moor outside the houses.

Low-key **Ste-Maxime** ⓱ offers an old-fashioned taste of the Côte with its palm trees, promenade

BELOW: Pampelonne bay.

and golden beaches. Facing the port, the stone **Tour Carrée** (place de l'Eglise; Wed–Sun 10am–noon, 3–6pm; charge) built in 1520 as a refuge against pirates, is now a small folk museum, after having served as barn, town hall and prison. A covered market (daily in summer, every morning except Monday in winter) is held a few streets back on rue Fernand Bessy.

Fréjus and St-Raphaël

Squeezed between the massifs of the Maures and Estérel, the next main resort heading east is **Fréjus** ⓲, which is scattered with Roman remains. Located on the Via Aurelia, it was founded as a port in 49 BC by Julius Caesar. It was developed into a naval base by Emperor Augustus – an alternative to unruly Marseille. The **Lanterne d'Auguste**, one of two towers that originally guarded the harbour, still survives. The Roman harbour has long since silted up. In its place there's a modern marina and apartment complex known as **Port-Fréjus**.

Fréjus' most impressive Roman remains are the 2nd-century **Arènes** (rue Henri Vardon; tel: 04 9451 3431; Tue–Sun 9.30am–12.30pm, 2–6pm, Nov–Apr until 5pm) on the western edge of town, which could once accommodate 10,000 spectators. Although substantially damaged, the amphitheatre is still used for rock concerts and bullfights.

In the centre of town overlooking place Formigé stands the medieval **Cathédrale St-Léonce** (Cité Episcopale; tel: 04 9451 2630; June–Sept daily 9am–5.30pm, Oct–May Tue–Sun 9am–noon, 2–5pm; charge). Begun in the 10th century, it is bordered by a 12th-century cloister that features a fantastical wooden ceiling decorated with animals and mythical beasts. You must take one of the frequent guided tours to see the cathedral's elaborately carved Renaissance wooden doors and the 5th-century baptistery, an octagonal structure with granite columns and carved marble capitals pilfered from Roman remains.

Nearby on place Calvini, the **Musée Archéologique** (tel: 04 9432 1598; May–Sept Tue–Sun 9.30am–

TIP

Les Bâteaux Verts (tel: 04 9449 2939, www. bateeauxverts.com) runs frequent ferries between Ste-Maxime and St-Tropez, an excellent way of beating the traffic jams. The company also runs sightseeing trips around the headlands and past celebrity villas on the St-Tropez peninsula.

Below: Port Grimaud.

Vineyard near St-Tropez, one of many producers of the Côtes de Provence wines made in the warm coastal hinterland.

BELOW: the old port, St-Raphaël.

12.30pm, 2–6pm, Oct–Apr Tue–Sun 9.30am–12.30pm, 2–5pm) has a good collection of Roman and early Ligurian tiles, mosaics and sculptures, including the two-faced bust of Hermes that has become the symbol of the town.

In addition to Fréjus's Roman and medieval attractions, there are a couple of very un-Gallic curiosities. A **Buddhist pagoda** sitting in an oriental garden, just off the DN7 to Cannes, commemorates the death of 5,000 Vietnamese soldiers in World War I, while a replica of the Missir **Mosque** in Mali lies unprepossessingly in the middle of an army camp off the D4 to Bagnols.

Merging into Fréjus to the east, lively **St-Raphaël ⑲** started life as a holiday resort for the Roman legionaries of Fréjus. In the 19th century, Napoleon landed in St-Raphaël on his return from Egypt, and this was also his departing point 14 years later when he was banished to Elba. St-Raphaël's status as a fashionable resort is largely down to Alphonse Karr, a former editor of *Le Figaro*, who discovered St-Raphaël in 1865

and encouraged his friends, Alexandre Dumas and Guy de Maupassant amongst them, to follow him. Now, though less trendy and marred by some huge apartment blocks, St-Raphaël has no lack of visitors, even if they're just here to lose a few euros at the rather hideous casino on the palm-lined seafront.

More fun is the daily fish market in the old port, where you can take boats in summer to St-Tropez, Port Grimaud and the Ile de Port-Cros. Behind here is the small, rather unkempt old town, with a good covered market on place Victor-Hugo. The **Musée Archéologique** (place de la Vieille Eglise; tel: 04 9419 2575; Tue–Sat 9am–noon, 2–6pm; charge), in the presbytery of the 12th-century Romanesque church of St-Pierre-des-Templiers, contains Roman amphorae and a display of underwater equipment.

The Massif de l'Estérel

The red porphyry rock of the Estérel tumbles down to the sea in a dramatic sweep of hills and ravines. Highwaymen and sundry criminal types ruled the impenetrable reaches of the **Massif de l'Estérel ⑳** for many centuries, the most notorious of them Gaspard de Bresse, who hung out at the village of Les Adrets de l'Estérel. Forested with pines, cork oak, juniper, rosemary and arbousiers (strawberry trees), in winter the hills turn yellow with mimosa.

The **Corniche d'Or** coast road (D559) makes a scenic alternative to the autoroute to Cannes, though the familiar pattern of private villas, hotels and apartments "de grand standing" blocking views and access to the sea can be very frustrating even here. East of St-Raphaël, the forested **Cap du Dramont** has some lovely stretches of coast path. The Plage du Dramont was one of the main landing beaches for Allied forces in the liberation of Provence: 20,000 America GIs, commemorated in a marble monument, landed here in less than 10 hours on 15 August 1944.

Nearby **Agay** has a sheltered bay with three sandy beaches that are wonderful for swimming. East of here between Anthéor and Trayas is the most picturesque stretch of road winding between rocky outcrops and deep sea inlets, with plenty of places to stop and admire the view. Inland, those with an eye for a panorama should head for **Mont Vinaigre** (at 618 metres/2,027ft, the highest point of the massif) or the Pic de l'Ours.

Further east the tiny port and sandy beach of **La Figueirette**, just before Théoule-sur-Mer, is the starting point for several footpaths into the Estérel. Follow the signs to **Notre-Dame d'Afrique**. Placed here in 2002, the 12-metre (39ft) -high statue facing across the Mediterranean is a copy of the black statue of the Virgin at Notre-Dame d'Afrique in Algiers. It is a place of pilgrimage for the French *pieds noirs* returned from Algeria, with a blessing ceremony each May.

Another curiosity to look out for high above the corniche is the **Palais Bulles** built in 1968 by experimental Finnish–born architect Antti Lovag for the couturier Pierre Cardin. Lovag rejected straight lines and angles: everything here is globular curves. The outside amphitheatre is the setting for an eclectic summer music festival.

Sitting on the seafront at **Mandelieu-la Napoule ㉑**, just west of Cannes, is the fantastical **Château de la Napoule** (www.chateau-lanapoule.com; mid-Feb–mid-Nov daily 10am–6pm, mid-Nov–mid-Feb Sat, Sun and school hols 10am–6pm, Mon–Fri 2–6pm; charge). Originally a fortress belonging to the powerful Villeneuve family, later a glass factory, it was acquired by eccentric American artist Henry Clews in 1918, son of a wealthy banking family. He and his wife gave the place a complete medieval make-over with turrets, crenellations and gargoyles, adding Clews' own weird sculptures and topiaried gardens. Today the castle is an arts foundation offering residences to writers and artists.   ❏

Gaspard de Bresse, the Robin Hood of the Estérel, was the most notorious of the brigands operating in the Estérel in the 18th century. He targeted tax officers and wealthy voyagers, always giving a portion of his proceeds to the poor. A gentleman thief who robbed without bloodshed, a prankster and a dandy, he won over several of his female victims. He was arrested for good at an inn in La Valette du Var and executed in 1781.

Below: Côte de l'Estérel.

Restaurants, Bars and Cafés

Restaurants

Prices for a three-course meal without wine. Many restaurants have a less expensive lunch menu:
€ = under €25
€€ = €25–40
€€€ = €40–60
€€€€ = over €60

Bormes-les-Mimosas
Restaurant de l'Estagnol
Parc de l'Estagnol
Tel: 04 9464 7111. Open L & D in summer. €€
Alfresco eating under the pines, set just back from the beach at l'Estagnol. The speciality is fresh fish and langoustines grilled on an open wood fire. Also serves a bouillabaisse.

La Tonnelle
place Gambetta
www.la-tonnelle-bormes.com
Tel: 04 9471 3484.
Open L Fri–Tue, D Thur–Tue. Closed mid-Nov–mid-Dec. €€
In a pleasant, airy dining room on the square, Gil Renard serves attractively presented modern Mediterranean cooking. Home-made bread and fruit-based desserts are particular highlights.

Cogolin
Grain de Sel
6 rue du 11 novembre
Tel: 04 9454 4686. Open D Mon–Sat. €€
Fresh seasonal bistro cooking, such as stuffed vegetables, roast lamb and fruit tarts, prepared in an open kitchen by a young haute cuisine-trained chef.

Collobrières
Hôtel-Restaurant des Maures
19 boulevard Lazare Carnot
Tel: 04 9448 0710. Open July–Aug L & D daily, Sept–June L daily. €
A popular, unpretentious family-run restaurant and bar with tables on the terrace spanning the Real Collobrier River. Sustaining rustic fare includes a wild boar stew.

Fréjus
L'Entrée des Artistes
63 place St-François-de-Paule. Tel: 04 9440 1160.
Open L & D Tue–Sat. €€
An appealing café-restaurant serving imaginative Provençal dishes, with tables on a small square in the old town.

Gassin
Villa Belrose
boulevard des Crêtes la Grande Bastide
www.villabelrose.com
Tel: 04 9455 9797. Open L & D daily (D only July–Aug, except Sun L & D). Closed Nov–Easter. €€€€
A luxurious hotel restaurant with elegant panelled dining room and a superb terrace overlooking the bay of St-Tropez.

Refined Mediterranean gourmet cooking.

Grimaud
Le Coteau Fleuri
place des Pénitents
www.coteaufleuri.fr
Tel: 04 9443 2017. Open L & D Wed–Mon (daily July–Aug). Closed Nov–Dec. €€€
In an 18th-century house, quietly situated in the old village. Renowned locally for its gastronomic take on regional cuisine by Jean-Claude Paillard.

Hyères
Les Jardins de Bacchus
32 avenue Gambetta
www.les-jardins-de-bacchus.com
Tel: 04 9465 7763. Open L Tue–Fri and Sun, D Tue–Sat. €€
Situated on the main street leading up to the old town, chef Jean-Claude Santorini prepares classic southern cuisine with cosmopolitan touches, such as stuffed sea bream, a white ratatouille (without tomatoes) and delicate violet ice cream.

Le Lavandou
Les Tamaris "Chez Raymond"
Plage de St-Clair
Tel: 04 9471 0270. Open Tue D, Wed–Mon L & D. Closed Nov–Jan. €€

Left: style and colour.

The most upmarket of the fish restaurants along the Plage de St-Clair is renowned for its *bourride* and the excellent daily catch.

Ramatuelle
Chez Camille
route de la Bonne Terrasse
Tel: 04 9812 6898. Open L & D Wed–Sun (D daily July–Aug). Closed Oct–Easter. €€€
Right at the Cap Camarat end of the Plage de Pampelonne, this ancient fisherman's shack draws *le tout St-Trop* for its bouillabaisse, fish soup, lobster and grilled fish.

La Farigoulette
rue Victor Léon
Tel: 04 9479 2049. Open L & D daily (D only July–Aug). Closed Oct–Mar. €€
A simple, informal bistro on the old rampart climb, serving grilled meats, an intense herby *daube de boeuf*, *anchoïade* and pasta dishes.

Rayol-Canadel
Maurin des Maures
boulevard du TCF
www.maurin-des-maures.com
Tel: 04 9405 6011. Open L and D daily. €€
This noisy, animated institution has lots of atmosphere, combining a popular restaurant where you are packed elbow to elbow down long tables, and a local bar with pinball and table football. Come for fish dishes and Prov-

ençal classics like *daube de boeuf* and rabbit. Book ahead.

St-Raphaël
L'Arbousier
9 l'angle de la rue Marius Allongue
www.arbousier.com
Tel: 04 9495 2500. Open L & D Tue–Sat. €€
Using seasonal produce and regional recipes, this cosy Provençal restaurant has become a local favourite for the cooking of Philippe Troncy. Magnolia-shaded terrace in warm weather.

St-Tropez
Brasserie des Arts
5 place des Lices
www.brasseriedesarts.com
Tel: 04 9440 2737. Open L & D daily. €€
The "BA" was reborn in 2008 as a sleek cream and teak affair for people-watching from the terrace. The menu ranges from carpaccios, risottos and crumbles to classic steak tartare, fish with olives and herby lamb, as well as brunch on Sunday. Dress up to look as cool as the staff. Service until 3am in peak season.

Le Girelier
quai Jean Jaurès
www.legirelier.fr
Tel: 04 9497 0387. Open Apr–Oct L & D Tue–Sun. Closed Nov–mid-Mar. €€
This harbourside fish and shellfish restaurant has gained a chic fisherman's shack-inspired

decor from designer Kristian Gavoille following a change of ownership. Fish *a la plancha* is a speciality along with Le Girelier's own take on bouillabaisse. Serves all day noon–midnight.

Le Gorille
1 quai Suffren
www.legorille.com
Tel: 04 9497 0393. Open July–Aug daily 24 hours; Sept–June 8am–1am; closed Jan. €
Against its designer neighbours the open-all-hours Gorille is refreshingly down to earth, serving coffees, steak tartare and *salade niçoise* all day, plus sustenance for après-clubbers in the dead of night.

Senequier
quai Jean Jaurès
www.senequier.com
Tel: 04 9497 2020. Open daily. Closed mid-Jan–mid-Feb. €€
This St-Tropez institution, which opened as a patisserie specialising in nougat in 1887 (still available at 4 place aux Herbes), has had a makeover by hot young designer Noé Duchaufour-Laurence but happily kept the rows of red directors' chairs for surveying the portside scene. Not cheap but a must at apéritif time.

Spoon Byblos
Hôtel Byblos, avenue Maréchal Foch
www.byblos.com
Tel: 04 9456 6820. Open Apr–Oct D daily. Closed

Nov–Mar. €€€€
Alain Ducasse's world food concept located within the fashionable Byblos hotel has a sultry mood popular with the glitterati. There are now two menus: Spoon Origins allows you to mix and match different sauces and condiments to accompany your John Dory or *boeuf tournedos*, while Spoon Now features new inventions.

La Table du Marché
38 rue Georges Clemenceau
www.christophe-leroy.com
Tel: 04 9497 8520. Open L & D daily. €€
The relaxed bistro of celeb chef Christophe Leroy. At the front *le snack* serves up quiches, tarts and patisseries; at the rear the bistro has a Franco-Mediterranean menu.

RIGHT: the enchanting terrace at Alain Ducasse's Spoon Byblos.

TROPICAL GARDENS

The Riviera's mild climate and abundant sunlight have made it a paradise for a remarkable range of flora

All sorts of tropical and subtropical plants have been naturalised in the Riviera region – not just cultivated in gardens and public parks, but growing wild, like the mimosa trees that thrive in the Estérel hills, and the eucalyptus in the Maures forests.

The Belle Epoque was the golden age of Riviera gardens. Most of these exotic edens were created between the 1890s and the 1920s, many of them by the foreigners who came to winter in the region. Almost as varied as the plants they contained were the people who created them: English aristocrats and colonels, American writers, Russian princesses, landscape designers, architects and artists, explorers, botanists and other scientists. Some gardens were created for scientific purposes, others as luxuriant backdrops to go with their exuberant *palazzi* and avant-garde villas.

These green-fingered eccentrics introduced countless new species to the native Mediterranean flora of herbs, parasol pines, olive trees and cork oaks, ranging from the agaves and date palms of desert regions to the dank ferns, banana trees and purple bougainvillea of the tropics. Against the formal restraint of traditional French gardens, with their gravel paths and neatly trimmed hedges, these places were often flamboyantly exotic creations bursting with colour.

LEFT: cactus fruit at the Jardin Exotique, Monaco.

ABOVE: Jardins d'Ephrussi Rothschild, St-Jean-Cap Ferrat. The seven themed gardens, created by Béatrice Ephrussi, are arranged around a central formal French garden with a pool and musical gardens.

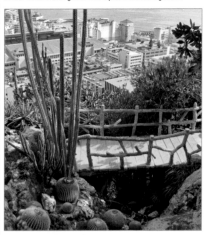

ABOVE: Monaco's Jardin Exotique. This collection, begun at the turn of the 20th century, has over 1,000 species of cacti and other succulent plants, as well as a cave with stalactites and stalagmites.

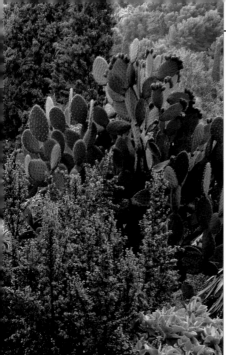

GARDEN TRAILS

1. The Route des Parcs et Jardins du Var (www. tourismevar.com) follows a 325km (200-mile) loop between Saint-Zacharie in the Ste-Baume Massif to Hyères, taking in tiny hill village, herb and scent gardens, historic chateau gardens and the arty gardens of Hyères, as well as addresses of some of the *département*'s best nurseries.

2. The Route des Jardins de la Riviera follows the Alpes-Maritimes coast between Mandelieu-la Napoule and Menton, visiting gardens, villas and grand hotels of the Belle Epoque, including the famous Villa Ephrussi, the gardens of Menton, Villa Eilen Roc in Antibes and the garden of actor-playwright Sacha Guitry at Cap d'Ail.

3. The Route du Mimosa (www.bormesles mimosas.com).

4. Menton, famed for its lemons *(above picture)* is the undisputed garden capital of the coast. Some of its gardens can be visited through the Service du Patrimoine de Menton (tel: 04 9241 7695, www. jardins-menton.fr).

ABOVE LEFT AND RIGHT: cacti in the exotic garden at Jardin d'Ephrussi Rothschild.
BELOW: Jardin Botanique Exotique Val Rahmeh, Menton. Over 700 species grow in profusion on a hilly site around a 1920s villa.

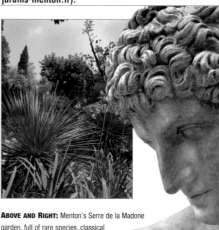

ABOVE AND RIGHT: Menton's Serre de la Madone garden, full of rare species, classical statuary and fountains.

ST-PAUL, VENCE AND THE GORGES DU LOUP

The hilly interior of the western Alpes-Maritimes is home to two shrines of modern art: the Fondation Maeght at St-Paul-de-Vence and Matisse's Chapelle du Rosaire at Vence. Around the Gorges du Loup are some classic *villages perchés*, and fragrant Grasse is the centre of perfume production

West of the River Var, the ancient city of Vence and historic hill towns such as St-Paul-de-Vence and Tourrettes-sur-Loup rest against a mountain backdrop. This part of the Alpes-Maritimes remained part of Provence, and later France, even when the Comté de Nice to the east was under Piedmontese-Sardinian sovereignty – hence some impressive fortifications put up by the French monarchy anxious to control the border. Less crowded and built-up than the coastal strip, the hinterland has an artistic and architectural heritage ranging from medieval chateaux to modern masterpieces, while the gentle climate favourable for flower cultivation has made Grasse a world centre for the perfume industry.

St-Paul-de-Vence

Sitting within ramparts on top of a hill, **St-Paul-de-Vence ❶** epitomises all that is best and worst about Provence: while undeniably picturesque, the village is easily overrun with tourists and any semblance of everyday life has been glossed over by arts-and-crafts galleries and souvenir shops. Thankfully, far more illustrious than the art touted in the old village are the works on show

at the **Fondation Maeght** (*see page 209*), outside the village. One of the finest collections of modern art in the world, it is a wonderful example of the integration of art with architecture and nature.

The village gained its reputation as an artistic centre in the 1920s. The **Auberge de la Colombe d'Or** became a meeting place for a bevy of artists – including Picasso, Bonnard, Chagall, Modigliani and Soutine – who, as the tale goes, left their canvases behind, sometimes to settle

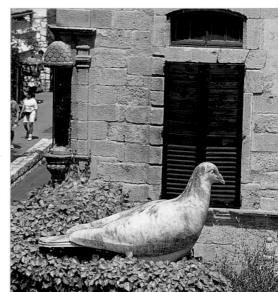

LEFT: Vence facade.
RIGHT: the Colombe d'Or.

For centuries, St-Paul served as a fortress guarding the border between France and the Comté de Nice. When King François I built the ramparts of the village in the 16th century, he uprooted all the inhabitants and packed them off to live in nearby La Colle-sur-Loup. Over 100 years later, new residents arrived: the monks of the Ordre des Pénitents Blancs.

BELOW:
a splash of colour in
St-Paul-de-Vence.

long-running accounts. Whatever the truth, the Colombe d'Or has now assembled its own priceless collection of paintings. You must dine or stay here, however, a delightful if pricey experience, in order to see the collection. Lesser mortals can at least take a seat opposite the Colombe d'Or at the **Café de la Place**.

Within the town walls, rue Grande forms a spine through the town, lined with art galleries and craft shops between the 14th-century Porte Nord (or Porte Royale) to the Porte Sud (or Porte de Nice). About halfway along, at the place de la Grande Fontaine, a street climbs to a small square at the top of the village. Here you'll find the **Eglise Collégiale**, in which is a painting attributed to Tintoretto, the **Chapelle des Pénitents Blancs**, the Mairie (town hall) housed within the remains of the castle keep, and the small **Musée de l'Histoire Local** (Apr–Oct daily 10am–noon, 3–6pm, Dec–Mar 2–5pm; closed Nov; charge)

where costumed figures illustrate key moments in St-Paul's history. Outside the south gate is the cemetery in which the painter Marc Chagall is buried. You can also follow the path along the western ramparts, which provides good views over vineyards and luxury villas to the coast.

Vence

Modern-art pilgrims should also make for **Vence ❷**, just 4km (2½ miles) further north, and its **Chapelle du Rosaire** (468 avenue Henri Matisse; tel: 04 9358 0326; Mon, Wed, Sat 2–5.30pm, Tue, Thur 10–11.30am, 2–5.30pm; charge), on the edge of town on the route de Ste-Jeannet. It was designed between 1948 and 1951 by the elderly Henri Matisse (1869–1954), who had moved to the Villa le Rêve in Vence during World War II, encouraged by the Dominican nun Sister Jacques-Marie (*see margin right*).

The chapel is strikingly pure and bright: the roof in glazed blue-and-

St-Paul, Vence and the Gorges du Loup

white pantiles, and the only colour in its white interior contributed by the stained-glass windows and the reflections they create. The figurative tiles on three of the walls capture Matisse's fluid mastery of line in the single stroke of his drawings. On the simple stone altar lies a tiny bronze crucifix. In an adjacent room you can see Matisse's preparatory sketches.

A spiritual testament by the aged artist, Matisse called the chapel his most satisfying work. He was not the only artist attracted to Vence: Chagall also lived here, and the writer D.H. Lawrence came here after having been diagnosed with tuberculosis.

Within the city walls

Vence's walled city centre contains many traces of its days as a powerful bishopric. Its strategic mountain position made it a trophy for successive Ligurians, Lombards, Romans, countless Christians and Saracens, and the Germans and Italians of World War II, who all passed through here.

Begun in the 4th century, the **Ancienne Cathédrale**, in place Clemenceau on the site of a Roman temple, reflects the town's battle-torn past. The building is a patchwork of styles and eras, with its simple Baroque facade, Gothic windows, Roman tablets incorporated into the porch, fragments of the earlier Carolingian church, 15th-century carved choir stalls and a delicate 1979 mosaic by Chagall of Moses in the baptistery.

Behind here pleasant place Godeau contains an ancient Roman column, while rue de l'Evêché, which has some interesting craft galleries and artists' studios, leads to place du Peyra and its restaurant terraces. On one side of the square, abutting a medieval tower, is the **Château de Villeneuve-Fondation Emile Hugues** (www.museedevence.com; tel: 04 9358 1578; July–Sept 10am–6pm, Oct–June Tue–Sun 10am–12.30pm, 2–6pm, closed between exhibitions; charge), the 17th-century baronial residence of the powerful Villeneuve family, now used for high-quality exhibitions of modern and contemporary art. Outside the Porte du Peyra, place du Frêne contains a venerable ash tree supposedly planted by

TIP

The Villa le Rêve in Vence, where Matisse lived from 1943 to 1949, is now used for painting courses and artists' residences. Half- or one-day visits can be arranged by appointment: 261 avenue Henri Matisse, tel: 04 9358 8268.

BELOW:
Giacometti sculpture, Fondation Maeght.

Fondation Maeght

The Fondation Maeght (623 chemin des Gardettes, St-Paul-de-Vence; www.fondation-maeght.com; tel: 04 9332 8163; daily July–Sept 10am–7pm, Oct–June 10am–6pm; charge) is arguably the most interesting of all the museums on the Côte d'Azur, inaugurated in 1964 to house the fabulous modern art collection put together by Paris art dealer Aimé Maeght and his wife Marguerite. The concrete building was designed by the Spanish architect José-Luis Sert, and is beautifully integrated with both landscape and artworks, inside and out. A series of pools, terraces and sculptures include funky, colourful ceramic fountains by Miró and tiled designs by Braque. Other sculptures, among them works by Giacometti and Calder, are dotted around the pine-shaded garden. All the structural features were devised to promote an understanding of 20th-century art, and the architect worked directly with some of the artists, principally Miró and Chagall, to achieve this. A few of the holdings are sometimes on loan and the collection is rehung for themed exhibitions each summer, but with reserves this large there is always something to see.

Around a dozen families still make their living cultivating violets in Tourrettes-sur-Loup. The fragrant purple flowers are harvested between mid-October and mid-March; between May and July the leaves are picked and delivered to the perfume factories in Grasse. The end of the flower harvest is celebrated in March by the Fête des Violettes, with a Mass, dancing and a floral procession.

François I in 1538. Just beyond here square du Grand-Jardin is the setting for the farmers' market (mornings daily) and Les Nuits du Sud, Vence's summer world music festival.

The Gorges du Loup

From Vence it's a scenic drive along D2210 to the attractive hilltop village of **Tourrettes-sur-Loup** ❸, dubbed the "city of violets" *(see left)*. Now home to the requisite Provençal clan of potters, painters and woodcarvers, Tourrettes was a Roman and subsequently Saracen stronghold. The only evocations of war today come from the 15th-century chateau, once marking the entrance to the village, now at its centre and occupied by the Mairie (town hall).In the main square, the church conceals a triptych by the Bréa school.

The road from Tourrettes descends through woodland into the river valley at **Pont-du-Loup** – home to the much publicised **Confiserie Florian** (tel: 04 9359 3291; free), an old-fashioned sweet manufacturer open to visitors. Here you can decide to head southwards towards

Le Bar-sur-Loup or upstream on the D6 along the imposing **Gorges du Loup** ❹, where the torrential Loup River has scythed its way through a gorge of grey rock. It is punctuated by some impressive waterfalls, notably the **Cascade de Courmes** which plunges down about 50 metres (160ft) halfway along the Gorges, the smaller **Cascade des Desmoiselles**, and, further up, **Saut du Loup** (Wolf's Leap). Signs advise on sudden rises in the water level, dependent on the hydroelectric station upstream.

In the other direction, **Le Bar-sur-Loup** is a relatively ungentrified village whose church (closed for restoration) contains a fascinating if macabre painting of the dance of death.

Gourdon

If the term *village perché* needed a perfect example, **Gourdon** ❺ would be it. One whole side of the village teeters on the edge of a rocky cliff, obviating the need for any fortress walls to repel invaders.

A brief walk up through the village's main street (cars are not allowed)

BELOW: playing boules in Tourrettes-sur-Loup.

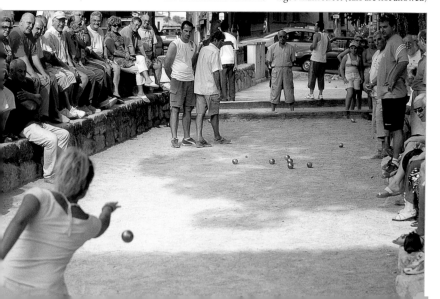

brings you to the feudal **Château de Gourdon** (www.chateau-gourdon.com; tel: 04 9309 6802; historic and Art Deco museums can be seen on guided visits; the gardens are open to groups by reservation; no children under 12; charge). Inside it contains two museums: the historic museum tracing the castle's history, along with a large collection of weapons, and **Musée des Arts Décoratifs et de la Modernité**, which contains a superb collection of furniture and lighting by avant-garde designers, such as Eileen Gray, Ruhlmann and Chareau.

From Gourdon the D3 zigzags down to Grasse. On your way you might choose to detour to **Valbonne** ❻. Valbonne immediately stands out from its neighbours as it was laid out in the 16th century on a strict rectangular grid plan by monks from the Abbaye de Chaalis, on the southern edge of the town.

Another very different planned city lies east of here on the Plateau de Valbonne. Founded in the early 1970s, **Sophia-Antipolis** is southern France's answer to Silicon Valley, a brave new world of high-tech companies, research institutes and a branch of the university of Nice.

Grasse, the perfume capital

Literature fans may recognise **Grasse** ❼ as the setting for Patrick Süskind's novel, *Perfume*. France's sprawling perfume capital is not one of Provence's most attractive towns, and the hilly geography and winding boulevards make finding your bearings difficult. But the municipality is at last making an effort to revive the rather run-down town centre through restoration and pedestrianisation.

Between 1138 and 1227 Grasse was a free city, allied to Pisa and Genoa, and governed by a consulate, like the Italian republics, before being annexed by the counts of Provence. When Provence was united with France in 1482, Grasse continued to trade with Italy, importing animal skins and selling linen and high-quality leather goods. In the 16th century, the fashion for perfumed gloves encouraged the perfume industry in Grasse, but it was not until the 18th century that tanning

TIP

Running into the southern edge of Grasse is Mouans-Sartoux, whose main appeal is the Espace de l'Art Concret (www. espacedelartconcret.fr; tel: 04 9375 7150; July–Aug daily 11am–7pm, Sept–June Wed–Sun noon–6pm; charge) at the Château de Mouans. The gallery was founded by artist Gottfried Honegger and the widow of Josef Albers in 1990 to exhibit their collection of minimalist abstract art.

BELOW: Gourdon.

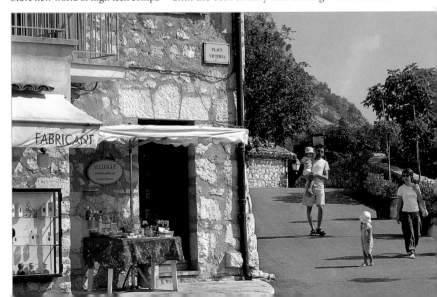

Perfumes of Provence

Although best known for making perfumes for the world's biggest fashion houses, Grasse's "noses" also concoct fragances for use in cleaning products

The perfume industry in Grasse originated with an immigrant group of Italian glove-makers in the 16th century. They discovered the wonderful scents of the flowers in the area and began perfuming their soft leather gloves, a fashion introduced by Catherine de Medici and a favourite way to use perfume at a time when the odour of the general populace definitely required masking.

Demand for the floral perfumes steadily grew in the 18th and 19th centuries, and Grasse prospered as a perfume mecca. Local production of the raw material declined, however, after World War II due to competition from countries such as Turkey, Egypt and Bulgaria, where labour costs were much lower. On top of this, the gentle climate attracted many wealthy people to the area, pushing land prices sky-high and causing acres to be sold off as building plots.

Nonetheless, each morning you can still see vast mountains of rose petals, vats of mimosa or jonquils and spadefuls of violets and orange blossom just picked and waiting to be processed.

The flowers must be picked early in the day, when the oil is most concentrated, and delivered immediately. It takes vast quantities of blooms to produce the tiniest amounts of "absolute" (concentrated) perfume: around 750kg (1,650lbs) of roses for just 1kg (2.2lbs) of rose absolute and about 4,000kg (8,800lbs) for 1kg of essential oil.

Various methods are used to create the absolutes and essential oils that the perfumier mixes to create a fragrance. The oldest method is steam distillation, now used mainly for orange blossom. Water and flowers are boiled in a still, and the essential oils are extracted by steam.

Another ancient, though expensive, method is *enfleurage*. The flowers are layered with a semi-solid mixture of lard, spread over glass sheets and stacked in wooden tiers. When the fat is fully impregnated with perfume, the scent is separated out by washing the *axonge* (fat) with alcohol. A more modern method is extraction by volatile solvents, leaving a final dose of concentrated essence.

The highly trained perfumiers or "noses" can identify and classify hundreds of fragrances. In creating a fragrance, a perfumier is rather like a musician, blending different "chords" of scent to create a harmony. The desired result is a complex perfume that will radiate around the body in a slow process of diffusion – what the French call *sillage*. Nowadays, many of the raw ingredients are imported, with the exception of jasmine and may rose; others, such as musk, formerly made from animals, are chemically synthesised. But the perfumiers' know-how keeps Grasse at the forefront of the industry, not just with perfumes for the great fashion houses but with the fragrances used in household cleaning products and food-industry flavourings. ❏

LEFT: visiting the Parfumerie Fragonard factory.

and perfumery began to develop as separate trades.

Perfume museum

On a still day, Grasse lives up to its reputation as a scent capital: a sweet aroma lingers in the air. Huge hoardings announce factory visits to the three big perfumiers – Fragonard, Molinard and Galimard – all actually located some way outside the town centre. The **Musée International de la Parfumerie** (2 boulevard du Jeu de Ballon; www.museesdegrasse.com; tel: 04 9705 5800; May–Sept daily 10am–7pm, until 9pm Sat, Oct and Dec–Apr Wed–Mon 11am–6pm, closed Nov; charge) in an 18th-century mansion and its modern extension provides an imaginative introduction to the art of perfumery and the sense of smell, with displays of the assorted plants, minerals, roots and animal matter used to make perfumes. The museum has a vast collection of perfume bottles, a greenhouse containing olfactory plants and materials to sniff and touch, a reconstruction of a medieval apothecary's shop and works by contemporary artists.

Near by is the **Musée Provençal du Costume et du Bijou** (2 rue Jean Ossola; tel: 04 9336 4465; Easter–Oct daily 10am–1pm, 2–6pm, Nov–Easter Mon–Sat; charge), where 18th- and 19th-century regional costumes and jewellery are attractively presented around the upstairs rooms of a period house, with a Fragonard perfume shop below. The perfume company's original factory, the **Usine Historique de Fragonard** (20 boulevard Fragonard; daily 9am–6pm, 7pm July–Aug; free), opened in 1926, is just down the hill. A few perfumes, soaps and cosmetics are still made here.

Grasse cathedral

Rue Jean-Ossola is the best way into the largely pedestrianised old town and is lined with fine facades, among them that of the Hôtel Luce at No. 14, where swashbuckling musketeer d'Artagnan is said to have stayed. On place du Petit-Puy are a fortified watchtower, the Hôtel de Ville (once the bishop's palace) and the **Cathédrale Notre-Dame-de-Puy**, a much altered, rather gloomy Romanesque

TIP

The Moulins de la Brague (www.moulin-opio.com; tel: 04 9377 2303; Mon–Sat) at Opio has been run by the Michel family for over 150 years. Although water power has now been replaced by electricity, traditional methods are still used to make high-quality olive oil from the tiny purple *caillette* or "olive de Nice".

BELOW: gathering jasmine, Grasse.

Carved statue representing the perfumier's art outside the Parfumerie Fragonard, one of Grasse's oldest perfume-making establishments.

BELOW: cradle vaulting of Grasse cathedral.

structure. It contains three paintings by Rubens and a rare religious subject, *The Washing of the Feet*, by Jean-Honoré Fragonard (1732–1806), who was born in Grasse.

The Fragonard connection

Although the town makes the most of its connection with Fragonard, he actually spent most of his career in Paris or on the Grand Tour of Italy with aristocratic patrons, and it was only after the French Revolution that he took refuge in Grasse in the house of a wealthy cousin, now the **Villa-Musée Fragonard** (23 boulevard Fragonard; www.museesdegrasse.com; guided visits only June–Sept daily 10am–7pm, Oct and Dec–May Wed–Mon 10am–6pm, closed Nov; free). The most remarkable aspect of the house is its stairwell, decorated with grisaille frescos by Fragonard's son when he was only 13 years old. In a neighbouring building, the **Musée de la Marine** (Mon–Fri 10am–12.30pm, 2.30–5.30pm, closed most of Nov; free), commemorates the life of Admiral de Grasse, who defeated the British fleet at the battle of Chesapeake during the American War of Independence.

Another fine neoclassical residence contains the **Musée de l'Histoire de Provence** (2 rue Mirabeau; June–Sept daily 10am–7pm, Oct and Dec–May Wed–Mon 10am–6pm; charge) devoted to Provençal life, with rooms furnished in period style.

Grottes de St-Cézaire

Napoleon passed by Grasse after escaping from Elba. The former N85 road (now D6185/D6085), known as the Route Napoléon, roughly follows the route he took through Provence on his return to Paris for the Hundred Days. From Grasse, the route climbs over the Col du Pilon pass before reaching the hamlet of St-Vallier-de-Thiey.

From here you can continue to Castellane *(see page 158)* or turn off on the D5 to the **Grottes de St-Cézaire ❽**, a cave complex with stalactites in extraordinary shades of dark red and pink. From St-Cézaire you can return to Grasse via the village of **Cabris** (6km/4 miles from Grasse on the D4 road), which commands an impressive view from its castle ruins. ❑

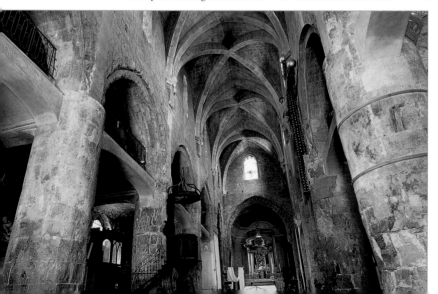

RESTAURANTS AND BARS

Restaurants

Prices for a three-course meal without wine. Many restaurants have a less expensive lunch menu:
€ = under €25
€€ = €25–40
€€€ = €40–60
€€€€ = over €60

Le Bar-sur-Loup
L'Hostellerie du Château
6–8 place Francis Paulet
www.lhostellerieduchateau.com
Tel: 04 9342 4110. Open L & D Thur–Tue. €€€
In the former castle of the counts of Grasse, artistically presented modern southern cooking is served in a pared-down dining room with panoramic views over the Loup valley. In summer, you also have the choice of eating in a simpler café which opens onto the village square.

Cabris
Auberge du Vieux Château
place du Panorama
www.aubergeduvieux
chateau.com
Tel: 04 9360 5012. Open L & D Wed–Sun (plus D Mon & Tue July–Aug). €€
Set in the former castle guardroom, this place is very popular among Grasse's anglophone

expats, thanks to its terrace views and a frequently changing, Mediterranean menu.

Grasse
La Bastide St-Antoine
48 avenue Henri Dunant
www.jacques-chibois.com
Tel: 04 9370 9494. Open L & D daily. €€€€
Difficult to find but well worth the search, this restaurant is set in an old olive grove outside Grasse, and is fashionable for the gourmet cuisine of Jacques Chibois. In season, truffles and wild mushrooms are house specialities.

Café des Musées
1 rue Jean Ossola
Tel: 04 9260 9900. Open summer L & D daily, winter L & D Mon–Sat. €
This stylish modern café is conveniently located between the perfume and costume museums (Musée International de la Parfumerie and Musée Provençal du Costume et du Bijou). It's ideal for a drink or a light lunch of salads, savoury tarts and home-made desserts.

St-Paul-de-Vence
La Colombe d'Or
1 place du Général de Gaulle
www.la-colombe-dor.com
Tel: 04 9332 8002. Open L

& D daily. Closed Nov–22 Dec. €€€€
Once frequented by penniless artists who persuaded the owner to accept their paintings in payment for meals and board, this legendary hotel and restaurant now displays works by Miró, Picasso, Modigliani, Matisse and Chagall for a jet-set clientele. Serves classic cuisine and has arguably the most beautiful terrace in the region.

Vence
Les Bacchanales
247 avenue de Provence
www.lesbacchanales.com
Tel: 04 9324 1919. Open L & D Thur–Mon. €€€
Chef Christophe Dufau

has moved from Tourrettes-sur-Loup to a modern dining room in a 19th-century villa on the edge of Vence, towards the Matisse chapel (Chapelle du Rosaire). His beautifully presented regional cooking is characterised by the use of wild herbs and edible flowers in dishes.

La Litote
5 rue de l'Evêché
www.lalitote.com
Tel: 04 9324 2782. Open L & D Tue–Sat, L Sun. €€
This friendly bistro in the old town brings an imaginative whiff of modernity to Provençal cuisine. There are concerts on Thursday nights.

RIGHT: spectacularly situated restaurant, Gourdon.

MERCANTOUR NATIONAL PARK AND THE ARRIÈRE-PAYS NIÇOIS

Away from the coast, the eastern Alpes-Maritimes is characterised by wild mountains, plunging gorges, clear sparkling rivers and Italianate villages with frescoed churches

The rugged, sparsely populated Mercantour Massif provides a startling contrast to the built-up coast. Ice and fast mountain torrents have cut deep gorges through the rock. Flowing roughly north to south, the River Cians, the Tinée and Vésubie all empty into the River Var, while further east lie the Bévéra and Roya rivers. The scenery ranges from olive groves grown on the lower slopes to pines and edelweiss, mountain lakes and bare Alpine peaks, many of them over 2,000 metres (6,560ft). The area is a paradise for hikers and mountaineers in summer and skiers in winter.

In addition to its spectacular scenery, this Alpine region by the Italian border also has a little-known architectural and artistic heritage that reflects a period when it was more heavily populated, largely because of the active trade routes, notably the salt route, linking the Comté de Nice, Piedmont and Liguria. Chapels, often decorated with ornate frescos, were put up as protection against the frequent outbreaks of plague, and during the Counter-Reformation, fine Baroque churches were constructed as the Catholic Church sought to reassert its authority against the Protestant Reformation.

The Arrière-Pays Niçois

Even a few kilometres inland from Nice or Monaco, you soon find yourself in a mountain environment studded with medieval villages. Unspoilt **Peillon**, 15km (9 miles) northeast of Nice, clings like an eagle's eyrie onto a jagged ridge above the River Paillon. Vaulted alleys and steep stairways are lined with 16th-century houses, and the Chapelle des Pénitents Blancs is decorated with dramatic 15th-century frescos of the Passion of Christ.

LEFT: ibex roam the Mercantour Massif.

Further along steep narrow roads and hairpin bends stands the perched village of **Peille**, with some lovely Renaissance and Gothic fountains, doorways and stonework amid the cobbled alleyways.

Coaraze ❶, another delightful village balancing at an altitude of 650 metres (2,100ft), calls itself *le village du soleil*. Wander through the narrow cobbled streets looking out for the sundials, which have been a feature here since Jean Cocteau decorated the town hall with one. Next to the lizard mosaic on place Félix-Giordan is a poem relating the local legend of how the villagers caught the devil, who cut off his tail to escape. (Coaraze derives from the Provençal words 'coa raza' meaning 'cut tail'.) On the edge of the village is the **Chapelle Bleue**, named after the blue murals created by Ponce de Léon in 1965.

Parc National du Mercantour

Covering a large swathe of the region is the **Parc National du Mercantour** (www.mercantour.eu) **❷**, a huge national park created in 1979, which joins the Parco Naturale Alpi Maritime around the Argentera Massif in Italy. It consists of two zones: the highly protected, largely uninhabited central zone, and the peripheral zone where the villages are situated.

Botanists now believe that more than half of the 4,000 or so species of wild flowers found in France grow in the Mercantour, including 63 varieties of orchid. Wildlife includes ibex, chamois, marmots, the ptarmigan, black grouse, golden eagle and rare species of owl. More controversial are the wolves that have returned to the area after crossing the border from Italy, now a source of heated argument between environmentalists and the shepherds who claim that the wolves are killing their sheep.

Vallée des Merveilles

At the heart of the national park lies the mysterious **Vallée des Merveilles ❸**, where the mountains shelter a remarkable display of over 40,000 prehistoric rock engravings by early Bronze Age settlers. First recorded in the 17th century, these carvings are similar to ones found in the

Thousands of Bronze Age drawings can be seen in the Vallée des Merveilles.

BELOW: Alpine flowers.

TIP

Snow and ice are often present from October until June, and the weather can change without warning or differ considerably from one valley to the next. Even in summer, mist can close around you. The locals and the *gendarmes* (police) are familiar with the conditions and certainly won't laugh at people wearing heavy gear in summer or requesting a mountain guide.

Camerino valley near Bergamo in Italy. The French carvings are exceptional, though, in that they depict a race of shepherds rather than hunters: the scarcity of wild game in the region forced the Bronze Age tribes to turn to agriculture and cattle-raising. These primitive inscriptions served as territorial markers for the area's tribes.

However, the drawings are also open to some less earthbound interpretations. Anthropomorphic figures represent domestic animals and chief tribesmen but also dancers, devils, sorcerers and gods. Such magical totems are in keeping with Mt-Bégo's *(see page 219)* reputation as a sacred spot. Given the bleakness of the terrain, it is hardly surprising that the early shepherds looked heavenwards for help. Nowadays, as then, flocks of cows, sheep and goats graze by the lower lakes. However, the abandoned farms and shepherds' outhouses attest to the unprofitable nature of mountain farming.

Some demanding hiking

There are two main points of access into the Vallée des Merveilles: from **St-Dalmas-de-Tende** in the Roya valley on the eastern side, and from **Madone de Fenestre** in the Vésubie valley to the west. The valley is accessible only in summer and only on foot (although a few all-terrain vehicles are permitted). Much of the terrain is really only suitable for those hikers with limbs and lungs strong enough to endure a day or two of solid walking and with hiking gear to match. Hardened hikers can probably make do with a large-scale map – arm yourself with the IGN 1:25,000 map and a Topoguide. If an overnight stay is necessary, try one of the simple mountain refuges administered by the Club Alpin Français (www.cafresa.org; tel: 04 9362 5999). Often, there aren't even any paths, let alone signposts if you lose your way. For the less experienced hiker, a mountain guide is essential, or join

Mercantour National Park and the Arriere-Pays Niçois

one of the regular guided walks to some of the more accessible engravings, organised by the national park (June–Sept, information from Maisons du Parc and tourist offices, *see margin right*). They last about three hours and leave from the Refuge des Merveilles or Refuge de Fontanalbe (the latter is the easiest to reach, from Castérino west of St-Dalmas-de-Tende).

The area between **Mt-Bégo** and the 2,934-metre (9,626ft) **Mont du Grand Capelet** makes for a good, if tough, hike, with several lakes on the way. There are mountain refuges either end of the 60km (40-mile) valley. If a thunderstorm strikes, don't panic: shepherds working in the valleys below more than 3,000 years ago treated Mt-Bégo like a temple, a place where sheep were sacrificed in an attempt to appease terrifying storms. In contemporary and less superstitious times, the mountain is simply seen as an effective lightning conductor.

Tende

The main base for excursions into the Mercantour, especially the Val-lée des Merveilles, is **Tende ❹**. When the rest of the Comté de Nice rejoined France in 1860, this upper part of the Roya valley, the favourite hunting ground of king Vittorio Emanuele II, was granted to Italy, joining France only in 1947. The stacked houses, many of them dating from the 15th century, are built in local green-hued schist and have balconies and overhanging roofs. The 15th-century **Eglise Collégiale Notre-Dame de l'Assomption** (summer daily 9am–6pm; winter daily 9am–5pm) has a belfry shaped like two stacked barrels and a Baroque interior with 17th-century organ loft.

The **Musée des Merveilles** (www. museedesmerveilles.com; tel: 04 9304 3250; May–mid-Oct Wed–Mon 10am– 6.30pm, daily July–Sept, mid-Oct–Apr Wed–Mon 10am–5pm, closed 2 weeks in Mar, 2 weeks in Nov; free), in a striking modern building, has an exhibition devoted to the prehistory of the park, including original fragments from the rock drawings and mouldings of the most famous motifs.

TIP

There are Maisons du Parc providing information about the Parc National du Mercantour (www. mercantour.eu) in St-Etienne-de-Tinée, St-Martin-Vésubie and Tende. They are open in summer and during school holidays.

BELOW LEFT: the national park is dotted with refuges for hikers.
BELOW: on the trail to Pas des Ladres in the park.

BELOW: restored mill by the Roya River.

Vallée de la Vésubie

Within easy reach of Nice and the coast, the glorious **Vallée de la Vésubie ❺** leads you away from a Mediterranean landscape to the fresher Alpine scenery of dark-green pines, waterfalls near Le Boréon and green pastures at Roquebillière. The main town, **St-Martin-Vésubie ❻** offers cool respite as a mountaineering centre in the summer. This is a sleepy and unpretentious place, disturbed only by the rush of water down a 1-metre (3ft) -wide canal. The twin torrents of Le Boréon and the Madone de la Fenestre converge in the town to form the River Vésubie.

Summer for a Vésubian inhabitant starts on 2 July, when a procession wends its way out of St-Martin carrying an 800-year-old wooden statue of Notre-Dame-de-Fenestre 12km (7 miles) east to the sanctuary at **Madone de Fenestre** (open daily). Winter begins when the procession makes the return journey in the third week of September. A few kilometres to the west of St-Martin-Vésubie is a small skiing resort at **La Colmiane**, complete with a few old chalets.

The **Gorges de la Vésubie** begin at St-Jean-la-Rivière; there is a spectacular panorama from above the fortified village of **Utelle**, at **Madone d'Utelle ❼**. The sanctuary here (www.madone dutelle.com; tel: 04 9303 1944; daily)is on the site of an ancient shrine to a statue of the Virgin, destroyed in the French Revolution. The new church, consecrated in 1806, is still a place of pilgrimage, with simple accommodation and a restaurant.

Tinée valley

The Gorges de la Vésubie end at the Plan du Var. Leaving the D6202 at the Pont de la Mescla, the D2205 heads up the Tinée valley through the **Gorges de la Mescla ❽**, where spectacular slabs of rock overhang both road and river. Further up, the old village of **Isola** is today largely a doorway to the modern ski resort of **Isola 2000 ❾** *(see box below)*, near the Italian frontier, but it does have several of the chapels indicative of the once fervent religious life of these valleys, three *lavoirs* (wash houses) and a communal bread oven in use until 1950.

Winter Sports in the Alpes-Maritimes

In winter, the 85 percent of the population of the Alpes-Maritimes resident near the coast suddenly seems to acquire a taste for the backcountry. The right bank of the Var becomes a fashionable artery as the Niçois head to the skiing resorts: Auron and Isola 2000 for the *sportif* in search of a conversation piece; Valberg and Beuil for the less pretentious or those more keen on cross-country skiing. **Valberg** (www.valberg.com) is a family-oriented resort with good facilities for children, and a snowboarding park. Its *domaine* is now linked to **Beuil** (www.beuil.com), an ancient village which was once the seat of the Grimaldis. **Auron** (www.auron.com) lines up a full range of slopes and trails for the inveterate skier, as well as a modern snowpark for snowboarders. The modern chalets, flats and ski lifts dotting the pastures are the inland equivalent of the concrete structures on the coast, although it is possible to stay in some of the more charming villages in the area. Inaugurated in 1971, **Isola 2000** (www.isola2000.com) has space-age architecture, and its 120km (75 miles) of pistes have been joined by high-thrill snowboarding and heli-skiing options.

Further up the valley at 1,140 metres (3,740ft), rural **St-Etienne-de-Tinée** ⑩, though largely rebuilt after a fire in the 1930s, has an important religious heritage. The walls and vault of the **Chapelle St-Sébastien** (contact tourist office for visits: St-Etienne tel: 04 9302 4196; Auron tel: 04 9323 0266, generally Mon and Thur 4pm in summer) are covered with paintings telling the life of the martyr saint, attributed to Jean Canavesio and Jean Baleisoni, dating from 1492. Even the nearby ski resort of **Auron** *(see box)* contains the frescoed 14th-century **Chapelle St-Erige**, unlikely survivor amid the modern apartment blocks.

Sospel

On the southeastern edge of the Parc National is the charming Italianate town of **Sospel** ⑪. It's popular with the Mentonnais for a day out, for walking (the GR52 long-distance footpath runs through here) or for hunting in autumn. Successively under the rule of the counts of Ventimiglia, Provence and Nice, it was the second-most important town in the Comté de Nice in the Middle Ages, when it had a flourishing religious life. In the early 18th century it was known for its literary circle. The Bévéra, a tributary of the Roya, runs through it, leaving a series of islets around the **Vieux Pont** (old bridge). The bridge is an oddity, with a toll gate in the middle for levying tax on the salt route. Today it contains the tourist office.

The oldest part of the town is a cluster of buildings with wooden balconies overlooking the river. By the river, a sheltered *lavoir* filled with water even at the height of summer still survives. On the southern side of the bridge, houses come in weathered shades of orange, yellow, ochre or red stucco, and the 17th-century Baroque **Cathédrale St-Michel** lords it over an attractive cobbled square. Inside is an altarpiece by Francesco Brea, a member of the celebrated Niçois dynasty of painters.

You can also visit the reinforced concrete **Fort St-Roch** (tel: 04 9304 0070; June–Sept Tue–Sun 2–6pm, Apr, May, Oct Sat–Sun 2–6pm; charge), built as part of the Maginot Line (there's another one at Ste-Agnès,

TIP

Each August, the Festival International des Orgues Historiques gives people the chance to hear the historic organs housed in many of the churches of the Roya and Bévéra valleys. For details, tel: 04 93 04 22 20; www.royabevera.com

BELOW: road to Sospel.

further south near Menton), the defensive system of partially underground fortresses built along the eastern border of France in the 1930s.

Northwest of Sospel, the D2566 climbs through deep pine forests to the **Col de Turini** (from where you can join the Vésubie valley or return to Nice via Lucéram), with a small ski resort and a good starting point for some relatively gentle walks. The nearby **Plateau d'Authion** was a battlefield on more than one occasion; you'll find the **Cabanes Vieilles** (ruins of Napoleonic barracks) there, destroyed during combat with retreating German troops at the end of World War II.

Roya Valley and Saorge

Northeast of Sospel, the D2204 takes you over the Col de Brouis (Brouis pass) to join the Roya valley just north of **Breil-sur-Roya** ⑫. On a flat expanse of valley, the wide Roya has here been turned into an artificial lake that lies along the edge of town. Breil produces excellent olive oil, using a variety of olive, the *cailletier*, found only in the Alpes-Maritimes.

The **Vallée de la Roya** was retained by the Italians until October 1947, because it was the only link with the Mercantour and the hunting grounds of the king of Italy.

North of Breil, the road, which shares the valley with the railway, gets more dramatic, passing through steep gorges on the way to the spectacularly situated town of **Saorge** ⑬, which still has the appearance of a mountain stronghold. Packed into a cliff face, it takes a trek on foot to reach the centre, through some of the steepest cobbled alleyways imaginable. Tall, narrow houses tower over dark streets. Some people do still live here, but the young tend to be quick to move out to search for employment elsewhere. The contemporary exodus contrasts with ancient times, when it seemed like everyone was trying to invade the fortified village – unsuccessfully. Such was its reputation for impregnability that would-be invaders eventually gave up trying.

The steepness does not rule out the existence of a fine Renaissance church, **St-Sauveur**, with a red-and-gold altar. The finely carved church

BELOW: Saorge.

Mountain Trains

Three railway lines run into the interior of the Alpes-Maritimes. The SNCF-run Nice–Cuneo line follows the Peillon, Bévéra and Roya valleys through long tunnels and over numerous viaducts, stopping at Peillon, Sospel, Breil-sur-Roya, Saorge, La Brigue and Tende. In summer, a special tourist train, dubbed the "Train des Merveilles", leaves Nice at 9am, arriving at Tende at 10.46am. It provides a tourist commentary and slows down for photo opportunities. In winter the "train des neiges" is a special service for skiers, consisting of a shuttle from Tende to Castérino. Another line joins this one from Ventimiglia in Italy to Breil-sur-Roya.

organ was made in Genoa in the 19th century. Its installation, and even the building of the church, would not have been possible without the strength and agility of the mules used to carry materials up the hill. Saorge has not forgotten the contribution the animals made (and still make) to life in the village: one of the village festivals is dedicated to St Eloi, patron saint of mules.

Saorge Monastery

Amid olive trees at the top of town, the **Monastère de Saorge** (www.monum.fr; tel: 04 9304 5556; Wed–Mon 10am– noon, 2–6pm, until 5pm in winter; charge), founded in 1633, no longer has Franciscan monks; instead its tranquil atmosphere now serves for writers' retreats and workshops. The church is a fine example of the local Baroque style, with an elaborate master altar with barley-sugar columns surrounding a statue of the Virgin. The whitewashed two-storey cloister is painted with several ornate sundials.

The valley here apparently has a good echo, a feature that allowed 20th-century soldiers to communicate from the ruined castle above with a nearby chateau.

La Brigue

At St-Dalmas-de-Tende, side roads lead off in one direction towards the Vallée des Merveilles, and in the other to **La Brigue** , another of those mountain villages clearly once more populated and prosperous than it is today. It has some finely carved lintels, Baroque churches, arcaded medieval houses and the ruins of the 14th-century Château Lascaris, which is floodlit at night.

However, the main reason to pause here lies 4km (2½ miles) further east, where the simple exterior of the isolated **Chapelle de Notre-Dame-des-Fontaines** (tel: 04 9379 0934; summer daily 10am–12.30pm, 2–5.30pm) does little to prepare you for the extraordinary wealth of frescos within. Attributed to Jean Baleison and Jean Canavesi, the 15th-century cycle of the life of the Virgin, the Passion and the Last Judgement has earned it the nickname "the Sistine Chapel of the southern Alps". ❏

The chapel of Notre-Dame-des-Fontaines, near La Brigue, is a local place of pilgrimage, renowned for its vivid frescos, painted in 1492 by Canavesi of the Niçoise school.

RESTAURANTS AND BARS

Restaurants

La Brigue
Le Mirval
3 rue Vincent Ferrier
www.lemirval.com
Tel: 04 9304 6371. Open D Mon–Fri, L & D Sat–Sun. Closed Dec–Mar. €
Delightful riverside restaurant. Both Italian and Niçois dishes available.

Peillon
Auberge de la Madone
3 place Auguste Arnulf, Peillon Village. Tel: 04 9379

9117. Open L & D Thur–Tue. Closed Nov–Jan, except Christmas hols. €€€
Father and son duo Christian and Thomas Millo produce an imaginative version of regional cuisine.

St-Dalmas-de-Tende
Le Prieuré
rue Jean Médecin
www.leprieure.org
Tel: 04 9304 7570. Open L & D daily. €
This restaurant is linked to an employment

scheme for the disabled. The chef finds inspiration in the local mountains, producing *tourte brigasque*, terrines and mountain ham. Lovely views. Summer terrace.

St-Martin-Vésubie
Le Boreon
Quartier La Cascade, Le Boreon
www.hotel-boreon.com
Tel: 04 9303 2035. Open L & D daily. Closed Nov–Jan. €
A pretty lakeside chalet 5km north of St-Martin-Vésubie. where cooking includes game stews and duck fillet with honey.

Sospel
Restaurant Bel Aqua
Hôtel des Etrangers,
7 boulevard de Verdun
www.sospel.net
Tel: 04 9304 0009. Open L & D Thur–Mon. Closed Nov–Feb. €€
This restaurant is a favourite with locals and Mentonnais. Specialities include the local trout.

Prices for a three-course meal without wine. Many restaurants have a less expensive lunch menu:

€ = under €25
€€ = €25–40
€€€ = €40–60

NICE

Queen of the Riviera, capital of the Côte d'Azur, Nice is a gem of a city, with a wealth of museums, lively old town markets, and enough gardens, fountains and palm trees to raise the alfresco lifestyle to an art form

France's fifth city was founded around 350 BC by the Greeks, Called "Nikaea", it was built on the hill by the waterfront. Later, the Roman settlement of Cemenelum developed further inland on the Cimiez hill. In the Middle Ages, Nice ❶ asserted its independence from Provence as a mini-republic ruled by consuls. When Provence was incorporated into France in 1486, Nice and its hinterland remained a quasi-independent *comté*, under the protection of the dukes of Savoy, and was often a pawn between the rival ambitions of the French crown and the Holy Roman Empire. After the Revolution, Nice briefly became part of France under Napoleon, before returning to the kingdom of Piedmont-Sardinia. In 1860, the population voted to become French.

Nice's Italianate legacy can be seen in the city's culinary specialities, such as ravioli (which the Niçois claim to have invented), and in the Genoan-style painted facades in the old town. Nice was first embraced as a fashionable winter resort by English aristocrats in the late 18th century. In the 1820s and 30s, the promenade des

Anglais was laid out and railways, hotels, villas and gardens were all built to serve the needs of the Riviera royalty that followed in their wake. The fashion for sun- and sea-bathing arrived in the 1920s, attracting artists and writers.

Today, the city's traditional mellow lifestyle co-exists with its business status as France's second-largest convention city after Paris; its high-tech industry is growing rapidly, rivalling tourism as the city's main revenue generator. A new business district

Main attractions

COURS SALEYA MARKET, VIEUX NICE
CHAPELLE DE L'ANNONCIATION, VIEUX NICE
PALAIS LASCARIS, VIEUX NICE
COLLINE DU CHÂTEAU
VIEUX PORT
MAMAC
PROMENADE DES ANGLAIS
CATHÉDRALE ORTHODOXE RUSSE
MUSÉE DES BEAUX-ARTS JULES CHERET
PARC FLORAL PHOENIX
MUSÉE NATIONAL CHAGALL
MUSÉE MATISSE

LEFT: Nice's most famous hotel, the Negresco, built in 1912.
RIGHT: the market on cours Saleya.

Matisse lived in many locations in Nice before settling in Cimiez. One of his homes was in the big yellow house at the end of cours Saleya (1 place Charles Félix). Here, Matisse painted odalisques, drawing inspiration from the views of the sea and the flower market below.

has developed and mayor Christian Estrosi has plans for an ambitious "Eco-Vallée" with port facilities, congress centre and football stadium along the Var River on the city's western edge.

Orientation

Nice divides up neatly into old and new parts, with the medieval streets of Vieux Nice to the east, and the broad avenues and squares of the new town behind the promenade des Anglais to the west. Elegant residential districts, such as Costebelle and Cimiez, sit on the hills inland.

Vieux Nice

Vieux Nice is a maze of lively, narrow streets, where tiny grocers rub shoulders with clothes shops, art and craft galleries, souvenir outlets and quirky bars. The old town gained pretty much the appearance it has today in the 16th and 17th centuries, when the population was forced down

from the medieval upper town. The best place to start exploring is the **cours Saleya** Ⓐ, lined with cafés, a vibrant flower market (Tue–Sat 6am–5.30pm, Sun until 1pm) and a fruit and vegetable market every morning except Monday, when there's a flea market instead. Early risers can also hit the small fish market on place St-François (Tue–Sun mornings).

Between cours Saleya and quai des Etats-Unis are **Les Ponchettes**, a row of low white buildings once used by fishermen, now mostly galleries and restaurants. To the north the former palace of the Sardinian kings now houses the Préfecture. On rue de la Poissonnerie, a discreet facade hides the exuberantly decorated Baroque **Chapelle de l'Annonciation** Ⓑ (daily 7am–noon and 2.30–6.30pm), known as the Eglise Ste-Rita to locals who light candles to Rita, patron saint of lost causes, in the chapel to the left of the entrance. At the eastern end of the cours is the pedimented **Ancien**

Sénat, which administered justice on behalf of the Dukes of Savoy.

West of the cours on rue St-François-de-Paule are Nice's town hall and the **Opéra de Nice** , a feast of Second Empire opulence, with a colonnaded marble facade. On the place du Palais de Justice is Nice's imposing law court, the **Palais de Justice** , inaugurated in 1892, and facing it, an 18th-century clocktower and the russet-coloured facade of the Palais Rusca. The pavement cafés are an ideal spot to enjoy this newly renovated square, and on Saturdays there's a market here selling pottery and books.

On rue Droite, once the town's main north-south thoroughfare, is the **Palais Lascaris** (15 rue Droite, Wed–Mon 10am– 6pm; free), a grand 17th-century mansion reflecting the city's Genoese past, with a splendid balustraded staircase and salons with painted ceilings. There is also a collection of historical musical instruments, as well as an 18th-century pharmacy by the entrance.

At the heart of Vieux Nice on place Rossetti is the Baroque **Cathéd-rale de Ste-Réparate** (daily 9am–noon, 2–6pm), named after the patron saint of the city, a young virgin brought here in the 4th century from Israel in a boat pulled by angels. Her landing place is now known as the Baie des Anges (Angels' Bay). The cathedral has a dome of glazed tiles and an 18th-century belltower. The square itself is a great spot for coffee or ice cream. The elegant 18th-century arcaded **place Garibaldi**, at the northeastern corner of Vieux Nice, is named after the popular hero of Italian unification, who was born in the city and is buried in the cemetery on Le Château.

Le Château and the Vieux-Port

The old town's eastern extremity is flanked by **Le Château** , site of the original medieval hill town and the citadel demolished by Louis XIV in 1706. Today it is a pleasant park, with an artificial waterfall, a playground and some scant medieval ruins, as well as three cemeteries (Catholic, Protestant, Jewish) with some splendidly melodramatic funerary monuments.

TIP

Nice's most famous gelateria is Fenocchio at 2 place Rosetti, in front of the cathedral in Vieux-Nice, with a huge choice of ice creams and sorbets.

BELOW: Nice's old town.

The Museum of Modern and Contemporary Art (MAMAC) has an important collection of French and American art from the 1960s onwards. Le Relève (16 bis rue Delille) is a bar and restaurant conveniently located for the museum, with good music and art exhibitions.

BELOW:
the Russian Cathedral.

Most people make the climb for the marvellous panoramic views of the city; if you don't want to walk, you can take the lift at the end of quai des Etats-Unis up to the **Tour Bellanda** – a mock fortified tower where composer Hector Berlioz lived in the 1840s – or the tourist train that leaves from the Jardins Albert 1er.

East of the castle hill, past the stirring World War I **Monument aux Morts** is Nice's picturesque **Vieux-Port** (old port). This departure point for cruise ships sees swish yachts moored alongside small fishing boats. Quai des Deux Emmanuel is lined with bars and fish restaurants, while on place de l'Ile de Beauté, Genoese-style *trompe l'oeil* painted facades frame the neo classical church **Eglise Notre-Dame du Port**. Behind here on rue Catherine Ségurane and rue Antoine Gauthier is a cluster of antiques dealers and arcades.

On the eastern side of place de l'Ile de Beauté, boulevard Carnot marks the start of the Basse Corniche coast road, which loops around Mont Boron past extravagant villas and mock castles towards the Italian frontier *(see page 244)*. A fascinating curiosity at No.25 (entrance on impasse Terra Amata) is the **Musée de Paléontologie Humaine de Terra Amata** (www.musee-terra-amata.org; Tue–Sun 10am–6pm; free), located on the spot excavated in 1966 where a nomadic tribe of elephant hunters had camped out on the beach some 400,000 years ago.

Place Masséna and the Promenade des Arts

Symbolic heart of Nice and junction between Vieux Nice and the new town, **Place Masséna** ⓗ was laid out in the 1840s as part of the grandiose town-planning schemes of King Charles-Albert of Turin. Towards the sea, the Jardin Albert 1er provide a swathe of greenery, dotted with statuary and modern sculptures, covering over what was the mouth of the River Peillon. Heading inland along the promenade des Arts esplanade are the modern Théâtre de Nice and the **Musée d'Art Moderne et d'Art Contemporain** ❶ (MAMAC; www.mamac-nice.org; tel: 04 9713 4201; Tue– Sun 10am–6pm; free), a striking building of octagonal marble towers joined by glass walkways. The focus is on French and American art from the 1960s to the present, including some iconic Pop Art pieces by Andy Warhol and Roy Lichtenstein, a room devoted to local hero Yves Klein, and a large collection of Nikki de Saint-Phalle's colourful papier-mâché figures.

Promenade des Anglais and the New Town

The palm-lined **promenade des Anglais** ❶, funded in the 1820s by Nice's English colony, runs for 5km (3 miles) along the seafront. Although it's become a busy main road, the 'prom' is still *the* place for a stroll or a spot of people-watching. Much of the long shingle beach is taken up with private beach concessions with sun loungers and restaurants, although there are decent public stretches. The other side of the road is lined with grand hotels and apartment blocks. At No. 15 the **Palais de la Méditerranée** is a modern casino and luxury hotel behind a striking Art Deco facade. Set in tropical gardens, the **Musée d'Art et d'Histoire Palais Masséna** (Wed–Mon 10am–6pm; free), in a lavish villa built in 1898, has grand reception rooms and a winter garden downstairs. The museum upstairs contains portraits, costumes and memorabilia of the aristocrats and intellectuals who shaped the town's Belle Epoque glory. Next door at No.37 is the **Negresco**, Nice's most famous hotel built in 1912.

Behind the promenade des Anglais lies the new town, laid out in the late 19th and early 20th centuries with garden squares, fanciful villas and Belle Epoque and Art Deco buildings. Cutting inland from place Masséna towards the station, **avenue Jean Médecin** is a busy shopping street, now pedestrianised with the tramway running down the centre. The town's most upmarket fashions can be found on rue de Paradis, rue Alphonse Karr and avenue de Verdun.

A couple of blocks west of the station, the **Cathédrale Orthodoxe Russe** (boulevard Tzarewitch; daily 9am–noon, 2.30–5pm, June–Sept until 6pm; charge) is a startling reminder of Nice's once thriving Russian colony. Complete with five onion domes, precious icons and an ornate gilded iconostasis, this is more 17th-century Moscow than Belle Epoque France.

On the Baumettes hill, a Belle Epoque villa built for a Ukrainian princess houses the **Musée des Beaux-Arts Jules Cheret** (33 avenue des Baumettes; www.musee-beaux-arts-nice. org; tel: 04 9215 2828; Tue–Sun 10am–6pm; free). Here you can see European fine arts from the 17th to 20th centuries, with highlights from Brueghel, Fragonard, Dufy, Bonnard, Sisley, Van Dongen and Rodin, as well as pastels by poster artist Jules Cheret. In the Fabron district further west, the 1920s villa of perfumier François Coty contains the **Musée International d'Art Naïf Anatole Javovsky** (avenue Val Marie; Wed–Mon 10am–6pm; free), an exceptional collection of charming, often

Roman ruins in Cimiez, part of the archaeological park known as Les Arènes.

BELOW: floats parade at the Carnaval de Nice.

Carnaval de Nice

Nice celebrates Mardi Gras with the largest pre-Lent carnival in France (www.nicecarnaval.com), culminating in a spectacular explosion of fireworks above the Baie des Anges. For two weeks around Shrove Tuesday huge papier-mâché floats proceed through the town amid bands, confetti battles and throngs of spectators. Highlights include the *bataille des fleurs*, when thousands of fresh flowers are tossed into the crowds, and the ceremonial burning of *Sa Majesté Carnaval*, the carnival king, on the promenade des Anglais at the end of the festival. If you want to join in the spectacle, make sure you book your accommodation well in advance.

obsessively detailed paintings by Naive artists (self-taught, often mentally ill artists) including Bombois, Seraphine and Grandma Moses.

At the western end of promenade des Anglais, you'll come to the exotic, flower-filled **Parc Floral Phoenix** (daily 9.30am–7.30pm, until 6pm in winter; charge), with its vast glass and steel tropical greenhouse *(see margin)*. Set by a lake on the edge of the park, the **Musée des Arts Asiatiques** (www. arts-asiatiques.com; tel: 04 9229 3700; Wed–Mon 10am–5pm, May–mid-Oct until 6pm; free), in a spectacular circular building designed by Japanese architect Kenzo Tange, has a fine collection of Asian artefacts and a tea pavilion, where the tea ceremony is performed some weekends (reservation necessary, tel: 04 9229 3702).

Cimiez

In the fashionable residential area of Cimiez you'll find palm-filled gardens, extravagant Belle Epoque villas and vast former hotels (now apartments), with the crowning jewel being the Hôtel Excelsior Régina (corner of boulevard de Cimiez and avenue Régina), built in 1895. A statue of Queen Victoria in front commemorates her frequent visits here. It was later converted into apartments, one of which Matisse lived in during World War II.

About halfway up the hill, the **Musée National Marc Chagall** (avenue du Docteur Ménard; www. musee-chagall.fr; tel: 04 9353 8720; Wed–Mon 10am–5pm, July–Sept until 6pm; charge) contains a phenomenal collection of Chagall's works, centred around 12 vast, exuberant canvases illustrating stories from the Old Testament.

Cimiez is also the site of Roman Nice. Almost opposite the Régina are the **Arènes**, the scant remains of Nice's amphitheatre, today the venue for the city's outdoor jazz festival in July. Behind here, the **Musée Archéologique** (160 avenue des Arènes de Cimiez; Wed–Mon 10am–6pm; free) consists of a museum displaying Roman statues and artefacts, and an archeological site with extensive remains of three Roman bath complexes.

Henri Matisse

Set amid olive groves in Les Arènes park is the **Musée Matisse** (164 avenue des Arènes de Cimiez; tel: 04 9381 0808; Wed–Mon 10am–5pm, Apr–Sept until 6pm; free), in a redochre Genoese villa and its modern underground extension. Matisse loved Nice and its "clear, crystalline, precise, limpid" light; before his death in 1954 he bequeathed many works to the city, which form the core of this fabulous collection.

Matisse and Raoul Dufy are buried in the cemetery of the Franciscan **monastery** (place du Monastère de Cimiez; tel: 04 9381 0004); the adjoining church has three medieval masterpieces by Louis Bréa. The monastery's gardens are in a beautiful setting, with climbing roses, and a sweeping panorama of the Baie des Anges. ❏

BELOW: Musée Matisse.

RESTAURANTS AND BARS

Restaurants

Prices for a three-course meal without wine. Many restaurants have a less expensive lunch menu:
€ = under €25
€€ = €25–40
€€€ = €40–60
€€€€ = over €60

L'Auberge de Théo
52 avenue Cap de Croix
Tel: 04 9381 2619. Open L & D Tue–Sat, L Sun. €€
This cheerful, family-run Italian trattoria, with a rustic decor of hayracks, farm implements and Neapolitan crib figures, is one of the rare restaurants in Cimiez. Authentic dishes include mixed antipasti, pasta with swordfish, beef tagliata and little babas doused in limoncello. French and Italian wines.

Bistrot Antoine
27 rue de la Préfecture
Tel: 04 9385 2957. Open L & D Tue–Sat. €€
The up-and-coming address in Vieux Nice has made its mark with rejuvenated regional fare and light, market-inspired *plats du jour*.

Le Bistrot des Viviers
22 rue Alphonse Karr
www.les-viviers-nice.fr
Tel: 04 9316 0048. Open L & D Mon–Sat. Closed Aug. €€
Side by side Les Viviers and Le Bistrot des Viviers

share the same excellent chef Jacques Rolange and polished service but the bistro is less formal and less expensive.

L'Escalinada
22 rue Parolière
Tel: 04 9362 1171. Open L & D daily. €
The two whitewashed dining rooms and prized terrace are always packed at this Vieux Nice shrine to timeless Niçois specialities, such as sardines *à l'escabèche*, stuffed courgette flowers, ravioli and gnocchi. No credit cards.

Keisuke Matsushima
22 ter rue de France
www.keisukematsushima.com
Tel: 04 9382 2606. Open D Mon, L & D Tue–Sat. €€€
Japan meets Provence with brilliant young chef Keisuke Matsushima, who trained with some of France's top chefs to become one of Nice's gastronomic successes. Subtly lit slate tables provide a suitable setting for his artistically presented creations – think green, purple and wild asparagus with lemon froth or scallops with truffles, peas and wasabi.

La Merenda
4 rue Terasse. No phone. Open L & D Mon–Fri. €€
This tiny bistro in the old town is considered by many to serve the best

traditional Niçois cuisine, although the lack of phone (stop by ahead to bag a table) makes eating here difficult.

La Petite Maison
11 rue St-François-de-Paule
Tel: 04 9385 7153. Open L & D Mon–Sat. €€€
One of the most fashionable restaurants in Nice draws a celebrity clientele for luxurious renditions of Niçois cooking.

Le Safari
1 cours Saleya
www.restaurantsafari.com
Tel: 04 9380 1844. Open L & D daily. €€
This atmospheric brasserie draws an eclectic mix of locals and visitors. Serves Niçois specialities and wood-fired pizzas all afternoon.

Le Vin sur Vin
18 bis rue Biscarra
www.restaurant-20survin.com
Tel: 04 9392 9320. Open L & D Mon–Sat.
This friendly wine bar and shop is popular with young Niçois natives for wines by the glass. Think 20 out of 20 for a good steak, red mullet with risotto or grilled swordfish served with tabouleh and melon juice.

Le Zucca Magica
4 bis quai Papacino
www.lazuccamagica.com
Tel: 04 9356 2527. Open L & D Tue–Sat. €€
The magic pumpkin is that rare thing in France: a vegetarian restaurant and, what's more, one with culinary ambition.

RIGHT: the salade Niçoise originates in, of course, Nice.

THE RIVIERA FROM CANNES TO CAGNES

This stretch of the azure coast saw the birth of the Riviera as a summer destination. Here lovely (if crowded) beaches alternate with historic Antibes and Cagnes, luxuriant secluded peninsulas and the party towns of Cannes and Juan-les-Pins

Originally a winter destination favoured by the British and Russians, the stretch of coast from Cannes to the Italian border was dubbed the French Riviera by the Italians and the Côte d'Azur by the French – the latter term coined in 1887 by French writer Stephen Liégeard, who was inspired by the deep blue of its sea.

In 1923, the Hôtel du Cap stayed open over the summer for the first time, heralding the birth of the summer season and a new era in tourism, kick-started by glamorous American visitors. Scott Fitzgerald, Ernest Hemingway and Dorothy Parker were joined by artists and writers, Colette and Picasso among them. They helped build the Riviera myth with its jazz-age images of a hedonistic lifestyle centred on the new pastimes of sunbathing, water-skiing and cocktail parties.

An even greater revolution came with the advent of paid holidays, introduced by France's first socialist government in 1936, and the continued democratisation of holiday-taking after World War II. Consequently, the coast oscillates between two extremes: the Côte d'Azur of the very rich – a privileged world of yachts and villas – versus the campsites and cheap hotels catering for backpackers and budget travellers.

Cannes

Long an insignificant fishing village, **Cannes ❷** was first put on the map in 1834 when the British Lord High Chancellor, Lord Brougham, was forced to winter here due to an outbreak of cholera in Nice. Brougham, whose statue stands on the allées de la Liberté, was so taken with Cannes

Main attractions

LA CROISETTE, CANNES
LE SUQUET, CANNES
ILE SAINTE-MARGUERITE
MARCHÉ PROVENÇAL, VIEUX ANTIBES
MUSÉE PICASSO, VIEUX ANTIBES
MARINELAND, ANTIBES
CHÂTEAU-MUSÉE GRIMALDI, HAUT-DE-CAGNES

LEFT: the Carlton hotel on the promenade of La Croisette.
RIGHT: this is the life – Cannes' seafront.

The Hôtel Martinez has the largest private beach along La Croisette.

that he had a villa built here, starting a trend for wintering in the town. Within three years, 30 new villas had been built and the shoreline avenue, now called La Croisette, was laid.

Cannes's international status was cemented with the establishment of the town's film festival *(see page 236)*, inaugurated in 1946. For ten days each May, the town becomes the centre of the film universe, thronged by movie magnates, film stars and fans. Yet for all its glamour, Cannes has a pleasantly lived-in feel. Year-round trade fairs and conferences give it a permanent population and an economy not entirely reliant on tourism.

La Croisette

Sweeping east along the seafront is **La Croisette**, a palm tree-lined promenade bordered by plush hotels and apartments on one side, manicured beaches and smart beach clubs on the other. It is a focus for strolling and people-watching, with a constant stream of open-topped cars in summer. At No. 1 is the **Palais des Festivals et des Congrès**, nicknamed "the bunker", which since 1983 has been home to the

Film Festival, celebrated for the famous climb up "les marches", its red-carpeted stairs – a great photo op for acting out your own film star fantasies. It is also used for congresses, trade fairs and rock concerts and is home to the tourist office and the Croisette Casino. Film stars and directors have left a trail of handprints in the esplanade outside.

Cannes's grandest hotels are all on La Croisette, bearing testimony to the resort's glamorous history. At No. 14, the Belle Epoque **Majestic** has kept up its palatial status with a new wing of luxurious suites added in 2010, and its own private jetty stretching towards the sand across the street. At No. 47, **La Malmaison** (July–Sept Tue–Sun 11am–8pm, mid-Sept–June Tue–Sun 10am–1pm, 2–6pm; charge) is the only surviving part of the original Grand Hotel – 19th-century forerunner of today's seafront giants, since replaced by a 1970s high-rise. The building now houses temporary art exhibitions.

At No. 58, the **Carlton** has a wedding-cake facade that has barely changed since it was built in 1912. The pepper-pot cupolas at each end are said to be modelled on the breasts of la Belle Otero, a celebrated dancer and courtesan. Further down the drag, at No. 73, is the Art Deco **Hôtel Martinez**, the largest hotel in France when it opened in 1929.

The Port-Vieux and Le Suquet

West of the Palais des Festivals sits Cannes's old harbour, which still has a few fishing boats among the luxury yachts, and the allées de la Liberté, with its bandstand and *pétanque* players. Behind rue Félix Faure with its fish restaurants lies pedestrianised rue Meynardier and the excellent covered food market, **Marché Forville** (mornings daily in summer, Tue–Sun in winter). Cannes' oldest neighbourhood, **Le Suquet**, winds up the hill behind, past the 16th-century church **Notre-Dame d'Espérance**, whose parvis is used for the Nuits du Suquet classical music festival in July. At the top on shady **place de la Castre**, the castle and watchtower were built by Lérins monks in the 11th century to guard against Saracen attack. The castle houses the **Musée de la Castre** (tel: 04 9338 5526; July–Aug daily 10am–7pm, Apr–June and Sept Tue–Sun 10am–1pm, 2–6pm, Oct– Mar Tue–Sun 10am–1pm, 2–5pm; charge), an eclectic ethnographic and archaeological collection, plus a couple of rooms of Provençal and Orientalist paintings. In the museum courtyard, you can climb the Tour du Suquet for panoramic views.

West of Le Suquet, above the Plage de la Bocca (a good bet for bathing if you don't fancy one of the expensive private beaches), the Croix des Gardes district was the first part of Cannes to be built up by foreign aristocrats. Several of their fantastical villas remain, including **Villa Rothschild** (1 avenue Jean de Noailles), now the municipal library, whose exotically planted gardens have become a public park, and the **Château de la Tour** (10 avenue Font de Veyre), a crenellated mock castle, now a hotel.

Le Cannet

Up boulevard Carnot, on the hill above Cannes, **Le Cannet ❸**, once a separate hill village now more or less engulfed by its bigger neighbour, still has a villagey appeal. Le Cannet is notable as the former home of the painter Pierre Bonnard, who lived in the Villa du Bosquet from 1926 until

TIP

Boats run all year from Cannes to the Iles de Lérins. Trans Côte d'Azur (tel: 04 9298 7130, www.trans-cote-azur. com) and Horizon (tel: 04 9298 7136) run services to Ile Ste-Marguerite. Planaria (tel: 04 9298 7138) runs services to Ile St-Honorat. Note that you cannot combine the two islands in one trip.

Cannes Film Festival

You can't beat the Festival de Cannes for true A-lister glamour. Film industry outsiders can join in the atmosphere at the film screenings at Cinéma de la Plage

For ten days in May, over 30,000 film producers, directors, distributors and actors, and 4,000 international journalists descend on Cannes for the Festival de Cannes (www.festival-cannes.com). The public crowds the railings in front of the Palais des Festivals in hope of autographs and paparazzi snap stars in glamorous evening wear as they make the legendary climb up the Palais' red-carpeted steps.

Both public and media remain fascinated by the festival, debating the merits or not of the films projected, whether the stars are out in force and, of course, whether the right film has been awarded the Palme d'Or. The festival likes to arouse controversy and to spring some surprises: in 2009, jury president Isabelle Huppert was accused by some of manipulating the jury to award the

Palme d'Or to Michael Haneke; in 2010, it was awarded to little-known Thai director Apichatpong Weerasethakul.

The festival was originally conceived by the French government in the 1930s to provide an alternative to the Venice Film Festival, where only films meeting the approval of Mussolini's censors were shown. Cannes was elected for its "sunny and enchanting location". The first festival was scheduled for 1939, but plans were scuppered by World War II, and it was not until 20 September 1946 that glasses were raised at the belated inaugural festival.

Each year the festival's board of directors chooses a 10-member international jury: nine artists and a president. Past presidents range from Jean Cocteau (1953 and 1954) to the first woman president Olivia de Havilland (1965) and, more recently, Martin Scorsese (1998), Wong Kar Wai (2006) and Tim Burton (2010). The jury awards the prestigious "Palme d'Or" for Best Film, as well as prizes including Best Actor, Best Actress and Best Screenplay. Enduring past winners include Fellini's *La Dolce Vita* in 1960, Mike Leigh's *Secrets and Lies* and Tarentino's *Pulp Fiction*.

The festival is fascinatingly international – recent years have seen an enormous rise in the number of Asian, Middle Eastern and Eastern European films and relatively low numbers of US films.

The Cannes Festival is also a major venue for the hard-nosed buying and selling of film rights, with some 1,500 films screened outside the competitions in the important Marché du Film.

The festival is supposed to be for industry insiders only, with tickets to screenings notoriously difficult to come by. However, if you're determined to see the stars, have a talent at charming bodyguards, and your budget stretches to the luxury hotels along La Croisette, you may yet get to take part in the action. The public do get to see some films, as the festival organises the outdoor Cinéma de la Plage (public screenings on the beach). Pick up invitations at the tourist office. ❑

LEFT: 1953 festival: Dany Robin, Kirk Douglas, Olivia de Havilland and Edward G. Robinson.

his death in 1947. The Belle Epoque Hôtel-Villa St-Vianney, adjoining the town hall, is being converted into the **Musée Bonnard** (due to open 2011, www.rmn.fr), a museum devoted to the artist.

The Iles de Lérins

If you want to escape the crowds, take a boat from quai Laubeuf, in Cannes' Vieux-Port, and head for the delightful **Iles de Lérins**.

At a mere 400 metres (1,300ft) in width, **Ile St-Honorat ❹**, mainly covered by eucalyptus and cypresses, is the smaller of the two Lérins islands. Although it seems like a quiet backwater, the island has an impressive ecclesiastical history, dating back to a monastery founded by St Honorat in the 5th century. For centuries it was a religious centre where many important bishops – including Ireland's St Patrick – trained. It was so powerful that it owned much of the land along the Mediterranean coast, including Cannes. Note there are no restaurants on the island, so bring a picnic.

Ste-Marguerite ❺, the larger island, named after Honorat's possibly non-existent sister, is home to the impressive **Fort Royal**, begun by Richelieu in the early 17th century and occupied by the Spanish during the Thirty Years War. The keep now contains the **Musée de la Mer** (June–Sept daily 10.30am–5.45pm, Oct–Mar Tue–Sun 10.30–1.15pm, 2.15–4.45pm; charge) where you can see ancient amphoras and other artefacts salvaged from shipwrecks, and the prison cells where Protestants were held after the Revocation of the Edict of Nantes in 1685. Some of the cells have been decorated with murals by artist Jean le Gac but the most evocative is the heavily barred cell of the Man in the Iron Mask, immortalised by Alexandre Dumas. The prisoner's identity is still a mystery, although numerous, often far-fetched, suggestions

include Louis XIV's twin brother, disgraced civil servant Nicolas Fouquet, playwright Molière and the son of Oliver Cromwell. The island is perfect for a day's excursion with a small beach west of the harbour and rocky inlets for bathing, a nature reserve for waterfowl around the Etang de Batéguier, a botanical trail and plenty of picnic spots.

Mougins

Five km (2½ miles) inland from Cannes, **Mougins ❻**, which overshadowed the former during the Middle Ages, has guarded its image as a pristine hill village. Its steep streets, terraces trailing flowers, concealed mansions, and some of the Côte's best restaurants make it a chic place for Cannes conferencegoers to hang out.

In the 1920s and 1930s, when it became the done thing to holiday on the Côte d'Azur, artists Cocteau and Man Ray arrived, and Picabia built his eccentric Château de Mai here. Picasso lived in Mougins from 1961 until his death in 1973. The town's artistic connections are nowadays reflected in its

Most of the monastic buildings on Ile St-Honorat date from the 11th and 12th centuries. However, the abbey church (www. abbayedelerins.com; open daily, closed for Sun services) was built in the late 19th century by the Cistercian monks who bought the island in 1869. There's a small museum and a shop where the monks sell a herb-based liqueur called Lérina.

BELOW: Bonnard's former home, Le Cannet.

The 12th-century chapel Notre-Dame-de-Vie in Mougins.

BELOW RIGHT: Picasso in 1948.

numerous art and craft galleries. At the top of the village, the **Musée de la Photographie** (67 rue de l'Eglise; tel: 04 9375 8567; Tue–Sun 10am–12-.30pm, 2–7pm, until 6pm in winter; charge) has numerous photographs of Picasso, as well as works by master snapper Robert Doisneau.

Vallauris

Another town with strong links to Picasso is **Vallauris** ❼, east of Cannes, where the artist turned his hand to pottery in the 1940s; the **Madoura Pottery** (avenue Suzanne et Georges Ramié; open Mon–Fri) still retains the copyright to Picasso's ceramics. Ceramics have been the mainstay of Vallauris for more than four centuries, continuing the tradition with countless pottery workshops and the Biennale de la Céramique every even-numbered year. Unfortunately the main shopping street is now clogged with tacky pottery outlets and the old town largely dwarfed by modern housing blocks. Uphill, however, visitors can experience the more highbrow side to Vallauris in the shape of the town's three museums, all housed in the largely Renaissance chateau.

In the chateau chapel, the **Musée National Picasso La Guerre et La Paix** (www.musee-picasso-vallauris.fr; tel: 04 9364 7183; July–Aug daily 10am–6.45pm, rest of summer Wed–Mon 10am–noon, 2–6pm, until 5pm in winter; charge) contains Picasso's ode to peace, completed in 1952, with its two massive panels *War* and *Peace*, and a third panel depicting figures of the four continents around a dove. Some of the pottery made by Picasso during the six years when he had his Fournas atelier (now 95 avenue Pablo Picasso) is exhibited in the **Musée de la Céramique** (same hours), also in the chateau. The collection traces the pottery heritage of Vallauris, from early domestic wares, via Art Nouveau forms by the Massier dynasty, to modern art pottery. A third museum, the **Musée Magnelli** (same hours) contains works by abstract painter Alberto Magnelli. Just outside the chateau stands Picasso's bronze of a man holding a sheep, which he presented to the town in 1949.

Picasso's Pots

In 1946, Picasso discovered Vallauris when he visited a pottery exhibition and the Madoura workshop of Suzanne and Georges Ramié. In 1948, he settled in the town with his companion Françoise Gilot. Although he had experimented with ceramics in Paris in the 1920s, this was the start of a true fascination with clay and a burst of creativity that saw the production of some 4,000 pieces of pottery before his death in 1973. To begin with, Picasso did not make the plates and jugs himself but worked in close collaboration with the Ramiés and their craftsmen, painting the pots with wonderfully free designs of faces, fish or bullfighting scenes that often show him at his most joyful. If some items were merely series decorated by the artist (and he also licensed Madoura to produce some of his designs in limited editions), he was later to mould and pummel the damp clay to create new forms in zoomorphic vessels. His heads, owls or birds and tanagra-shaped vases are true sculptural one-offs. Long dismissed by art critics as "not proper Picasso" and by art potters as "not proper pottery", Picasso's pots are now seen as a true aspect of the artist's oeuvre and a contribution to the vitality of modern ceramics.

Antibes-Juan-les-Pins

Back on the coast, the historic port of **Antibes** ❶ contrasts with the villas and tropical vegetation of the Cap d'Antibes and the indulgent party town of **Juan-les-Pins**, renowned for its clubs, expensive boutiques and casinos. Founded by the Phoenician Greeks, who named it Antipolis, Antibes was a keystone in French naval strategy. Having been sacked twice by Emperor Charles V in the 16th century, kings Henri II and Henri III added fortifications; in 1680 Louis XIV brought in his military engineer Vauban to give it the star-shaped ramparts and bastions that line the shore. The largest yachting marina in Europe ensures that Antibes is lively all year round with a large spin-off industry of yacht brokers and ship chandlers, and a big English expat community.

Vieux Antibes

Behind the ramparts, Antibes has a splendid cobble-stoned old town with a covered food market on **cours Masséna** (Tue–Sun mornings; every morning June–Sept).

In summer there's a craft market here in the afternoons. Off the marketplace, the orange and yellow baroque facade of the **Eglise de l'Immaculée Conception** hides the simple, earlier structure of what was once a cathedral. Next door is the severe **Château Grimaldi**, once the bishop's palace, later residence of the Grimaldi family, the king's governor and a barracks before becoming an archaeological museum. In 1946, Picasso had a studio here, often using Ripolin household paint due to the scarcity of art materials after the war. The castle now houses the beautifully refurbished **Musée Picasso** (tel: 04 9290 5420; mid-June–mid-Sept Tue–Sun 10am–6pm, mid-Sept–mid-June Tue–Sun 10am–noon, 2–6pm; charge), which features his celebrated work *Joie de Vivre (Joy of Life)* and the triptych *Satyre, Centaure, Faune*, as well as several of his nudes and still lifes, including *Le Gobeur d'Oursins (Sea Urchin Eater)*, pottery and drawings. Works by other artists who lived in Antibes are also on display, such as abstract paintings by Hans Hartung,

TIP

The Musée Peynet in Vieux Antibes (place Nationale; Tue–Sun 10am–noon, 2–6pm; charge) presents comic drawings by cartoonist Raymond Peynet (creator of "Les Amoureux", The Lovers) and other drawings by newspaper cartoonists.

BELOW: Plage de la Garoupe, Cap d'Antibes.

TIP

Held each July in the Pinède Gould, Jazz à Juan is one of the world's leading jazz festivals and the place to catch first-rate names in American jazz, blues and fusion, such as B.B. King, Dizzy Gillespie, Wayne Shorter and Keith Jarrett, in a stunning setting against the Mediterranean Sea. Recently established Jazz Révélations is a smaller festival in April seeking out new acts. See www.antibes-juanlespins.com

and Russian-born Nicolas de Staël's last unfinished canvas *Le Grand Concert* (sometimes removed during temporary exhibitions). Outside on the terrace are sculptures by Miró and Arman and elongated bronze figures by Germaine Richier. The villagey streets of old Antibes' Commune Libre du Safranier form a bohemian arty district which proudly declared its "independence" in 1960.

At the southern end of the ramparts, the gunpowder stores of the Bastion St-André contain the **Musée d'Archéologie** (Tue–Sun 10am–noon, 2–6pm; 5pm in winter; charge), with remnants of ancient Antipolis, Roman stelae and mosaics, and the mysterious Galet d'Antibes, a large stone with mysterious inscriptions dating from the 5th century BC. Antibes' best public beach, the **Plage de Salis** (boulevard James Willie) is a 15-minute walk from here.

On a promontory on the port's northern side is the bastioned fortress of **Fort Carré** (guided visits every 30 mins Tue–Sun 10am–6pm, 4.30pm in winter; charge).

Juan-les-Pins and Cap d'Antibes

Wooded Cap d'Antibes is an exclusive millionaires' paradise, home to jet-setters' favourite, Hôtel du Cap-Eden-Roc, the hotel that set the trend for the summer season, and colossal villas belonging to Russian oligarchs and Arab princes. On the western side of the promontory, **Juan-les-Pins** ❾ reputation for hedonism is well established: the F. Scott Fitzgeralds and other wealthy American socialites were swinging here as early as the 1920s. La Garoupe, the sandy beach on Cap d'Antibes, is still the place to sunbathe, and there are some public stretches between the snooty private beach concessions. It is also the starting point for the Sentier Tir-Poil coastal footpath, which leads to the **Villa Eilen Roc** (Sept–June house Wed 9am–noon, 1.30–5pm; gardens Tue–Wed 9.30am–5pm; free), designed by Charles Garnier of Paris and Monte Carlo opera houses fame. Its gardens are the setting for the Musiques au Cœur classical music festival every July. On the top of the peninsula,

BELOW: relaxing among the fishing boats in Juan-les-Pins. **BELOW RIGHT:** Golfe Juan.

Jardin de la Villa Thuret (41 boulevard du Cap; Mon–Fri summer 8am–6pm, winter 8.30am–5.30pm; free), with its jungle-like tangle of plants, is one of the Riviera's oldest botanic gardens.

Biot

Heading east from Antibes, **Marineland** (www.marineland.fr; Feb–Dec daily 10am–7pm; charge) is a huge marine theme park with afternoon whale and dolphin shows. On the same site are the aquatic fun park Aquasplash (open June–Sept; charge), crazy golf, and the cowboy-themed farm, La Petite Ferme du Far West (open daily; charge).

The artist Fernand Léger (1881–1955) adopted **Biot** ⑩, another medieval perched village, as his outpost. At the foot of the village, the **Musée National Fernand Léger** (tel: 04 9291 5030; Wed–Sun 10am–noon, 2–6pm, Sept–June until 5pm; charge) has a vast ceramic mosaic on its exterior, and is the permanent home of nearly 400 of the artist's paintings, tapestries, stained glass and ceramics, surrounded by a garden with giant versions of some of his sculptures.

Like Vallauris, Biot was long known for its potteries. Since 1956, however, it has been more associated with glass and the beautiful creations of the **Verrerie de Biot**, famed for its bubble glass. You can watch the master glassblowers at work in the factory located at the foot of the village; adjoining it are a shop, a small glass museum and the Galerie Internationale du Verre, exhibiting the work of international art glassmakers.

Villeneuve-Loubet

The resort of **Villeneuve-Loubet** ⑪ is often associated with the gigantic pyramidal forms of the **Marina Baie des Anges** development (contact tourist office for visits, tel: 04 9202 6616). Built in the 1970s, it was long decried as one of the monstrosities of coastal over-construction, though today its stepped-back terraces and roof gardens seem positively restrained compared to the urban sprawl that surrounds it.

Villeneuve-Loubet also has its old medieval hill town, located 3km (2 miles) inland. Above the village is the medieval **castle** where French king François I stayed for three weeks in 1538 for the signature of the Treaty of Nice. Although the castle is still privately owned, it is open for guided visits (reserve with tourist office, tel: 04 9202 6616; July–Aug Wed and Sun, Sept–June two Sundays a month).

Lower down the hill, the **Musée Escoffier de l'Art Culinaire** (www.fondation-escoffier.org; Dec–Oct Sun–Fri 2–6pm, 7pm in summer; charge) preserves the memory of Auguste Escoffier, "king of chefs and chef of kings", in the house where he was born in 1846. Exhibits include Escoffier's handwritten recipe book and photographs of Australian soprano Dame Nelly Melba, for whom he invented the Peach Melba.

TIP

The Chapelle de la Garoupe (daily 10am–noon, 2.30–5pm) on Cap d'Antibes has been a site of pilgrimage for centuries. It's a pleasant walk up the stony Chemin de Calvaire, past the stations of the Cross, from the Port de Salis.

BELOW: bubble glass (*verre à bulles*) of Biot.

Inside the Château-Musée Grimaldi.

Cagnes-sur-Mer

Cagnes-sur-Mer splits into three parts. At the lower end, Cros-de-Cagnes is a rather downmarket modern seaside resort, with a race-track, a pebbly beach backing onto the road and the added disadvantage of aircraft noise. Cagnes-sur-Mer, with its public park and a covered market (mornings only) occupies the middle ground. Rising up above both of them is the medieval village of **Haut-de-Cagnes**, where plentiful restaurants make it a popular night out for Niçois. Crowning the village is the crenellated tower of the **Château-Musée Grimaldi** (May–Sept Wed–Mon 10am–noon, 2–6pm, Oct–Apr until 5pm, closed 2 weeks Nov; charge).

Originally a watchtower, it was transformed into a Renaissance residence by Jean-Henri Grimaldi. On the ground floor, a small museum pays homage to the olive tree, while upstairs are paintings of the Montparnasse cabaret singer Susy Solidor by artists such as Cocteau, and a collection of contemporary Mediterranean art. The highlight, however, is the grand ceremonial room on the first floor, whose ceiling, painted by Italian artist Giulio Benso Pietra, is a vertiginous feat.

The elderly Renoir lived in Cagnes from 1906 to 1919. The house he built at Les Collettes, just east of Cagnes-sur-Mer, is now the **Musée Renoir** (May–Sept Wed–Mon 10am–noon, 2–6pm, Oct–Apr Wed–Mon until 5pm, closed 2 weeks Nov; charge). It remains much as it was when the artist lived here. Paintings of his garden, of his granddaughter Coco, and a version of his *Large Bathers* reflect the high tonality of his late works. There are also several of the bronze sculptures Renoir increasingly turned to at the end of his life.

Cagnes-sur-Mer has a varied programme of festivals throughout the year. The main sporting events revolve around the Hippodrome (racecoure), the second-largest in France, with both sand and grass tracks, as well as a trotting (harness racing) track. The Fête de la Châtaigne (Chestnut Festival) in November is a more traditional option. ❑

RESTAURANTS AND BARS

Restaurants

Prices for a three-course meal without wine. Many restaurants have a less expensive lunch menu:

€ = under €25
€€ = €25–40
€€€ = €40–60
€€€€ = over €60

Antibes-Juan-les-Pins

Les Pêcheurs
10 boulevard Maréchal Juin, Cap d'Antibes
www.lespecheurs-lecap.com
Tel: 04 9293 1330. Open mid-Mar–Oct. Les Pêcheurs D, Le Cap L. €€€€
This waterside restaurant and hotel complex with private sandy beach has rejuvenated the local scene with the acclaimed cooking of Nicolas Sole. Lunch is in the simpler Le Cap on the beach.

Taverne du Safranier
1 place du Safranier, Vieux-Antibes. Tel: 04 9334 8050. Open July–Aug D Mon–Tue, L & D Wed–Sat; Sept, Oct and Mar–June L & D Tue–Sat, L Sun. €€
An animated bistro popular with arty locals. Specialities include marinated sardines, ravioli and a gigantic lemon meringue tart.

Les Temps des Mets
7 rue James Close, Antibes
www.restaurantlestemps desmets.fr. Tel: 04 9294 0731. Open D daily. €

Cosmopolitan modern cooking served by very friendly staff, in Vieux Antibes. Generous wok dishes are the speciality along with other French and world flavours.

Biot

Café-Galerie des Arcades
16 place des Arcades
Tel: 04 9365 0104. Open L daily, D Tue–Sat. Closed Nov. €€
This popular village inn doubles as an art gallery. Provençal cuisine is served indoors or under the medieval arcades.

Cagnes-sur-Mer

Josy-Jo
2 rue du Planastel, Haut-de-Cagnes
www.restaurant-josyjo.com
Tel: 04 9320 6876. Open L & D Mon–Fri, D Sat. Closed mid-Nov–mid-Dec. €€€
A Cagnes institution for 40 years. Self-taught Josy Bandecchi serves courgette flower fritters and chargrilled steaks in the ancient village house where artists Modigliani and Soutine stayed.

Cannes

Astoux et Brun
27 rue Félix Faure
www.astouxbrun.com
Tel: 04 9339 2187. Food served all day daily. €€
At this brasserie over-

looking the old port, it's not the decor that counts but the people-watching and the excellent shellfish.

Aux Bons Enfants
80 rue Meynardier. No phone. Open L & D Mon–Sat. Cash only. €
Opened in 1935 and still run by the same family, this bistro is popular for its generous home cooking. Expect starters like grilled sardines, followed by beef *daube*.

Caffé Roma
1 square Merimée
www.cafferoma.fr
Tel: 04 9338 0504. Open L & D daily. €€
The terrace at this big café is popular for an espresso, cocktails and Italian specialities, as well as the ringside view of comings and goings from the Palais des Festivals.

Mougins

Brasserie de la Mediterranée
Place de la Mairie
www.restaurantlamediterranee.com. Tel: 04 9390 0347. Open L & D daily. €€
A casual-chic restaurant with trad brasserie decor and an appealing choice of southern favourites.

Le Rendez-Vous de Mougins
place du Commandant Lamy
www.au-rendez-vous-mougins.com
Tel: 04 9375 8747. Open L & D daily. €
Simple Provençal specialities in a convivial atmosphere on the village square.

RIGHT: fantastically well-presented food.

THE RIVIERA FROM VILLEFRANCHE TO MENTON

East of Nice towards the Italian frontier, arid limestone mountains descend almost directly into the sea. Historic ports, such as Villefranche-sur-Mer and Italianate Menton, mix with exclusive residential peninsulas, while the mild climate has peppered the area with exotic gardens

Three corniche roads snake eastwards from Nice towards the Italian border. The Basse Corniche (D6098), or Corniche Inférieure, hugs the coast, winding between villas and apartment blocks and providing an overview of how heavily built-up it has become – though still interspersed by old harbours and exclusive headlands. The Moyenne Corniche (D6007) is the shortest and probably the most stylish of the three routes, while the Grande Corniche (D2564), roughly tracing the Roman Via Aurelia, is the highest of the three corniches, passing through a sparsely vegetated limestone landscape. It is also the longest route from Monaco to Nice, though not necessarily the slowest, since heavy traffic often clogs the coast road. For those in a hurry, the A8 *autoroute* runs parallel to it, slightly further inland.

Villefranche-sur-Mer

The Basse Corniche leaves the Vieux-Port of Nice climbing up round the fantastical villas of Mont Boron. First stop to the east, the town of **Villefranche-sur-Mer** ⑬ was established in the 14th century as a *villefranche* or customs-free port by Charles II d'Anjou, and was long the principal port of the Comté de Nice. In 1557, to protect the port, Philibert of Savoy built

a massive **citadelle**, now home to the town hall, congress centre and four minor museums. These include sculptures by Antoniucci Volti and the **Musée Goetz-Boumeester of modern paintings** (June–Sept Mon–Sat 10am–noon, 3–6.30pm; Sun 2–6.30pm; Oct–May Mon–Sat 10am–noon, 2–5.30pm, Sun 1.30–5pm; free). British and American ships still use the sheltered harbour, which is one of the deepest in the world, as do cruise ships and a small fishing fleet.

The town is well restored but not bijou, with tall painted stucco houses and lively fish restaurants lining quai Courbet. Here you'll also find the **Chapelle St-Pierre** (Tue–Sun summer 10am–noon, 3–7pm, winter 10am–noon, 2–6pm; charge), also known as the Cocteau Chapel, one of the most extraordinary works by Surrealist writer, artist and filmmaker Jean Cocteau. He restored the medieval chapel dedicated to St Peter, patron saint of fishermen, painting it with quirky fishing scenes and episodes from the saint's life. Behind the quay, the old town is also worth exploring. It contains the curious rue Obscure, a covered, vaulted street where the townspeople sheltered in times of siege, and steep, narrow streets that climb up to the Baroque church of St-Michel, which contains an expressive, 17th-century figwood sculpture of the Dead Christ.

Cap Ferrat

Continuing east along the bay from Villefranche, a side road leads to **Cap Ferrat ⑭**. Hideout of the seriously rich and famous, this is one of the

few areas of the coast that guards its aura of exclusivity. Much of it lurks behind security fences and guard-dog warnings, but the Plage Passable is a pleasant little beach, not far from the former villa of King Leopold II of Belgium, from where you can join the coastal path round the Cap.

The pink-and-white **Fondation Ephrussi de Rothschild** (www.villa-ephrussi.com; Feb–Oct daily 10am–6pm, July–Aug until 7pm, Nov–Jan Mon–Fri 2–6pm, Sat, Sun and school hols 10am–6pm; charge) was built in 1905–12 to house the art collection of Baroness Ephrussi de Rothschild (1864–1934). Around a Venetian Gothic-style central courtyard, panelled rooms are laden with 18th-century French furniture, a ceiling painted by Tiepolo, and precious Sèvres and Vincennes porcelain, but its greatest attraction are its 7 hectares (17 acres) of exotic gardens. They spread along the crest of the Cap with gorgeous views on all sides.

Not far away, the **Zooparc du Cap Ferrat** (www.zoocapferrat.com; tel: 04 9376 0760; daily 9.30am–7pm, until 5.30pm in winter; charge) is like a

TIP

The main attraction of the Fondation Ephrussi de Rothschild is its nine themed gardens. A meandering promenade takes you past roses, exotic cacti and Provençal flora, through a French formal garden with musical fountains, a Japanese garden with gravel and little shrines, an Italian Renaissance garden, and the romantic lapidary garden with its fragments of Gothic architecture and medieval statuary.

FAR LEFT: an ideal way to travel along the coast.
BELOW:
St-Jean-Cap Ferrat.

TIP

For beach restaurants, try fashionable **Plage Restaurant La Paloma** (tel: 04 9301 6471) on Paloma Beach at Cap Ferrat. It's casual at lunchtime, with grilled fish and salads, more romantic (and expensive) for candlelit dinners. At Cap d'Ail, laidback **L'Eden** (tel: 04 9378 1706) serves good-value traditional French cooking amid a Balinese-style tropical decor on the idyllic Plage Mala. It can be reached by boat or on foot down steps from the coast path.

BELOW: the casino in Beaulieu-sur-Mer.

lushly planted garden itself, where crocodiles, zebras, lemurs, gibbons and wild cats live amid its pools, palm trees, islands and waterfalls. Recent additions include a panther canyon and a nocturnal environment for rats and bats. Further round the Cap, **St-Jean-Cap Ferrat** has a chic harbour frequented by the yachting fraternity.

Across the bay from Villa Ephrussi you can spot another glamorous mansion. On the water's edge at **Beaulieu-sur-Mer**, the **Villa Kerylos** (www.villa-kerylos.com; Feb–Oct daily 10am–6pm, July–Aug until 7pm, Nov–Jan Mon–Fri 2–6pm, Sat, Sun and school hols 10am–6pm; charge) is a 1902–8 reconstruction of an ancient Greek villa by wealthy German scholar Theodor Reinach. Together with architect Emmanuel Pontremoli he created what is not so much a replica villa as an idealised version, with marble columns and cool courtyards open to the sea and sky, which houses a large collection of mosaics, frescos and furniture.

Beaulieu-sur-Mer ⓯ itself is a genteel retirement town with a Belle

Epoque casino, luxury hotels and elegant rest-homes reclining in the sheltered climate. From here the Basse Corniche passes through the sprawling resort of Eze-Bord-de-Mer and Cap d'Ail before reaching Monaco.

Eze and La Turbie

Impaled on a rocky spike some 400 metres (1,300ft) above the sea is picturesque **Eze Village ⓰**, with its cluster of pantiled medieval houses and Baroque church. Access is from the Moyenne Corniche or by donkey track from the coast, and its entrance, through a small hidden archway, comes after a short winding climb from the main road – the village is closed to motor vehicles. Few other *villages perchés* command the popularity of Eze, and pushing through the crowded narrow streets at the height of summer can be trying. However, the village's current prosperity belies its troubled past, mostly as a charred ruin: razed successively over several centuries, enslaved by Arabs, its citizens regularly tortured and burnt.

These days, one undoubtedly flourishing aspect is the **Jardin**

Exotique (Mar–Aug daily, closed Sept–Feb; charge), a fine collection of cacti and succulents, interspersed with terracotta sculptures. This garden was planted in 1950 around the ruins of the chateau, which had been dismantled in 1706.

High up on the Grande Corniche east of Eze, the white marble columns of the ruined Roman monument at **La Turbie** ⓱ stand out against the sky. The village derives its name from the Latin *tropaea*, meaning trophy, after the vast monument **la Trophée des Alpes** (18 avenue Albert I; http://la-turbie.monuments-nationaux.fr; daily mid-May–mid-Sept 9.30am–1pm, 2.30–6.30pm, mid-Sept–mid-May 10am–1.30pm, 2.30–5pm; charge). It was erected here in 6 BC in honour of Emperor Augustus's victory over 44 Alpine tribes, whose names are inscribed inside.

The Trophy dominates the narrow streets of the medieval village, which still has its fortified gateways. The **Eglise St-Michel** is an 18th-century Baroque offering, full of gaudy red marble that might befit a film star's villa in St-Tropez.

Roquebrune Cap-Martin

Between Monaco (*see page 253*) and Menton lies **Roquebrune Cap-Martin** ⓳. The Cap is an exclusive millionaire's haunt: Empress Eugénie and Winston Churchill stayed here, as did some less desirable characters, Emperor Bokassa among them. Much of it is off-limits, although you can walk round the Sentier du Littoral, which hugs the sea edge, with opportunities for bathing from the rocks. Just west of the Cap, within easy reach of Roquebrune Cap-Martin station, the pleasant beach of Cabbé sits under the gardens of the elegant Villa Mangano. It is largely pebble, but has some sand at low tide, unlike the shingle beach of more downmarket suburb, Carnolès (on the Menton side).

Up on the coast path sits the **Cabanon** (visits Tue and Fri 10am; reserve several days ahead with tourist office, tel: 04 9335 6287; charge), the tiny log cabin constructed by Le Corbusier in 1951–2. It's not the only avant-garde building here: Eileen Gray's groundbreaking Villa E-1027 was designed by the Irish-born decorator and architect in 1929. After being abandoned for several years, it is currently being restored.

Perched high up above Carnolès is old **Roquebrune Village**, a picturesque tangle of alleys and houses built into the rock, with terraces offering superb views over the skyscrapers of Monte-Carlo below. Its **Château** (tel: 04 9335 0722; daily July–Aug 10am–12.30pm, 3–7.30pm, Feb–June, Sept–Oct 10am–12.30pm, 2–6pm, Nov–Jan 10am–12.30pm, 2–5pm; charge) dates back to the 10th century when Conrad I, count of Ventimiglia, built it to keep out the Saracens. In the cemetery next to the village, Le Corbusier, who drowned while swimming in the sea in 1965, is buried alongside his wife in a tomb of his own design.

The Trophée des Alpes was built by the Roman Senate as a reward to Emperor Augustus for his successful campaign against the remaining 44 rebellious Alpine tribes.

BELOW:
the village of Eze.

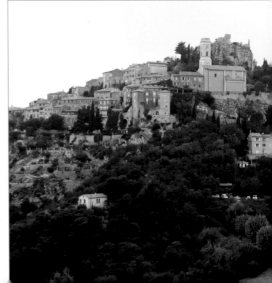

TIP

The attractive town of Ventimiglia just across the Italian border from Menton is a popular hop for locals thanks to its vast food and general goods market every Friday. Beware the fake designer handbags sold here: people are regularly stopped at the border customs post and may incur large fines for smuggling.

Roquebrune's other popular landmark, along the steep footpath that runs down to the lower town, is the wonderfully gnarled **Olivier Millénaire**, an ancient olive tree that is probably even older than its name (1,000-year-old olive tree) claims.

Menton: lemon capital

Sheltered by mountains, **Menton** basks in an enchanted setting with 300 days of sun a year and a climate at least two degrees warmer than that of Nice. Mexican and North African vegetation, as well as citrus fruit, flourish in this subtropical greenhouse.

In the second half of the 19th century, Menton was renowned as a winter sanatorium, thanks to Dr Bennet, an English doctor, who promoted Menton's mild climate as perfect for invalids. As a result British and Germans flocked here in winter, as did Russians, who added another of the Riviera's Russian Orthodox churches to the town. Royal visitors such as Queen Victoria helped the town acquire a reputation as the most aristocratic and anglophile of all the resorts on the Riviera. Along the sea-front and in the hills surrounding the Italianate old town, grand hotels and romantic villas were built.

Nowadays, most of the grand hotels have been demolished or converted into apartments, and the mild climate has given Menton the reputation of a cosy retirement home. However, the town has been rejuvenated since 1993 when Menton and Ventimiglia together became the European Union's first joint urban community, combining frontier posts and municipal and business activities (*see margin left*).

Surrealism fans will be interested to learn that the Salle des Mariages, where marriage ceremonies are held in Menton's **Hôtel de Ville** (town hall) was decorated with murals by Jean Cocteau in the 1950s (reservation advised tel: 04 9210 5000; visits Mon–Fri 8.30am–12.30pm, 2–5pm; charge). A tiny bastion on quai Monléon, by the harbour, contains the **Musée Jean Cocteau** (Wed–Mon 10am–noon, 2–6pm; charge), conceived by the artist, with his own quirky pebble mosaics by the entrance and a display of his pottery,

BELOW: Menton, beach and old town.

drawings and prints. A second Cocteau museum (due to open 2011, www.tourisme-menton.fr; call tourist office for information, tel: 04 9241 7676), in an exciting building designed by Bandol architect Rudy Ricciotti, is under construction on the quay near the market to house the Séverin Wunderman collection of works by Cocteau and other modern artists.

Next to the **place aux Herbes** is the excellent **covered market** and the place du Marché with its flower stalls. Running behind them, pedestrianised rue St-Michel and avenue Félix-Faure hum with shops and restaurants.

The old town

The Italianate old town occupies the hill, all narrow shady streets stacked with houses. Flights of steps decorated with black-and-white pebble mosaics lead up from quai Bonaparte to Baroque **Basilique St-Michel Archange** (daily July–Aug 3–5.15pm, Sept–June 10am–noon, 3–5.15pm), which has a pink-and-orange campanile and sculptures on its facade. The square in front

is the main venue for Menton's prestigious chamber music festival each August. A second Baroque church stands across the square, the **Chapelle de la Conception** (open Wed 3–5pm), its walls ringed by life-size statues of saints.

Built in tiers where the castle once stood, the **Cimetière du Vieux-Château**, at the top of the hill, holds the tombs of many of the Russian and British families who settled here from the end of the 19th century, including those of illustrator Aubrey Beardsley and William Webb Ellis, creator of the modern game of rugby.

At the western end of the town, behind the seafront apartments and hotels of the promenade du Soleil, is the 18th-century pink-and-white **Palais Carnolès**, the former summer residence of the Monaco royal family, still with its fine staircase and some of its original panelling and painted ceilings. Today it contains the **Musée des Beaux Arts** (3 avenue de la Madone; Wed–Mon 10am–noon, 2–6pm; free), including a Madonna by Louis Bréa, Flemish

Menton celebrates its little yellow lemons with a flamboyant annual festival starting in mid-February and continuing into March. Over two weeks, lemons and oranges are piled high into incredible sculptures in the Jardin des Biovès, and on the Sundays, floats and bands parade along the seafront. For details, contact www.feteducitron.com

BELOW: view of the inland hill village Castellar and the mountains beyond.

Walking the Caps

Although the Riviera's exclusive headlands can seem like the preserve of the rich and famous, everyone has the right to walk along the French seashore, a right increasingly enforced by the local authorities as they maintain and improve the signposting on the Sentier du Littoral (coastal path). The path takes you around three of the region's most beautiful headlands: Cap Ferrat (footpath from Plage Passable to Port St-Jean), Cap d'Ail (footpath from Plage Mala to Plage Marquet), and Cap Martin (along the Sentier Corbusier, between the Plage du Cabbé and Carnolès). At times the path hugs the water or crosses beaches, with opportunities for bathing from the rocks or in surprisingly wild coves, inaccessible from the road and surrounded by Mediterranean vegetation and azure seas – or with surreal views of Monaco's tower blocks. At other times, steps climb up the cliffs and the path skirts the rear of private grounds, offering glimpses of Belle Epoque villas, tropical gardens and the lifestyle of the privileged few. The Conseil Général des Alpes Maritimes publishes a Randoxygène guide, *Rando Pays Côtier*, available from tourist offices. Also try www.randoxygene.org for more details.

and Dutch paintings, and works by Suzanne Valadon, Raoul Dufy and Graham Sutherland. Surrounding it, the **Jardin des Agrumes**, run by INRA (the state agricultural research institute), has many different species of citrus tree.

A horticulturalist's paradise

Menton boasts a remarkable number of exotic gardens – two of these are easily accessible to the public. The **Jardin Botanique Exotique Val Rahmeh** (avenue St-Jacques; www. mnhn.fr; tel: 04 9335 8672; Apr–Sept 10am–12.30pm, 3.30–6.30pm, Oct–Mar Wed–Mon 10am–12.30pm, 2–5pm; charge), arranged around a 1920s villa, proves that everything can indeed grow in Menton. A winding trail leads between magical and medicinal plants, dry and wet environments, towering palms, dank tropical ferns, forests of bamboo and exotic cocoa, avocado, banana, guava and citrus fruits, tea bushes and spice trees. This garden is also one of the institutions cultivating the *sophoro toromiro* tree in the hope

of introducing it back into the wild *(see margin left)*.

The **Serre de la Madone** (route de Gorbio; www.serredelamadone.com; tel: 04 9357 7390; Tue–Sun 10am–6pm, Dec–Mar until 5pm, closed Nov; charge) is a romantic garden designed in the 1920s by Lawrence Johnson, creator of the garden at Hidcote Manor in England. It is laid out with geometrical pools, terraces, fountains and classical statues that create different perspectives and environments for irises, acanthus, camellias, water plants, toxic daturas and flora from all over the globe.

Interesting gardens that can only be visited on tours organised by the Service du Patrimoine (tel: 04 9210 3366, *see page 205*) include the **Jardin des Colombières** (July–mid-Aug only, by appointment, tel: 04 9210 9710), inspired by Greek and Roman mythology, the **Jardin de la Fontana Rosa** (Mon and Fri 10am), which has ceramic motifs paying tribute to Don Quixote, and the grounds full of tropical and sub-tropical plants at **Villa de la Maria Serena** (Tue 10am). ❏

BELOW: the Serre de la Madone garden.

RESTAURANTS AND BARS

Restaurants

Prices for a three-course meal without wine. Many restaurants have a less expensive lunch menu:

€ = under €25
€€ = €25–40
€€€ = €40–60
€€€€ = over €60

Eze

Château de la Chèvre d'Or
rue du Barri
www.chevredor.com
Tel: 04 9210 6661. Open L & D daily. Closed mid-Nov–Feb. **€€€**
Luxurious dining with spectacular views. As well as the gastronomic restaurant, in summer you can also eat on the terrace (light, regional specialities at lunch, Asian-inspired cuisine at dinner) and in the informal Café du Jardin.

La Turbie

Café de la Fontaine
4 avenue du Général de Gaulle
www.hostelleriejerome.com
Tel: 04 9328 5279. Open L & D daily. **€**
Bruno Cirino of the Hostellerie Jérôme has brilliantly revived the village café as a casual but chic bistro, with a superb-value blackboard menu of homely specials, such as marinated sardines,

Nice-style rabbit and home-made fruit tarts. Open for breakfast or afternoon drinks as well.

Menton

Mirazur
30 avenue Aristide Briand
www.mirazur.fr
Tel: 04 9241 8686. Open July–Aug D Tue–Fri, L & D Sat–Sun; Sept–June L & D Tue–Sun. **€€€**
In the hands of adventurous young Argentine chef Mauro Colagreco, staid Menton now has one of the most exciting restaurants on the coast. Daring combinations of the finest ingredients, including fruit and vegetables from his kitchen garden, meet impeccable technique in specialities like low temperature pigeon. The dining room offers panoramic views over the bay. Make a reservation to secure a table.

Le Nautic
27 quai de Mauléon
Tel: 04 9335 7874.
Open L Tue, Wed, Fri–Sun, D daily. **€€**
A good fish restaurant with friendly Italian owners. Fried squid, John Dory with courgettes or sea bass cooked in a salt crust might appear on the menu. Try the strawberry *sabayon* for dessert.

Roquebrune Cap-Martin

Les Deux Frères
place des Deux Frères
www.lesdeuxfreres.com
Tel: 04 9328 9900. Open summer L Wed–Sun, D Tue–Sun; winter L Tue–Sun, D Tue–Sat. Closed mid-Nov–mid-Dec. **€€€**
The old village school is now a pleasant small hotel and restaurant. Attractive southern dishes might include artichoke salad or red mullet in a herb crust.

St-Jean-Cap-Ferrat

La Voile d'Or
Port de Plaisance, 7 avenue Jean-Mermoz
www.lavoiledor.fr
Tel: 04 9301 1313. Open L & D daily. Closed Oct–

Easter. **€€€€**
Luxurious fish and shellfish and grand French classics are served in a dining room overlooking the yachting marina; there's also a beach restaurant at lunch.

Villefranche-sur-Mer

Le Cosmo
11 place Amélie Pollonnais
www.lecosmo.fr
Tel: 04 9301 8405. Open L & D daily, service all day mid-June–mid-Sept. **€€**
This brasserie and cocktail bar has a big terrace overlooking the Cocteau chapel and is good for inventive salads, steak tartare, pasta or the fish catch of the day.

MONACO

Monaco is Europe's second-smallest independent country after the Vatican, with a huge concentration of wealth and sky-high property prices to match. The Principality has a busy cultural and sporting season and a legendary casino, plus all the trappings of a mini state

Seen from across the bay, Monaco ⑳ is a surreal sight with its cluster of skyscrapers against a backdrop of mountains, like Hong Kong on the Mediterranean. Indeed, comparisons with Hong Kong are not unjustified: a tiny, densely populated state squeezed between coast and mountains, a mix of modernity and Belle Epoque splendour and an important banking centre.

Of the 32,000 residents, only 7,000 are Monégasque citizens, and of the 40,000 people who work in Monaco to serve its tax exiles, gamblers and holidaymakers, many don't actually live in the state itself but commute in from more affordable lodgings in surrounding towns. High property prices are due not only to the rich residents and high-income tourists, but also because Monaco is bursting at the seams. One of the quandaries for the royal oligarchy is how to extend the city, not just building upwards but through continued projects of land reclamation over the sea or through colonisation of neighbouring France: the swanky Monte-Carlo Country Club at the end of avenue Princesse Grace is actually in Roquebrune-Cap Martin, while the Monte-Carlo Golf Club is at La Turbie.

A new Grimaldi

In 2005 Prince Albert II *(see box, page 254)* acceded to the throne, on the death of his father, Prince Rainier III, after 56 years as head of state. In theory Monaco is a constitutional monarchy, with a Minister of State who heads a cabinet of four ministers and a legislature of 24 elected by Monégasque citizens, but in practice the Prince remains enormously powerful. The Minister of State is chosen by the prince and approved by the French government.

Main attractions

PALAIS PRINCIER
MUSÉE OCÉANOGRAPHIQUE
JARDIN EXOTIQUE
MARCHÉ DE LA CONDAMINE
PORT HERCULE
CASINO DE MONTE-CARLO

LEFT: the skyscrapers of Monaco.
RIGHT: changing of the guard.

Orientation

Monaco is split into six districts: medieval Monaco-Ville or the old town, La Condamine port area, glamorous Monte-Carlo, the Larvotto beach district further east, La Fontvieille west of the Rocher, and residential Monaghetti on the hill behind. Although the state is tiny, it's very hilly. If you're on foot, there's a system of lifts and stairways, as well as five bus routes for getting around.

Princess Grace, formerly American film star Grace Kelly, who married Prince Rainier in 1956 and died in a car crash in 1982, is buried in the cathedral cemetery, along with numerous other members of the Grimaldi dynasty.

Le Rocher

Monaco-Ville, the core of Monaco, is often referred to as "Le Rocher" (the Rock), since it sits on a precipice which juts into the sea between Port Hercule and the modern port of Fontvieille. Le Rocher is crowned by the royal palace, the **Palais Princier** Ⓐ (place du Palais; www.palais.mc; daily May–Sept 9.30am–6.30pm, Apr 10.30am–6pm, Oct 10am–5.30pm; charge). The audio-guided visit takes in the Cour d'Honneur and sumptuous 17th- and 18th-century state apartments, including the Salon Louis XV and the Throne Room. You can also watch the changing of the

BELOW: Prince Albert II at his coronation.

guard that takes place on the square outside each day at 11.55am. An adjacent entrance leads to the **Musée des Souvenirs Napoléoniens** (June–Sept daily 9.30am–6pm, Oct–11 Nov daily 10am–5pm, mid-Dec–May Tue–Sun 10.30am–noon, 2–4.30pm; charge), a collection of Napoleonic memorabilia, including Napoleon's cradle and famous black hat, as well as an exhibition of documents from Monaco's history.

The old town's pristine streets lead to the neo-Byzantine **Cathédrale** Ⓑ (4 rue Colonel Bellando del Caste; open daily), which was built in white stone from La Turbie during the 19th century, and contains tombs of the Grimaldis. Near by, the **Musée de la Chapelle de la Visitation** (place de la Visitation; tel: +377 9350 0700; Tue–Sun 10am–4pm; charge) houses a collection of Baroque religious paintings, including works by Rubens and Ribera. Also worth a look is the **Chapelle de la Miséricorde** Ⓒ (daily 10am–6pm), which has a stripey marble interior and a painted wood sculpture of the Dead Christ, attributed to 18th-century

Albert II

The year 2005 saw the arrival of a new head of Europe's second-smallest but richest state with the coronation of Albert II, hitherto best known for his sporting achievements (a member of Monaco's Olympic bobsleigh team) and succession of glamorous female companions, including Claudia Schiffer, Naomi Campbell and Brooke Shields. Will it be a new style of monarchy? Prince Rainier III had done much to transform the Monaco economy in his 56-year reign but was increasingly surrounded by octogenarian councillors. Fifty-three-year-old Prince Albert II has brought in a younger team of ministers and advisers, is actively engaged against climate change and for sustainable development – and female staff are now being allowed to wear trousers for the first time. He has also involved Monaco more deeply in humanitarian causes, giving financial aid to countries in the wake of natural disasters, such as Haiti and Pakistan. As to the important question of an heir to the throne, a royal wedding is at last on the cards as Albert is set to marry long-term girlfriend, former South African swimming champion Charlène Wittstock in July 2011.

local sculptor François-Joseph Bosio, that is paraded through town on Good Friday.

On the edge of the Rock, the **Musée Océanographique** (avenue St-Martin; www.oceano.mc; daily Apr–June and Sept 9.30am–7pm, July–Aug until 7.30pm, Oct–Mar 10am–6pm; charge) is a great hit with kids for its illuminated tanks of tropical fish and crustaceans, a shark lagoon and coral reef. It also contains a collection of whale skeletons, preserved specimens and navigation equipment related to the oceanographic voyages of explorer-prince Albert I, who founded the museum in 1910.

Climbing up the cliffside in the Moneghetti district behind Le Rocher, the **Jardin Exotique** (boulevard du Jardin Exotique; tel: +377 9330 3365; daily 15 May–15 Sept 9am–7pm, 16 Sept–14 May 9am–6pm or dusk; charge) is a display of prickly cacti and succulents from deserts and other dry zones. At the foot of the garden, is **Grotte de l'Observatoire** (guided tours only), a cave complex with stalactites and stalagmites. Nearby, the 1920s Villa Paloma is being renovated as Monaco's new fine art museum, the **Nouveau Musée National de Monaco** (56 boulevard du Jardin Exotique; www.nmnm.mc; tel: +377 9898 1962; charge), with fine art and stage sets and costume designs from the Salle Garnier.

The harbours

La Condamine district is Monaco's old harbour area and site of a daily food market on place d'Armes. In 2002, Port Hercule was expanded with a huge new semi-floating jetty. The port is lively with bars and restaurants, has an outdoor swimming pool (ice rink in winter) on quai Albert Ier and is a prime vantage point for the Monaco Grand Prix.

Fontvieille was a new residential district created on reclaimed land in the 1980s around a modern marina.

TIP

Monaco has a different dialling code to France. If you're calling Monaco from abroad – including the surrounding Côte d'Azur – you'll need to use the international dialling code (00 377). To call France from Monaco, dial 00 33 and leave off the 0 at the start of French phone numbers.

The Monaco Grand Prix is the most glamorous on the F1 circuit and involves 78 laps around the Principality's hairpin bends at the end of May. Book many months in advance to secure grandstand places.

BELOW: a Ferrari draws up outside Monte-Carlo's Casino.

Just back from the port, constructed rather bizarrely over a shopping centre on the Terrasses de Fontvieille, is a cluster of small museums: the **Collection de Voitures Anciennes** (daily 10am–6pm; charge), the late Prince Rainier's collection of vintage cars and carriages, the **Musée des Timbres et des Monnaies** (Stamp and Coin Museum; daily July–Sept 10am–6pm, Oct–June 10am–5pm; charge); the **Musée Naval** (www.musee-naval.mc; daily 10am–6pm; charge), and the **Jardin Animalier** (www.palais. mc; tel: +377 9325 1831; daily June–Sept 9am–noon, 2–7pm, Oct–Feb 10am–noon, 2–5pm, Mar–May until 6pm; charge), a small zoo.

You'll also find the **Roseraie Princesse Grace** (Princess Grace Rose Garden), laid out with 4,000 rose bushes planted amid Mediterranean pine and olive trees, a lake and a collection of modern sculpture.

Monte-Carlo

For most people the district that epitomises Monaco is Monte-Carlo – or more particularly the ensemble of the Casino, Café de Paris and the Hôtel de Paris – with its ornate Second Empire architecture, luxury boutiques and swarms of Ferraris and Rolls-Royces. This is the area that made the Principality's fortune when Prince Charles III built the casino on a hill (hence Monte Carlo) previously used for cultivating lemons. He handed its management to entrepreneur François Blanc, founder of the Société des Bains de Monaco, which still owns the Principality's grandest hotels and casinos. You can visit the chocolate-box **Casino** **G** (place du Casino; tel: +377 9216 2000; Mon–Fri 2pm until late, Sat–Sun noon until late; open to over 18s only, ID required), built in the late 19th century, awash with gilt and cherubs. Opera and ballet are performed in the Casino's painstakingly restored **Salle Garnier**, a feast of coloured marble, mosaics and chandeliers.

Next door the domed Café de Paris – where great chef Auguste Escoffier once held sway – also has a casino, decorated with a Grand Prix theme, while its brasserie terrace offers perfect opportunities to watch the Hôtel de Paris' clientele coming and going. If you really want to blow your budget, visit überchef Alain Ducasse's Louis XV Restaurant on the ground floor of the hotel or go shopping on the avenue des Beaux-Arts.

Along the seafront below the Casino, accessible by a series of lifts, the ornate stucco **Villa Sauber** is used for art shows as part of the **Nouveau Musée National de Monaco** (17 avenue Princesse Grace; daily summer 11am–7pm, winter 10am–6pm; charge; *see page 255*).

Almost opposite is a modern **Japanese garden** and the angular, glass-sided **Grimaldi Forum** (10 avenue Princesse Grace; www.grimaldiforum. com; tel: +377 9999 2000), used for exhibitions, concerts and dance. Further along the avenue are Monaco's man-made beach at Larvotto, and the famous Sporting Club d'Eté complex, home to Jimmy'z nightclub. ❑

RESTAURANTS AND BARS

Restaurants

Prices for a three-course meal without wine. Many restaurants have a less expensive lunch menu:

€ = under €25
€€ = €25–40
€€€ = €40–60
€€€€ = over €60

Le Café de Paris

place du Casino, Monte-Carlo
www.montecarloresort.com
Tel: +377 9216 2020. Open daily noon–2am. €€
Completely renovated in 1920s style, the place where the crêpe Suzette was supposedly invented by accident for Edward VII (and named after one of his mistresses) is one of the sights of Monte-Carlo. Classic brasserie food and great terrace for people-watching.

Joël Robuchon Monte-Carlo

Hôtel Metropole, 4 avenue de la Madone, Monte Carlo
www.metropole.com
Tel: +977 9315 1515. Open L & D daily. €€€€
After Paris, Robuchon has brought his contemporary global tapas concept to Monte-Carlo in the hands of chef Christophe Cusset, with a succession of inventive dishes and sometimes daring combinations of flavours, although there

is also a more conventional rotisserie menu.

Karément

Grimaldi Forum, 10 avenue Princesse Grace
www.karement.com
Tel: +377 9999 2020. Open L & D daily. €€
The smart neo-Baroque bar and restaurant is absolutely the place to be, whether for breakfast on the terrace overlooking the sea, Provençal, Japanese and Chinese food at lunch or cocktails and DJs at night.

Le Louis XV

Hôtel de Paris, place du Casino, Monte-Carlo
www.alain-ducasse.com
Tel: +377 9806 8864. Open L & D Thur–Mon (plus Wed D in summer). Closed Dec and 2 weeks in Mar. €€€€
The flagship of the Ducasse empire, in the hands of Franck Cerruti, a native of Nice, serves lavish seasonal Mediterranean cuisine in the palatial dining room of the Hôtel de Paris. Smart dress required.

Polpetta

2 rue Paradis, Monte-Carlo
Tel: +377 9350 6784. Open L & D Sun–Fri, D only Sat. €€
Once frequented by Frank Sinatra, this bistro offers hearty Italian food, and is among the best value for money in Monaco.

St-Benoît

10 ter avenue de la Costa
Tel: +377 9325 0234. Open L & D Tue–Sun.€€€
A favourite with locals, in a rooftop position with views over the marina. The emphasis is on classic fish and shellfish.

Stars and Bars

6 quai Antoine 1er
www.starsnbars.com
Tel: +377 9797 9595. Open L & D June–Sept daily, Oct–May Tue–Sun. €€
Burgers and Tex-Mex are the name of the game at this hugely popular American restaurant, which has racing cars hanging from the ceiling and crash barriers around the bar inside. Has a huge terrace over-

looking Port Hercule. There's a friendly welcome for all, from small children to racing drivers and pop stars. Service all day.

Tip Top

11 avenue des Spélugues, Monte-Carlo
Tel: +377 93 50 69 13. Open L & D Mon–Sat noon–dawn, D Sun 7pm–dawn. €€
A busy convivial bistro and café frequented by an enormously eclectic crowd, ranging from local office workers to Albert II and scores of Formula 1 drivers, as photos on the walls reveal. The speciality is steak with matchstick chips, but they'll also do you a pizza in the dead of night.

RIGHT: ice cream sundaes at Le Café de Paris.

INSIGHT GUIDES TRAVEL TIPS

PROVENCE

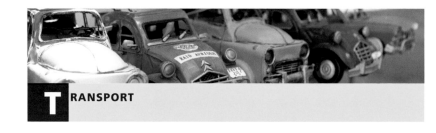

TRANSPORT

GETTING THERE AND GETTING AROUND

By Air

The main gateway to the south of France is Nice-Côte d'Azur Airport, France's second airport, which has two terminals served by numerous international airlines.

From the UK and Ireland

Online bookings often provide the cheapest rates. As well as booking direct with different airlines (listed below), well-established ticketing sites include www.expedia. com (UK and US sites), www.cheap-flights.com (UK), www.cheaptickets.com (US), www.lastminute.fr (France) and www.opodo.com (France and UK); www.travelsupermarket.com is a price-comparison website.
British Airways tel: 0844 4930 787 (UK); 800 247 9297 (US); 08 2582 5400 (France); www.british airways.com operates flights to Marseille from Gatwick, and to Nice from Heathrow, Gatwick and London City.
Bmibaby tel: 0905 828 2828 (UK); from abroad tel: +44 8458 101 100, www.bmibaby.com flies from Birmingham and East Midlands to Nice.
EasyJet tel: 0905 821 0905 (UK); 0899 651 011 (France); www. easyjet.com operates flights from

Belfast, Edinburgh, Newcastle, Liverpool, Luton and Stansted to Nice, and from Bristol and Gatwick to Marseille.
Flybe tel: 0871 700 2000 (UK); + 44 1392 268 529 (from abroad), www.flybe.com goes from Southampton, Birmingham, Exeter and Manchester to Avignon, and from Southampton to Nice.
Jet2 tel: 0871 226 1737; www.jet2. com flies from Leeds and Manchester to Nice, and from Leeds to Avignon.
Ryanair tel: 0906 270 5656 (UK); 1530 787 787 (Ireland); 08 9278 0210 (France); www.ryanair.com flies from Dublin, Edinburgh and Stansted to Marseille, from Dublin to Nice, from Liverpool and Luton to Nîmes, and from Stansted to Toulon-Hyères.
Aer Lingus tel: 0871 718 5000 (UK); 0818 365 000 (Ireland), 0821 23 02 67 (France), www. aerlingus.com flies from Dublin to Marseille and Nice, and from Cork to Nice.

From the US

Delta tel: 800 221 1212 (US); 08 1164 0005 (France); www.delta. com has a daily flight from JFK-New York to Nice. Otherwise flights from the US go via Paris. To reach Provence from Paris, **Air France** tel: 0871 6633 777 (UK); 800 237 2747 (US); 3654 (France); www.airfrance.fr flies

from Paris to Nice, Marseille, Avignon and Toulon-Hyères, and from Cork to Nice.

Getting from the Airport

Nice-Côte d'Azur airport (www.nice. aeroport.fr). The 20-minute taxi ride to the centre of town can be expensive (€20–30), but there is a vast network of bus services covering the entire region as far as Marseille and Genoa. Useful routes include 98 to Nice town centre and gare routière (bus station), 99 to Nice train station, 110 express line to Monaco and Menton, 210 to Cannes, and 250 to Golfe-Juan/Vallauris via Antibes.
Héli Air Monaco, tel: 00 377 9205 0050; www.heliairmonaco.com runs regular helicopter services between Nice airport and Monaco for not necessarily much more than a taxi.
Marseille Provence Airport (www. marseille.aeroport.fr) is at Marignane. and has regular buses to Marseille Gare St-Charles (about 25 mins, €8.50), as well as direct buses to Aix-en-Provence, Manosque, Digne, St-Maximin and Brignoles. A shuttle bus runs to Vitrolles Aéroport train station for destinations including Marseille, Arles, Nîmes, Avignon, Cavaillon and L'Isle-sur-la-Sorgue. A taxi to Marseille will cost about €40–50.
Toulon-Hyères airport (www.toulon-

hyeres.aeroport.fr) is actually located at Hyères, and is convenient for St-Tropez. Bus No. 7803 runs from the airport to St-Tropez via La Londe, Bormes-les-Mimosas, La Môle and Cogolin. Bus No. 102 runs from the airport to Hyères and Toulon town centres. See www.transports.var.fr for information.
Avignon airport (www.avignon.aero port.fr) is at Montfavet on the eastern edge of the city; taxis to the centre cost around €20.
Nîmes airport (www.nimes-aeroport.fr) is located between Nîmes and Arles. A shuttle bus (*navette*) timed to coincide with flights runs to Nîmes train station (buy the €5 ticket on the bus). Prepare to pay around €25 for a taxi to Nîmes, around €30 to Arles.

By Train

The TGV high-speed track has now reached Marseille and Nîmes, reducing the journey time from Paris Gare de Lyon to only around 3 hours. There are between 10 and 12 TGVs per day from Paris to Marseille, 9 per day to Nice (around 6 hours) and 15 a day to Avignon (approx. 3 hours). Other stations served include Orange, Aix-en-Provence TGV, Les Arcs, St-Raphaël, Cannes and Menton.

From the UK, Eurostar trains run to Lille and Paris Gare du Nord; it is possible to book through tickets from all over the UK to stations in Provence on www.eurostar.com, making London to Marseille, for example, a journey of 6 hours 30 minutes with a change at Lille. From mid-July to mid-September, there is also a direct train between London St Pancras and Avignon Centre every Saturday.

Tickets

In the UK, tickets for journeys in France can be booked at the Rail Europe Travel Centre (1 Lower Regent Street, SW1, tel: 08448 464 064) or online at www.rail europe.co.uk. As well as individual journeys, a variety of passes are available including InterRail passes for use in up to 28 Euro-

ABOVE: the TGV on the corniche d'Estérel.

pean and North African countries. and InterRail France passes for 2 to 8 days within France only.

In the US, call Rail Europe at 877 257 2887 or book online at www.raileurope.com. Non-Europeans and non-North Africans can buy a **Eurailpass** (www.eurail.com). Assorted options allow first- or second-class travel in France only, in 2 to 5 countries or in up to 20 other participating countries, but must be purchased before your arrival in Europe.

In France, buy tickets in any SNCF train station or by phone on 3635 (France only). You can also book, pay and find web discounts on the Internet site: www.voyages-sncf.com. Journeys on the TGV require a seat reservation. There are often good disounts and special offers on www.voyages-sncf.com for early reservations (Prems), last-minute reservations and idTGV electronic TGV tickets.

Remember that before you get on the train you have to date-stamp your ticket ("compostez votre billet") in the *composteur* machine at the entrance to the platforms.

By Car

If you don't mind a long drive, and want to have a car to tour when you get to Provence, then driving from the UK is a good option. However, note that in July and August – particularly on Saturdays around the 14 July and 15

August public holidays – the motorways get extremely busy. Traffic bulletins on Autoroute FM (107.7FM) are useful, with hourly bulletins in English in summer.

Road distances to the South are as follows:
• Calais–Nice: 1,167km (725 miles)
• Caen–Nice: 1,161km (721 miles)
• Dieppe–Avignon: 854km (531 miles)
• Calais–Avignon: 965km (600 miles)
The fastest route to Provence is from Calais via Paris, the A6 Autoroute to Lyon and the A7 down the Rhône valley. All autoroutes have *péage* toll booths, where payment may be made in cash or by credit card.

Another option is to drive to Paris and then put your car on the train. The SNCF has an "Auto/Train" service from Paris to Avignon, Marseille, Toulon, Fréjus/St-Raphaël and Nice (see www.voyages-sncf.com/autotrain), though note that you do not travel on the same train as your car.

Car Ferry Operators

The following companies operate across the English Channel:
Brittany Ferries sails from Portsmouth to Caen, Cherbourg or St-Malo; from Plymouth and Cork to Roscoff; and, May–Oct only, from Poole to Cherbourg. Tel: 0870 366 5333 (UK); 08 2582 8828 (France), www.brittany-ferries.com

Norfolkline sails from Dover to Dunkerque in 1 hour 45 minutes. Tel: 0870 870 1020 (UK); 03 2828 9550 (France); www.norfolk line-ferries.com

P&O sails from Dover to Calais in 90 minutes. Tel: 0870 598 0333 (UK); 08 2512 0156 (France); www.poferries.com

SeaFrance sails between Dover and Calais. Tel: 0871 423 4119 (UK); +44 845 458 0666 (from abroad), www.seafrance.com

Transmanche and LD Lines runs from Newhaven to Dieppe and Dover to Boulogne-sur-mer. Tel: 0800 917 1201 (UK); 08 0065 0100 (France); www.transmanche ferries.com

Eurotunnel

Eurotunnel carries cars and their passengers from Folkestone to Calais on a simple drive-on-drive-off train system (journey time 35 minutes). Payment is made at toll booths (which accept cash, cheques or credit cards). For the best prices and to avoid queues, it is best to book ahead (tel: 0870 535 3535 (UK); 08 1063 0304 (France); www.eurotunnel.com).

GETTING AROUND

Although it is possible to get around Provence by train and bus, a car (or, if you're energetic, a bicycle) is essential to explore the region independently. Bus and train services are adequate between main towns and cities, especially along the coast, but there may only be one bus a day – and sometimes no buses at all – to small villages.

Public Transport

Public transport within larger towns is fairly efficient but can be limited between towns and in rural areas. Marseille has a metro system, two tramlines and an extensive bus network; Nice has a large bus network and a tramline.

By Bus

Details of routes and timetables are available from tourist offices and bus stations (gares routières). Both should also be able to give details of coach tours and sightseeing excursions.

For information on bus routes and timetables between towns, visit the site www.lepilote.com for the Bouches-du-Rhône département, www.vaucluse.fr for the Vaucluse, www.varlib.fr for the Var, www.lignes dazur.com for the coastal zone of the Alpes-Maritimes and www.cg06. fr. Note that many bus services are geared towards transporting teenagers to school and that frequency may well be reduced during the summer holidays.

By Train

There is a reasonably good SNCF rail network in the south of France, especially in the Rhône Valley and along the coast. You can pick up free local timetables from railway stations (gares SNCF) or visit www.voyages-sncf.fr.

Services range from the high-speed TGV lines, which stop only at main stations, to the local TER services, which run along the Côte d'Azur, stopping at all stations between Marseille and Venti-miglia, and the scenic line along the Côte Bleue west from Marseille to Martigues. See www.ter-sncf.com for timetables.

Out-of-town stations usually (but not always) have a connecting navette (shuttle bus) to the town centre. Sometimes the SNCF runs a connecting bus service (indicated as "Autocar" in timetables) to stations where the train no longer stops or along disused lines; rail tickets and passes are valid on these routes. Children under 4 years old travel free, those from 4 to 12 have reduced rates. Before boarding the train remember to composter (validate) your ticket at a machine in the station.

Two scenic mountain lines depart from Nice. The **Roya Valley line** (www.ter-sncf.com/paca) runs from Nice to Tende through the Paillon and Roya-Bévéra valleys. The privately operated **Train des Pignes** (www.trainprovence.com; tel: 04 9703 8080) has four return journeys from Nice Gare de Provence that run up the Var valley to Digne-les-Bains. Vintage steam trains run on Sundays in summer.

By Car

Between cities: roads to and around the main resorts get completely choked up during July and August, and you can spend as much time getting to the beach as you spend on it. Try to avoid weekends, mid- to late mornings (when everyone's going to the beach), and late afternoons (when everyone's going home from the beach).

BELOW: cycling past the Pont St-Bénézet in Avignon.

Motorways *(autoroutes)* are designated "A" roads, National Highways *(routes nationales)* "N" or "RN" roads. Local roads are known as "D" routes and very small "C" communal roads. Note that many roads have recently been renumbered, as former N roads have come under local control and have been renumbered as D routes.

Parking in the main resorts is often costly; parking meters have been replaced by *horodateurs*, (pay-and-display machines), which take coins and/or special parking cards that can be bought at a tobacconist *(tabac)*.

British, US, Canadian and Australian licences are all valid in France. You should always carry your vehicle's registration document and valid insurance. Additional insurance cover, in some cases including a "home-return" service, is offered by a number of organisations, including the British Automobile Association (www.theaa.com), European breakdown service tel: 00 800 88 77 66 55 or French landline 04 72 17 12 00) and Europ-Assistance (www.europ-assistance.co.uk; tel: +44 844 338 55 33).

Speed Limits

Speed limits are as follows, unless otherwise indicated: 130 kph (80mph) on motorways; 110 kph (68mph) on dual carriageways; 90 kph (56mph) on other roads, except in towns where the limit is 50 kph (30mph) and occasionally 30 kph (20mph); there are a growing number of speed radars. Speed limits are reduced by 20 kph (12mph) on motorways in wet weather and during periods of high pollution.

Rules of the Road

• Drive on the right.
• The minimum age for driving in France is 18. Foreigners may not drive on a provisional licence.
• Full or dipped headlights must be used in poor visibility and at night; sidelights are not sufficient unless the car is stationary.

Beams must be adjusted for right-hand-drive vehicles.
• The use of seat belts (front and rear) is compulsory.
• Children under 10 are not allowed to ride in the front seat, except rear-facing baby seats.
• Carry a red warning triangle to place 50 metres (165ft) behind the car in case of a breakdown or accident, and a fluorescent yellow jacket. In an accident or emergency, call the police (dial 17) or use the free emergency telephones (every 2km/1 mile) on motorways. If another driver is involved, lock your car and go together to call the police. It is useful to carry a European Accident Statement Form (obtainable from your insurance company), which will simplify matters in the event of an accident.

Traffic on major roads generally has priority, with traffic being halted on minor approach roads by means of one of the following signs:
Cédez le passage – give way
Vous n'avez pas la priorité – you do not have right of way

If an oncoming driver flashes their headlights it is to indicate that he or she has priority – not the other way around.

Car Hire

To hire a car you need to be at least 21 years old and must have held a driving licence for at least a year. Some hire companies will not rent to people under 26 or over 60. Expect to pay about €245 a week for a small car with insurance and 1,700km (1,056 miles) included. You can sometimes find good weekend deals, usually from Friday evening to Monday morning. Watch out for cheaper companies that may balance a low hire cost with high charges in the event of damage to the vehicle. Fly-drive packages, or arranging car hire in advance, can work out slightly cheaper than hiring once you arrive. The SNCF offers substantial discounts with train-plus-car rental packages under

its "Voyage Alacarte" scheme (www.voyages-sncf.com).

Avis, tel: 08 2005 0505
www.avis.com
Budget, tel: 08 2500 3564
www.budget.com
Europcar, tel: 08 2535 8358
www.europcar.com
Hertz, tel: 01 3938 3838
www.hertz-europe.com

Bicycles

If you're planning to bring your own bike, most long-distance trains have special areas designated for bicycle transport. You must reserve in advance and pay a small fee. Alternatively, if you partially dismantle your bicycle and put it in a carrier (available at most bicycle shops) you can carry it on as luggage for no extra fee. Most regional trains also make provisions for bicycles, as does the Eurostar. Within the region, Aix, Avignon, Marseille and Nice all have inexpensive municipal bike hire schemes, where you pick up the bike at one spot and leave it at another. To hire a bike by the half-day, day or longer, try Holiday Bikes (www.holiday-bikes.com; tel: 0810 809 609), which has outlets in numerous towns.

Taxis

Taxis are normally available at railway stations and official taxi ranks in city centres. Outside the cities, hotels and tourist offices should have information on local companies or check the *pages jaunes* telephone directory.
Aix tel: 04 4227 7111,
www.taxisradioaixois.com
Avignon tel: 04 9082 2020,
www.taxis-avignon.fr
Cannes tel: 08 9071 2227,
www.taxicannes.fr
Marseille: tel: 04 9102 2020,
www.taximarseille.com
Menton tel: 08 2090 8980,
www.taxis-radio-mento.com
Monaco tel: 08 2020 9898,
www.taximonacoprestige.com
Nice: tel: 04 9313 7878.

ACCOMMODATION

WHERE TO STAY

Hotels

All hotels in France carry star ratings, set down by the Ministry of Tourism, ranging from one star to extremely luxurious five stars. Even the simplest hotels may be perfectly clean and acceptable, though you shouldn't expect much in the way of room service or facilities such as air conditioning or lifts. Grand five-star establishments will have spacious rooms, restaurants and bars, spas and sports facilities and often literally hundreds of staff ready to cater to every whim. Don't rely too heavily on the star system, however – although it has recently been overhauled, it depends on criteria such as room size, presence of a lift, business centres and languages spoken by reception, rather than the quality of welcome or good taste. Country hotels and grand hotels will often have a restaurant.

Hotel Associations

As well as international groups such as Accor (www.accor.com), which has hotels ranging from budget Formule 1 and Etap, via Ibis, Mercure and Novotel to the luxury Sofitel brands, and Kyriad (www.kyriad.com), both of which have branches in the main cities, there are assocations of independent hotels, to which several

of the hotels in this guide belong. Most offer centralised booking services. These include:

Châteaux & Hôtels Collection tel: 08 1174 3742 (France); +33 1 7272 9202 (outside France); www.chateauxhotels.com. Mid- to high-end hotels, restaurants and rooms in private chateaux.

Exclusive Hotels +33 8 2513 1010; www.exclusive-hotels.com. Two hundred stylish, urban boutique hotels, including several in the PACA region, with good internet booking rates.

Logis de France www.logishotels. com. Federation of over 3,000 private hotels, mainly in the budget to mid-range category in villages and small towns. Many have good, simple restaurants.

Relais & Châteaux tel: 08 2532 3232 (France); 00 800 2000 00 02 (UK), +1 800 735 2478 (US/ Canada); www.relaischateaux.com. Luxury hotels, often with gourmet restaurants.

Relais du Silence 01 4449 9000; www.relaisdusilence.com). Mid- to high-end hotels "de charme" in particularly peaceful settings, often in the country.

Prices and Reservations

Paradoxically for an area that boasts some of the most expensive hotels in the world, Provence and the Côte d'Azur has many remarkably inexpensive decent

hotels: it is quite possible to spend anything from €45 for a night in a double room to well over €1,000. In tourist destinations rates are often highest in July and August, while in more business-oriented cities, such as Marseille and Toulon, you may find that rates are actually lower in August and at weekends. Some places shoot up prices for special events such as the Monaco Grand Prix, Nice Carnaval, Cannes Film Festival and the *féria* in Nîmes. Note that prices are charged per room not per person, and generally do not include breakfast. Details of room prices should be visible either outside or in reception, as well as on the back of bedroom doors. Supplements may be charged for an additional bed or a cot (*lit bébé*). Some seaside hotels try to insist on *demi-pension* or a minimum of two or three nights in summer.

When reserving, the hotel may ask for your credit card number; some will demand a non-refundable *arrhes* (deposit). Try to book ahead for the peak summer season, key events or the Easter and May public holidays. If you arrive without a reservation, the tourist office should be able to tell you which hotels have rooms available for the night and may even have a hotel reservation service.

Bed and Breakfasts

Bed and breakfast (chambres d'hôtes) accommodation is increasingly widely available in Provence and can be anywhere from a working farm or simple village house to a sumptuous château – with correspondingly large variations in price. Home-cooked evening meals, often eaten at a communal table d'hôte, are sometimes available. Under French regulations, chambres d'hôtes have a maximum of five bedrooms and fifteen people, with breakfast included in the price.

Bed and Breakfast in France lists B&Bs. UK booking service, tel: 0871 781 0834; www.bedbreak. com. **Fleurs de Soleil** (www.french-guesthouse.com) is an independent association of B&Bs.

Gîtes, Villas and Flat Rentals

Self-catering accommodation can be a good way to holiday in the south. Gîtes are found in rural areas, mostly away from the coast, sometimes on working farms or in converted farm buildings. On the coast, accommodation can vary from modern apartment complexes to luxury villas. There are several national networks of gîtes, the largest of which is **Gîtes de France** (www.gites-de-france.fr), whose members are regularly inspected by the national federation and rated between one and five "épis" (ears of corn). The other main network is **Clévacances** (www.clevacances.com), which has furnished seaside apartments, country cottages and B&Bs, with its own system of key ratings. Many tourist offices also have details of rental accommodation. Rentals generally run Saturday to Saturday, although it may be possible to rent for a weekend in low season.

At the luxury end of the market, **Balfour France** (www.balfourfrance.com; UK tel: 020 7367 0960) concentrates on luxury villa rentals, generally with pools

and often with maid and chef service thrown in, with properties in Provence, on the Var coast around St-Tropez and around Grasse and Cannes.

Falling somewhere between hotel and apartment are apart-hotels (rooms with kitchenette), such as the Suitehotel and Citadines groups, and holiday apartment complexes such as Latitudes and Pierre et Vacances.

Various UK-based tour operators also offer a range of self-catering accommodation as part of a package holiday. Try:
Allez France, www.allezfrance.com
Chez Nous, tel: 0845 268 1102; www.cheznous.com
French Life, tel: 0870 444 8877; www.frenchlife.co.uk

Gîtes d'Etape

Gîtes d'Etape offer basic, inexpensive accommodation for walkers or cyclists, often in remote mountain areas; expect communal accommodation, bunk beds and shared bathrooms. You will need to make reservations, especially in busy periods.

Mountain refuges (refuges) offer similar accommodation and some also provide meals. Many refuges are open from June to September only, and they should always be booked in advance. Lists of refuges are available from local tourist offices.

Youth Hostels

To stay in most youth hostels (auberges de jeunesse) you need to be a member of the Youth Hostel Association (YHA) or the **Fédération Unie des Auberges de Jeunesse** (FUAJ), tel: 01 4489 8727; www.fuaj.org, which is affiliated to the International Youth Hostel Federation (www.hihostels.com), although it is possible to take up temporary membership for the night. There are FUAJ-affiliated hostels in Arles, Cassis (Calanques), Fontaine-de-Vaucluse, La Palud-sur-Verdon, Manosque, Marseille, Menton, Nice, Nîmes and Tarascon.

Camping

French campsites (campings) are often remarkably well appointed. Look for those with the Camping Qualité label, which adhere to a national quality charter, with 139 adherent sites in the PACA region (see www.campingqualité.com). The **French Federation of Camping and Caravanning** (FFCC) website www.campingfrance.com contains a bilingual listing of campsites.

Most campsites open between March or April and September or October. Prices range from around €15–30 per night for two people with a car, caravan or tent. On the coast during high season the campsites can be extremely crowded. Although camping rough (camping sauvage) is generally not permitted, it may be worth asking the owner of the land for permission if there is nowhere official to pitch up near by. Fire is an ever-present risk in the region, so be particularly careful when cooking.

Campsites are graded from one-star (minimal comfort, water points, showers and sinks) to four-star luxury sites, which allow more space for each pitch and offer above-average facilities, such as pools and restaurants. For something more rural, look out for signs designated Aire naturelle de camping and Camping à la ferme .

UK Reservation Services

The following offer camping holiday packages with ferry transport and tent or mobile home pitch:
Canvas Holidays (UK), tel: 0845 268 0827; www.canvasholidays.co.uk
Select Site (UK), tel: 0844 406 0127; www.select-site.com
Vacansoleil, tel: 0333 700 5050, www.vacansoleil.co.uk

Hotel Listings

Hotels are listed according to the chapters in this book, and thereafter by place, then hotel name, in alphabetical order.

AVIGNON

Avignon

Hôtel Cloître St-Louis
20 rue du Portail Boquier
Tel: 04 9027 5555
www.cloitre-saint-louis.com
Set around a pleasant cloister, the Cloître St-Louis combines a wing of a former monastery with a dramatic, modern steel-and-glass wing, with a swimming pool on top. The modern wing was designed by French architect Jean Nouvel who designed the iconic Torre Agbar building in Barcelona . **€€€**

Hôtel d'Europe
14 place Crillon
Tel: 04 9014 7676
www.hotel-d-europe.fr
Set at the rear of a lovely courtyard, in an antique-filled 16th-century mansion, this elegant hotel has resided here for more than 200 years. Guests have ranged from Napoleon, Lamartine, Victor Hugo and John Stuart Mill to more recent politicians and actors. **€€€**

Hôtel de Blauvac
11 rue de la Bancasse
Tel: 04 9086 3411
www.hotel-blauvac.com
A lovely budget option on a narrow street in the heart of town. The 17th-century former residence of the Marquis de Blauvac is simple but alluring. The 16 rooms have exposed stone walls and newly re-done bathrooms. **€**

Hôtel de la Mirande
4 place de la Mirande
Tel: 04 9014 2020
www.la-mirande-avignon.com
The faultlessly decorated Mirande offers 20 personalised rooms in the 17th-century Hôtel de Vervins, situated just behind the Palais des Papes. The salons and glazed-in courtyard still have the feel of a private house and you can take cookery courses in the old kitchens. **€€€€**

Hôtel Mignon
12 rue Joseph Vernet
Tel: 04 9082 1730
www.hotel-mignon.com
This sweet little hotel with 16 colourful rooms is surprisingly adequate for its category and price. It's not luxurious, but the location is central and the bathrooms sparkle. **€**

La Ferme
chemin des Bois,
Ile de la Barthelasse
Tel: 04 9082 5753
www.hotel-laferme-avignon.com
A beautiful farm in a peaceful spot on an island, yet within easy reach of the city centre. Pleasant rooms, fresh, simple cuisine, and a swimming pool. **€**

Mercure Cité des Papes
1 rue Jean Vilar
Tel: 04 9080 9300
www.mercure.com
If you are determined to stay next door to the lovely Palais des Papes, consider the modern 73-roomed Cité des Papes. Request one of the quiet back rooms with palatial views. **€€**

Villeneuve-lès-Avignon

Hôtel-Restaurant La Magnaneraie
37 rue Camp de Bataille
Tel: 04 9025 1111
www.hostellerie-la-magnaneraie.com
If you're having trouble finding somewhere to stay in Avignon, you could consider staying in Villeneuve. This hotel is housed in a 15th-century silk farmhouse built of honey-coloured stone, and is set in large gardens with ponds, palms and ancient oaks. More contemporary facilities include a large swimming pool and tennis courts; you can also hire bicycles. **€€–€€€**

ORANGE AND THE MONT VENTOUX

Carpentras

Le Fiacre
153 rue Vigne
Tel: 04 9063 0315
www.hotel-du-fiacre.com
An interesting old town house and an excellent choice if you want to stay somewhere central. **€€€€**

Hôtel du Forum
24 rue du Forum
Tel: 04 9060 5700
www.hotel-forum-provence.com
A friendly purpose-built hotel just outside the old town with comfortable, good-sized bedrooms, friendly staff and a courtyard terrace. **€**

Châteauneuf-du-Pape

La Sommellerie
route de Roquemaure
Tel: 04 9083 5000
www.la-sommellerie.fr
In the heart of the famous vineyards, 4 km (2½ miles) from the village centre, this restored 17th-century farm has pleasant rooms with rustic furnishings.

Dining room serves regional cuisine. Has a swimming pool. **€€**

Orange

Hôtel Le Glacier
46 cours Aristide-Briand
Tel: 04 9034 0201
www.le-glacier.com
A straightforward hotel in a good location on the edge of the old town. Very friendly staff. No restaurant. **€**

Hôtel Arène
place des Langes
Tel: 04 9011 4040

www.hotel-arene.fr
This good central hotel on a tranquil square has a mix of Provençal-style rooms and modernised "executive" rooms. Good restaurant and a coffee bar with internet access. **€€**

Sault

Hostellerie du Val de Sault
route de St-Trinit
Tel: 04 9064 0141
www.valdesault.com
This is an elevated modern hotel with gardens and a swimming pool looking out onto Mont Ventoux. There are rooms with terraces, and the cuisine served is typical of the region and tasty. Closed Nov–Mar. €€€

Uchaux

Château de Massillan
chemin Hauteville
Tel: 04 9040 6451
www.chateau-de-massillan.com
This luxury hotel-restaurant in a historic chateau a few kilometres northeast of Orange has been given a modern interior by London-based Birgit Israel Interiors. Extensive grounds include a courtyard, pool, kitchen garden and vineyard. €€€

Vaison-la-Romaine

Hostellerie le Beffroi
rue de l'Evêché
Tel: 04 9036 0471
www.le-beffroi.com
Le Beffroi is a delightful 16th-century hostelry in two adjoining houses. Located in the medieval upper town with period decor and a good restaurant (open from April to October). The terrace swimming pool has lovely views. €€

ABOVE: Avignon.

THE LUBERON

Bonnieux

Bastide de Capelongue
Les Claparèdes, chemin des Cabanes
Tel: 04 9075 8978
www.capelongue.com
Beautiful modern stone *mas* in the midst of the *garrigue* plateau above the village, with spacious rooms, two pools and a first-rate restaurant in the hands of top chef Edouard Loubet. There are also stylish apartments to rent at the Ferme de Capelongue. €€€€

Gordes

La Bastide de Gordes
route de Combe
Tel: 04 9072 1212
www.bastide-de-gordes.com
A fine Renaissance building on the ramparts with elegant rooms, wonderful views and many modern facilities, including a salubrious spa, solarium and sauna. Visits to local vineyards can be arranged. Has 29 rooms and two suites. €€€€

L'Isle-sur-la-Sorgue

Mas de Cure Bourse
120 chemin de la Serre
Tel: 04 9038 1658
www.masdecurebourse.com
Set in orchards 3km (2 miles) from the town, this former 18th-century coaching inn has pleasant, traditionally decorated rooms, a restaurant, large garden and swimming pool. €€

Lourmarin

Le Mas de Guilles
route de Vaugines
Tel: 04 9068 3055
www.guilles.com
A quiet and relaxing *mas*, set amid vineyards at the end of a long avenue of olive trees, just outside Lourmarin. Most rooms are spacious and attractive with big old Provençal wardrobes. There is a swimming pool and tennis courts in the grounds. Dinner is served either in a vaulted dining room or on the terrace. €€

Ménerbes

Hostellerie Le Roy Soleil
route des Beaumettes, D103
Tel: 04 9072 2561
www.roy-soleil.com
A relaxed hotel in an 18th-century manor amid vineyards beneath the village, with flamboyantly decorated rooms and a pool. As well as the gastronomic restaurant, there's a simpler bistro for weekday lunch. Closed mid-Nov–mid-Mar. €€

St-Saturnin-sur-Apt

Domaine des Andéols
Tel: 04 9075 5063
www.domainedesandeols.com
This painstakingly restored hamlet has brought conceptual design to deepest Provence. The nine achingly hip "houses" are furnished with modern design classics and contemporary artworks. There's an immaculate garden and a restaurant overseen by Paris chef Guy

Martin. Dine al fresco by candlelight in the summer. Stylish indoor and outdoor pools, library and hamman. Closed from Nov–Mar. €€€€

Vaugines

Hostellerie du Luberon
Tel: 04 9077 2719
www.hostellerieduluberon.com
A simple, Provençal *mas* with a friendly, family-run atmosphere. The restaurant looks out onto the pretty gardens and a pool. €€

PRICE CATEGORIES

Price categories are for an average double room in high season:
€ = under €100
€€ = €100–180
€€€ = €180–300
€€€€ = more than €300

MARSEILLE AND THE CALANQUES

Marseille

Hôtel Alizé
35 quai des Belges
Tel: 04 9133 6697
www.alize-hotel.com
This much-loved budget address has recently refurbished Provençal-style rooms and a prime position on the Vieux-Port: ask for a room with a port view. **€**

Hôtel Le Corbusier
280 boulevard Michelet
Tel: 04 9116 7800
www.hotellecorbusier.com
The hotel in Le Corbusier's Cité Radieuse is a cult address for architecture fans. Rooms vary from simple monastic cabins with shared bathrooms to mini-suites for four. There's also the original

bar, an adventurous restaurant, and the use of the Cité's rooftop gym and paddling pool.

Mercure Grand Hôtel Beauvau
4 rue Beauvau
Tel: 04 9154 9100
www.mercure.com
Occupying a prime site on the Vieux-Port, this grand hotel has welcomed such luminaries as George Sand, Chopin and Alfred de Musset. Many of the 73 rooms, including some family duplexes with balcony, overlook the Vieux-Port. **€€€**

Radisson Blu Marseille Vieux Port
40 quai du Rive Neuve
Tel: 04 8892 1950
www.radissonblu.com/hotel-marseille
An airy modern hotel spread over two buildings on either side of an outdoor pool and sunbathing deck. 189 rooms come with Provençal or African-inspired minimalist decoration. Bar, Mediterranean restaurant and a brasserie. **€€€**

Résidence du Vieux-Port
18 quai du Port
Tel: 04 9191 9122
www.hotelmarseille.com
This 1950s hotel has great views to Notre-Dame-de-la-Garde. The spacious balconied rooms have been redecorated in a reinterpretation of their original '50s style with high-tech bathrooms. A neo-50s brasserie is downstairs. **€€€**

Cassis

Les Jardins de Cassis
avenue Auguste Favier
Tel: 04 4201 8485
www.hotel-lesjardinsde-cassis.com
A lovely Provençal-style hotel situated on the hillside above the town centre, sitting in a palm tree-filled garden. The rooms are clean and well maintained. Nineteen of the 36 rooms have baclonies or private terraces. Also has a pool. **€€**

AIX-EN-PROVENCE

Grand Hôtel Nègre Coste
33 cours Mirabeau
Tel: 04 4227 7422
www.hotelnegrecoste.com
This hotel may not be as grand as it once was (its original reception rooms have lost out to a pizzeria and the decor is a little tired, but the reasonably sized bedrooms offer views of cours Mirabeau at the front and over pantiled

rooftops to the cathedral at the rear. **€€**

Hôtel Artéa
4 boulevard de la République
Tel: 04 4227 3600
www.hotel-artus-aix-en-provence.com
Located near La Rotonde, the 18th-century town house that was once home to composer Darius Milhaud has been undergoing substantial refurbishment but remains good value, with smart new bathrooms. No lift. **€€**

Hôtel Cardinal
24 rue Cardinal
Tel: 04 4238 3230
www.hotel-cardinal-aix.com
A charming budget hotel near the Musée Granet, in an 18th-century

building cluttered with antique furniture and paintings. **€**

Hôtel Cézanne
40 avenue Victor Hugo
Tel: 04 4291 1111
www.hotelaix.com
The Cézanne has been transformed into a lovely modern boutique hotel with a relaxing downstairs bar with neo-Baroque armchairs, individually decorated rooms and new king-size beds. Helpful staff. **€€€**

Hôtel des Augustins
3 rue de la Masse
Tel: 04 4227 2859
www.hotel-augustins.com
Housed in a building that was an Augustine convent until the French Revolution of 1789, it became a hotel in the 1890s. Conveniently

located near the cours Mirabeau, this place has comfortable rooms and an imposing vaulted reception area. **€€–€€€**

Hôtel des Quatre Dauphins
54 rue Roux Alphéran
Tel: 04 4238 1639
www.lesquatredauphins.fr
Overlooking the dolphin fountain in the Quartier Mazarin, this small hotel has lots of fans. It is inexpensive but not without character and comfort. No lift. **€**

Le Pigonnet
5 avenue du Pigonnet
Tel: 04 4259 0290
www.hotelpigonnet.com

This historic bastide is a luxurious and tranquil retreat just a short walk from the city centre. Has an upmarket restaurant, swimming pool and loungers, rose garden and shady, verdant grounds in which Cézanne once painted a view of the Montagne Ste-Victoire. €€€

ST-RÉMY AND LES ALPILLES

Fontvieille

Hôtel La Peireiro
36 avenue des Baux
Tel: 04 9054 7610
www.hotel-peireiro.com
Constructed in the 1970s in old stone quarries in the Alpilles and sitting in lovely gardens, La Peireiro has 43 rooms, a pool, sauna and mini-golf. €€

Les Baux-de-Provence

L'Oustau de Baumanière
Route d'Arles
Tel: 04 9054 3307
www.oustaudebaumaniere.com
A legendary luxury hotel in a superbly renovated 16th-century farmhouse outside Les Baux, with a magnificent view and celebrated gastronomic restaurant. Closed Jan–Feb. €€€€

St-Rémy-de-Provence

Hôtel Château des Alpilles
D31
Tel: 04 9092 0333
www.chateaudesalpilles.com
Sophisticated 19th-century chateau in its own park includes accommodation in restored farmhouse and chapel. Has a pool, and restaurant serving excellent regional dishes. €€€

Hôtel du Cheval-Blanc
6 avenue Fauconnet
Tel: 04 9092 0928
www.hotelcheval-blanc.com
A simple and slightly eccentric hotel, but the reasonably sized rooms and bargain prices, plus a town-centre location, make this a long-standing budget favourite. The owners do insist you pay upfront. Closed from Nov to early Mar. €

Hôtel les Ateliers de l'Image
36 boulevard Victor Hugo
Tel: 04 9092 5150
www.hotelphoto.com
Occupying a former music hall, this is a very stylish hotel. Particularly lovely is the Japanese-inspired garden with its pools and pathways. The garden is expansive and has sun loungers surrounding the pool. The hotel also offers a modern restaurant, sushi bar, photography courses and exhibitions. €€€

Salon-de-Provence

Abbaye de Ste-Croix
D16, Val de Cuech
Tel: 04 9056 2455
www.hotels-provence.com
This secluded luxury hotel outside Salon has a unique setting in a former Benedictine abbey, complete with medieval chapel and 25 rooms and suites occupying former monks' cells. Closed Nov–Mar. €€€

ARLES AND THE CAMARGUE

Arles

Grand Hôtel Nord-Pinus
place du Forum
Tel: 04 9093 4444
www.nord-pinus.com
This luxury hotel with its fashionable bar is an Arles institution. The stairway decorated with *féria* bullfighting posters and Peter Beard photos shows the town's dual interests. €€€

Hôtel Calendal
5 rue Porte de Laure
Tel: 04 9096 1189
www.lecalendal.com
Welcoming hotel with Provençal-style rooms in a cluster of old houses set around a pretty courtyard. Good location behind the Arena; some rooms have views of the Théâtre Antique. There's a restaurant, tea room and spa. €€

Hôtel d'Arlatan
26 rue du Sauvage
Tel: 04 9093 5666
www.hotel-arlatan.fr
A chic address in a historic mansion with a pool, an enclosed garden and a scattering of Roman archaeological remains. 34 rooms and seven suites. €€

Hôtel du Forum
place du Forum
Tel: 04 9093 4895
www.hotelduforum.com
With 18 old-fashioned rooms, the family-run Forum may lack the style of the Grand Hôtel Nord-Pinus, but it is comfortable and has the advantage of a swimming pool in a secluded courtyard. Has a private bar with billiard table. Closed Nov–Mar. €

Hôtel du Musée
11 rue du Grand Prieuré
Tel: 04 9093 8888
www.hoteldumusee.com
A 17th-century mansion

tucked away on a winding street near the Rhône, with a pretty courtyard for breakfast, vaulted lounge and its own art gallery. €

Le Sambuc

Le Mas de Peint
D36, between Arles and

TRANSPORT

ACCOMMODATION

ACTIVITIES

A – Z

LANGUAGE

Salin-de-Giraud
Tel: 04 9097 2062
www.masdepeint.com
This elegant period farmhouse offers the full rural Camargue experience, with eleven rustic chic bedrooms,

and delicious Provençal meals *à la table d'hôte* (by reservation only). Bulls and horses roam the 1300-acre (526-hectare) estate. Relax by the pool or take a ride to view the wildlife. €€€

Stes-Maries-de-la-Mer

Hôtel Camille
13 avenue de la Plage
Tel: 04 9097 8026
www.hotel-camille.camargue.fr
This hotel offers very

reasonable rates for the Camargue, though be prepared to pay a little more for those with sea views. No frills but friendly, and situated right on the beach. Closed 11 Nov–Apr. €

NÎMES AND THE PONT DU GARD

Nîmes

Hôtel de L'Amphithéâtre
4 rue des Arènes
Tel: 04 6667 2851
On a side street behind the Roman arena, this excellent budget hotel's main selling points are its location and friendly staff. Rooms have antique furniture and are clean, but pretty dated. €
Hôtel Imperator Concorde
quai de la Fontaine

Tel: 04 6621 9030
www.hotel-imperator.com
The low-key façade hides comfortable, traditional rooms, a good restaurant, a vintage lift and a luxuriantly planted garden. This is where toreadors have traditionally stayed – and, of course, bull-fighting fan Ernest Hemingway. €€€
New Hôtel La Baume
21 rue Nationale
Tel: 04 6676 2842
www.new-hotel.com

Occupies a fine 17th-century *hôtel particulier* with a magnificent galleried interior courtyard. The spacious rooms are comfortable and decorated with richly coloured furnishings. €€
Royal Hôtel
3 boulevard Alphonse Daudet
Tel: 04 6658 2827
www.royalhotel-nimes.com
The Royal Hôtel is a cult address with its artfully casual boho decor, worn

leather armchairs, wood floors, modern art and friendly staff. Most rooms overlook the place d'Assas, where its trendy tapas bar, La Bodeguita, has tables on the pavement. €€

THE GORGES DU VERDON

Castellane

Nouvel Hôtel de Commerce
18 place Marcel Sauvaire
Tel: 04 9283 6100
www.hotel-fradet.com
Reasonably priced rooms in a 19th-century building and its modern extension, plus an

excellent restaurant in the hands of a former student of Alain Ducasse. €€

Moustiers-Ste-Marie

La Bastide de Moustiers
chemin de Quinson

Tel: 04 9270 4747
www.bastide-moustiers.com
This beautifully restored ancient *bastide* was the first of Alain Ducasse's country *auberges*, with just 12 gloriously romantic rooms exuding luxury and rural calm, and an excellent restaurant. It has extensive grounds with lawns and a terrace, kitchen garden, swimming pool and helicopter pad. €€€–€€€€
La Bonne Auberge
Le Village
Tel: 04 9274 6618
A reasonable inexpensive hotel in the village. Features a rustic restaurant serving regional dishes, and a pool. Closed Nov–Mar. €

Trigance

Château de Trigance
route du chateau
Tel: 04 9476 9118
www.chateau-de-trigance.fr
This lovely 11th-century fortress towers over the hilltop village of Trigance just south of the Gorges. It has appropriately medieval themed bedrooms with four poster beds and a good restaurant in the vaulted arms room. Closed Nov–Mar. €€

BELOW: Moustiers-Ste-Marie.

Digne and the Southern Alps

Digne-les-Bains

Hôtel le Grand Paris
19 boulevard Thiers
Tel: 04 9231 1115
www.hotel-grand-paris.com
Le Grand Paris, a
17th-century former
convent with an old-
fashioned ambience, is
family-run and is the
place to stay in Digne.
The hotel has sixteen
rooms and three suites,
an excellent restaurant,
a plane tree-shaded
patio and stylish health
centre. €€€€

Mane

Couvent des Minimes
chemin des Jeux de Maï
Tel 04 9274 4444
www.couventdesminimes-
hotelspa.com
A warm, golden stone
17th-century
monastery just south of
Forcalquier has been
turned into a swish
hotel by the Occitane
beauty group, with
elegant, pared-back
rooms, a restaurant
and a spa. The terraced
gardens contain pool,

tennis court and a
typically Provençal
pétanque pitch. €€€

Super Sauze

Hôtel Pyjama
Super-Sauze,
Enchastrayes
Tel: 04 9281 1200
http://lepyjama.jimdo.com
Ski addicts should make
for this homely winter-
sports hotel in the
Ubaye valley. Geared for
the snow-seeker, it is
also open in summer.
Some rooms have

mezzanines to
accommodate families.
No restaurant, but
breakfast can be taken
in your room, in front of
the log fire in winter, or
on the terrace in
summer. Closed mid-
Sept–mid-Dec. €

Toulon and the Western Var

Bandol

L'Ile Rousse
25 boulevard Louis-
Lumière, Plage de
Renecros
Tel: 04 9429 3300
www.ile-rousse.com
This waterfront hotel
and thalassotherapy
centre was totally
renovated in 2010, and
has 67 comfortable
rooms, most with a sea
view and direct access
to its two private
beaches. Refined
cuisine served in the
restaurant. €€€

Below: cookery course.

La Cadière d'Azur

Hostellerie Bérard
avenue Gabriel Péri
Tel: 04 9490 1143
www.hotel-berard.com
An atmospheric hotel
with 40 rooms in a
cluster of buildings
(including a monastery)
in a hill village perched
above the coast. It has a
renowned restaurant, a
simpler bistro and a spa
focused on aroma-
therapy. Also runs
cookery courses. €€€

St-Maximin la-Sainte-Baume

Hôtellerie Le Couvent Royal
place Jean Salusse
Tel: 04 9486 5566
www.hotelfp-saintmaximin.com
Occupies a royal monas-
tery founded in 1295
adjoining the finest
Gothic church in Pro-
vence. The former
monks' cells have been
converted with good
taste into 67 bedrooms.

Meals are served in the
vaulted chapterhouse or
in the cloister. €€–€€€

Sanary-sur-Mer

Hôtel de la Tour
24 quai General de Gaulle
Tel: 04 9474 1010
www.sanary-hoteldelatour.com
The best-placed hotel in
Sanary, located next to
the Saracen tower, with
most rooms overlooking
the port. The hotel has
an old-fashioned charm,
24 pretty rooms and
friendly owners, plus a
restaurant specialising
in seafood. €€

La-Seyne-sur-Mer

Kyriad Prestige
1 quai du 19 mars 1962
Tel: 04 9405 3400
www.kyriad-prestige-toulon-la-
seyne-sur-mer.fr
A striking modern hotel
right on the harbour at La
Seyne with views across
the bay to Toulon. 94
rooms with balconies and
an outdoor pool. €€€

Toulon

Le Grand Hôtel Dauphiné
10 rue Berthelot
Tel: 04 9492 2028
www.grandhoteldauphine.com
For a hotel in such a
central location by place
Puget in the old town, it
offers good value. Has
55 air-conditioned
rooms, and friendly
staff. €

Price Categories

Price categories are for
an average double room
in high season:
€ = under €100
€€ = €100–180
€€€ = €180–300
€€€€ = more than €300

ST-TROPEZ AND THE MAURES

Bormes-les Mimosas

Hôtel Bellevue
14 place Gambetta,
Bormes Village
Tel: 04 9471 1515
www.bellevuebormes.fr.st
A hotel-restaurant set on
the lively main square of
the old village. Most of
the twelve rooms are
decorated with Prov-
ençal print fabrics.
Closed mid-Nov to mid-
Jan. €

Hôtel de la Plage
boulevard de la Plage,
La Favière
Tel: 04 9471 0274
www.hotelbormes.com
This family-oriented
hotel in Bormes' beach
resort of La Favière has
been run by the same
family since it opened in
1939. Most of the 45
air-conditioned rooms
have balconies or ter-
races, and there's a res-
taurant serving dinner if
desired. *Pétanque* and
ping pong outside.
Closed Oct–Easter. €

Fréjus

Hôtel L'Aréna
145 boulevard Général
de Gaulle
Tel: 04 9417 0940
www.arena-hotel.com
Situated in the old town
with 39 Provençal-style
rooms, a pool, and a
pleasant garden and an

excellent regional
restaurant. €€

Grimaud

Hostellerie du Coteau Fleuri
place des Pénitents
Tel: 04 9443 2017
www.coteaufleuri.fr
A welcoming 1930s
inn on the outskirts
of town with views
over the vineyards.
The restaurant serves
traditional Provençal
cuisine. €€€€

La Boulangerie
route de Collobrières
Tel: 04 9443 2316
www.hotel-laboulangerie.com
A small but comfortable
and friendly hotel
situated in the quiet of
the Massif des Maures.
The hotel's amenities
include a pool and
tennis courts. Closed
mid-Oct–Easter. €€

Ile de Porquerolles

Mas du Langoustier
Tel: 04 9458 3009
www.langoustier.com
A warm Provençal *mas*
that is luxurious if a bit
precious, surrounded by
gardens. Fabulous res-
taurant. Free transport
from the port to the
hotel. Closed Oct–
Easter. €€€

Ile de Port Cros

Le Manoir
Tel: 04 9405 9052
The only hotel on the
no-smoking, no-car
island of Port Cros.
Rooms in the colonial-
style 19th-century
building are cosy and
some have balconies.

Large garden. Closed
Oct–Apr. €€€

La Croix-Valmer

La Pinède Plage
Tel: 04 9455 1616
www.pinedeplage.com
Comfortable hotel set
amid parasol pines on
the Plage de Gigaro.
Great for sporting types:
you can step almost
straight onto the sand,
where there are free
kayaks, pedalos and
windsurfers, and the
chance to jet- and water-
ski. €€€€

Le Lavandou

Les Roches
1 avenue des trois Dauphins,
Aiguebelle Plage
Tel: 04 9471 0507
www.hotellesroches.com
A luxurious modern
hotel built into the
cliffside. Private beach,
saltwater swimming
pool and restaurant with
great sea views. Closed
in winter. €€€€

Le Rayol-Canadel

Le Bailli de Suffren
Tel: 04 9804 4700
www.lebaillidesuffren.com
The curved 1960s build-
ing – all rooms with bal-
conies or terraces and
sea views – is set on the
beach below the gardens
of the Domaine de Rayol.
Pool, private beach, bar,
restaurant and hire boats
to explore the St-Tropez
peninsula without the
traffic jams. €€€€

Plan-de-la-Tour

Mas des Brugassières
1.5km (1 mile) south of

the village
Tel: 04 9455 5055
www.masdesbrugassieres.com
In the Maures hills,
10km (6 miles) from
Ste-Maxime, this
intimate hotel was
modelled on a Provençal
mas, or farmhouse. The
large garden includes a
small pool; many rooms
open onto a semi-
private terrace. Closed
mid-Oct–Mar. €€

Ramatuelle

La Ferme d'Augustin
Plage de Tahiti
Tel: 04 9455 9700
www.fermeaugustin.com
This lovely old farm-
house is set in vineyards
next to Tahiti Beach. The
46 bedrooms overlook
the gardens, and many
have balconies and sea
views. The restaurant
(for hotel guests only)
favours produce from
the hotel's kitchen gar-
den. Heated swimming
pool. Most guests are
regulars so reserve well
ahead. Closed mid-Oct–
Mar. €€€

Hostellerie Le Baou
avenue Gustave Etienne
Tel: 04 9812 9420
www.hostellerie-le-baou.com
This big upmarket hotel
just below the village
has good-sized modern
rooms with balconies or
private garden terraces.
Restaurant. €€€–€€€€

ABOVE: Les Roches, Le Lavandou.

St-Tropez

Hôtel Les Palmiers
26 boulevard Vasserot.
Tel: 04 9497 0161
www.hotel-les-palmiers.com
Proof that good-value,
no frills accommodation
exists even in St-Tropez,
Les Palmiers has a great
location by place des
Lices, though the hotel
itself is set back in a
tropical garden. Rooms
are simple but clean. €€

Hôtel Sube
Port de St-Tropez
Tel: 04 9497 3004
A long-established hotel
right on the port where
all the action is (though
it can be noisy). Best
rooms have views of the
port. The hotel bar is a
favourite meeting place
for yachtie types.
€€–€€€

Kube Hotel Saint-Tropez
route de Saint-Tropez (D98),
Gassin
Tel: 04 9497 2000
www.kubehotel.com
The offshoot of the
trendy Paris Kube has
kept the trademark
glass-and-steel
reception cube and ice
bar but has more of a
resort feel. A gorgeous
minimalist marble pool
stretches between
shady lawns where you
can eat in summer.
There's also a smaller
heated pool, outdoor
cocktail bar and rooftop
champagne bar. €€€€

La Mistralée
1 avenue du Général Leclerc.
Tel: 04 9812 9112
www.hotel-mistralee.com
The white stucco villa of
Alexandre "hairdresser
to the stars" de Paris
has been turned into
a sophisticated small
hotel, with boudoir-style
conservatory, outdoor
pool in the walled garden
and a restaurant where
the chef will personally
concoct your menu.

The eleven rooms each
have a different theme
ranging from colourful
"chinoise" to manly
brown and white-striped
Hemingway. €€€€

La Ponche
3 rue des Remparts
Tel: 04 9497 0253
www.laponche.com
Discreet, exclusive
retreat conjured out of a
group of old fishermen's
cottages next to the Port
des Pêcheurs. Some bed-
rooms have private roof
terraces and sea views.
Good regional cooking in
the restaurant. Private
garage. Closed Nov–mid-
Feb. €€€€

Le Yaca
1 boulevard d'Aumale
Tel: 04 9455 8100
www.hotel-le-yaca.fr
An attractive old
Provençal residence,
tastefully refurbished.
Accommodation is built
around a pool and
gardens. Le Patio
restaurant serves Italian
cuisine. €€€€

INLAND VAR HILL VILLAGES

Fayence

Moulin de la Camandoule
Chemin de Notre-Dame
des Cyprès
Tel: 04 9476 0084
www.camandoule.com
This ancient olive mill in
the valley below Fay-
ence has been elegantly
converted into a small,
peaceful hotel with a
good restaurant serving
traditional Provençal
fare. Nine bedrooms
and two duplex-suites,
all with en suite. Lunch
and dinner are often
served on the terrace in
summer. Swimming
pool. €€

Les-Arcs-sur-Argens

Logis du Guetteur
Place du Château
Tel: 04 9499 5110
www.logisduguetteur.com
Pleasant, atmospheric
hotel with romantic
rooms in part of the
11th-century castle
dominating the village.
Good restaurant and
swimming pool. €€

Seillans

Hôtel des Deux Rocs
place Font d'Amont
Tel: 04 9476 8732
www.hoteldeuxrocs.com
This converted 18th-

century residence is set
in a lovely spot at the top
of the town and is com-
plete with 14 beautifully
decorated rooms, a
good restaurant and
lovely terrace. €€

Tourtour

Bastide de Tourtour
route de Flayosc
Tel: 04 9810 5420
www.bastidedetourtour.com
Palatial 25-room hotel
built in 1967 in tradi-
tional tufa stone, set in
a park with fabulous
views over the Var and
beyond. The facilities
include a heated pool,
billiard room, tennis

court and a good
restaurant. €€€

Villecroze

Auberge des Lavandes
place Général de Gaulle
Tel: 04 9470 7600
A small, good-value
auberge with Norwegian
owners, plus a good
restaurant. Closed mid-
Oct–Mar. €

PARC DU MERCANTOUR AND ALPINE VALLEYS

Breil-sur-Roya

Hôtel Le Roya
place Bianchéri
Tel: 04 9304 4810
www.hoteleroya.com
A simple pink stucco
hotel next to the village
car park (market here on
Tuesdays) offering B&B
for those on a budget. €

Lantosque

**Hostellerie
de l'Ancienne
Gendarmerie**
Quartier du Rivet
Tel: 04 9303 0065
www.hotel-lantosque.com
Hotel in the former
gendarmerie with a
rustic but elegant
interior. Eight brightly
decorated bedrooms.

The restaurant looks out
onto the swimming pool
and the valley. Friendly
welcome. €–€€

Peillon

Auberge de la Madone
Tel: 04 9379 9117
www.auberge-madone-peillon.com
Located at the gates of
the hilltop village of
Peillon, this *auberge*
offers a flowery terrace
with a wonderful view, a
one-star Michelin restau-
rant and gorgeous rooms
fitted with antiques. €€

St-Dalmas-sur
Tende

Le Prieuré
rue Jean Médecin
Tel: 04 9304 7570

www.leprieure.org
Three-star hotel with a
pleasant restaurant, set
in a lovely valley. Has
a policy of employing
people with disabilities.
Organises summer
trips to the Vallée
des Merveilles within
Mercantour Park. €

Sospel

Hôtel des Etrangers
9 boulevard de Verdun
Tel: 04 9304 0009
www.sospel.net
A Sospel institution
with popular restaurant
and a pool overhanging
the river. English is
spoken, and the
proprietor is an expert
on local history. Closed
Nov–Feb. €

Tende

Le Chamois d'Or
Hameau de Casterino
Tel: 04 9304 6666
www.hotelchamoisdor.net
A traditional mountain
chalet on the threshold
of the Vallée des
Merveilles. The large
rooms are furnished in a
contemporary,
montagnard style.
Regional cuisine served
in the restaurant. 22
rooms. €€

ST-PAUL, VENCE AND GRASSE

Biot

Hôtel des Arcades
16 place des Arcades
Tel: 04 9365 0104
www.hotel-restaurant-les-
arcades.com
Quirky, antique-filled
hotel in a 15th-century
mansion. The restaurant
is also an art gallery. €

Grasse

**Hôtel des Parfums
(Odalys)**
rue Eugène Charabot
Tel: 04 9242 3535
www.hoteldesparfums.com
This purpose-built hotel
on the fringes of the old
town has moderately
priced rooms with
gorgeous views.
Facilities include a
jacuzzi, hammam, pool
and fitness room. €€

**La Bastide Saint-
Antoine**
48 avenue Henri Dunant
Tel: 04 9370 9494
www.jacques-chibois.com
This 18th-century
bastide has stark but
chic, modern rooms and
offers wonderful views
of the mountains and
sea. It has a pool, olive
grove and organises reg-
ular art exhibitions. It's
best known for its gas-
tronomic restaurant.
€€€€

St-Paul-de-Vence

**Hostellerie des
Remparts**
72 rue Grande
Tel: 04 9332 0988
www.hostellerielesremparts.com
A cheap, slightly eccen-
tric option right in the
heart of the old village.

Friendly staff and a res-
taurant. Closed mid-
Nov–mid-Dec and Jan. €
La Colombe d'Or
place des Ormeaux
Tel: 04 9332 8002
www.la-colombe-dor.com
The 16-roomed
Colombe d'Or was once
frequented by unknown,
penniless artists who
persuaded the original
owner, Paul Roux, to
accept their paintings in
payment for meals and
board. Works by Miró,
Picasso, Modigliani,
Matisse and Chagall
can now be viewed by
guests of the hotel and
restaurant. €€€€
Mas d'Artigny
chemin des Salettes
Tel: 04 9332 8454
www.mas-artigny.com
Sprawling hotel in the
woods between St-Paul

and La Colle. Splendid
views of the sea and
the mountains. Has 85
rooms, the suites hav-
ing their own private
garden and pool. Spa
and tennis courts on-
site. €€€

PRICE CATEGORIES

Price categories are for
an average double room
in high season:
€ = under €100
€€ = €100–180
€€€ = €180–300
€€€€ = more than €300

Vence

Château St-Martin
route de Courségoules
Tel: 04 9358 0202
www.chateau-st-martin.com
True luxury in the former castle of the Knights Templar, on the hills above Vence with views to the coast.

Rooms are classic and the restaurant has an ever-growing reputation. Extensive grounds include tennis court and infinity pool. €€€€

Mas de Vence
539 avenue Emile Hugues
Tel: 04 9358 0616
www.azurline.com
A ten-minute walk from

the old town, this neo-Provençal *mas* has comfortable though functional air-conditioned rooms and a decent restaurant; what really stands out are the pleasant outdoor pool and friendly staff who will go out of their way to help. €–€€

La Villa Roseraie
14 avenue Henri Giraud
Tel: 04 9358 0220
www.villaroseraie.com
This pretty Belle Epoque villa has a lovely garden, pool and 12 rooms (some small). A five-minute walk from the old town of Vence. No restaurant. €€

NICE

Hi Hotel
avenue des Fleurs
Tel: 04 9707 2626
www.hi-hotel.net
The colourful trendy Hi aims to make you reconsider the way you stay at a hotel with nine different bedroom concepts for music-lovers, computer nerds, movie fans and so on. There's a garden courtyard, DJ bar and rooftop sundeck with minuscule swimming pool. €€€

Hôtel Aria
15 avenue Auber
Tel: 04 9388 3069
www.aria-nice.com
This renovated 19th-century hotel overlooks an attractive garden square amid the Belle Epoque and Art Deco buildings of the new town. Rooms are light and high-ceilinged, decorated in sunny colours. Good value. 30 rooms. €€

Hôtel Beau Rivage
24 rue St François-de-Paule
Tel: 04 9247 8282
www.nicebeaurivage.com
Matisse, Nietzsche and Chekhov all stayed at the 118-room Beau Rivage, located near the opera in the old town. It's been given a suave, minimalist refurbishment by architect Jean-Michel Wilmotte. Also has a fashionable private beach. €€€€

Hôtel Grimaldi
15 rue Grimaldi
Tel: 04 9316 0024
www.le-grimaldi.com
A lovely intimate hotel with prettily furnished rooms in two Belle Epoque houses in the new town. €€–€€€

Hôtel Negresco
37 promenade des Anglais
Tel: 04 9316 6400
www.hotel-negresco-nice.com
This flamboyant Belle Epoque hotel is an

opulent vestige of Nice's golden era. The 150 rooms and apartments are magnificently furnished with antiques, priceless paintings and tapestries. The celebrated Chantecler restaurant is acknowledged as one of the best tables in the region. €€€€

Hôtel du Petit Palais
17 avenue Emile Bieckert
Tel: 04 9362 1911
www.petitpalaisnice.com
One of the few hotels still up in Cimiez in the former villa of actor-playwright Sacha Guitry. It has friendly staff and attractive rooms, some with small terraces or balconies giving rooftop views to the Baie des Anges. €€

Hôtel Suisse
15 quai Raubà Capéù
Tel: 04 9217 3900
www.hotels-ocre-azur.com
Behind a period facade

virtually built into the cliff face of castle hill, the Hôtel Suisse has been stylishly modernised with an airy ground-floor salon and breakfast room and a different colour scheme on each floor. Most rooms have a sea view and balcony. €€

Hôtel Windsor
11 rue Dalpozzo
Tel: 04 9388 5935
www.hotelwindsornice.com
From the outside it looks like a 19th-century hotel, but inside this boho arty establishment boasts a hammam, aviary, exotic garden, and rooms commissioned by different contemporary artists. €€

THE RIVIERA FROM CANNES TO CAGNES

Antibes–Juan les-Pins

Belles Rives
boulevard Edouard-Baudoin, Juan-des-Pins
Tel: 04 9361 0279
www.bellesrives.com
Close enough to town to

enjoy the lively atmosphere, yet sufficiently far away from the noise and crowds. The Belles Rives has retained all the attraction of the stylish Art Deco period, when it was the home of Zelda and F. Scott

Fitzgerald. It has a gourmet restaurant, piano bar and beach restaurant. €€€€

Garden Beach Hotel
15–17 boulevard Edouard Baudoin, Juan-des-Pins
Tel: 04 9293 5757
www.juanlespinshotel.fr

ABOVE: a suite with a stunning sea view.

A modern 175-room hotel located on the seafront with direct acces to its own private sandy beach. There's also an indoor pool. €€€

Grand Hôtel du Cap-Eden-Roc
boulevard Kennedy, Cap d'Antibes
Tel: 04 9361 3901
www.hotel-du-cap-eden-roc.com
A jet-setters' destination in wooded grounds, this is the ultimate in Riviera glamour and a favourite with Hollywood actors. A serious splurge. €€€€

Hôtel des Mimosas
rue Pauline, Juan-des-Pins
Tel: 04 9361 0416
www.hotel-mimosas.fr
A large, early 20th-century house set in quiet gardens just a five-minute walk from the beach. Attractive bedrooms, swimming pool. No restaurant. Closed Oct–Apr. €€

La Jabotte
13 avenue de Max Maurey, Antibes
Tel: 04 9361 4589
www.jabotte.com
Adorable – and affordable – lodgings with bright decor just up the street from the Plage de Salis. The original artwork in the rooms is the work of one of the owners. Closed Nov and Christmas week. Ten rooms. €–€€

Relais du Postillon
8 rue Championnet, Vieux Antibes
Tel: 04 9334 2077
www.relaisdupostillon.com
It's hard to find a bargain in high season on the Côte d'Azur, but the Relais du Postillon in the old town of Antibes comes pretty close, with 15 characterful rooms and a homely bar. €

Cannes

3.14 Hotel
5 rue François Einesy
Tel: 04 9299 7200
www.3-14hotel.com
A gloriously over-the-top creation of the sort that you could only get away with in Cannes. Five floors of bedrooms are each themed according to a continent. A glass fountain, lovebirds at reception, bar, restaurant and lounge are on the ground-floor "earth" and a pool on the rooftop "sky". €€€€

Carlton Intercontinental
58 La Croisette
Tel: 04 9306 4006
www.intercontinental.com/cannes
The legendary palace hotel where the jury always stays during the film festival has sumptuous suites. However, it helps to have film-star means as standard rooms can be disap-

pointingly small. Avoid those at the rear without sea views. Includes two restaurants, a health club, swimming pool and private beach with watersports facilities. €€€€

Hôtel Molière
5 rue Molière
Tel: 04 9338 1616
www.hotel-moliere.com
There's a relaxed mood at this small hotel, set at the rear of a long garden between La Croisette and rue d'Antibes. Rooms sport modern minimalist tones, and most have good-sized balconies. €€

Hôtel Splendid
4–6 rue Félix-Faure
Tel: 04 9706 2222
www.splendid-hotel-cannes.fr
A sparkling white Belle Epoque edifice in the heart of the action, virtually opposite the Palais des Festivals. Rooms have been comfortably updated while retaining period flourishes; breakfast is served on a large sunny terrace. €€€

Le Cavendish
11 boulevard Carnot
Tel: 04 9706 2600
www.cavendish-cannes.com
Attractive Belle Epoque building on the big boulevard that descends towards La Croisette. The comfortable period town-house style was conceived as in homage to the English lords who once frequented the coast, with some wonderful circular rooms in the corner turret. €€€

Le Mistral Hôtel
13 rue des Belges
Tel: 04 9339 9146
www.mistral-hotel.com
This is a stylish budget discovery just a couple

of streets back from the Palais des Festivals. The eleven rooms, named after different winds (chinook, scirocco, etc), are decked out in warm colours and stripey wood; larger ones can accommodate three people and have daylit bathrooms. No lift. €–€€

Martinez
73 La Croisette
Tel: 04 9298 7300
www.hotel-martinez.com
A glitzy Art Deco extravaganza. When it opened, it was France's largest hotel. A major facelift in 2003 saw the creation of two vast rooftop suites and a luxurious Givenchy spa, and renovation of the splendid facade, grand staircase and hall. €€€€

Mougins

Le Mas Candille
boulevard Clément Rebouffel
Tel: 04 9228 4343
www.lemascandille.com
A luxurious hotel on the edge of the old village. Choose the rooms in the main *mas*, decorated with light Provençal colours and antique furniture, rather than the rather dark Asian-themed rooms in the modern *bastide* annexe. Spacious gardens, a lovely pool and a Shiseido spa. Good modern Provençal cooking in the restaurant. €€€€

PRICE CATEGORIES

Price categories are for an average double room in high season.
€ = under €100
€€ = €100–180
€€€ = €180–300
€€€€ = more than €300

THE RIVIERA FROM VILLEFRANCHE TO MENTON

Beaulieu-sur-Mer

La Réserve de Beaulieu
5 boulevard du Général Leclerc
Tel: 04 9301 0001
www.reservebeaulieu.com
A grand Riviera dowager opened in 1905, with luxurious rooms, spa and billiards room, a swimming pool in the garden and a private beach and harbour. Located right on the sea-front. Closed mid-Oct–mid-Dec. €€€€

Eze

Château de la Chèvre d'Or
rue de Barri
Tel: 04 9210 6666
www.chevredor.com
Staying here is an unforgettable experience. The 28-room hotel created out of old village houses combines a warm provincial elegance with Riviera élan, and the restaurant has magnificent coastal views. €€€€

Menton

Hôtel Aiglon
7 avenue de la Madone
Tel: 04 9357 5555
www.hotelaiglon.net
A 19th-century white stucco mansion converted into an atmospheric hotel. The Belle Epoque bar/salon is a delight; rooms are less elaborate, with old-fashioned charm. Set in large gardens, there's an outdoor pool and a play area and ping pong for children. €€

Hôtel Napoléon
29 Porte de France
Tel: 04 9335 8950
www.napoleon-menton.com
This modern seafront hotel is near Val Rahmeh gardens. Bedrooms at the front have balconies overlooking Garavan Bay, while those at the rear have mountain views. There's a bar, garden with banana trees and outdoor pool and gym. Also owns the Plage Napoléon across the street, with beach restaurant overseen by Mauro Colagreco. €€

Roquebrune-Cap-Martin

Les Deux Frères
Roquebrune Village
Tel: 04 9328 9900
www.lesdeuxfreres.com
A hotel and restaurant occupying the old school-house, it has ten different rooms, ranging from veiled bridal room to Moorish-inspired. €–€€

St-Jean-Cap Ferrat

Brise Marine
58 avenue Jean Mermoz
Tel: 04 9376 0436
www.hotel-brisemarine.com
An authentic late 19th-century villa with fairly small but immaculate rooms, some overlooking the sea, and a steeply terraced garden that leads down to the sea. Closed Nov–Jan. €€

Grand Hôtel du Cap Ferrat
71 boulevard Général de Gaulle
Tel: 04 9376 5050
www.grand-hotel-cap-ferrat.com
This Riviera grand dame was brought up to date in 2009. Bedrooms in the

main building feature vast beds and walk-in dressing rooms, while ground-floor suites in the modern annex each have a private spillover pool. There's also a new spa, although it's hard to beat the beauty of the original outdoor pool. €€€€

Villefranche-sur-Mer

Hôtel Welcome
3 quai Amiral Courbet
Tel: 04 9376 2762
www.welcomehotel.com
With the best location in Villefranche, it's hardly surprising that this historic hotel has welcomed many illustrious guests. The spacious rooms nearly all have balconies overlooking the port, and there's a stylish wine bar. Closed mid-Nov–Christmas. €€

MONACO

Hôtel de France
6 rue de la Turbie, La Condamine
Tel: +377 9330 2464
www.monte-carlo.mc/france
A rare bargain option, located on a side street near the train station and convenient for the port and palace, with 26 fresh, colourful rooms. €

Hôtel de Paris
place du Casino,

Monte-Carlo
Tel: +377 9806 3016
www.montecarloresort.com
This palatial hotel boasts Alain Ducasses's three-star restaurant, the Louis XV. It is the most magnificent and glamorous place to stay in Monaco. Direct access to the luxurious Thermes Marins spa. €€€€

Le Méridien Beach Plaza
22 avenue Princesse Grace, Monte-Carlo
Tel: +377 9330 9880
www.lemeridienmontecarlo.com
The huge modern Méridien Beach is very popular with the new fortunes from Russia and eastern Europe. Contemporary art in the lobby and a 24-hour restaurant where you

can watch the chefs cooking. Outdoor and indoor pools, plus private beach. €€€€

TRANSPORT

ACCOMMODATION

ACTIVITIES

A – Z

LANGUAGE

A CTIVITIES

FESTIVALS, THE ARTS, NIGHTLIFE, OUTDOOR ACTIVITIES AND SHOPPING

FESTIVALS

Festivals abound in Provence, especially in summer, when world-class music, theatre and dance are staged here, such as the Avignon theatre festival, jazz in Nice and Juan-les-Pins, and opera in Aix-en-Provence and Orange. All year round you'll find traditional celebrations of everything from bullfighting and patron saints to lemons and the wine harvest. For a programme of the region's summer festivals pick up the annual booklet *Terre des Festivals* at tourist offices or download it at www.laregie-paca.com.

January

Isola 2000: *Trophy Andros.* Car-racing tournament on ice.
Monaco: Monte-Carlo Rally; International Circus Festival (www.montecarlofestival.mc)

February

Avignon: *Les Hivernales.* Contemporary dance (www.hivernales-avignon.com).
Bormes-les-Mimosas: *Corso Fleuri.* Mimosa festival with flower-decorated floats.
Marseille: *Fête de la Chandeleur.* Candlemas procession and blessing of *navettes* biscuits at the Abbaye St-Victor.
Menton: *Fête du Citron.* Carnival-time lemon festival with parade, bands and incredible citrus fruit sculptures (www.feteducitron.com).
Nice: *Carnaval.* Decorated floats parade behind the Roi du Carnaval; flower battles on the promenade des Anglais.
Villefranche-sur-Mer: *Combat Naval Fleuri.* Flower jousting on traditional *pointu* fishing boats.

March

Monte-Carlo: *Les Printemps des Arts.* Biennial of dance and classical music (odd years) until mid-April (www.printempsdesarts.com).
Vallauris-Golfe-Juan: *Fête Napoléon.* First weekend in March locals re-enact Napoleon's landing at Golfe Juan on 1 March 1815.

April

Antibes: *Salon des Antiquaires.* Antiques fair by the Port Vauban (www.salon-antiquaires-antibes.com).
Arles: *Féria de Pâques.* Easter *féria* bullfighting and festivities in the Roman arena (www.feriaarles.com).

May

Banon: cheese fair – celebration of the local Banon goat's cheese.

Cannes: Film Festival *(see page 236).*
Fréjus: *Bravade St-François.* Festival in honour of the patron saint of Fréjus.
Grasse: *Expo Roses.* Rose show.
Monaco: Formula 1 Grand Prix.
Nîmes: *Féria de Pentecôte.* Bull-fighting, music and *bodegas.*
St-Tropez: *Bravades (16–18)* with costume parades to celebrate the town's patron saint and military history.
Stes-Maries-de-la-Mer: *Pèlerinage de Mai.* France's biggest gypsy gathering.
Vaucluse: *Fête de la Vigne et du Vin.* Wine festival.

June

France: *Fête de la Musique* on 21 June sees free concerts held on midsummer's day. *Fête de la Saint-Pierre* on 27 June is the festival of the patron saint of fishermen, celebrated in numerous fishing ports.
Antibes: International Young Soloist Festival.
Monte-Carlo: *Fête de la St-Jean* (23 and 24 June). Traditional *fêtes* of St-John the Baptist.
Nice: *Festival du Musique Sacré.* Religious music in Vieux Nice churches.
Tarascon: *Fête de la Tarasque.* Celebrating the legend of the monster that terrorised the town.

July

France: Bastille Day (14 July). Fireworks and dancing commemorate the French Revolution.

Aix-en-Provence: *Festival d'Art Lyrique.* International opera *(see page 116)*.

Antibes-Juan-les-Pins: *Jazz à Juan.* International jazz. *Musiques au Coeur.* Opera).

Arles: *Les Rencontres d'Arles.* International photography festival with exhibitions until September *(see page 138); Suds à Arles.* World-music festival until mid-August (www.suds-arles.com).

Avignon: *Festival d'Avignon* and *Le Off.* International theatre festival and its fringe offshoot *(see page 64)*.

Cannes: *Les Nuits Musicales du Suquet* classical concerts (www.nuitsdusuquet-cannen.com).

Fréjus: Féria; *Forum des Arts et de la Musique.* Concerts, dance, theatre.

Hyères: *Design Parade.* Modern design competition and debates at the Villa Noailles. Exhibitions last until September.

Lacoste: *Festival de Lacoste.* Opera, dance and theatre in a Luberon hill village (until early August).

Ménerbes: *Les Musicales du Luberon.* Classical concerts in the village church.

Marseille: *Mondial du Pétanque.* Over 12,000 competitors enter the world *pétanque* championships.

Monte-Carlo: Concerts in the courtyard of the Palais Princier; Fireworks Festival; *Les Nuits de la Danse*; Monte-Carlo Sporting Summer Festival.

Nice: Nice Jazz Festival. Eclectic jazz in the Roman arena and Jardin des Arènes in Cimiez (www.nicejazzfestival.fr).

Orange: *Les Chorégies d'Orange.* First-rate lyric opera in the Théâtre Antique (until mid-August) *(see page 70)*.

La Roque d'Antheron: *Festival International de Piano.* Leading pianists perform in the château gardens and Luberon churches (www.festival-piano.com).

La Seyne-sur-Mer: Jazz festival in the Fort Napoléon.

Vaison-la-Romaine: *Vaison Danses.* Contemporary dance in the Roman theatre (www.vaison-danses.com).

Vallauris: *Biennale Internationale de Céramique.* Pottery Festival, until October, even years.

Vence: *Les Nuits du Sud.* World music until early August (www.nuitsdusud.com).

August

Brignoles: *Festival de Jazz.*

Cannes: *Festival Pantiero.* Electronic music and DJs (www.festivalpantiero.com).

Fréjus: *Fête du Raisin.* Wine-tasting and feasting.

Grasse: Festival of Jasmine.

Menton: International Chamber Music Festival (www.musiquementon.fr).

Nice: *Fierà de la San Bertoumieu.* Craft and regional-produce fair, with traditional music and games.

Ramatuelle: theatre and comedy festival.

Salon-de-Provence: *Musique à l'Emperi.* Chamber music at the Château de l'Emperi (www.festival-salon.fr)

St-Rémy-de-Provence: *Féria Provençale.* Bull-running and music.

September

Antibes: *Festival d'Art Sacré.*

Religious music in the old cathedral.

Arles: *Fêtes des Prémices du Riz.* Rice festival and bullfighting.

Cassis: *Ban des Vendanges.* Wine harvest celebration.

Cavalaire-sur-Mer: *Grand Prix de France Jet Offshore.* Jet-skiing.

France: *Journées du Patrimoine.* Third weekend in September when historic monuments and official buildings are open to the public free.

Grasse: *Bio-Grasse Foire.* Organic produce fair.

October

Collobrières: *Fêtes de la Châtaigne.* Chestnut harvest festival on three Sundays in October.

Marseille: *Fiesta des Suds.* World music festival in the Dock des Suds (www.dock-des-suds.org).

Roquebrune-sur-Argens: *Fête de Miel.* Honey festival.

November

Arles: *Salon International des Santonniers* (until mid-Jan). Exhibition of Christmas crib figures; *Marché de Noël.*

Carpentras: *Foire St-Suffrein.* Truffle fair.

Marseille: *Foire-aux-Santons* (late Nov until mid-Jan). Provençal Christmas crib figures market dating back to 1803.

Monte-Carlo: 19 Nov, National Holiday: parades, ceremonies and spectacles (fireworks the previous evening).

WHAT'S ON AND TICKETS

César, a weekly listings magazine, is distributed free in the Gard, Vaucluse and Bouches-du-Rhône *départements.*

Friday editions of newspapers are a good source of information on the local nightlife: see *La Provence* and *La Marseillaise.* Also visit www.nicematin.fr and www.laprovence-presse.fr. The major cities produce brochures of the main events –enquire at the tourist office.

Tourist offices may also have ticket offices for local music, theatre or cultural events. Many theatre and opera box offices accept credit card telephone or internet bookings. In major cities, FNAC (www.fnac.com) and Virgin stores are ticket agents for local gigs. Tickets can also be bought via **France Billet** (tel: 08 9269 2192; www.francebillet.com).

TRANSPORT

ACCOMMODATION

ACTIVITIES

A – Z

LANGUAGE

December

Bandol: *Fêtes du Millésime.* Tastings of the new Bandol wine vintage.
Fréjus: *Foire aux Santons.* Provençal crib figures and Christmas market.
Nice: *Crèche vivante.* Living Christmas nativity scene on place Rossetti.
St-Raphaël: *Fêtes de la Lumière.* Involves fireworks and street theatre.

THE ARTS

Outside the summer festival season, performing arts are largely found in the main cities, such as Marseille, Nice, Avignon, Aix, Arles, Toulon or Monte-Carlo, where you will find opera, theatre and cinema venues. Respected resident companies include the Théâtre de Nice, Ballets de Monte-Carlo and the Ballet Preljocaj in Aix. In summer, you'll also find touring circuses, outdoor rock concerts and film screenings all along the coast.

Venues

Aix-en-Provence

Ballet Preljocaj–Pavillon Noir, 530 avenue Mozart; tel: 04 4293 4800; www.preljocaj.org. Exciting contemporary dance from international visiting companies and the resident Ballet Preljocaj.
Cinéma Renoir, 7 rue Villars; tel: 04 4291 3332. Three auditoriums, one with a big screen. Shows art-house and box-office films in their original language.
Cité du Livre, 8–10 rue des Allumettes; tel: 04 4293 5419; www.citedulivre-aix.com. Multidisciplinary arts centre with annual literary festival.
Théâtre des Ateliers, 29 place Miollis; tel: 04 4238 1045; www.theatre-des-ateliers-aix.com. Contemporary theatre.

Antibes

Théâtre Antibea, 15 rue Georges Clemenceau; tel: 04 9334 2430; www.theatre-antibea.com. Small theatre with a varied repertoire. Some English-language plays.

Arles

Cargo de Nuit, 7 avenue Sadi-Carnot; tel: 04 9049 5599; www.cargodenuit.com. Venue for world music and jazz concerts.

Avignon

Théâtre des Carmes, 6 place des Carmes; tel: 04 9082 2047. Avignon's oldest theatre company, based in a restored Gothic cloister.
Théâtre Municipal, 20 place de l'Horloge; tel: 04 9085 0232. The main permanent theatre in Avignon. Stages official festival productions in July.
Utopia, 4 rue des Escaliers Ste-Anne; tel: 04 9082 6536. Avignon's main 'VO' or *version-originale* (original-language) cinema, with a bohemian bistro and café.

Cannes

Palais des Festivals et des Congrès, 1 boulevard de la Croisette; tel: 04 9339 0101. The venue for the Film Festival is also used for plays, ballets and concerts.
Théâtre Alexandre III, 19 boulevard Alexandre; tel: 04 9394 3344; www.theatredecannes.com. A former cinema, this theatre stages plays, including classics and modern interpretations.

Cavaillon

Théâtre de Cavaillon, rue du Languedoc; tel: 04 9078 6464; www.theatredecavaillon.com. A state-subsidised theatre putting on theatre, dance, music and multidisciplinary projects, as well as a programme of nomadic pieces and events in nearby Luberon villages.

Marseille

L'Intermédiaire, 63 place Jean-Jaurès; tel: 04 9147 0125. Jazz, blues, rock and traditional southern French music.
Opéra de Marseille, 2 rue Molière; tel: 04 9155 1110. Opera, ballet and classical music.
Théâtre du Gymnase, 4 rue du Théâtre-Français; tel: 04 9124 3535/08 2000 0422. Restored vintage theatre staging innovative drama.
Théâtre National de la Criée, 30 quai Rive Neuve; tel: 04 9154 7054; www.theatre-lacriee.com. Renowned theatre in the old fish market.

Monaco

Salle Garnier, place du Casino, Monte-Carlo; tel: +377 9806 2828; www.opera.mc. Glamorous opera.
Théâtre de Princesse Grace, 12 avenue d'Ostende; tel: +377 9350 0345. Concerts, spectacles and classic theatre.

Nice

Cinémathèque de Nice, Acropolis, 3 esplanade J.F. Kennedy; tel: 04 9204 0666, www.cinematheque-nice.com. A cinema screening classic and recent movies in VO (*version originale* with subtitles).
Opéra de Nice, 4 rue St-François-de-Paule; tel: 04 9217 4000; www.opera-nice.org. Classic venue for symphony concerts, ballet and opera.
Théâtre National de Nice, promenade des Arts; tel: 04 9313 9090; www.tnn.fr. Theatre renowned for premiering new drama by its own troupe and visiting companies.

Nîmes

Théâtre de Nîmes, 1 place de la Calade; tel: 04 6636 6510; www.theatredenimes.com. Hosts a varied programme of theatre as well as visiting contemporary dance companies.

Toulon

Opéra de Toulon, place Victor Hugo; tel: 04 9492 7078; www.operadetoulon.fr. Ornate municipal opera house staging opera and Baroque and classical concerts.

ABOVE: Monaco aquarium.

MUSEUMS AND GALLERIES

Provence has a magnificent legacy of art, and many major art museums. There are also numerous smaller museums and galleries offering a variety of art and crafts. Most museums charge an entrance fee (although municipal museums in Nice are now free), but look out for discounts for families, or off-peak periods. As a rule, national museums are closed on Tuesday, while municipal museums shut on Monday. Opening times vary. Most museums close from noon to 2 or 2.30pm, although major sites are often open continuously, especially in summer.

NIGHTLIFE

The Côte d'Azur is famed for its nightlife, in particular its legendary casinos, which nowadays often incorporate nightclubs, cabarets and restaurants. The larger cities have a variety of late-night bars and clubs. Several Parisian clubs migrate to Cannes for the Cannes Film Festival, and in high summer special events are hosted all along the coast. St-Tropez and Juan-les-Pins are legendary party destinations, but in smaller towns and villages there is usually little going

on at night unless a festival is taking place. Most will have a bar or café that stays open until midnight or later though.

Casinos and Cabaret

Roulette and black jack are all part of the Riviera's glamorous image. As well as the fashionable casinos listed here, there are also lower-key casinos with a variety of table games and slot machines at other resorts including Bandol, Beaulieu, Menton and Cavalaire, and inland at Aix-en-Provence and Grasse. You have to be over 18 to enter a casino (bring ID).

Cannes

La Croisette Casino Barrière, Palais des Festivals, Cannes; tel: 04 9298 7800, www.lucien barriere.com.
Palm Beach Casino, 57 boulevard F. Roosevelt; tel: 04 9706 3690. Casino, restaurant and piano bar (11pm–5am).

Monte-Carlo

Casino de Monte-Carlo, place du Casino; tel: +377 9216 2300. The original and still the most famous casino on the Côte d'Azur. Formal dress is required. Open all year: main salon from noon, private rooms from 3pm. Has a separate cabaret and several restaurants.

Nice

Casino Ruhl, 1 promenade des Anglais; tel: 04 9703 1222; www. lucienbarriere.com. Glitzy casino with gaming tables, slot machines and a cabaret at weekends.

Nightclubs

Antibes–Juan-les-Pins

La Siesta, rte du Bord de Mer, Antibes; tel: 04 9333 3131, www. lasiesta.fr. Large seafront complex with restaurant, bar, casino and club.
Le Village, 1 boulevard de la Pinède, Juan-les-Pins; tel: 04 9293 9000. Extremely popular club playing the latest music.

Avignon

Le Bokao's, 9 bis boulevard du quai St-Lazare; tel: 04 9082 4795; www.bokaos.fr. Big trendy dance club.
L'Esclave, 12 rue du Limas; tel: 04 9085 1491; www.lesclavebar. com. Predominantly gay bar and disco. Popular during the summer theatre festival.

Cannes

Le Bâoli, Port Canto, La Croisette; tel: 04 9343 0343; www.lebaoli.com. Glamorous all-night restaurant, sushi bar and discothèque in a tented Arabian Nights setting.
Zanzibar, 85 rue Félix-Faure; tel: 04 9339 3075. Established gay bar and club.

Marseille

Le Trolleybus, 24 quai de Rive Neuve; tel: 04 9154 3045; www. letrolley.com. Huge club in old vaulted port buildings offering techno, salsa, jazz and rock DJs and concerts.
The New Cancan, 3 rue Sénac-de-Meilhan; tel: 04 9148 5976; www.newcancan.com. The most popular gay club in Marseille.

Monaco

La Rascasse, quai Antoine; tel: +377 9325 5690. All-night pub with an outdoor terrace and a restaurant. Plays jazz and rock.
Le Sporting d'Eté, avenue Princesse Grace; tel: +377 9216 2277. Fashionable Euro-trash rendezvous, with restaurants, Jimmy'z nightclub, concerts and the Summer Casino. Open during summer season only.

Nice

Le Bar des Oiseaux, 5 rue St-Vincent; tel: 04 9380 2733; www. bardesoiseaux.com. Live jazz, chanson and café-théâtre in a characterful Vieux Nice bar and restaurant.
Le Ghost, 3 rue de la Barillerie; tel: 04 9392 9337; www.leghost-pub.com. A cool Vieux Nice bar-club with good cocktails and thumping electro DJs.
Le Klub, 6 rue Halévy; tel: 04 9316 8726; www.leklub.net.

Predominantly house music for a mixed gay and straight crowd.

St-Tropez

Les Caves du Roy, Hôtel Byblos, avenue Paul Signac; tel: 04 9456 6800; www.byblos.com. Legendary jet-set club in Hôtel Byblos. Closed Nov-Mar.

Le Papagayo, Résidence du Port; tel: 04 9479 2950; www.papagayo-club.net. Opened in the 1960s and still the place for party people.

Le VIP Room, Résidences du Nouveau Port; tel: 04 9497 1470; www.viproom.fr. St-Tropez's most fashionable club and restaurant.

OUTDOOR ACTIVITIES

Provence offers a huge range of opportunities for sports enthusiasts, whether you're after a bucolic cycle ride or serious rock-climbing or sailing. Golf is very popular, as is tennis, and even fairly small villages often have tennis courts, though you may have to become a temporary member to use them. First port of call for finding out about facilities should be the *départemental* tourist board websites *(see page 293)* and local tourist offices, which can provide information on boat and bike hire facilities, tennis courts, horse-riding and swimming lessons. Several UK travel firms offer holidays tailored to specific activities *(see page 293)*.

Cycling

Cycling is a wonderful way to enjoy Provence *(see page 263 for advice on transporting your own bike)*. If you don't have a bike, you can rent cycles locally. You could consider a package cycling holiday, with accommodation booked in advance and your luggage transported for you. The Luberon and the Alpilles are particularly popular cycling areas, while the Mont Ventoux ascent is a famed Tour de France challenge. For the Vaucluse, www.provence-cycling.co.uk

is an excellent English-language website providing information on itineraries, short breaks, cycle hire and bike-friendly hotels and restaurants.

The IGN (Institut Géographique National) 906 Cycling France map gives details of routes, clubs and places to stay. Information is also available from the Touring Department of the **Cyclists Touring Club** (www.ctc.org.uk; tel: 0870 873 0060). Its service to members includes competitive cycle and travel insurance and free detailed touring itineraries, whilst its tours brochure lists trips to the region, organised by members. The club's French counterpart is **Fédération Française de Cyclotourisme**, www.ffct.org; tel: 01 56 20 88 87.

Diving

The Iles de Lérins, the Iles d'Hyères and the Calanques offer some of the best diving in the Mediterranean. Diving centres in Marseille, Cassis, Nice and Cannes offer diving courses and initiation sessions for beginners as well as trips for experienced divers.

Fishing

Here you have a choice of sea- or freshwater fishing. The season opens around the second Saturday in March. For freshwater fish-

ing you will need to be affiliated to an association. For general information and addresses of local fishing associations contact local tourist offices.

Golf

Provence has many excellent golf courses, and the Mediterranean climate means golf can be played all year round. Most clubs offer lessons. First-rate 18-hole courses include: Royal Mougins Golf Club (www.royalmougins.fr; tel: 04 9292 4969) near Cannes; Golf Terre Blanche at the Four Seasons Resort Provence (www.fourseasons.com/provence), near Fayence, and the Monte-Carlo Golf Club (tel: 04 9241 5070) at La Turbie.

Hiking and Climbing

There is a vast network of sign-posted footpaths, including several long-distance footpaths *(sentiers de grande randonnée)*, as well as opportunities for rock-climbing, notably in the regional and national parks, such as the Parc du Mercantour, the Gorges de Verdon, the Calanques and the Luberon, and in the Massif des Maures and the Estérel ranges. Ensure you are suitably equipped with water, warm clothing, good boots and a map. There are also stretches of scenic coast path *(Sentier du Littoral*

BELOW: canoe trip on the Gardon river under the Pont du Gard's arches.

or *Sentier des Douaniers*). In high summer, footpaths in some of the massifs may be closed due to fire risk.

Some local tourist offices or ramblers' organisations put on guided walks of local sights, plants or wildlife; for example the Office National des Forêts organises walks in the Maures (information at the tourist office in Bormes-les-Mimosas), the Maison de Gorges de Verdon at La Palud-sur-Verdon organises walks in the Gorges de Verdon and the Nice branch of the Club Alpin Français (www.cafnice.org) organises walking, climbing and skiing trips in the Mercantour National Park. For specialised guides who can take you walking in the Mercantour contact the tourist office or Maison du Parc in Tende.

Maps/Walking Guides

The French Ramblers' Association (**Fédération Française de la Randonnée Pédestre**; FFRP; www.ffrandonee.fr) in Paris publishes **Topo-guides** (guide books in French incorporating IGN 1:50,000 scale maps) to France's footpaths, including guides to the grandes-randonnées and guides to different areas with walks of varying lengths and difficulties. These are available from map retailers (high-street stores or online) and from all good bookshops in the region.

IGN Blue series (*Série Bleue*) maps at a scale of 1:25,000 are ideal for walkers; IGN also publish maps of the national parks and produce walking maps on CD-ROM under the **IGN Rando** logo – the *Série Bleue* and the Top 25 are for walkers.

Horse-riding

Horse-riding and pony-trekking are popular activities in Provence, with *centres équestres* (equestrian centres) all over the region, in rural areas, in the mountains, less inhabited parts of the coast, and especially in the Camargue.

Skiing

The Alpes-Maritimes are very popular for skiing, with several large resorts, such as Auron, Valberg and Isola 2000 in the Mercantour (www.stationsdumercantour.com) for downhill skiing (see page 220). Smaller Val Casterino and Le Boréon are more geared to cross-country skiing. They are only a few hours from the coast, and at certain times of the year you can combine the beach and skiing in one day. Other small stations include Gréolières-les-Neiges north of Grasse and Mont Serein on Mont Ventoux in the Vaucluse.

Watersports

Sailing and Windsurfing

Antibes and Cannes are major yachting centres, while Juan-les-Pins is said to have been the birthplace of water-skiing. If you're interested in yacht or speedboat hire, all the main marinas have yacht brokers and ships' chandlers. Many private beaches have a good range of equipment for hire, such as dinghies, catamarans, sea kayaks, and surfing and water-skiing equipment. There are dinghy sailing schools at Bormes-les-Mimosas, Mandelieu-la Napoule and Menton; the Base Nautique (50 boulevard Franck Pilatte) near the Vieux Port in Nice is home to assorted rowing, sailing and diving clubs and schools. Noted windsurfing spots include Six-Fours-les-Plages, west of Toulon, and the Plage de l'Almanerre at Hyères.

Inland, you'll find sailing clubs and boat hire on several lakes, such as the Lac de St-Cassien, near Montouroux, and the Lac de St-Croix and Lac d'Esparron in the Gorges de Verdon.

Canoeing and Kayaking

Several companies, mainly based in Castellane, organise canoeing, canyoning and white-water rafting

trips in the Gorges de Verdon. There is also gentler kayaking on the Sorgue River at Fontaine-de-Vaucluse and L'Isle-sur-la-Sorgue. Many beaches also hire out sea kayaks.

Spectator Sports

Equestrian Events

The major horse-racing venue is the Côte d'Azur Hippodrome at Cagnes-sur-Mer, where meetings are held during the day from December to May and in the evenings in July and August. There are also racetracks at Hyères (Hippodrome de la Plage, for flat racing, steeplechasing and trotting) and Marseille (Hippodrome Borély for flat racing and trotting). There are international show-jumping competitions in Cannes in May and Monaco in June, and an international polo event at St-Tropez in July.

Football and Rugby

Marseille (Olympique Marseille), Nice and Monaco all have premier division football teams, as does the newly promoted AC Arles-Avignon team, which plays in Avignon. Toulon rugby team plays in the French Top 14.

Golf

The Monaco **Golf Tournament** takes place in early July. Another golfing event is the **Professional Golf Open** at Mougins (near Cannes), held every April.

Motor Sports

Motor racing's big social and sporting event is the **Monaco Grand Prix** in May, one of the most decisive contests in the Formula 1 championship, which takes place around the streets and tight bends of the principality; hotels and the best grandstand views are booked up months ahead. In January, the Monte-Carlo Car Rally, first staged in 1911, takes in the region's snowy mountains before finishing in Monte-Carlo.

TRANSPORT

ACCOMMODATION

ACTIVITIES

A – Z

LANGUAGE

SPAS & THALASSOTHERAPY

More luxury hotels now have spas offering a variety of beauty treatments and massages. Historic spa towns offering the benefits of natural warm water springs include Aix-en-Provence, Digne-les-Bains and Gréoux-les-Bains. Along the coast, some resorts have thalassotherapy centres offering saltwater treatments, notably at L'Ile des Embiez, Bandol, Hyères, Fréjus, Antibes and Monaco. For information see www.france-thalasso.com

Sailing and Windsurfing

Les Voiles d'Antibes in June starts off the classic yacht racing season, followed by the Régates Royales at Cannes in September. This coincides with the Cannes International Boat and Yacht Show and **Les Voiles de St-Tropez** (late September-early October), a spectacular gathering of vintage and modern sailing yachts.

Tennis

The Monte-Carlo Open men's tournament is held in April, with the Nice Tennis Open in May.

SHOPPING

Shopping Areas

Over the years, many French towns have kept the town centre for small boutiques and individual shops. Large supermarkets, furniture stores and DIY outlets are often grouped on the outskirts of the town, mostly designated as a *centre commercial*. This laudable intent is somewhat marred by the horrendous design of some of these centres – groups of garish functional buildings that make the town's outskirts very unattractive. In the case of Nice, for example, there are vast hypermarkets, beyond the airport to the west of town at St-Laurent-du-Var.

Centres commerciaux are fine for bulk shopping, self-catering or finding a selection of wine to take home at reasonable prices, but it is in the town centres that you will find the individual souvenirs that give a taste of the region.

What to Buy

Local crafts: There are countless opportunities to buy local crafts, although be aware that some of the garish "Provençal" fabrics and mass-produced pottery may well have been imported. Among specialities to look out for are *santons* (clay Christmas crib figures in various sizes depicting typical Provençal villagers and pastimes – the baker, the shepherd, the fishwife, etc), pottery and faience (famous centres include Vallauris, Apt and Moustiers-Ste-Marie), printed fabrics and table linen, hand-woven baskets, soaps and toiletries, olive wood bowls and utensils. Some towns are linked with particular products, such as hand-blown glass from Biot, earthenware in Vallauris, leather goods and bullfighting costumes in Arles and the Camargue, and perfumes in Grasse.

Antiques and Collectables

Antiques can be another good buy in the south. The flea market at L'Isle-sur-la-Sorgue *(see page 92)* has the largest concentration of antiques dealers outside Paris. Also worth a look are the antiques district of Nice behind the Vieux-Port *(see page 228)*, the streets between the Préfecture and the Palais de Justice in Marseille, and the Quartier Mazarine and streets around place des Trois-Ormeaux in Aix-en-Provence. Monaco has upmarket antiquaires along boulevard des Moulins and branches of the international auction houses. Particularly southern articles are "Beaucaire" mirrors carved with grapes and vines, antique printed fabrics and quilts

and faience from Apt, Marseille and Moustiers.

Fashion and Accessories

Aix-en-Provence, Marseille, St-Tropez, Cannes, Nice and Monaco are all major fashion shopping destinations. In Nice, you'll find everything from mainstream to designer to new agey organic wear in Vieux Nice. In Cannes, La Croisette and rue d'Antibes are where to find glitzy film-star evening wear and jewellery; St-Tropez is the place for summer party wear – as well as the famous tropézienne sandals from Atelier Rondini and mens' swimming trunks at Villebrequin. Beach resorts generally have an excellent choice of swimwear.

Food and Wine

Foodie treats to take home include olive oil and jars of *tapenade*, dried herbs and *saucisson sec*, mountain honey and sweets such as the *calissons* of Aix *(see page 43)*.

With wines varying from celebrated Châteauneuf-du-Pape and sweet Beaumes-de-Vénise to the pale pink rosés from Côtes de Provence, Provence offers numerous opportunities to buy direct from vineyards. Good sources of information for visiting wine producers, tastings and wine courses include: Maison des Vins des Côtes de Provence (Les Arcs; tel: 04 9499 5020), Maison des Vins de Châteauneuf-du-Pape (8 rue Maréchal Foch, Châteauneuf-du-Pape; tel: 04 9083 7069; www. vinadea.com), and Maison de la Truffe et du Vin in Ménerbes (tel: 04 9072 3837).

Tax Refunds (Détaxes)

A refund (average 13 percent) of value-added tax (TVA) can be claimed by non-EU visitors if they spend over €180 on the same day in any one shop. The shop will supply a *détaxe* form, which you will need to have stamped by customs on leaving the country. Send

MARKET ETIQUETTE

In a market all goods by law have to be marked with the price. Prices are usually by the kilo or by the *pièce*, that is, each item priced individually. Usually the stallholder (*marchand*) will select the goods for you. Sometimes there is a serve-yourself system – observe everyone else to see whether this is the case or not. With some foods, you may be offered a taste to try first: *un goûter*.

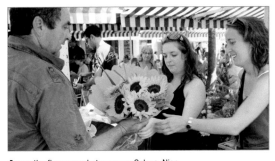

ABOVE: the flower market on cours Saleya, Nice.

a copy back to the shop, which will refund you by bank transfer or through your credit card. *Détaxe* does not cover food, drink, antiques or works of art.

Markets

Virtually every town and village in Provence will have its open-air market, which is both a social rendezvous and the place where chefs stock up. In smaller towns and villages, the market will usually be one or two mornings a week, in larger towns there may be a daily morning market or covered market open morning and afternoon. Expect to find locally produced vegetables, fruit, herbs, goat cheese, dried sausages, meat and poultry, fish, honey, olives and olive oil; you may also find household goods, kitchenware and clothing. Below are some of the best.

Alpes-de-Haute-Provence

Castellane: Wed, Sat
Colmars-les-Alpes: Tues
Digne-les-Bains: Wed, Sat
Forcalquier: Mon
Manosque: Sat
Moustiers-Ste-Marie: Fri
Sisteron: Wed, Sat

Alpes-Maritimes

Antibes: Tues–Sun; daily in summer
Cannes Marché Forville: Tues–Sun; daily in summer
Grasse: Tues–Sun

Menton Halles Municipales covered market: daily
Nice Cours Saleya: Tues–Sun
St-Etienne-de-Tinée: Fri
Sospel: Thur, Sun
Tende: Wed
Vallauris: Tues, Sun
Vence: Tues, Fri

Bouches-du-Rhône

Aix-en-Provence: main market daily; flower market Mon, Wed, Fri, Sun
Arles: Wed, Sat
Cassis: fish market daily; food and general market Wed, Fri
Fontvieille: Mon, Fri
La Ciotat: Tues, Sun
Marseille: Vieux Port fish market daily; avenue du Prado food and general market Mon–Sat.
St-Rémy-de-Provence: Wed, Sat
Stes-Maries-de-la-Mer: Mon, Fri
Salon-de-Provence: Wed, Fri
Tarascon: Tues

Gard

Aigues-Mortes: Sun
Nîmes Les Halles covered market: Tues–Sun

Monaco

Marché de la Condamine: daily

Var

Collobrières: Sun, Thur
Draguignan: Wed, Sat
Fayence: Tues, Thur, Sat
Hyères: Tues, Sat
La Londe-des-Maures: Sun
Le Lavandou: Thur
Salernes: Sun
St-Tropez: Tues, Sat

Ste-Maxime: covered market Tues–Sun; farmers' market Thur.
Sanary-sur-Mer: Wed
Toulon Cours Lafayette: Tues–Sat

Vaucluse

Apt: Sat, farmers' market Tues.
Avignon Les Halles covered market: Tues–Sun; produce and flea market Sat and Sun
Cadenet: Mon
Carpentras: Fri
Cavaillon: Mon
Châteauneuf-du-Pape: Fri
Coustellet farmers' market: Sun, except Jan–Feb, and Wed evening June–Aug
Cucuron: Tues
Roussillon: Wed
Vaison-la-Romaine: Tues; farmers' market Sat, plus Thur summer.

SIZE CONVERSION CHART

WOMEN		
France	UK	US
38	10	8
40	12	10
42	14	12
44	16	14
46	18	16
48	20	18
MEN		
France	UK	US
32	32	42
34	34	44
36	35	46
38	36	48
40	37	51
42	38	54

TRANSPORT

ACCOMMODATION

ACTIVITIES

A – Z

LANGUAGE

A – Z

A HANDY SUMMARY OF PRACTICAL INFORMATION, ARRANGED ALPHABETICALLY

A dmission Charges

Entrance fees for museums and galleries generally fall between €4 and €8 per adult, with free admission for children – check on the qualifying age, since for some places it is under 18 and others under 12 or 7 years of age. Look out for special rates for students and over 60s. Municipal museums in Nice are free. National museums and monuments, including the Musée Chagall in Nice, Musée Léger in Biot and Musée Granet in Aix are free to all European Union nationals aged under 26, although there may be a charge for temporary exhibitions.

Various passes, such as Passion in Avignon, Pass Monuments in Arles and the ticket Nîmes

Romaine, provide discounts to museums and monuments, and sometimes reduced prices on guided tours and transport as well. Most tickets can be bought at the local tourist office or the museums themselves.

Age Restrictions

Minimum ages: consent 15, marriage 18, buying alcohol 16, drinking wine or beer in a bar 16, drinking spirits in a bar 18, driving 18, entering a casino 18.

B udgeting for your Trip

Expect to pay:
25cl (un demi) of draught lager €3.50; glass of house wine €4–7; main course in a budget

(€8–12), moderate (€15–25) and expensive (€30–50) restaurant, although there are often good-value fixed price menus, especially at lunch. Expect prices to be higher along the coast than in inland villages. Allow the following for a double room in a cheap (€60–80), moderate (€120–160) and deluxe hotel (€300+) in high season, not including breakfast.

C hildren

Sightseeing with children is only likely to be difficult in steep hill villages with lots of steps, which can be difficult to negotiate with a pushchair.

A wide range of activities can be found to suit children of all ages, from riding, cycling and river-bathing, to rambling through the countryside and exploring castles. Most towns and villages have swimming pools, tennis courts and playgrounds.

The beach and the sea are of course the easiest way to amuse children, and private beach concessions with sun-loungers and parasols are the easiest of all. Inflatables are often provided, and there are sometimes also bouncy castles.

Many seaside resorts have children's clubs on the beach, where, for a fee, children can be left under supervision for a few hours to take part in organised sports and fun events. At some resorts you'll be able to find swimming lessons and sailing courses (usually in Optimists).

Circuses often tour the seaside resorts in summer, while the Cirque Alexis Gruss takes up summer quarters at Piolenc, north of Orange. Look out also for summer fireworks festivals in Cannes and Monaco.

When hiring a car, be sure to book any baby seats in advance, although larger hire companies do usually have a few ready to go.

Hotels and Restaurants

Most hotels have family rooms *(chambre triple ou quadruple)* or can often add an extra bed *(lit supplémentaire)* in a double room so

that children do not have to be separated from their parents. A cot *(lit bébé)* can also often be provided, sometimes for a small supplement, although it is a good idea to check this in advance.

Eating out is easy, especially during the day, as going out for a meal is a quintessential part of French culture and all but the poshest restaurants welcome young children. Many restaurants offer a children's menu, will split a prix-fixe menu between two children, or even give you an extra plate to share your own meal.

Shopping

French shops are well provided with all child necessities. Disposable nappies *(couches jettable)* are easy to find, and French baby food is often of gourmet standard, though watch out for added sugar.

Children's Attractions

Museums and Monuments
The Egyptian collections and African sculptures at the Vieille Charité in Marseille, Matisse's colourful paintings and cut-outs at the Musée Matisse in Nice, the Musée d'Art Moderne et Contemporain in Nice, the medieval siege instruments at the Château des Baux in Les Baux-de-Provence, the Arènes (Roman amphitheatre) in Nîmes, the Musée de la Préhistoire at Quinson in the Gorges de Verdon, the

Musée International de la Parfumerie in Grasse and the Collection de Voitures Anciennes (vintage cars) in Monaco all have plenty to interest children.

Zoos, Parks and Aquariums
Child-friendly zoos and nature parks include the Musée Océanographique in Monaco, Zoo de la Barben near Salon-de-Provence, the Zoo de St-Jean Cap Ferrat, and the Zoo de Mont Boron (plus the ride up in the *téléferique*) at Toulon. There is a children's trail at the Marais de Vigueirat nature reserve in Camargue, and the Parc Floral Phoenix in Nice, but the most popular attraction is likely to be the Marineland complex just east of Antibes, with its whale and dolphin displays, and adjoining water fun park, crazy golf and wild west park.

Boat Trips
Enjoyable boat trips include the Ile Ste-Marguerite from Cannes or Ile de Porquerolles and Port-Cros from the Presqu'île de Giens, Hyères and Le Lavandou, to the Iles de Frioul and Calanques from Marseille and Cassis, around the port of Toulon. Several companies also offer marine viewing trips in glass-bottomed boats.

Climate

Provence and its Côte d'Azur are renowned for their sunshine. Each year there are typically more than 300 sunny days and less than 850 mm (33½ inches) of rain. When it does rain, however, it pours. Average temperatures range from 48°F (8°C) in winter to 84°F (26°C) in summer – however, maximum temperatures in summer can easily reach the high 30°Cs, so it is advisable to keep in the shade between noon and 3pm. If walking outside during the hottest hours, wear a hat and carry plenty of drinking water, and apply sunscreen regularly. Winters are usually mild and sunny, and summers are typically hot and dry. Inland, the plains around

BELOW: summer fun on L'Isle-sur-la-Sorgue.

TRANSPORT

ACCOMMODATION

ACTIVITIES

A – Z

LANGUAGE

CLIMATE CHART

Provence

☐ Maximum temperature
☐ Minimum temperature
— Rainfall

Carpentras and Aix-en-Provence have a more continental climate which means that summers can be stiflingly hot, but be prepared for the drop in temperature in high mountain areas such as Mont Ventoux and the Mercantour.

Climate varies between the high country and low country. However, the whole region experiences the sporadic virulence of the legendary northwest wind, the mistral, from late autumn to early spring. There have also been violent storms in the area in recent years, causing major floods and damage.

When to Visit

The tourist season starts around Easter and continues to the end of October. Many restaurants and hotels close at the end of the season, especially along the coast. During the peak period from 15 July to the end of August reservations are essential. Other popular times to come are during Nice Carnaval and Menton lemon festival in February and the Monaco Grand Prix in May. Always reserve in advance if you're visiting the ski resorts in winter, especially at weekends and during French school holidays.

What to Wear

The clothing you bring depends on your destination and when you travel; you will only need to dress

up for chic restaurants in the cities or casinos. Bring plenty of light clothing in summer but dress appropriately for visiting churches and synagogues; a scarf or shirt are always useful cover-ups. Try not to wander around the streets in swimwear – in Monaco it is formally forbidden. Even in summer, a sweater, wrap or light jacket is useful for cooler evenings, and a waterproof coat or jacket will be needed from October to April. Comfortable shoes are advisable for sightseeing.

Weather Information

For weather information tel: 08 92 68 02 followed by the number of the *département* (eg. 13 for Bouches-du-Rhône, 83 for Var, etc) or visit www.meteo.fr

Temperatures are always given in Celsius (centigrade). To convert to Fahrenheit, see below:

$0°C = 2°F$	$20°C = 68°F$
$10°C = 50°F$	$25°C = 77°F$
$15°C = 59°F$	$30°C = 86°F$

Crime and Safety

Incidents of violent crime against visitors are rare, but you should apply the usual precautions when wandering about late at night. Try not to carry large amounts of cash, never leave valuables in your car, and be on the lookout for pickpockets, especially in crowds. In Nice and Marseille, be aware there have been incidents of bags and

watches snatched through open car windows when waiting at traffic lights. Any loss or theft should be reported immediately to the nearest *commissariat de police* in main towns and *gendarmerie* in rural areas.

Customs Regulations

You may take any quantity of goods into France from another EU country as long as they are for personal use and you can prove that tax has been paid on them in the country of origin. Customs officials still have the right to question visitors.

Quantities accepted as being for personal use are as follows:
• 800 cigarettes, 400 small cigars, 200 cigars or 1 kg of loose tobacco.
• 10 litres of spirits (more than 22 percent alcohol), 90 litres of wine (under 22 percent alcohol) or 110 litres of beer.

For goods brought in from outside the EU, the recommended quantities are:
• 200 cigarettes or 100 small cigars, 50 cigars or 250 g of loose tobacco.
• 1 litre of spirits (over 22 percent alcohol) and 2 litres of wine and beer (under 22 percent alcohol).
• 50 g of perfume.

Visitors may also carry up to €7,600 in currency.

If you go to the very popular Friday street market in Ventimiglia (Vintimille in French) just across

BELOW: the beach at Cannes.

the border in Italy, be careful about buying counterfeit goods. Customs checks are frequent at the Menton border post and you could be prosecuted.

D isabled Travellers

Disabled access is often difficult in historic buildings or the stepped streets of old hill towns, but many of the south's recently renovated museums do have wheelchair access. All hotels built since 1978 should have at least one specially adapted bedroom, while public buildings, such as town halls, museums and hospitals built since 1978 should also be accessible, though it's always wise to check beforehand exactly what is meant by this. The Association des Paralysés de France (www.apf.asso.fr) publishes an annual *Guide Vacances*. A new label Tourisme & Handicap (www.tourisme-handicaps.org) is gradually being introduced to indicate tourist facilities accessible for physically, visually, aurally or mentally handicapped travellers, with information about labelled hotels, gîtes, campsites, restaurants, tourist sights and local transport on the different *départemental* websites *(see tourist information, page 293)*. There is also wheelchair access to some beaches – designated *handiplages*.

Disabled parking places are widespread and are indicated with a wheelchair sign. The international blue disabled parking disc scheme is recognised in France. To hire a wheelchair or other equipment enquire at the local pharmacy.

For further information in the UK contact: Tourism for All UK, tel: 0845 124 9971; www.tourismforall.org.uk. In the US contact sath, tel: (212) 447 7284; www.sath.org

Transport

Eurotunnel (UK tel: 0870 535 3535; France tel: 0810 63 03 04) – the Channel Tunnel car-on-a-train service – allows disabled

passengers to stay in their vehicle. Eurostar trains (UK special requests, tel: 0870 518 61 86; www.eurostar.com) give special-rate wheelchair-user fares and a reduced rate for one travelling companion.

Most ferry companies offer facilities for disabled travellers if they are contacted in advance of travel.

For rail travel, the SNCF runs the Service Accès Plus (tel: 0890 640 650, then press 1; www.accesplus.sncf.com, or with reservations on www.voyages-sncf.fr) to help disabled voyagers. For help boarding the train, reservations should be made at least 48 hours in advance. *Le Guide du Voyageur à Mobilité Réduite SNCF* is available free in train stations. Reduced tolls are charged on *autoroutes* for vehicles fitted to accommodate the disabled.

E lectricity and Gas

220-volt, 50-cycle AC is universal, generally with a three-pin plug. British visitors should buy an adaptor (*adaptateur*); American visitors will need a transformer (*transformateur*).

In many rural areas butane gas is used for cooking and heating water. Campers and caravanners needing replacement gas canisters will find them on sale at local shops, garages and supermarkets (return the empty one).

Embassies and Consulates

Australia: (Embassy) 4 rue Jean-Rey, 75015 Paris; tel: 01 4050 3300; www.france.embassy.gov.au
Canada: (Consulate) 35 avenue Montaigne, 75008 Paris; tel: 01 4443 2902; www.international.gc.ca
Ireland: (Embassy) 12 avenue Foch, 75116 Paris; tel: 01 4417 6700; www.embassyofirelandparis.com
UK: (Consulate) 24 avenue du Prado, 13006 Marseille; tel: 04 9115 7210; http://ukinfrance.free.gov.uk
US: (Consulate) 7 avenue Gustave V, 06000 Nice; tel: 04 9388 8955; http://france.usembassy.gov/consulara.html
Place Varian Fry, 13006 Marseille; tel: 04 9154 9200; www.amb-usa.fr/marseille
7 avenue Gustave V, 06000 Nice; tel: 04 9388 8955; www.amb-usa.fr/marseille/nice

Etiquette

Madame/Mademoiselle and Monsieur are widely used in French. Unless you know someone well or are talking to children, use the formal *vous* rather than *tu* form. It is polite to shake hands when meeting someone. Don't kiss cheeks with someone you don't know, unless they propose to *"donne la bise"* – a polite peck on either side. Note that topless bathing (very common in the 80s and 90s) has gone totally out of fashion. See also What to Wear, under Climate.

G ay & Lesbian Travellers

France is generally gay tolerant, although gay bars and clubs are mainly restricted to the larger towns, such as Nice, Cannes, Avignon, Toulon and Marseille. Coco Beach east of Nice's Vieux Port is a popular Gay beach, and there are lively Gay Pride parades in June in Nice and Marseille. The brochures *Nice Practical Guide* and *www.Cannes*, published by the respective tourist offices, list gay and gay-friendly bars and hotels. See also regional listings magazines, such as *L'Excès* (www. exces.com) or visit www.gay.com for all gay travel information.

Health & Medical Care

Healthcare is generally of an extremely high standard in France and the Côte d'Azur has the highest concentration of specialist doctors in France outside Paris. There are no compulsory vaccinations or particular health risks. Tap water is safe to drink, unless marked *eau non potable*. However you should be careful to avoid sunburn: wear sunhats and avoid exposure to the powerful midday sun. Other potential hazards are mosquitoes at night (many people use plug-in anti-mosquito diffusers) and, some years, invasions of jellyfish (*méduses*) in the sea, usually indicated at the entrance to beaches.

EU nationals staying in France are entitled to use the French Social Security system, which refunds up to 70 percent of medical expenses. British nationals should obtain a European Health Insurance Card before leaving the UK. These are available online at www.ehic.org.uk. This is not a substitute for insurance though, and does not cover repatriation in case of an accident. If you're ill, your hotel can probably recommend an English-speaking doctor or dentist; make sure it is a *médecin conventionné* (affiliated to the social security system). The main cities have hospitals with 24 casualty departments (*Urgences*). Consultations and prescriptions have to be paid for in full in France and are reimbursed, in part, on receipt of a completed *fiche* (form).The doctor will give you a prescription and a *feuille de soins* (statement of treatment), allowing you to claim back part of the cost when you return to the UK. Nationals of non-EU countries should take out travel and medical insurance before leaving home.

Pharmacies

Pharmacies in France are good, but expensive. The staff in pharmacies are well qualified, however, and should be able to advise on many minor ailments. All pharmacies can be identified by a neon green cross. Most open from 9 or 10am until 7 or 8pm Monday to Saturday.

If the pharmacy is closed there will be a sign – or the police station should be able to provide information – giving details of a *pharmacie de garde*, which will offer a night-time or Sunday service.

Internet

Most hotels now have internet access. Wifi is widespread and often, though not always, free (check at reception), otherwise hotels may have a computer in the lobby with internet access for use of guests. Wifi hotspots can also often be found at airports, train stations and some cafés and brasseries. Tourist offices should be able to supply addresses of internet cafés.

Lost Property

To report a crime or loss of belongings, go to the local police station (*gendarmerie* or *commissariat de police*). Telephone numbers can

BELOW: Saintes-Maries-de-la-Mer.

be found at the front of local telephone directories. If you lose your passport, you should report it firstly to the police and then to your consulate or embassy. The SNCF (French railways) has its own lost property system.

Maps

Hotels and tourist offices can usually supply a town street map (*un plan*). For driving, a 1:200,000 or 1:250,000 scale road atlas or sheet map (*carte routière*) of Provence Côte d'Azur is useful. If you're planning to do any serious hiking, buy 1:25,000 scale maps published by IGN.

Stockists of French maps in the UK include: The Travel Bookshop, 13 Blenheim Crescent, London W11, tel: 020 7229 5260, www.thetravelbookshop.co.uk; Stanfords (www.stanfords.co.uk) have stores in Covent Garden, London (tel: 020 7836 1321), Bristol and Manchester. Online, try www.map kiosk.com or www.amazon.co.uk

Media

Newspapers and Magazines

The French press is very regional. Popular papers in the south include *Nice-Matin, La Provence, Var-Matin, Le Dauphiné Vaucluse* and *La Marseillaise,* though for more weighty news you'll generally need to look at the national dailies *Le Monde, Le Figaro* and *Libération*. Foreign newspapers are widely available in the main cities and resorts. The local English-language magazine *Riviera Reporter* is good for regional information and local politics.

Television

France has six terrestrial TV channels (TF1, France 2, France 3, Arte, M6 and the subscription channel Canal+). Most hotels will also have cable, satellite or TNT channels, which often include some foreign channels, such as CNN and BBC World.

ABOVE: Le Café de Paris, Monaco.

Radio

The following is just a selection of what is available (wavelengths are given in MHz):

87.8 France Inter. A state-run, middle-of-the-road channel offering music and international news.

91.7–92.1 France Musique. Another state-run channel, offering classical music and jazz.

93.5–93.9 France Culture. Highbrow state culture station.

bfm. Business and economics news. Aix-en-Provence 93.8, Cannes and Nice 104.4, Hyères 87.9, Marseille 93.8.

93.4 Radio FG FM. Gay station with music and lonely hearts: www.radiofg.com

rtl. A popular mix of music and chat. Avignon 107.2, Cannes and Nice 97.4, Marseille 101.4.

Europe 1. News, press reviews and sports. Avignon 94.6, Cannes and Nice 101.4, Marseille 104.8.

105.5 France Info. Tune in for 24-hour news, economic updates and sports news.

107.7 Radio Trafic. Gives regular traffic bulletins in English.

BBC World Service. This can be received in France on shortwave between 6.195 and 12.095 MHz. One local radio station is Kiss FM: 90.9FM and 94.6FM for Cannes.

Money

Currency

France is part of the euro (€) zone. Banknotes are available in denominations of 500, 200, 100, 50, 20, 10 and 5 euros; avoid the largest denominations as many shops will not accept €200 and €500 notes. There are coins for 2 and 1 euros and for 50, 20, 10, 5, 2 and 1 cent. ATMs are the simplest, and usually cheapest, way of obtaining cash in euros. They are plentiful in large cities, though may be scarce in rural areas. Travellers' cheques are rarely used in France.

Credit cards (cartes de crédit)

Credit cards are widely accepted, especially Visa and Mastercard. There may be a minimum sum (often €15).

For lost and stolen credit cards: Groupement des Cartes Bancaires tel: 0892 70 57 05; American Express tel: 01 4777 7200; Diners Club tel: 0810 31 41 59; Eurocard/Mastercard tel: 08 0090 1387; Visa tel: 08 9270 5705.

Tipping

A 10–15 percent service charge is included in hotel and restaurant bills, so any further tip is purely optional, although you may want to round off bills with a few coins or small notes. Taxis also include service charges but it is common to round up to the nearest 5 or 10. It is also the done thing to hand hotel porters, tour guides, filling station attendants, etc, a euro or two for their services.

O pening Hours

Shops generally open Mon–Sat 9.30 or 10am to 7pm; small shops often take a long lunch break, closing at noon and re-opening at 3 or 4pm. Bakeries generally open 8am–8pm and may open on Sunday, closing one other day a week; some supermarkets remain open until 9 or 10pm.

Restaurants usually serve noon–2 or 2.30pm, 7.30 or 8pm–9.30 or 10pm, and may close one or two days a week; cafés and brasseries often open from early morning until late.

Banks generally open Mon–Fri 9am–noon, 2–5pm; some open Saturday morning and close on Monday.

Museums usually open 10am–5 or 6pm (sometimes later in summer) and often close on either Monday or Tuesday; smaller museums often close for lunch.

P ostal Services

Post offices (www.laposte.fr) open Mon–Fri 9am–noon and 2–6pm, Sat 9am–noon. In large towns they may not close for lunch, but in small villages they may only be open for a short time in the morning.

In larger post offices, each counter has specific services, so check you are in the right queue (look for *"Timbres"* if you only want stamps) or use one of the self-service machines. You can also buy stamps at tobacconists *(bureaux de tabac)* and some shops selling postcards. Letter boxes are yellow. You should use Monaco stamps to send letters from Monaco.

Urgent post can be sent *par exprès*. The Chronopost system is also fast but is expensive.

Poste Restante

Mail can be kept for collection when addressed to you at: Poste

Restante, Poste Centrale (for the main post office) plus the town postcode and name. A small fee will be charged and you will need to show your passport to collect your post.

Public Holidays

Banks, post offices, public offices and many museums and shops close on public holidays (*jours fériés*); public transport often runs on Sunday schedules. It is common practice if a public holiday falls on a Thursday or Tuesday for French businesses to *faire le pont* ("bridge the gap") and take the Friday or Monday as a holiday as well.

The most strongly respected *jours fériés* are I January, 1 May, 14 July, 15 August and 25 December. While the shops may be shut, there will often be a *fête* on 14 July and 15 August. Foreign embassies and consulates observe French public holidays as well as their own.

1 January Nouvel An
New Year's Day
March/April Lundi de Pâques
Easter Monday
1 May Fête du Travail
Labour Day
8 May Fête de la Victoire 1945
VE Day
May Ascension
Ascension
May/June Lundi de Pentecôte
Whit Monday
14 July Fête Nationale/le Quatorze juillet Bastille Day
15 August Assomption
Assumption
1 November Toussaint
All Saints' Day
11 November Fête de l'Armistice
Armistice Day
25 December Noël
Christmas

TIME ZONE

France is always one hour ahead of the UK (i.e. Greenwich Mean Time +1 in winter, and GMT+2 in summer).

R eligion

The French Republic has officially been a lay state since the French Revolution and does not have an established religion. However, the church calendar determines most of the public holidays and the majority of the population is nominally Roman Catholic, with substantial minority Protestant, Muslim and Jewish communities. Non-Catholic services are called *cultes*; Protestant churches are known as *temples*. Roman Catholicism is the established religion in Monaco.

There are Anglican churches with regular services in English in Nice, Cannes, Menton, Monaco and Vence.

S moking

Smoking is prohibited in all state-owned buildings and public places, including post offices, stations, cinemas and museums, on public transport, and in restaurants, bars, cafés, discothèques and casinos, except in specially ventilated sealed-off *fumoirs* or outside on café terraces. Smoking is banned in the public areas of hotels, but not in hotel bedrooms unless they are designated non-smoking rooms.

T elephones

French phone numbers are all 10 figures including two-digit regional prefixes as follows: numbers in Southeast France all start with 04 (when dialling from outside France, omit the initial zero). They are always written and spoken in two-digit numbers (eg 01 25 25 25 25). Mobile phone numbers start 06 (07 numbers are also due to be introduced). 08 numbers have special rates varying from 0800 freephone numbers to premium rates such as 0836. Directory enquiries are available from various providers, including 118000, 118007, 118008 and 118218.

TOILETS

Anyone may use the toilet in a bar or café, whether they are a customer or not, unless there is a sign specifying that this is not allowed, but it is polite to at least order a coffee at the bar. (Ask for *les toilettes* or *le WC*, which is pronounced "vay-say").

Public Phones

Many public telephones only accept *télécartes* (phone cards), available from post offices and tobacconists. A surcharge will usually be added for calls made from your hotel room.

International Calls

When dialling France from abroad, dial the French country code 00 33 and omit the 0 at the start of the 10-digit number. To dial overseas from France, dial 00, followed by the country code (UK: 44; Canada & US: 1; Australia: 61; Monaco: 377) and then the number, usually omitting the initial zero. International directory enquiries: 3212.

Tourist Information

Every town and city, and almost every small village, has its own *office de tourisme*, sometimes also referred to as the *maison* (or *bureau*) *de tourisme*. These are usually located on or near the

BELOW: Antibes' town hall.

main square, and sometimes also at main stations. In smaller villages, where the tourist office is only open for limited hours it may be called the *syndicat d'initiative*, often located at the *mairie* (town hall). Tourist offices can usually supply good town plans and local maps, as well as information about restaurants, accommodation, sights, festivals and events, guided tours and sporting facilities. Tourist office staff should be able to give you impartial advice or point you to the piles of free advertising leaflets, which are left by hotels, shops, museums and the like. Some bigger tourist offices, such as Aix and Nice, offer efficient hotel booking services if you arrive without accommodation, and ticket booking services.

Before you travel, you may want to get hold of information from the Maison de France in your country (see www.franceguide.com for addresses). See also the useful bilingual tourist board websites for the Alpes-de-Haute-Provence (www.alpes-haute-provence.com), Alpes-Maritimes (www.guideriviera.fr), the Bouches-du-Rhône (www.visitprovence.com), Var (www.visitvar.fr), Vaucluse (www.provenceguide.com) and PACA regional tourist board (www.decouverte-paca.fr).

Principal tourist offices

Aix-en-Provence place de la Rotonde; tel: 04 42 16 11 61; www.aixenprovencetourism.com
Antibes 11 place du Charles de Gaulle; tel: 04 97 23 11 11; www.antibes-juanlespins.com
Arles esplanade Charles de Gaulle, boulevard des Lices; tel: 04 90 18 41 20; www.arlestourisme.com
Avignon 41 cours Jean Jaurès; tel: 04 32 74 32 74; www.avignon-tourisme.com
Cannes Palais des Festivals, La Croisette; tel: 04 92 99 84 22; www.cannes.fr/tourisme
Grasse 22 cours Honoré Cresp; tel: 04 93 36 66 66; www.grasse.fr
Marseille 4 La Canebière; tel: 04 91 13 89 00; www.marseille-tourisme.com

ABOVE: antiques for sale on L'Isle-sur-la-Sorgue.

Menton Palais de l'Europe, 8 avenue Boyer; tel: 04 92 41 76 76; www.menton.fr
Monaco 2a boulevard des Moulins, Monte Carlo; tel: +377-92 16 61 16; www.visitmonaco.com
Nice 5 promenade des Anglais, tel: 08 92 70 74 07; www.nicetourisme.com; branches at Nice train station (avenue Thiers) and Aéroport Nice Côte d'Azur (T1).
Nîmes 6 rue Auguste; tel: 04 66 58 38 00; www.ot-nimes.fr
St-Tropez quai Jean Jaurès; tel: 08 92 68 48 28; www.ot-saint-tropez.com
Toulon place Louis Blanc, Bas Cours Lafayette; tel: 04 94 18 53 00; www.toulontourisme.com
Vence 8 place du Grand Jardin; tel: 04 93 58 06 38; www.vence.fr

Tour Operators

The following organise special tours and holidays to Provence.
Ace Cultural Tours
Tel: 01223 835 055; www.acestudytours.co.uk
Cultural tours.
Body and Soul Holidays (Erna Low)
www.bodyandsoulholidays.info
Offer spa and thalassotherapy holidays.
Cycling for Softies
Tel: 0161 248 8282
www.cycling-for-softies.co.uk
NatureTrek
Tel: 01962 733051
www.naturetrek.co.uk
Wildlife holidays to the Camargue

and Luberon.
Prospect
Tel: 01227 743 307
www.prospecttours.com
Music and art tours.
Responsible Travel
www.responsibletravel.com
Environmentally conscious cycling, walking, cooking and scuba diving trips.
vfb Holidays
Tel: 01452 716840
www.vfbholidays.co.uk
Holiday rentals and guided holidays.

V isas and Passports

European Union visitors do not need a visa to enter France, but should have a valid passport or identity card. Citizens of the US, Canada, Australia or New Zealand and certain other countries only need a visa for stays of more than three months. Check with the French consulate in your country.

Non-European Union nationals who intend to stay in France for more than 90 days should apply for a *carte de séjour* (or *titre de séjour*).

W eights and Measures

The metric system is used in France for all weights and measures. For a handy reckoning, bear in mind 80km equals 50 miles, 1kg is about 2lbs, and 50cl about 1 pint.

TRANSPORT

ACCOMMODATION

ACTIVITIES

A – Z

LANGUAGE

LANGUAGE

KEY FRENCH WORDS AND PHRASES

Useful Words and Phrases

yes/no *oui/non*
OK *d'accord*
I'm sorry *Excusez-moi/Pardon*
please *s'il vous/te plaît*
thank you (very much) *merci (beaucoup)*
excuse me *excusez-moi*
hello *bonjour* ("allo" on telephone)
goodbye *au revoir*
good evening *bonsoir*
here/there *ici/là*
big/small *grand(e)/petit(e)*
good/bad *bon(ne)/mauvais(e)*
today *aujourd'hui*
yesterday *hier*
tomorrow *demain*
this morning *ce matin*
this afternoon *cet après-midi*
this evening *ce soir*
What is your name? *Comment vous appelez-vous?*
My name is… *Je m'appelle…*
Do you speak English? *Parlez-vous anglais?*
I am English/American *Je suis anglais(e)/américain(e)*
I don't understand *Je ne comprends pas*
Please speak more slowly *Parlez plus lentement, s'il vous plaît*
Can you help me? *Pouvez-vous m'aider?*
I'm looking for… *Je cherche…*
Where is…? *Où est…?*
I don't know *Je ne sais pas*

On Arrival

airport *l'aéroport*
train station *la gare (SNCF)*
bus station *la gare routière*
Métro stop *la station de Métro*
bus/coach *l'autobus/le car*
bus stop *l'arrêt*
platform *le quai*
ticket *le billet*
return ticket *aller-retour*
toilets *les toilettes/les WC*
I want to get off at… *Je voudrais descendre à…*
Is there a bus to…? *Est-ce qu'il y a un bus pour …?*
Which line do I take for…? *Quelle ligne dois-je prendre pour…?*
Validate your ticket *Compostez votre billet*

At the Hotel

I'd like a (single/double) room… *Je voudrais une chambre (simple/double)…*
….with shower *avec douche*
….with a bath *avec bain*
Does that include breakfast? *Est-ce que le petit déjeuner est compris?*
washbasin *le lavabo*
key *la cléf*
elevator *l'ascenseur*
air-conditioned *climatisé*
swimming pool *une piscine*

On the Road

Where is the nearest garage? *Où est le garage le plus proche?*
Our car has broken down *Notre voiture est en panne*
I want to have my car repaired *Je veux faire réparer ma voiture*
left/right *gauche/droite*
straight on *tout droit*
roundabout *rond-point*
far/near *loin/près d'ici*
on foot *à pied*
by car *en voiture*
road map *la carte*
street *la rue*
give way *céder le passage*
motorway *l'autoroute*
toll *péage*
speed limit *la limitation de vitesse*
petrol *l'essence*
unleaded *sans plomb*
diesel *le gasoil*
water/oil *l'eau/l'huile*
puncture *un pneu crevé*

Shopping

Where is the nearest bank/post office? *Où est la banque/Poste la plus proche?*
I'd like to buy/try on… *Je voudrais acheter/essayer…*
How much is it? *C'est combien?*
Do you take credit cards? *Prenez-vous les cartes de crédit?*
Have you got…? *Avez-vous…?*

NUMBERS

0 zéro	**11** onze	**30** trente
1 un, une	**12** douze	**40** quarante
2 deux	**13** treize	**50** cinquante
3 trois	**14** quatorze	**60** soixante
4 quatre	**15** quinze	**70** soixante-dix
5 cinq	**16** seize	**80** quatre-vingts
6 six	**17** dix-sept	**90** quatre-vingt-dix
7 sept	**18** dix-huit	**100** cent
8 huit	**19** dix-neuf	**1000** mille
9 neuf	**20** vingt	**1,000,000**
10 dix	**21** vingt-et-un	un million

cheap bon marché
expensive cher
a piece of un morceau de
each la pièce (eg ananas, 0.5
la pièce)
bill/receipt la note/le reçu

Dining Out

Prix fixe or **menu** are fixed-price
menus. **A la carte** means dishes
from the menu are charged sep-
arately.
breakfast le petit déjeuner
lunch le déjeuner
dinner le dîner
meal le repas
first course l'entrée
main course le plat
drink included boisson compris
wine list la carte des vins
the bill l'addition
plate l'assiette
glass le verre

Basics

beurre **butter**
confiture **jam**
crêpe **pancake**
croque-monsieur **ham-and-
cheese toasted sandwich**
croque-madame **ham-and-
cheese toasted sandwich with
a fried egg on top**
fromage **cheese**
fromage de chèvre **goat's
cheese**
galette **savoury pancake**
oeuf **egg**
oeuf à la coque **boiled egg**
oeuf sur le plat **fried egg**
oeufs brouillés **scrambled eggs**
pain **bread**
poivre **pepper**

sel **salt**
sucre **sugar**

L'Entrée (Starters)

anchoïade **sauce of olive oil,
anchovies and garlic, served
with raw vegetables**
rillettes **rich fatty paste of
shredded duck, rabbit or pork**
soupe/potage/velouté **soup**
tapenade **olive and anchovy
paste**

Viande (Meat)

bleu **extremely rare**
saignant **rare**
à point **medium**
bien cuit **well done**
agneau **lamb**
blanquette **stew of veal or lamb
with a creamy egg sauce**
…à la bordelaise **with red wine
and shallots**
…à la bourguignonne **cooked in
red wine, onions and mushrooms**
boeuf en daube **Provençal beef
stew with red wine, onions and
tomatoes**
brochette **kebab**
canard **duck**
carré d'agneau **rack of lamb**
cassoulet **stew with beans, sausages, pork and duck, from
southwest France**
cervelle **brains**
confit **duck or goose preserved
in its own fat**
coq au vin **chicken in red wine**
côte d'agneau **lamb chop**
dinde **turkey**
entrecôte **beef rib steak**
escargot **snail**
faisan **pheasant**

faux-filet **sirloin**
foie **liver**
foie gras **fattened goose/duck
liver**
gardiane de boeuf **rich beef stew
with olives and garlic**
cuisses de grenouille **frog's legs**
gibier **game**
grillade **grilled meat**
hachis **minced meat**
jambon **ham**
lapin **rabbit**
lardons **small pieces of bacon**
lièvre **hare**
oie **goose**
porc **pork**
poulet **chicken**
ris de veau veal **sweetbreads**
rognons **kidneys**
rôti **roast**
sanglier **wild boar**
saucisse **fresh sausage**
saucisson sec **dried cured
sausage (salami)**
veau **veal**
volaille **poultry**

Poisson (Fish)

Armoricaine **cooked with white
wine, tomatoes, butter and
cognac**
anchois **anchovies**
bar (or loup) **sea bass**
bouillabaisse **Provençal fish
soup, served with grated**

EMERGENCIES

Help! Au secours!
Stop! Arrêtez!
Call a doctor Appelez un
médecin
Call an ambulance Appelez
une ambulance
Call the police Appelez la
police
Call the fire brigade Appelez
les pompiers
**Where is the nearest
telephone?** Où est le
téléphone le plus proche?
**Where is the nearest
hospital?** Où est l'hôpital le
plus proche?
I am sick Je suis malade
**I have lost my passport/
purse** J'ai perdu mon
passeport/porte-monnaie

cheese, garlic croutons and
rouille, a spicy sauce
calmars squid
coquillage shellfish
coquilles St-Jacques scallops
crevette prawn (UK), shrimp (US)
daurade (or dorade) sea bream
espadon swordfish
fruits de mer seafood
homard lobster
huître oyster
langoustine large prawn
lotte monkfish
moule mussel
moules marinières mussels in
white wine and onions
mulet grey mullet
raie skate
rascasse scorpion fish
rouget red mullet
saint-pierre John Dory
saumon salmon
thon tuna
truite trout

Légumes (Vegetables)

ail garlic
artichaut artichoke
asperge asparagus
aubergine aubergine (eggplant)
avocat avocado
champignon mushroom
courgette courgette (zucchini)
chips potato crisps
chou cabbage
chou-fleur cauliflower
crudités raw vegetables
fenouil fennel
frites chips, French fries
gratin dauphinois sliced potatoes baked with cream
haricot bean
navet turnip
oignon onion
panais parsnip
petits farcis stuffed vegetables
poireau leek
pois pea
poivron bell pepper
pomme de terre potato
salade niçoise salad with egg,
tuna, olives, onions and
tomato
tomate tomato

Miscellaneous

biologique organic
pâte pastry
pâtes pasta

tarte open tart or quiche
tourte closed/double tart

Fruits (Fruit)

ananas pineapple
cerise cherry
citron lemon
citron vert lime
figue fig
fraise strawberry
framboise raspberry
mangue mango
noix walnut
noisette hazelnut
pamplemousse grapefruit
pêche peach
poire pear
pomme apple
raisin grape
prune plum
pruneau prune

Sauces (Sauces)

aioli garlic mayonnaise
béarnaise sauce of egg, butter,
wine and herbs
forestière with mushrooms
hollandaise egg, butter and
lemon sauce
lyonnaise with onions
meunière fried fish with butter,
lemon and parsley sauce
pistou Provençal sauce of
basil, garlic and olive oil;
vegetable soup with pistou
sauce
à la provençale with tomatoes,
garlic, white wine and olives

Dessert (Puddings)

clafoutis baked pudding of bat-
ter and cherries
coulis purée of fruit or
vegetables
gâteau cake
île flottante meringue in custard
crème anglaise custard
poire Belle Hélène pear with ice
cream and chocolate sauce
tarte Tatin upside-down tart of
caramelised apples
crème caramel caramelised
egg custard
crème Chantilly whipped cream

In a Café

coffee *café*
...with milk/cream *au lait/crème*

**I would like to reserve a
table** *Je voudrais réserver
une table*
I am a vegetarian *Je suis
végétarien(ne)*
I am on a diet *Je suis au
régime*
What do you recommend?
*Qu'est-ce que vous
recommandez?*
**Do you have local
specialities?** *Avez-vous des
spécialités locales?*
I'd like to order *Je voudrais
commander*
That is not what I ordered
*Ce n'est pas ce que j'ai
commandé*
Is service included? *Est-ce
que le service est compris?*
May I have more wine?
Encore du vin, s'il vous plaît!
Enjoy your meal *Bon
appétit!*

...decaffeinated *déca/
décaféiné*
...black/espresso *noir/express*
tea *thé*
herb infusion *tisane*
hot chocolate *chocolat chaud*
milk *lait*
mineral water *eau minérale*
still/fizzy *plat/gazeux*
jug of tap water *carafe d'eau*
**fresh lemon juice served with
sugar** *citron pressé*
freshly squeezed orange juice
orange pressé
fresh or cold *frais, fraîche,
froid(e)*
beer *bière*
...bottled *en bouteille*
...on tap *à la pression*
with ice *avec des glaçons*
neat *sec*
red *rouge*
white *blanc*
rosé *rosé*
dry *sec, brut*
sweet *doux*
house wine *vin de maison*
local wine *vin de pays*
pitcher *carafe/pichet*
...of water/wine *d'eau/de vin*
cheers! *santé!*

FURTHER READING

Former English adman Peter Mayle could be credited as the man who introduced the Luberon to most foreigners with **A Year in Provence** (Penguin), in 1991, his enjoyable and often spot-on account of his first year in the Luberon doing up a house in Ménerbes, later followed up by *Encore Provence* and *Toujours Provence*. Since then he has also turned to fiction in *Chasing Cézanne, Hôtel Pastis* and *Anything Considered*.

Non-Fiction

France in the New Century: Portrait of a Changing Society by John Ardagh (Penguin). Weighty tome on modern France.
Côte d'Azur: Inventing the French Riviera by Mary Blume (Thames & Hudson). Excellent account of *emigré* Riviera.
The Identity of France by Fernand Braudel (HarperCollins). Unputdownable analysis, weaving major events with everyday life, by one of France's best historians.
France on the Brink: A Great Civilization Faces the New Century by Jonathan Fenby (Arcade).

Below: a good place to read.

Controversial and witty account of French politics and life.
The French by Theodore Zeldin (Random House). Irreverent, penetrating analysis of the French character. Although written in the 1980s, it has become a classic.

Food

At Home in Provence by Patricia Wells (Prentice Hall). Recipes prepared in the American food critic's Provençal farmhouse.
A Table in Provence by Leslie Forbes (Penguin). Recipes.

Fiction

The Avignon Quintet by Lawrence Durrell (Faber). Classic travel writing from Durrell.
Bonjour Tristesse by Françoise Sagan (Penguin). The story of a teenager and her father, living the hedonistic Riviera life.
The Count of Monte-Cristo by Alexandre Dumas (Various editions). Gripping account of prison life and revenge at the Château d'If, near Marseille.
The Horseman on the Roof by Jean Giono (Harvill). Provence in the 1830s.
Jean de Florette and **Manon of the Springs** by Marcel Pagnol (Picador). Peasant struggles in rural Provence. Novels that inspired award-winning films.
Perfume by Patrick Süskind (Penguin Modern Classics). Sinister but gripping tale of an 18th-century Grasse perfumier.
The Rock Pool by Cyril Connolly (Persea). Satirical novel set in 1930s Riviera.
Super-Cannes by J G Ballard (Harper Perennial). A futuristic thriller set in a gated business park on the Riviera, loosely

inspired by Sophia-Antipolis.
Tender is the Night by F. Scott Fitzgerald (Penguin). Wealth and decadence on the Riviera.
Total Chaos by Jean-Claude Izzo (Europa Editions). The first of Izzo's Marseille crime trilogy featuring cop Fabio Montale (followed by **Chourmo** and **Solea**).

Other Insight Guides

Insight Step by Step Guides are self-guided walks and tours produced by local writers; this series covers *Paris* and *Nice & the French Riviera*. **Insight Fleximaps** are durable, laminated maps and cover the *French Riviera*.

SEND US YOUR THOUGHTS

We do our best to ensure the information in our books is as accurate and up-to-date as possible. However, some mistakes and omissions are inevitable and we are reliant on our readers to put us in the picture.

We would welcome your feedback on any details related to your experiences of using the book "on the road". The more details you can give us (particularly with regard to addresses, emails and telephone numbers), the better.

We will acknowledge all contributions, and we'll offer an Insight Guide to the best letters received.

Please write to us at:
   Insight Guides
   PO Box 7910
   London SE1 1WE
   United Kingdom
Or email us at:
   insight@apaguide.co.uk

ART AND PHOTO CREDITS

Philippe Achache 246
Ping Amranand 255
Apa 46, 75, 94, 95, 122T 128T,
129T 143T, 144T, 147T, 166, 141,
148T, 161L, 166, 167R, 168
171L, 171R, 171T, 172, 178,
181T, 182T, 186, 187, 198, 204,
205T, 205R, 206T, 207T, 213T,
201, 213L, 213R, 213T, 214T,
214L, 215, 216R, 218L, 218T,
221T, 222T, 242, all small cover
pictures except back cover left and
back flap bottom
BBC Hulton Picture Library
33, 36, 38
Natasha Babaian 170
Bank of England Museum 218R
Martin Black 80/81, 159
Nelly Boyd/Robert Harding 85
Ian Bradshaw 206
British Museum 67, 68, 69
John Bulmer 163L
Julian Calder 126, 203
Mark Cator/Impact 127, 158,
183
Conran Restaurants 93
Dennis Severs' House 232
Chris Donaghue 258/259
Andrew Eames 174/175, 210,
211
English Tourist Board 256
Sally Fear 162
Fortnum & Mason 158T
Lee Foster 205L
Geffrye Museum, London 233
Glyn Genin 6/7, 16, 17, 37, 43,
44, 45, 47L, 47R, 48, 49, 56, 66,
75L, 75R, 88, 89, 91, 96/97,
98/99, 108, 109, 110, 114T, 114,
134/135, 138, 139, 140, 156T,
156, 160, 169, 192, 193, 194T,
194, 196T, 196, 198T, 199T, 199,
214T, 216T, 217, 220, 222, 239,
244, 244T, back cover left and
back flap bottom
Dennis Gilbert 74, 109
Tim Graham 62
David Gray 18, 53, 130, 195T,
210L, 234/235
Susan Griggs Agency 177
David Haiden 57
Robert Harding 92, 112T, 223
Brian Harris 241, 218L
Historic Royal Palaces 223
Anthony Howarth 40, 219

Britta Jaschinski 14, 82, 83L,
83R, 84, 85, 86, 179
Richard Kalina/Shakespeare's
Globe 77
John Kegan 200/201
Landscape Only 188, 250/251
Alain Le Garsmeur 8/9, 23, 34,
123, 145, 152/153, 164
Libera Design/P. Libera 146, 197
John Londei 41
London Docklands Development
Corporation 231
Mike McQueen/Impact 133, 184,
228
Neil Menneer 50/51, 54, 55, 59,
108L, 132, 119, 144, 147L, 147R,
173, 241, 245
J. Miller/Robert Harding
100/101
Museum of London 18/19, 20,
21, 22, 28, 29, 30, 31, 35
Museum of London/HIP/Topham
24/25
Natural History Museum 71R
Julian Nieman 163, 185
Richard T. Nowitz 10/11, 52, 70,
120, 123, 125, 147L&R, 149,
151, 163L, 163R, 176, 177, 181,
182, 176, 221L, 221R, 250/251
Tony Page 247
David Reed 229
Tim Rooke/Rex Features 79
Brian Rybolt 218
Science & Society Picture Lib. 72
Skyscan Photolibrary 226/227
Ted Spiegel 189T
Mike St Maur 155
Stapleton Collection/Corbis 70
Liz Stares/Collections 238T
Tony Stone Worldwide 139, 131,
245, 257
Homer Sykes 219
Ray Tang/Rex Features 78
Liba Taylor/Collections 180L,
260
Topham Picturepoint 39 , 41, 58,
76, 112, 116, 160T, 183R
Bill Varie/Corbis 71L
Victoria and Albert Museum 74
Victoria and Albert Museum/
Derry Moore 73
Alex Wallerstein/Impact 110
Bill Wassman 42, 87, 115, 141,
125L, 154, 240
R. Williams 126T, 127T, 128, 129

Adam Woolfitt 157L&R, 158R,
189, 180R, 202, 207, 216L, 212R,
218, 236,
Adam Woolfitt/Robert Harding
12/13, 15, 90, 102, 120,
118/119, 161R
Gregory Wrona 117
Ian Yeomans 167L

PHOTO FEATURES

Pages 64/65: Clockwise from top:
Collections/Brian Shuel; Mary
Evans Picture Library; Libera
Design Ltd; Collections/
Bartholomew; Collections/Brian
Shuel; Collections/Brian Shuel;
Network/B. Hermann.
Pages 150/152: Top left: Glyn
Genin. Paintings by courtesy of the
National Gallery, London. Top right:
Courtesy of the National Portrait
Gallery, London
Pages 190/191: Clockwiase from
top left: Mary Evans Picture Library;
Apa; Collections/John Miller;
Collections/Liba Taylor;
Collections/Brian Shuel; Network/
Sunil Gupta; Collections/Michael
George
Pages 224/5: Clockwise from top
left: Apa; London Aerial Photo
Library; Apa; Apa; Apa; Collections/
James Bartholomew; Apa;
Collections/James Bartholomew;
Pages 240/241: Clockwise from
left: Pictorial Press (Audrey
Hepburn); Ben Edwards/Impact;
Collections/ Michael St Maur Sheil;
Rex Features; Piers
Cavendish/ Impact; Johnathan
Trapman/Ace (Wimbledon Cup)
Collections/Liba Taylor;
Collections/Geoff Howard

Map Production: Apa Cartography
Department

©2011 Apa Publications GmbH & Co.
Verlag KG, Singapore Branch

Production: Tynan Dean, Linton
Donaldson and Rebeka Ellam

GENERAL INDEX